T0207230

Communications
in Computer and Information Science 1873

Rationale

The CCIS series is devoted to the publication of proceedings of computer science conferences. Its aim is to efficiently disseminate original research results in informatics in printed and electronic form. While the focus is on publication of peer-reviewed full papers presenting mature work, inclusion of reviewed short papers reporting on work in progress is welcome, too. Besides globally relevant meetings with internationally representative program committees guaranteeing a strict peer-reviewing and paper selection process, conferences run by societies or of high regional or national relevance are also considered for publication.

Topics

The topical scope of CCIS spans the entire spectrum of informatics ranging from foundational topics in the theory of computing to information and communications science and technology and a broad variety of interdisciplinary application fields.

Information for Volume Editors and Authors

Publication in CCIS is free of charge. No royalties are paid, however, we offer registered conference participants temporary free access to the online version of the conference proceedings on SpringerLink (http://link.springer.com) by means of an http referrer from the conference website and/or a number of complimentary printed copies, as specified in the official acceptance email of the event.

CCIS proceedings can be published in time for distribution at conferences or as post-proceedings, and delivered in the form of printed books and/or electronically as USBs and/or e-content licenses for accessing proceedings at SpringerLink. Furthermore, CCIS proceedings are included in the CCIS electronic book series hosted in the SpringerLink digital library at http://link.springer.com/bookseries/7899. Conferences publishing in CCIS are allowed to use Online Conference Service (OCS) for managing the whole proceedings lifecycle (from submission and reviewing to preparing for publication) free of charge.

Publication process

The language of publication is exclusively English. Authors publishing in CCIS have to sign the Springer CCIS copyright transfer form, however, they are free to use their material published in CCIS for substantially changed, more elaborate subsequent publications elsewhere. For the preparation of the camera-ready papers/files, authors have to strictly adhere to the Springer CCIS Authors' Instructions and are strongly encouraged to use the CCIS LaTeX style files or templates.

Abstracting/Indexing

CCIS is abstracted/indexed in DBLP, Google Scholar, EI-Compendex, Mathematical Reviews, SCImago, Scopus. CCIS volumes are also submitted for the inclusion in ISI Proceedings.

How to start

To start the evaluation of your proposal for inclusion in the CCIS series, please send an e-mail to ccis@springer.com.

Rafael Valencia-García ·
Martha Bucaram-Leverone ·
Javier Del Cioppo-Morstadt · Néstor Vera-Lucio ·
Pablo Humberto Centanaro-Quiroz
Editors

Technologies and Innovation

9th International Conference, CITI 2023
Guayaquil, Ecuador, November 13–16, 2023
Proceedings

 Springer

Editors
Rafael Valencia-García 🆔
Universidad de Murcia
Murcia, Spain

Martha Bucaram-Leverone 🆔
Universidad Agraria del Ecuador
Guayaquil, Ecuador

Javier Del Cioppo-Morstadt 🆔
Universidad Agraria del Ecuador
Guayaquil, Ecuador

Néstor Vera-Lucio 🆔
Universidad Agraria del Ecuador
Guayaquil, Ecuador

Pablo Humberto Centanaro-Quiroz 🆔
Universidad Agraria del Ecuador
Guayaquil, Ecuador

ISSN 1865-0929   ISSN 1865-0937 (electronic)
Communications in Computer and Information Science
ISBN 978-3-031-45681-7   ISBN 978-3-031-45682-4 (eBook)
https://doi.org/10.1007/978-3-031-45682-4

This Springer imprint is published by the registered company Springer Nature Switzerland AG
The registered company address is: Gewerbestrasse 11, 6330 Cham, Switzerland

Paper in this product is recyclable.

Preface

The 9th edition of the International Conference on Technologies and Innovation (CITI 2023) took place from November 13th to 16th, 2023, in Guayaquil, Ecuador. The CITI conference series aims to establish itself as a global platform and focal point for professionals primarily involved in research, development, innovation, and university teaching in the field of Computer Science and Technology applied to various innovative domains. CITI 2023 was structured as a knowledge-sharing event, presenting numerous papers on today's cutting-edge technologies. These papers address paramount facets and future potentials from academic, inventive, and scientific points of view. The primary objective of the conference was to explore the viability of advanced and pioneering methodologies and techniques, along with their application in diverse domains within the field of Computer Science and Information Systems, embodying innovation in today's society.

We would like to express our gratitude to all the authors who submitted papers to CITI 2023, and our congratulations to those whose papers were accepted. There were 51 submissions this year. Each submission was Single-blind reviews by at least three Program Committee (PC) members. Only the papers with an average score of ≥ 1.0 were considered for final inclusion, and almost all accepted papers had positive reviews. Finally, the PC decided to accept 20 full papers.

We would also like to thank the Program Committee members, who agreed to review the manuscripts in a timely manner and provided valuable feedback to the authors.

November 2023

Rafael Valencia-García
Martha Bucaram-Leverone
Javier Del Cioppo-Morstadt
Néstor Vera-Lucio
Pablo Humberto Centanaro-Quiroz

Organization

Honor Committee

Martha Bucaram-Leverone   Universidad Agraria del Ecuador, Ecuador
Javier Del Cioppo-Morstadt   Universidad Agraria del Ecuador, Ecuador
Pablo Humberto   Universidad Agraria del Ecuador, Ecuador
    Centanaro-Quiroz
Teresa Samaniego-Cobo   Universidad Agraria del Ecuador, Ecuador

General Chairs

Rafael Valencia-García   Universidad de Murcia, Spain
Martha Bucaram-Leverone   Universidad Agraria del Ecuador, Ecuador
Javier Del Cioppo-Morstadt   Universidad Agraria del Ecuador, Ecuador
Néstor Vera-Lucio   Universidad Agraria del Ecuador, Ecuador
Pablo Humberto   Universidad Agraria del Ecuador, Ecuador
    Centanaro-Quiroz

Program Chairs

Rafael Valencia-García   Universidad de Murcia, Spain
Martha Bucaram-Leverone   Universidad Agraria del Ecuador, Ecuador
Javier Del Cioppo-Morstadt   Universidad Agraria del Ecuador, Ecuador
Néstor Vera-Lucio   Universidad Agraria del Ecuador, Ecuador
Pablo Humberto   Universidad Agraria del Ecuador, Ecuador
    Centanaro-Quiroz

Program Committee

Jacobo Bucaram-Ortiz   Universidad Agraria del Ecuador, Ecuador
Martha Bucaram-Leverone   Universidad Agraria del Ecuador, Ecuador
Rina Bucaram-Leverone   Universidad Agraria del Ecuador, Ecuador
Rafael Valencia-García   Universidad de Murcia, Spain
Ricardo Colomo-Palacios   Ostfold University College, Norway
Ghassan Beydoun   University of Technology Sydney, Australia

Antonio A. López-Lorca	University of Melbourne, Australia
Chunguo Wu	Jilin University, China
Siti Hajar Othman	Universiti Teknologi Malaysia, Malaysia
Anatoly Gladun	V.M. Glushkov Institute of Cybernetics of NAS of Ukraine, Ukraine
Aarón Ayllón-Benítez	Université de Bordeaux, France
Giner Alor-Hernández	Instituto Tecnológico de Orizaba, Mexico
José Luis Ochoa	Universidad de Sonora, Mexico
Ana Muñoz	Universidad Técnica Federico Santa María, Chile
Miguel Ángel Rodríguez-García	Universidad Rey Juan Carlos, Spain
Lucía Serrano-Luján	Universidad Rey Juan Carlos, Spain
Eugenio Martínez-Cámara	Universidad de Jaén, Spain
José Antonio García-Díaz	Universidad de Murcia, Spain
José Antonio Miñarro-Giménez	Universidad de Murcia, Spain
Catalina Martínez-Costa	Universidad de Murcia, Spain
Gema Alcaraz-Mármol	Universidad de Castilla-La Mancha, Spain
Gustavo Zurita	Universidad de Chile, Chile
Francisco M. Fernandez-Periche	U. Antonio Nariño, Colombia
Ali Pazahr	Islamic Azad University-Ahvaz Branch, Iran
Diego Gabriel Rossit	U. Nacional del Sur-CONICET, Argentina
Victor Rafael Bravo Bravo	Universidad de los Andes, Venezuela
Alvaro David Torrez Baptista	Universidade Federal do ABC, Brazil
Mónica Marrero	Delft University of Technology, The Netherlands
Ricardo Coelho Silva	Federal University of Ceará, Brazil
Alejandro Rodríguez-González	U. Politécnica de Madrid, Spain
Carlos Cruz-Corona	Universidad de Granada, Spain
Dagoberto Catellanos-Nieves	Universidad de la Laguna, Spain
Antonio Ruiz-Martínez	Universidad de Murcia, Spain
Manuel Quesada-Martínez	Universidad Miguel Hernández, Spain
Maria Pilar Salas-Zárate	Tecnológico Nacional de México/ITS de Teziutlán, Mexico
Mario Andrés Paredes-Valverde	Tecnológico Nacional de México/ITS de Teziutlán, Mexico
Luis Omar Colombo-Mendoza	Tecnológico Nacional de México/ITS de Teziutlán, Mexico
José Medina-Moreira	Universidad Agraria del Ecuador, Ecuador
Thomas Moser	St. Pölten University of Applied Sciences, Austria
Lisbeth Rodriguez Mazahua	I. Tecnológico de Orizaba, Mexico
Jose Luis Sanchez Cervantes	I. Tecnológico de Orizaba, Mexico
Cristian Aaron Rodriguez Enriquez	I. Tecnológico de Orizaba, Mexico
Humberto Marin Vega	Tecnológico N. de Mexico/I.T.S. Zongolica, Mexico

Salud M. Jiménez Zafra	Universidad de Jaén, Spain
M. Abirami	Thiagarajar College of Engineering, India
Gandhi Hernandez	U. Tecnológica Metropolitana, Mexico
Manuel Sánchez-Rubio	U. Internacional de la Rioja, Spain
Mario Barcelo-Valenzuela	Universidad de Sonora, Mexico
Alonso Perez-Soltero	Universidad de Sonora, Mexico
Gerardo Sanchez-Schmitz	Universidad de Sonora, Mexico
José Luis Hernández Hernández	U. Autónoma de Guerrero, Mexico
Mario Hernández Hernández	U. Autónoma de Guerrero, Mexico
Severino Feliciano Morales	U. Autónoma de Guerrero, Mexico
Guido Sciavicco	University of Ferrara, Italy
José Aguilar	Universidad de los Andes, Venezuela
Ángel García Pedrero	Universidad Politécnica de Madrid, Spain
Miguel Vargas-Lombardo	U. Tecnológica de Panamá, Panama
Denis Cedeño Moreno	U. Tecnológica de Panamá, Panama
Viviana Yarel Rosales Morales	I. Tecnológico de Orizaba, Mexico
Claudia Victoria Isaza Narvaez	Universidad de Antioquia, Colombia
Raquel Vasquez Ramirez	Instituto Tecnológico de Orizaba, Mexico
Janio Jadán Guerrero	Universidad Indoamérica, Ecuador
Yordani Cruz Segura	Universidad de las Ciencias Informáticas, Cuba
Freddy Tapia León	U. de las Fuerzas Armadas ESPE, Ecuador
Nemury Silega Martínez	U. de las Ciencias Informáticas, Cuba
Astrid Duque Ramos	Universidad de Antioquia, Colombia
Nelson Becerra Correa	U. Distrital Fco José de Caldas, Colombia
Alireza Khakpour	Ostfold University College, Norway
Mary Sánchez-Gordon	Ostfold University College, Norway
María José Marín Pérez	Universidad de Murcia, Spain
Ángela Almela	Universidad de Murcia, Spain
Ronghao Pan	Universidad de Murcia, Spain

Local Organizing Committee

Vanessa Vergara-Lozano (General Coordinator)	Universidad Agraria del Ecuador, Ecuador
Teresa Samaniego-Cobo	Universidad Agraria del Ecuador, Ecuador
Néstor Vera-Lucio	Universidad Agraria del Ecuador, Ecuador

Sponsoring Institutions

http://www.uagraria.edu.ec/

Contents

Natural Language Processing and Semantic Web

Computer Vision

Knowledge-Based Systems

Machine Learning

Towards a Model for the Detection of Firearms using Machine Learning Algorithms: A Case Study

Clifton Clunie[2] , Henry Acosta[1] , Hector Mendieta[1] , Henry Lezcano-Pittí[1] ,
Denis Cedeño-Moreno[1(✉)] , Luis Mendoza-Pittí[1] ,
Huriviades Calderon-Gómez[1] , Aristides Villarreal-Bravo[1,3] ,
Miguel Vargas-Lombardo[3(✉)] , and Boris Salvatierra-Gómez[3]

[1] Facultad de Sistemas Computacionales (FISC), Universidad Tecnológica de Panamá, Ciudad de Panamá, Panamá
{henry.lezcano,denis.cedeno,luis.mendoza1,huriviades.calderon,
aristides.villarreal}@utp.ac.pa

[2] Centro de Investigación TICs (CIDITIC), Universidad Tecnológica de Panamá, Ciudad de Panamá, Panamá
clifton.clunie@utp.ac.pa

[3] Universidad Tecnológica de Panamá, GISES, Ciudad de Panamá, Panamá
miguel.vargas@utp.ac.pa

Abstract. Every day, we face an increase in cases of violence and criminality committed by organized crime groups. This generates public safety problems and deteriorates the quality of life of inhabitants. Consequently, local authorities require more specialized security equipment. One kind is surveillance devices, but the monitoring process is very costly and fallible, and it is inefficient for human beings to analyze and process large amounts of data in an instant. Objective: In this contribution, we propose a prototype for the detection of firearms using deep learning algorithms with the objective of automating and optimizing this process. Methodology: To develop the firearm detection software, two important steps were carried out: creating a dataset with the presence of firearms and training a neural network to detect them. Results: Tests performed on the neural network YOLOv5 object detection model revealed a mAP of 0.645 and an average accuracy with 0.5 IoU at 0.915. Conclusions: The YOLO detection system allowed us to provide the developed model with the relevant image segments for firearm detection. In the future, low light detection can be improved and a more advanced version of YOLOv6 can be used to achieve higher accuracy in both images and videos.

Keywords: Machine learning · models machine learning · neural networks · real-time object detection · You Only Look Once

1 Introduction

The United Nations Office on Drugs and Crime (UNODC) estimated the homicide rate in Latin America and the Caribbean to be 15.5 per 100,000 inhabitants in 2011, more than double the global rate of 6.9 per 100,000 inhabitants, and almost five times higher

R. Valencia-García et al. (Eds.): CITI 2023, CCIS 1873, pp. 3–13, 2023.
https://doi.org/10.1007/978-3-031-45682-4_1

than the European rate of 3.5 per 100,000 [7]. While South America's homicide rate has followed the global trend of declining, rates in Central America and the Caribbean have been increasing. Most previous studies have addressed weapon detection in X-ray, millimeter, or RGB images using classical machine learning methods [1–5]. Currently, the most accurate object detection models are based on deep learning techniques, particularly CNN (convolutional neural network) based models. The emergence of these technologies provides us with countless new challenges and solutions to current problems, with software engineering being an indispensable area for the development of these solutions. One of them is surveillance devices, but the monitoring process makes it very difficult for humans to analyze and process large amounts of data in an instant. In many cases, these videos are used after the incident has occurred. Instead, with the help of an intelligent system that actively reports incidents of gun violence, it will be possible to optimize the alerts so the necessary personnel can proceed in the best way. By having AI integrated into one or several security cameras, it is possible to have better control and responses to cases of gun violence, sending an immediate alert to the authorities so that they can stop any type of violence.

The present study developed a firearm detection system using deep learning and addressing the detection problem, applied to recorded or live surveillance videos in these scenarios. Firearm detection in surveillance videos faces several challenges:

- Firearms can be handled in different ways, and a large part of the weapon can be occluded.
- Short-barreled firearms are small and the distance from the camera can be large, making detection more difficult.
- The process of designing a new dataset to successfully train the detection model is manual and time-consuming.

We build a new dataset that enables the model to successfully learn the distinctive features of firearms, then develop a firearm detection model suitable for real-life scenarios. This research proposes a deep learning model for handgun (pistol and revolver) detection to optimize real-time handgun monitoring and detection. On the social side, this may make people feel safer when leaving their homes. This research is divided into three sections. Section 2 explains the background of the research. Section 3 materials and methods for models. The Sect. 4, to present the results and discussion. Then the conclusions of this research are presented.

2 Background

In recent years, important advances have been made in the application of deep learning techniques for image recognition. Some related work has been published in these areas, for example, Redmon [17] proposed an object detection algorithm "You Only Look Once, YOLO" which was claimed to be more usable in real time than the prevailing algorithms due to its speed in object detection. An input image is divided into $S \times S$ grid cells, and some grid cells are responsible for detecting an object present in the image, i.e., only those where the center of the bounding box is in the cell. There were β bounding boxes, and the confidence scores for those boxes were predicted for each grid cell. The bounding box prediction is composed of five components: (x, y, w, h, c), where the coordinates (x, y) give the center of the box, (w, h) give the width and height of the box, and c gives the box's confidence score. There are in total $S \times S \times \beta \times 5$ outputs for an image input. The presence or absence of a bump can be determined from the confidence score. As in [17], we define the confidence score as where Pr(Object) is the probability of a pothole appearing in a grid cell and IoU is the intersection of the junction between the ground truth and the predicted boxes, as shown in Eq. (3). If no bump exists in that cell, the confidence score should be zero.

You Only Look Once (YOLOv5) was developed and published by Glenn Jocher, Ultralytics LLC, in 2020 as a GitHub repository [6]. There are four main YOLOv5 models based on the complexity of the architecture, i.e., XS, S, M, and L. This paper provides a performance analysis of the large (Yl), medium (Ym), and small (Ys) YOLOv5 models. The YOLOv5 models [6] include two main parts: the model backbone and the model head. YOLOv5 uses ResNet101 to develop the partial cross-stage bottleneck (CSP) that reduces the network parameters, extracts informative features from an input image [18], and reuses the captured features. Second, YOLOv5 develops the final detection part (model head) for feature aggregation. It is responsible for generating the final output vectors, including bounding boxes, confidence scores, and class probabilities. The final detection layers use the Sigmod activation function; however, the intermediate or hidden layers use Leaky ReLU activation functions. Finally, to filter out false predictions, in this work, we ignore any prediction that has a confidence score lower than 0.5. YOLOv5 uses the k-means clustering algorithm with different values of k to automatically determine the best anchor frames for that dataset and use them during training. In YOLOv5 calculates the total loss function from the regression loss, box_loss (based on GIoU; Eqs. (4)-(6)), obj_loss (based on IoU; Eqs. (3) and (7)), and the loss classification cls_loss. In this work, cls_loss is equal to zero because the prototype only detects firearms.

2.1 Faster R-CNN

The layers of the Faster R-CNN architecture are depicted in Fig. 2. It generates two region proposal networks (RPNs) for object detection. To generate the region proposal, a selective search approach is used. The anchors or region frames are classified by the RPN. This region proposal network takes as input the convolution feature map generated by the backbone layer and applies the anchors generated by sliding window convolution on the input feature map.

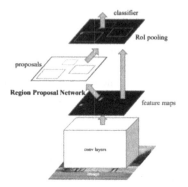

Fig. 1. Archictecture Faster R-CNN [20].

2.2 SSD (Single Shot Detector)

The SSD algorithm reached new milestones in terms of accuracy and detection performance. SSD speeds up the process by eliminating the need for a regional proposal network. To overcome the drop in accuracy, SSD brings some technologies, including preset frames and multi-scale functions. These enhancements allow SSD to match the accuracy of Faster R-CNN using lower-resolution images, which further increases speed. The average score is around 74% mAP and 59 FPS on the COCO dataset. COCO dataset. Figure 2 shows the SSD VGG-16 architecture [20–22].

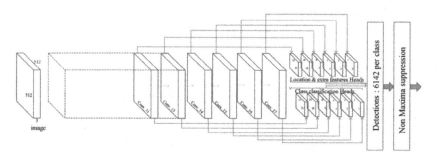

Fig. 2. MobileNet-V1 SSD architecture [22].

3 Materials and Methods for Proposed Model

Next, we present the set of data and the tools used to develop this work and explain in detail our proposed model. Figure 3 depicts the model proposed of weapon detection.

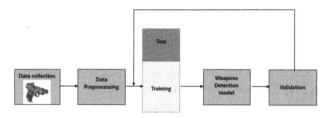

Fig. 3. Depicts the model proposed of weapon detection-Data Mining

3.1 Overview

First, we extract and pre-process the data set. With him training dataset, we train the model. We carry out the relevant evaluations, if it is necessary to readjust the values and re-train the model until this is the most adjusted possible.

3.2 Data Collection

In this research, data collection for criminal intent was collected on images of crimes with the intent to use firearms. The authors collected data on the intention to commit armed crimes in public using a public image dataset from the gun detection dataset.

3.3 Collection of the Dataset

The dataset must be prepared correctly. It is composed of image files and label files indicating the weapon objects in the images, which are then partitioned into the training set and the test set. The partitioned dataset needs to be converted into a TFRecord file, which is the data file format used for training the TensorFlow Model Zoo object detection model. This research uses the pre-trained Tensor-Flow Model Zoo model, which includes:

- SSD MobileNet-V1
- EfficientDet-D0
- Faster R-CNN Inception Resnet-V2

In the model training process, the split TFRecord files were used to feed image information through the network. The configuration pipeline file was used to set the iteration and other values for model training. The label map file is also needed to indicate the type of objects for the learning model. To evaluate the weapon detection model, the value of the results will indicate the location of the detected weapon in the images and the type of object classified. To analyze the correctness of the model, we use Mean Average Precision (mAP) and Intersection over Union (IoU).

3.4 Evaluation Model

The object detection result returns the predicted class and bounding box of the object. The evaluation deals with the standard loss function for the prediction class classification and bounding box location of the TensorFlow Pre-trained Object Detection Application Programming Interface (API) [23].

3.5 Evaluation

The metrics below were followed for the evaluation:

- P-R (Precision-Recall) curve: Precision is the fraction of relevant cases among the retrieved cases. Recall is the fraction of relevant cases retrieved over the total number of relevant cases [24]. The equations for these cases follow:

$$Pres = \frac{TP}{TP + FP} \tag{1}$$

$$Pres = \frac{TP}{P + FN} \tag{2}$$

- AP (Average Precision): This was proposed for the VOC2007 challenge [25] to evaluate the performance of detectors and is related to the area under the P-R curve of a class. The mAP is the average of the APs of all classes [24].

$$GIoU = \frac{Area + B_{det} \cap B_{gt-}}{Area + B_{det} \cup B_{gt-}} \tag{3}$$

where **B***gt* is the true ROI and **B***det* is the detected ROI. In this case, we have a TP if the IoU value greater than 0.5, otherwise it is FP. With these values, Eqs. (1) and (2) can be evaluated.

- GIoU: is used to evaluate how close the prediction bounding box (A) is to the ground truth box (B), where A, B $\subseteq$ S $\in$ R and the shape of the object (C), C $\subseteq$ S $\in$ R [26].

$$GIoU = IoU - \frac{\overset{C}{\&\, UB}}{|C|} \tag{4}$$

It calculates the loss related to the predicted bounding box position (x, y) and the actual position (x̂, ŷ) from the training data. This function computes a sum over each bounding box predictor (j = 0... β) of each grid cell (i = 0... s7)$]\!]$ $^{ob}8$. The object involved is the object$]\!]$ $^{ob}8$ that appears in cell i and$]\!]$ $^{ob}8$ indicates that the j-th bounding box predictor in cell i is responsible for that prediction.

$$\lambda_{coord} \sum_{i=0}^{S^2} \sum_{j=0}^{\beta} []^{obj} (x_i - \hat{x}_i)^2 + (y_i - \hat{y}_i)^2 \tag{5}$$

In the model training process, the split TFRecord files were used to feed image information through the network. The configuration pipeline file was used to adjust the iteration and other values for model training. The label map file is also needed to indicate the type of objects for the learning model. To evaluate the weapon detection model, the value of the results will indicate the location of the detected weapon in the images and the type of object.

- box_loss: calculates the loss related to the predicted bounding box position (x, y) and the actual position (x̂, ŷ) from the training data. This function computes a sum over each bounding box predictor (j = 0... β) of each grid cell (i = 0... s7)$]\!]$ ob; where *ob* implies the object that.

- obj_loss: loss related to the coordination error of the predicted box width/height. The square root is used to reflect that small deviations in large boxes matter less than those in small boxes. Therefore, we can predict the square root of the bounding box width and height instead of the width and height directly.

$$\lambda_{coord} \sum_{i=0}^{S^2} \sum_{j=0}^{\beta} \mathbb{1}_{ij}^{obj} \left[\left(\sqrt{w_i} - \sqrt{\hat{w}_i} \right)^2 + \left(\sqrt{h_i} - \sqrt{\hat{h}_i} \right)^2 \right] \tag{6}$$

- cls_loss: loss related to the classification error as a function of the confidence score for each bounding box predictor. Here, C is the confidence score and C^ is the intercept over the union of the predicted bounding box with the ground truth.

$$\sum_{i=0}^{S^2} \sum_{j=0}^{\beta} \mathbb{1}_{ij}^{obj} (C_i - \hat{C}_i)^2 + \lambda_{noobj} \sum_{i=0}^{S^2} \sum_{j=0}^{\beta} \mathbb{1}_{ij}^{noobj} (C_i - \hat{C}_i)^2 \tag{7}$$

4 Results and Discussion

For the weapon detection experiment, a dataset composed of weapon detection data was used. The pre-trained model of the TensorFlow framework was used for detection training:

1) SSD MobileNet-V1
2) EfficientDet-D0
3) Faster R-CNN Inception Resnet-V2
4) YOLOv5.

The model will adjust the location loss and classification loss to improve the accuracy of understanding the detection model data. The above losses can indicate the mathematical efficiency of incorrect prediction from type classification.

In Table 1, the weapon detection models appear in cell i, and⟧ ob;it indicates that the jth bounding box predictor in cell i is responsible for that prediction. The model will adjust the location loss and classification loss to improve the accuracy of understanding the detection model data. The above losses may indicate the mathematical efficiency of incorrect prediction from type classification. Table 1 shows the weapon detection models that were trained with Dataset 1, comprising 3973 gun images, 2400 training images, and 573 test images. The models achieved the highest mAP of 0.645, mAP at 0.5 IoU of 0.915.

Table 1. Weapons detection model evaluation.

Architecture	mAP	0.5IoU
SSD MobileNet-V1	0.562	0.787
EficienteDet-D0	0.431	0.771
Faster R-CNN Inception-V2	0.540	0.793
YOLO-V5	0.645	0.915

Table 2 shows the corresponding average accuracy (AP) values per gun class for the evaluation of the average accuracy value of the training dataset.

Table 2. Weapons detection model evaluation

Architecture	Precision	Recall	F1
SSD MobileNet-V1	78.7%	69.5%	73.81%
EficienteDet-D0	77.1%	59.9%	67.42%
Faster R-CNN Inception-V2	79.3%	68.6%	
YOLO-V5 (Ys)	94.03%	84.2%	-

In Table 2 show each study has a unique dataset, models, and measures to evaluate performance, the results may not be comparable. Each research attempt has its own set of testing circumstances, such as focusing only on images, videos, or high-resolution photographs. The performance metric implemented in several investigations is accuracy, while others use precision or mean accuracy (mAP). However, mAP is the most used. Therefore, we compare the findings in terms of mAP and accuracy at a standard IoU threshold of 0.50, as shown in Table 3, to evaluate weapon detection.

Compared to Carrobles et al. [14], Faster R-CNN-based weapon and knife detection for video surveillance uses CCTV angle-view images along with the image magnification method for preprocessing. From the results, our methods using Faster R-CNN Inception Resnet-V2 had an accuracy at 0.5 IoU of 79.3%, better than using Faster R-CNN GoogLeNet, which obtained a result of 55.25%. Gonzalez et al. [15] used Faster R-CNN Resnet50 FPN training on different datasets; the gun dataset achieved a 0.5 IoU accuracy of 88.1% and mAP of 0.652, while our similarly structured image dataset realized a 0.5 IoU accuracy of 78.71% and mAP of 0.562. Navalgund et al. [15] achieved a 0.5 IoU accuracy of 62.79% with SSD MobileNet-V1 training for weapon and non-weapon datasets. Compared to our method, SSD MobileNet-V1 achieves an accuracy of 78.7% at 0.5 IoU. Bushra et al. [27] used YOLOv5 training on different datasets; the gun dataset achieved accuracy of 98% and a mAP of 0.95 at 0.5 IoU, while our training achieved accuracy of 94.03% and a mAP of 0.645 at 0.5 IoU.

Table 3. Evaluation model

Case	Architecture	Precision	mAP
Carrobles et al. [14]	Faster R-CNN GoogleNet	55.45%	-
González et al. [16]	Faster R-CNN Resnet50 FPN (Handgun dataset)	88.1%	0.652
	Faster R-CNN Resnet50 FPN (Mock Attract Cam)	3.4%	0.009
Navalgund et al. [15]	Faster R-CNN Inception-V2	86.38%	-
	SSD MobileNet-V1	62.79%	-
Bushra et al. [27]	YOLOv4	84%	0.89
	YOLOv5	98%	0.95
Research	SSD MobileNet-V1	78.7%	0.562
	EficienteDet-D0	77.1%	0.431
	Faster R-CNN Inception-V2	79.3%	0.540
	YOLOv5 (Ys)	94.03%	0.645

5 Conclusions

This research presents a weapon detection model using object detection. The object detection method is based on the Model Zoo object detection API for specifying weapons in an image. The model provided accurate prediction and localization of the weapon type when using the dataset involving a medium to large object. Finally, the experimental report indicated the potential of deep learning algorithms for solving crime events. Based on the results obtained in the experimentation it can be concluded that:

- Increasing the dataset by implementing different techniques for the creation of new images provides complementary information, as the tests performed did not present strong overtraining in the initial stages of the network.
- The YOLO detection system allowed us to provide the developed model with the image segments that are relevant for firearm detection, allowing the whole system to focus only on the image segments where people with firearms appear and ignore the other areas of the image where firearms may not be present.
- Compared to all other YOLO families, identifying suspicious activities from video frames is a challenging task that requires processing multiple videos and images at the same time. However, it can help to make criminal activities occurring in the environment irrelevant to the current usual scenarios. In the future, low-light detection can be improved, and a more advanced version of YOLOv6 can be used to achieve higher accuracy in both images and videos.

Acknowledgments. We thank the to the national research system of Panama (SNI)-National Secretariat of Science, Technology and Innovation (SENACYT) and CIDITIC-UTP.

Authors Contribution.

Principal Author CLC, HM, HA; Conceptualization HA, HM, CLC, MVL; methodology CLC, HA; formal analysis CLC, LMP, HCG, BSG, HLP, AVB, DCM, MVL; research MVL, BSG, CMC, CLC, AVB; original-writing HA,HM, CLC, MVL; writing—review and edition MVL;HCG, LMP,BSG,HLP,AVB, DCM; Corresponding author DCM, MVL.

References

1. Flitton, G., Breckon, T.P., Megherbi, N.: A comparison of 3D interest point descriptors with application to airport baggage object detection in complex CT imagery. Pattern Recogn. **46**(9), 2420–2436 (2013)
2. Glowacz, A., Kmiec, M., Dziech, A.: Visual detection of knives in security applications using active appearance models. Multimedia Tools Appl. **74**(12), 4253–4267 (2015)
3. Tiwari, R.L., Verma, G.K.: A computer vision based framework for visual gun detection using harris interest point detector. Procedia Comput. Sci. **54**(1), 703–712 (2015)
4. Uroukov, I., Speller, R.: A preliminary approach to intelligent x-ray imaging for baggage inspection at airports. Signal Process. Res. **4**(1), 1–11 (2015)
5. Xiao, Z., Lu, X., Yan, J., Wu, L., Ren, L.: Automatic detection of concealed pistols using passive millimeter wave imaging. In: 2015 IEEE International Conference on Imaging Systems and Techniques (IST), pp. 1–4 (2015)
6. Jocher, G., et al.: ultralytics/yolov5: v5. 0-YOLOv5-P6. 1280, April 2021
7. Jocher, G., et al.: ultralytics/yolov5: v5.0 - YOLOv5- P6 1280 models, AWS, Supervisely and YouTube integrations, 4 (2021). [En línea]. https://doi.org/10.5281/ze-nodo.4679653
8. Buckchash, H., Balasubramanian, R.: A robust object detector: application to detection of visual knives. IEEE Multimedia Expo Workshops, 633–638 (2017)
9. Kmiec, M., Andrzej, G.: Object detection in security applications using dominant edge directions. Pattern Recogn. Lett. **52**(72), 79 (2015)
10. Tiwari, R.K., Verma, G.K.: A computer vision based framework for visual gun detection using SURF. In: Conference: International Conference on Electrical, Electronics, Signals, Communication and Optimization (EESCO) (2015)
11. Alahi, A., Ortiz, R., Vandergheynst, P.: FREAK: Fast Retina Keypoint, IEEE, **16**(21), 8 (2012)
12. Bhatia, S.K.: Adaptive K-Means clustering. In: FLAIRS Conference, pp. 695–699 (2004)
13. Huval, B., et al.: An empirical evaluation of deep learning on highway driving, arXiv preprint (2015)
14. Silver, D., et al.: Mastering the game of Go with deep neural networks and tree search. Nature, 529(7587), 484–489 (2016)
15. Morales, A., Fierrez, J., Sanchez, J.S., Ribeiro, B.: Pattern Recognition and Image Analysis: 9th Iberian Conference, IbPRIA 2019, Madrid, Spain, July 1–4, 2019, Proceedings, Part II, pp. 441–452, July 2019. https://doi.org/10.1007/978-3-030-31321-0_38
16. Navalgund, U.V., Priyadharshini, K.: Crime intention detection system using deep learning. In: 2018 International Conference on Circuits and Systems in Digital Enterprise Technology (ICCSDET), Kottayam, India, pp. 1–6 (2018). https://doi.org/10.1109/ICCSDET.2018.882 1168
17. Gonzalez, J.L.S., et al.: Real-time gun detection in CCTV: an open problem, Elsevier, vol. 132, pp. 297–308 (2020)
18. Redmon, J., Divvala, S., Girshick, R., Farhadi, A.: You only look once: unified, real-time object detection. In: Proceedings of the IEEE Conference on Computer Vision and Pattern Recognition (CVPR), Las Vegas, NV, USA, pp. 27–30 (2016)

19. Wang, C.-Y., et al.: CSP-Net: a new backbone that can enhance learning capability of CNN. In: Proceedings of the 2020 IEEE/CVF Conference on Computer Vision and Pattern Recognition Work-shops (CVPRW), Seattle, WA, USA, pp. 14–19 (2020)
20. Roeder, L.: Netron App Github (2021). [En línea]. Available: https://gi-thub.com/lutzroeder/netron. Accessed 11 Dec 2022
21. Biswas, A., Jana, A.P., Tejas, S.S.: Classification of objects in video records using neural network framework. In: International Conference on Smart Systems and Inventive Technology (2018)
22. Liu, W., Anguelov, D., Erhan, D., Szegedy, C., Reed, S., Fu, C.-Y., Berg, A.C.: SSD: Single Shot MultiBox Detector. In: European Conference on Computer Vision, vol. 169, pp. 20–31 (2017)
23. Jain, N., et al.: Performance analysis of object detection and tracking algorithms for traffic surveillance applications using neural networks. In: Third International conference on I-SMAC (IoT in Social, Mobile, Analytics and Cloud (2019)
24. tensorflow/models, GitHub, [En línea]. Available: https://github.com/ten-sorflow/models. Accessed 22 Nov 2022
25. Ramírez, J.: Curvas PR y ROC, bluekiri, 18 7 2018. [En línea]. Available: https://medium.com/bluekiri/curvas-pr-y-roc-1489fbd9a527. Accessed 15 Nov 2022
26. Everingham, M., et al.: The PASCAL Visual Object Classes (VOC) challenge. Int. J. Comput. Vis. **88**, 303–338 (2010)
27. Rezatofighi, H., Tsoi, N., Gwak, J.Y., Sadeghian, A., Reid, I., Savarese, S.: Generalized intersection over union: a metric and a loss for bounding box regression. In: Proceedings of the IEEE Conference on Computer Vision and Pattern Recognition, Long Beach, CA, USA, pp. 15–20 (2019)
28. Bushra, S.N., Shobana, G., Maheswari, K.U., Subramanian, K.: Smart video survillance based weapon identification using Yolov5 (2022)

Logistic Regression Model to Predict the Risk of Contagion of COVID-19 in Patients with Associated Morbidity Using Supervised Machine Learning

Vanessa Vergara-Lozano[1]([✉]) [ID], Katty Lagos-Ortiz[1] [ID], Jenny Chavez-Urbina[1] [ID], and Christian Rochina García[2] [ID]

[1] Facultad de Ciencias Agrarias, Universidad Agraria del Ecuador, Av. 25 de Julio, Guayaquil, Ecuador
{vvergara,klagos,jchavez}@uagraria.edu.ec

[2] Facultad de Ciencias Administrativas, Universidad Internacional del Ecuador, Av. Las Aguas y Av. Juan Tanca Marengo, Guayaquil, Ecuador
chrochinaga@uide.edu.ec

Abstract. This paper approaches the use of supervised machine learning techniques, the Logistic regression model indeed, to predict the risk of COVID-19 infection in patients with associated comorbidity rate. The objective is to develop a predictive model that can identify those patients with chronic diseases whose probabilities of acquiring the virus and other infectious diseases are high. Data obtained from the Mexican government are used which include information of patients with morbidities and their infection status. A review of the data is conducted and meaningful variables such as diabetes, hypertension, obesity, among others are selected for this study. A logistic regression model is developed by using the predictive variables priorly selected, and the parameters of the model are adjusted. It evaluates the accuracy of the model by comparing it with the known real values in a test dataset. An accuracy of the 66.67% of the model is obtained approximately. This study shows that comorbidities associated with pneumonia, diabetes, immunosuppression, hypertension, obesity, and tobacco are more closely related to a higher risk of COVID-19 infection. A model is proposed with these predictive variables, which achieves a similar accuracy to the initial model but with fewer predictive variables, making it easier to read.

In conclusion, the use of logistic regression models can be a very powerful tool to predict the risk of COVID-19 infection in patients with associated morbidities. However, permanent validation and refinement of the model, as well as consideration of other relevant factors, are required to obtain excellent results.

Keywords: Comorbidity · Infectious diseases · Supervised machine learning · Logistic regression model

R. Valencia-García et al. (Eds.): CITI 2023, CCIS 1873, pp. 14–26, 2023.
https://doi.org/10.1007/978-3-031-45682-4_2

1 Introduction

At the end of 2019, the emergence of COVID-19 caused a problematic situation that affected the entire world and led to an increase in emerging and re-emerging infectious diseases [1, 2]. It is known that coronaviruses are a large family of viruses and have caused many respiratory infections in humans.

The virus identified as SARS-CoV-2 is the causative agent of the coronavirus, and its transmission has been demonstrated through the presentation of various symptoms such as fever, fatigue, loss of taste, dry cough, nasal congestion, and other respiratory complications. Additionally, there were more severe cases such as pneumonia, sepsis, etc. This disease was declared a pandemic which affected the entire population [3].

More than 41 million people die annually from non-transmissible chronic diseases. Chronic diseases identified by scientists as the main risks closely related to COVID-19 complications include respiratory diseases such as chronic obstructive pulmonary disease (COPD), asthma, pulmonary fibrosis, cardiovascular conditions like hypertension, and metabolic conditions like diabetes [4]. Severe cases of COVID-19 are associated with advanced age [5], male gender [6], and the presence of comorbidities [7].

The identification of comorbidities associated with severe clinical presentation of COVID-19 is important for the appropriate therapeutic management of affected patients and for the development of health strategies aimed at the prevention and treatment of medical complications in the context of this disease.

Nowadays, there are reports that link the presence of comorbidities to a high or moderate risk of COVID-19 infection. However, the information available is scattered, and individual patient studies are necessary for precise conclusions. Therefore, the objective of this article is to analyze the risk of COVID-19 contagion in patients presenting clinical symptoms with associated comorbidities by creating a logistic regression model using machine learning [8].

This topic focuses on using supervised machine learning techniques, specifically the logistic regression model, to predict the risk of COVID-19 contagion in patients with underlying health conditions or diseases. The use of logistic regression models in this context allows us to leverage the relationship between input variables (such as prior health data, laboratory test results, among others) and the target variable (the risk of COVID-19 contagion) [9]. By training the model with data from previously diagnosed COVID-19 patients and variables associated with their health status, we can construct a model that learns to make predictions about the contagion risk in new patients with comorbidities.

This approach has several important implications. Firstly, it can help identify those patients with underlying health conditions who are at higher risk of contracting COVID-19. This can be useful in prioritizing the allocation of healthcare resources and making informed decisions regarding preventive measures and safety protocols.

Furthermore, the implementation of machine learning and predictive models might contribute to better the efficiency and accuracy of triage and early detection strategies [10]. By providing a tool capable of rapidly assessing the risk of contagion in patients who suffer associated morbidity, some effective preventive measures may be implemented and it would allow a successful management of healthcare resources.

Machine learning techniques, such as logistic regression, when combining with clinical and health data, have shown their effectiveness when predicting the severeness and outcomes of COVID-19. A group of scientists have developed a deep learning system for early triage of patients with early critical condition of COVID-19. This study has demonstrated that the logistic model and the input data allowed a precise classification of all the patients according to their cases of severity. As a consequence of that, it has facilitated an effective and immediate medical attention [11].

To fulfill the objective pursued by this research, logistic regression is a statistical technique that allows quantifying, in terms of probabilities, the risk of contagion of COVID-19 from the morbidity characteristics associated with an individual. Its ability to identify more related risk factors and its strength in the management of categorical variables makes it a successful technique to address this research.

These studies assure the idea that the utilization of logistic regression models in the context of COVID-19 and patients with associated morbidity may contribute with significant information for predicting the risk of contagion and the previous identification of patients with serious and severe complications. Nevertheless, it is primordial to emphasize that the continuous validation and refinement of these models are indispensable to certify their authenticity and effectiveness in a variety of clinical settings.

It is fundamental to take into consideration that the accomplishment of these models vastly depends on the quality and the representativeness of the data that have been used for this training. in addition to this, the models of logistic regression may have some limitations when capturing nonlinear relationships between variables y the interpretation of the model coefficients.

To come to the point, the implementation of logistic regression to make known in advance the risk of COVID-19 contagion in patients with associated morbidity portrays an optimistic application of machine learning. It might be used as a supplementary tool to prevent and detect high-risk patients and strengthen the strategies illness prevention and management. On the other hand, it is required a detailed validation and improvement of the models, as well as a comprehensive approach that unites clinical information with other significant factors to reach successful results.

2 Methodology

The research is based in the development of a model capable of making predictive analysis (PA) applied to authentic data from the patients, in order to provide the necessary and quick support when deciding clinical decision-making. The aim is to algorithmically recognize the combinations of clinical features (associated morbidities) of COVID-19 that forecast patients at higher risk of developing more alarming illnesses since its first stage [12]. This study strives to address the crucial need for a trustworthy prediction model for COVID-19 and in particular considering those individuals with chronic conditions such as cardiovascular diseases, chronic pulmonary illnesses, diabetes, obesity, renal diseases, and immunological disorders, who have a higher risk of serious complications if they contract COVID-19 [13].

For the current study, the statistical software R Studio was applied for the management, analysis and modeling of variables, utilizing various phases. In the first phase, a treatment and cleaning of the data was put in effect since there were unknown data in the predictor variables, which represents a minor percentage, less than 1%. In the second phase, an accurate and significant selection of variables was conducted, focusing mainly on the associated morbidities of the patients. In the third phase, the generation of the Logistic Regression model was obtained to prognosticate the risk of contracting the COVID-19 virus. The effectiveness of this predictive model was applied by using performance metrics, evidence that can be examined in the final stage. The whole proposed developmental process can be analyzed in the flowchart shown in Fig. 1.

Fig. 1. Flowchart of the Phases of Data Analysis and Modeling.

2.1 Data Processing

- Sample and Data Source

For the analysis and modeling, a dataset was utilized which was provided by the Mexican government [14].The data file includes a great amount of anonymized patient-related information, including preconditions. The dataset is composed of 21 unique features (discrete and Boolean variables) and 1,048,576 distinct patients. In the Boolean features, 1 indicates "yes," while 2 signifies "no". Additionally, the values 97 and 99 denote missing data [15]. Variables were extensively refined and recoded as can be seen in Table 1 in the observations.

Table 1. Description of each variable within the sample taken and the changes made to them.

Variables	Description	Observation
SEX	1 for female and 2 for male	It was recorded to 1 and 0, where 1 is female and 0 is male
AGE	The age of the patient when they were attended	Same encoding was used
CLASSIFICATION	COVID test results. Values 1–3 indicate that the patient was diagnosed with COVID at different degrees. If it was 4 or higher, it means the patient is not a COVID carrier or the test result is inconclusive	It was recoded to 1 and 0, where 1 represents a COVID diagnosis and 0 indicates the absence of the virus

(continued)

Table 1. (*continued*)

Variables	Description	Observation
TYPE OF PATIENT	The type of care the patient received at the facility. 1 for home return and 2 for hospitalization	Same encoding was used
PNEUMONIA	Whether the patient already has inflammation of the alveoli or not	Same encoding was used
PREGNANCY	Whether the patient is pregnant or not	Same encoding was used
DIABETES	Whether the patient has diabetes or not	Same encoding was used
COPD	Whether the patient has chronic obstructive pulmonary disease (COPD) or not	Same encoding was used
ASTHMA	Whether the patient has asthma or not	Same encoding was used
IMMUSUPR	Whether the patient is immunocompromised or not	Same encoding was used
HYPERTENSION	Whether the patient has hypertension or not	Same encoding was used
CARDIOVASCULAR	Whether the patient has a disease related to the heart or blood vessels	Same encoding was used
CHRONIC RENAL	Whether the patient has a chronic renal disease or not	Same encoding was used
OTHERS	Whether the patient has any other disease	Same encoding was used
OBESITY	Whether the patient is obese or not	Same encoding was used
TOBACCO	Whether the patient is a tobacco consumer or not	Same encoding was used
USMR	Whether the patient attended healthcare facilities of first, second, or third level	Same encoding was used
MEDICAL UNIT	Type of institution with the National Health System that provides healthcare	Same encoding was used
INTUBATED	Whether the patient was connected to the ventilator or not	Same encoding was used

(*continued*)

Table 1. (*continued*)

Variables	Description	Observation
ICU	Whether the patient was admitted to an Intense Care Unit (ICU) or not	Same encoding was used
DATE OF DEATH	If the patient passed away, indicate the date of death, and use 9999–99-99 otherwise	Same encoding was used

2.2 Significant Variables

A literature review was conducted to identify relevant but strongly confusing variables that could be associated with both the exposure of interest and the outcome of interest [16]. The most important variables were selected to be included in the regression model. The predictive variables for the modeling of the study included patient-related morbidities, with 12 types of Boolean variables to identify this important characteristic in the analysis. Each variable is presented with its descriptive statistical measures in Table 2.

Table 2. Predictive variables of the model with their descriptive statistical measures.

PNEUMONIA	PREGNANT	DIABETES	COPD
Min.:1.000	Min.:1.000	Min.:1.000	Min.:1.000
1st Qu.:2.000	1st Qu.:2.000	1st Qu.:2.000	1st Qu.:2.000
Median:2.000	Median:2.000	Median:2.000	Median:2.000
Mean:1.893	Mean:1.985	Mean:1.884	Mean:1.986
3rd Qu.:2.000	3rd Qu.:2.000	3rd Qu.:2.000	3rd Qu.:2.000
Max.:2.000	Max.:2.000	Max.:2.000	Max.:2.000
ASTHMA	INMSUPR	HIPERTENSION	OTHER_DISEASE
Min.:1.000	Min.:1.000	Min.:1.000	Min.:1.00
1st Qu.:2.000	1st Qu.:2.000	1st Qu.:2.000	1st Qu.:2.00
Median:2.000	Median:2.000	Median:2.000	Median:2.00
Mean:1.963	Mean:1.986	Mean:1.845	Mean:1.97
3rd Qu.:2.000	3rd Qu.:2.000	3rd Qu.:2.000	3rd Qu.:2.00
Max.:2.000	Max.:2.000	Max.:2.000	Max.:2.00
CARDIOVASCULAR	OBESITY	RENAL_CHRONIC	TOBACCO
Min.:1.000	Min.:1.00	Min.:1.000	Min.:1.000
1st Qu.:2.000	1st Qu.:2.00	1st Qu.:2.000	1st Qu.:2.000

(*continued*)

Table 2. (*continued*)

PNEUMONIA	PREGNANT	DIABETES	COPD
Median:2.000	Median:2.00	Median:2.000	Median:2.000
Mean:1.982	Mean:1.84	Mean:1.984	Mean:1.947
3rd Qu.:2.000	3rd Qu.:2.00	3rd Qu.:2.000	3rd Qu.:2.000
Max.:2.000	Max.:2.00	Max.:2.000	Max.:2.000

The missing data represented a very low percentage within the sample, that is why they were not part of the analysis. Additionally, it could be identified that there were higher percentages of morbidities in patients with diabetes (11.6%), hypertension (15.5%), obesity (16%) y pneumonia (10.7%) as shown in Fig. 2.

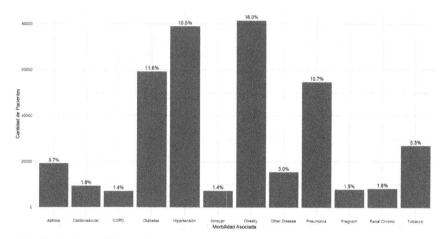

Fig. 2. Patients with associated morbidity that were assisted by symptoms of Covid-19

The selection of variables plays a fundamental role in identifying the most relevant characteristics in the process of building statistical models to contribute to the underlying relationships in the data [8]. A commonly used approach for this task is the evaluation of adjusted p-values. The adjusted p-value is a measure that quantifies the probability of observing an effect as extreme as that observed in the data, under the assumption that there is no real relationship between the independent variable and the dependent variable.

2.3 Predictive Model Launching

An automatic model of learning was developed based on Logistic regression to predict the risk of Covid-19 infection according to the 12 Boolean predictive variables which identified the associated morbidities in patients within the taken sample. There were used the selected characteristics as independent variables of the model [9]. The parameters of the model were adjusted by creating factors over the predictive variables due to the fact that they were working as binary variables (1 yes – 2 no).

The Logistic regression is useful for the cases in which the presence or the absence of a characteristic or result needs to be predicted according to the values of a set of predictors [10]. It is similar to a linear regression model, but it is adapted for models in which the dependent variable is binary, as in the case study in which the result of the variable is whether the patient contracts covid or not (1 – 0). The coefficients of Logistic regression can be used to calculate the probability of each variable regardless the model.

2.3.1 K-Fold Cross Validation

The robust evaluation of statistical models is essential to ensure the reliability of the results in the generation of this current model. K- fold cross-validation used as a reference methodology to address this challenge by offering an unbiased and strong evaluation of the performance of the models created [11]. This approach involves partitioning the dataset into k subsets equally. Through an interative process, each of these subsets is used as a test set while the remaining ones are used for model training.

With the implementation of this methodology, each observation participates in both the test conjunction and the training set is achieved, thus reducing the risk of bias and providing a more accurate evaluation of how the model generalizes to unseen data. K-fold cross-validation has become an essential tool for model selection and performance evaluation in various scientific fields, ensuring informed decision-making supported by empirical evidence.

2.4 Model Accuracy

The accuracy of the Logistic regression model that was stated in this paper refers to selection of cases properly classified by the model [12]. To calculate the accuracy, the predictions of the model must be compared with real known values in a test dataset as it is shown in the following formula:

$$Accuracy = (true\ positives + true\ negatives)\ /\ (true\ positives + False\ positives + true\ negatives + False\ negatives)$$

Sensitivity measures the ability of the model to identify positive observations in relation to all observations that are actually positive correctly [13]. In other words, sensitivity refers to the rate of true positives compared to the total positive observations.

Specificity measures the ability of the model to identify negative observations correctly in relation to all observations that are actually negative. It is the rate of true negatives compared to the total of negative observations [14]. 1 in 5 negative cases of risk of contagion of covid-19 were correctly predicted by the model.

3 Data Analysis

Automatic learning provides a number of techniques that help to find meaning from data, which are regularly grouped into supervised and unsupervised techniques. Within the group of supervised are the regression models that seek to predict a dependent variable from one or more independent variables or also known as predictors.

To accomplish the objective pursued by this research, logistic regression is a statistical technique that allows quantifying, in terms of probabilities, the risk of contagion of covid-19 from the morbidity characteristics associated with an individual. To identify more related risk factors and its strength in the management of categorical variables makes it a successful technique to address the present case of research.

Prior the application of the model, all the predictive variables will be converted into factual variables so that the presence or absence or morbidity in the patient will be identified as follows:

```
datos$PNEUMONIA <- as.factor(datos$PNEUMONIA)
datos$PREGNANT <- as.factor(datos$PREGNANT)
datos$DIABETES <- as.factor(datos$DIABETES)
datos$COPD <- as.factor(datos$COPD)
datos$ASTHMA <- as.factor(datos$ASTHMA)
datos$INMSUPR <- as.factor(datos$INMSUPR)
datos$HIPERTENSION <- as.factor(datos$HIPERTENSION)
datos$CARDIOVASCULAR <- as.factor(datos$CARDIOVASCULAR)
datos$RENAL_CHRONIC <- as.factor(datos$RENAL_CHRONIC)
datos$OTHER_DISEASE <- as.factor(datos$OTHER_DISEASE)
datos$OBESITY <- as.factor(datos$OBESITY)
datos$TOBACCO <- as.factor(datos$TOBACCO)
datos$CLASIFFICATION_FINAL <- as.factor(datos$CLASIFFICATION_FINAL)
```

Fig. 3. Conversion in factors of the predictive variables of the Logistic regression model.

A regression model is created as a first scenario that considers all available variables to determine the probability of risk of contagion of covid-19 from its associated morbidities. The results of the model can be identified in Fig. 4:

Evaluating the average validation indicators (precision, sensitivity and specificity) of the initial model that considers all the variables as shown in Fig. 5, it was possible to identify that 2 out of 3 predictions made by the model were correct; 9 out of 10 positive cases of risk of contagion of COVID-19 were correctly predicted and 1 out of 5 negative cases of risk of contagion of COVID-19 were correctly predicted.

K-fold method, which is an iterative and repetitive process, was used to have a strong evaluation of the statistical model and guarantee the reliability of the results. Repeating this process 5 times generates 5 independent estimates of model performance. Average indicators are obtained with these estimates, as an overall evaluation of performance, which facilitates the detection of patterns of overfitting and underestimation.

To select the most significant variables, the adjusted p-value method was applied, which quantifies the probability of observing an effect as extreme as that observed in the data. In this research, the significance threshold selected was less than 2e-16, which shown the variables with p-values below this threshold are considered statistically significant and they are selected to form part of our final model to predict the risk of contagion of covid-19, which it was possible to obtain 8 variables from among the 12 initially analyzed as can be seen in Fig. 6.

The average indicators of model performance when applying k-fold cru-zed validation can be seen in Fig. 7 below:

One of the characteristics to be evaluated to select the final model to be used corresponds to the appropriate number of independent variables. The preference for models with a small number of dependent variables compared to complex modes is rooted in

```
> summary(modelo_inicial)

Call:
glm(formula = CLASIFFICATION_FINAL ~ PNEUMONIA + PREGNANT + DIABETES +
    COPD + ASTHMA + INMSUPR + HIPERTENSION + CARDIOVASCULAR +
    RENAL_CHRONIC + OTHER_DISEASE + OBESITY + TOBACCO, family = binomial,
    data = datos_modelo)

Deviance Residuals:
    Min       1Q    Median       3Q       Max
-1.6021   -0.8601   -0.8601    1.4047    1.9975

Coefficients:
                   Estimate Std. Error   z value Pr(>|z|)
(Intercept)       -0.269508   0.054248    -4.968 6.76e-07 ***
PNEUMONIA2        -0.981833   0.009663  -101.610  < 2e-16 ***
PREGNANT2         -0.085686   0.024168    -3.545 0.000392 ***
DIABETES2         -0.278339   0.010030   -27.751  < 2e-16 ***
COPD2              0.153050   0.025926     5.903 3.56e-09 ***
ASTHMA2            0.136231   0.016039     8.494  < 2e-16 ***
INMSUPR2           0.276992   0.026323    10.523  < 2e-16 ***
HIPERTENSION2     -0.218766   0.009024   -24.244  < 2e-16 ***
CARDIOVASCULAR2    0.177714   0.022890     7.764 8.24e-15 ***
RENAL_CHRONIC2     0.205286   0.024249     8.466  < 2e-16 ***
OTHER_DISEASE2     0.132817   0.017851     7.440 1.00e-13 ***
OBESITY2          -0.283734   0.008137   -34.869  < 2e-16 ***
TOBACCO2           0.232002   0.013811    16.798  < 2e-16 ***
---
Signif. codes:  0 '***' 0.001 '**' 0.01 '*' 0.05 '.' 0.1 ' ' 1

(Dispersion parameter for binomial family taken to be 1)

    Null deviance: 662271  on 510040  degrees of freedom
Residual deviance: 644052  on 510028  degrees of freedom
AIC: 644078

Number of Fisher Scoring iterations: 4
```

Fig. 4. Results of the Logistic regression model.

```
> cat("Precisión promedio:", mean(precision_scores), "\n")
Precisión promedio: 0.6665464
> cat("Sensibilidad promedio:", mean(sensibilidad_scores), "\n")
Sensibilidad promedio: 0.9362015
> cat("Especificidad promedio:", mean(especificidad_scores), "\n")
Especificidad promedio: 0.1721259
> |
```

Fig. 5. Average Metrics of the Initial Logistic Regression

various theoretical and practical foundations. One of the fundamental reasons lies in the principle of parsimony, also known as "Occam's razor", which indicates that, between two equally valid explanations, the simpler is preferable. A model with fewer variables tends to be more interpretable and easier to communicate, allowing a clearer understanding of the relationships between variables and the outcome. Furthermore, the inclusion of non-relevant or redundant variables can be interpreted as bias and make it difficult to identify genuine patterns in the data. Also, models with an excessive number of variables are prone to overfitting, in which the model adapts too much to the training data and does not generalize well with new data. This can result in poor performance on unseen data sets and ultimately wrong decisions. In summary, choosing a model with a more limited and relevant set of independent variables not only improves interpretability and

```
Call:
glm(formula = CLASIFFICATION_FINAL ~ PNEUMONIA + DIABETES + ASTHMA +
    INMSUPR + HIPERTENSION + RENAL_CHRONIC + OBESITY + TOBACCO,
    family = binomial, data = datos_modelo)

Deviance Residuals:
    Min      1Q   Median      3Q      Max
-1.5859  -0.8595  -0.8595   1.4072   1.8834

Coefficients:
                  Estimate Std. Error  z value Pr(>|z|)
(Intercept)      -0.001530   0.038731   -0.040   0.968
PNEUMONIA2       -0.971456   0.009615 -101.030   <2e-16 ***
DIABETES2        -0.272439   0.010011  -27.213   <2e-16 ***
ASTHMA2           0.142442   0.016029    8.887   <2e-16 ***
INMSUPR2          0.316365   0.026104   12.119   <2e-16 ***
HIPERTENSION2    -0.204864   0.008950  -22.890   <2e-16 ***
RENAL_CHRONIC2    0.227281   0.024167    9.405   <2e-16 ***
OBESITY2         -0.279842   0.008130  -34.422   <2e-16 ***
TOBACCO2          0.238470   0.013802   17.278   <2e-16 ***
---
Signif. codes:  0 '***' 0.001 '**' 0.01 '*' 0.05 '.' 0.1 ' ' 1

(Dispersion parameter for binomial family taken to be 1)

    Null deviance: 662271  on 510040  degrees of freedom
Residual deviance: 644231  on 510032  degrees of freedom
AIC: 644249

Number of Fisher Scoring iterations: 4
```

Fig. 6. Summary of variables selected by the adjusted p-value method within the Model.

```
> cat("Precisión promedio:", mean(precision_scores), "\n")
Precisión promedio: 0.6663837
> cat("Sensibilidad promedio:", mean(sensibilidad_scores), "\n")
Sensibilidad promedio: 0.9354379
> cat("Especificidad promedio:", mean(especificidad_scores), "\n")
Especificidad promedio: 0.1730647
```

Fig. 7. Average metrics of the Logistic Regression Model applying K-Fold validation

communication, but also mitigates overfitting problems and increases the likelihood of obtaining consistent and reliable results across a variety of con-texts.

Based on the two proposed models, the model of the second scenario is selected, whose predictor variables were selected from p-value adjusted to a threshold of less than 2e-16. The summary table of indicators reveals that very little is sacrificed in terms of performance, especially in the accuracy and sensitivity of the model.

4 Conclusions and Further Investigation

Coronavirus disease (COVID-19) is an infectious disease caused by a coronavirus, most people infected with the COVID-19 virus experienced mild to moderate respiratory illness and recovered without requiring special treatment. Older people and those with underlying medical problems such as cardiovascular disease, diabetes, chronic respiratory diseases and cancer are more likely to develop severe diseases [15].

This study explored the predictive variables of morbidities associated with patients at risk of Covid-19 infection, through Log Regression modeling and validating it through the K-Fold method due to it is an effective tool to predict the probability of contracting a disease related to health conditions and other relevant factors. At the beginning, Logistic Regression was modeled with 12 variables of the morphologies associated with the patients, giving an accuracy of 0.6665434, but from the model obtained shown that the morbidities are associated with pneumonia, diabetes, asthma, immunosuppression, hypertension, kidney problems, obesity and tobacco being the most significant variables within the model and they are more related to the increase in the individual's vulnerability to contracting covid-19, It was modeled with these variables and obtained an accuracy of 0.6663867, that is, 0.0002 less than the accuracy of the initial version of this model, so this second version was chosen because it considered less valuable predictors, in exchange for an almost zero affectation in the accuracy of the model and gaining an understandable explanation for having a smaller number of predictive variables.

References

1. Pérez, A., Gómez, T., Dieguez, G.: Características clínico-epidemiológicas de la COVID-19. Rev Habanera Ciencias Médicas **2**, 1–15 (2020)
2. Tello Carhuanca, R., De La Calle Castro, A.I., Villegas Félix, T.L., Suasnabar Cueva, E.: Factores de comorbilidad y secuelas de covid 19 en trabajadores de un hospital nacional de Huancayo 2021. Visionarios en Cienc y Tecnol **6**, 111–121 (2022). https://doi.org/10.47186/visct.v6i2.97
3. Castro Amancio, A., Del-Carpio, S.: Relationship between comorbidities and COVID-19 morbidity and mortality. An la Acad Ciencias Cuba **11**, 936 (2021)
4. Díaz Pinzón, J.E.: Underlying comorbidities in Covid-19 related deaths by age group in Colombia. Rev Repert Med y Cirugía 117–121 (2020)
5. Wang, W., Tang, J., Fang, Q., Wei, F.: Updated understanding of the outbreak of 2019 novel coronavirus (2019-nCoV) in Wuhan, China. J. Med. Virol. 92, 441–447 (2020).https://doi.org/10.1002/jmv.25689
6. Jin, J.M., et al.: Gender differences in patients with COVID-19: focus on severity and mortality. Front Public Heal **8**, 545030 (2020). https://doi.org/10.3389/FPUBH.2020.00152/BIBTEX
7. Guan, W.J., et al.: Clinical characteristics of coronavirus disease 2019 in China. N. Engl. J. Med. (2020). https://doi.org/10.1056/NEJMoa2002032
8. Gutiérrez-Hernández, O., García, L.V.: Multiplicity Eludes Peer Review: The Case of COVID-19 Research (2021). https://doi.org/10.3390/ijerph18179304
9. Golas, S.B., et al.: A machine learning model to predict the risk of 30-day readmissions in patients with heart failure: a retrospective analysis of electronic medical records data. BMC Med. Inform. Decis. Mak. **18**, 1–17 (2018). https://doi.org/10.1186/s12911-018-0620-z
10. IBM Regresión logística binaria - Documentación de IBM. https://www.ibm.com/docs/es/spss-statistics/beta?topic=regression-binary-logistic. Accessed 10 Jul 2023
11. Gupta, V.K., Gupta, A., Kumar, D., Sardana, A.: Prediction of COVID-19 confirmed, death, and cured cases in India using random forest model. Big Data Min. Anal. **4**, 116–123 (2021). https://doi.org/10.26599/BDMA.2020.9020016
12. Steyerberg, E.W.: Clinical Prediction Models. (2019). https://doi.org/10.1007/978-3-030-16399-0
13. Nepomuceno, M.R., Klimkin, I., Jdanov, D.A., Alustiza-Galarza, A., Shkolnikov, V.M.: Sensitivity Analysis of Excess Mortality due to the COVID-19 Pandemic (2022). https://doi.org/10.1111/padr.12475

14. Kumleben, N., Bhopal, R., Czypionka, T., Gruer, L., Kock, R., Stebbing, J., Stigler, F.L.: The importance of sensitivity, specificity and predictive powers (2020). https://doi.org/10.1016/j.puhe.2020.06.006
15. Niziri, M.: COVID-19 Dataset | Kaggle (2021). https://www.kaggle.com/datasets/meirnizri/covid19-dataset?select=Covid+Data.csv. Accessed 9 Jul 2023

Analysis of CoI Presence Indicators in a Moodle Forum Using Unsupervised Learning Techniques

Mitchell Vásquez-Bermúdez[1,2](✉) ⓘ, Maritza Aguirre-Munizaga[1] ⓘ,
and Jorge Hidalgo-Larrea[1] ⓘ

[1] Facultad de Ciencias Agrarias "Dr. Jacobo Bucaram Ortiz", Universidad Agraria del Ecuador,
Avenida 25 de Julio y Pio Jaramillo, Guayaquil, Ecuador
{mvasquez,maguirre,jhidalgo}@uagraria.edu.ec
[2] Faculty of Mathematical and Physical Sciences, University of Guayaquil, Cdla. Salvador
Allende, Guayaquil, Ecuador
mitchell.vasquezb@ug.edu.ec

Abstract. This paper presents a study that uses unsupervised machine learning techniques to analyse CoI presence indicators (Social Presence, Teacher Presence and Cognitive Presence) in a Moodle forum. The objective of this study is to identify the profiles of the participants using unsupervised learning algorithms that detect patterns and common characteristics among them. To accomplish this, a plugin was developed in the Moodle forum to enable the meta-annotation of CoI presence indicators. Following that, various unsupervised learning algorithms, including Hierarchical clustering, Canopy, Cobweb, simple K-means, and more, were evaluated to identify the most suitable algorithm for detecting similar characteristics among groups of users in terms of their participation and activity levels in the forum and the topics they are most interested in and participate. Utilizing K-means, it became possible to determine whether the identified groups reflected varying levels of participation and particular user characteristics. Acquiring an understanding of user engagement and behavioral patterns provides valuable insights into community dynamics and leads to the development of strategies that enhance the online learning experience.

Keywords: Machine Learning · Meta-annotations · Community of Inquiry (CoI) Model · Indicators

1 Introduction

In recent years, the adoption of collaborative experiences in virtual environments has increased significantly, providing educational opportunities to a growing number of students around the world. In this context, asynchronous communication between students has been recognized as one of the most effective ways to foster collaboration. This approach allows students to interact at times of their choosing and have more control over

© The Author(s), under exclusive license to Springer Nature Switzerland AG 2023
R. Valencia-García et al. (Eds.): CITI 2023, CCIS 1873, pp. 27–38, 2023.
https://doi.org/10.1007/978-3-031-45682-4_3

the collaborative process. Several studies have confirmed that asynchronous communication is particularly beneficial in online learning environments, as it allows students to participate flexibly and autonomously [14]. However, distance learning presents unique challenges, especially when it comes to collaboration and interaction among participants. To overcome these limitations, the importance of implementing effective collaboration strategies in virtual learning environments has been highlighted. In this context, the presence inquiry (CoI) model [9] has been widely recommended. This model is based on the analysis of interactions between teachers and students in online courses [16], and allows us to understand the social presence, the instructional presence and the cognitive presence in the collaborative process.

The field of e-learning benefits from the CoI model as it provides a sound framework for analyzing interactions between teachers and students and improving collaboration in virtual learning environments [17]. Through this analysis, best practices and strategies can be identified to encourage active and meaningful participation.

This paper presents a plugin for an online learning environment, specifically for a Moodle forum. This plugin's main objective is the incorporation of CoI presence indicators through meta-annotations. Meta-annotation refers to the process of including additional information to forum interactions. In this case, it will be used to tag and categorize user contributions based on CoI presence indicators, which include social presence, teaching presence, and cognitive presence. These indicators are essential to assess the quality of the collaborative experience and the degree of student participation.

In addition, using unsupervised learning algorithms, such as Simple K-means, cluster groups were established that helped determine the most appropriate profile to identify groups of users with similar characteristics in terms of their participation, activity, and areas of interest in Moodle forum.

The algorithm's execution produced three clusters. Cluster 0 exhibits greater social and cognitive presence [3], whereas cluster 1 shows greater cognitive presence and cluster 2 has the most relevant social presence. As a result, collaborative groups can be classified based on their affective participation in online academic activities [16].

This article is organized into the following sections: Sect. 2 presents related works, which showcase some predictive machine learning models in Moodle associated with collaborative learning monitoring. Section 3 describes the methodology and algorithms used in the Machine Learning tool. Section 4 presents the results. Finally, the conclusions are explained.

2   Related Work

Fauszt et al. [7] propose a predictive machine learning model in Moodle with self-defined indicators, which allow educators to identify students at risk of academic failure and provide them with the necessary support to improve their performance. Nalli et al. [11] focuses on the use of machine learning to train heterogeneous groups in online course environments. The findings are relevant for the field of artificial intelligence, when exploring a promising application of machine learning, as well as for the educational field, when presenting an innovative strategy to improve learning results in online courses. Rivas et al. [13] focuses on the use of machine learning techniques to improve the academic performance of students using the Moodle e-learning platform at a European university [2].

Sha et al. [15] discuss the use of educational forums and emphasize the importance of automatic classifiers in assisting instructors to effectively implement their teaching methods. While automatic classifiers' accuracy has been extensively researched, this study evaluates the algorithmic fairness of these classifiers. This research offers a comprehensive outlook on the use of educational forums and stresses the need to consider both accuracy and fairness in automatic classifiers, which is essential for enhancing the learning experience in virtual environments.

Purwoningsih et al. [12] used exploratory data analysis and machine learning to process the data from the LMS and the sociodemographic profile of the students. Three potential groups of student behavior patterns in e-learning were identified, and a weak but significant relationship was found between context and student behavior. Taken together, these works demonstrate that machine learning can be an effective tool to improve the learning experience in virtual environments, both in terms of identifying students at risk of academic failure, forming heterogeneous groups, improving academic performance and promoting effective teaching practices. Besides, highlight the importance of considering both accuracy and fairness when applying automatic classifiers in educational settings [4].

Compared to related works that use self-defined indicators or focus on general behavioral patterns, this approach stands out for its holistic and specific approach based on CoI [1]. The combination of these three presences (social, pedagogical, and cognitive) [4] allows more accurate measurement of key aspects of online learning. The approach proposed in this study stands out from related research by outlining a set of specific indicators linked to the presences of the CoI model. Moreover, it is characterised by using unsupervised machine learning algorithms for data analysis, which makes it easier to detect hidden patterns and objectively group students based on their interaction and participation levels.

3 Methodology

The Moodle forum was modified to include a plugin that permits the use of Community of Inquiry (CoI) presence indicators. To enable students to reflect on their contributions, indicators based on meta-annotations were integrated. Using this interface, students can select from a list of indicators the one that best signalises their intention to work collaboratively, then expand on their selected indicator by entering free text [18]. Refer to Table 1 for a list of indicators corresponding to various forms of attendance.

The indicators chosen by participants during their interactions are saved in the database. Initially, the Moodle administrator manually enters and configures the Social Presence and Teacher Presence indicators. After that, the teacher adds the Cognitive Presence labels based on the addressed topic. Furthermore, the plugin enables the addition, editing and modification of metadata that can be configured based on the work context. To implement these indicators in forum interfaces, they have been incorporated as specific labels for each CoI presence, where participants have the option of searching for the meta-annotation to complete their message in a text area. See Fig. 1 for an example of a forum interface [8].

Table 1. Presence Type indicators

PRESENCES	TYPES OF INDICATORS
Social Presence	• Positive • Negative
Teacher Presence	• Role identification • Distribution of tasks by roles • Time management • Organize tasks • Tool Use Decision
Cognitive Presence	Labels are generated for the topics that are addressed as part of the collaborative slogan Example for a network design case: · Network hardware · Network topology · Equipment distribution · Network costs · Network link · Network advantage

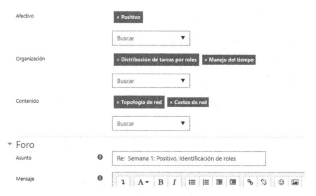

Fig. 1. Forum Interface

A plugin was implemented in the Moodle forum that allows the use of meta-annotations of CoI presence indicators. Data was collected from two groups of students, where they carried out their interactions in the forum, selecting the meta-annotation according to their participation in collaborative work, which focuses on a case study of a Network For this process, the KDD (Knowledge Discovery in Databases) methodology was applied [6]. In its first phase, the analysis of the scenario was carried out to identify the attributes of the problem oriented to the CoI presence in higher education students [5], identifying the following research questions:

- Are there different profiles of participants in the Moodle forum?
- What characteristics define each profile?

- Are there identifiable groups or communities within the forum?
- What are the most common engagement patterns among users?
- Are there differences in participation based on level of experience or type of course?

3.1 Data Preparation

During this phase, we extracted relevant data from the Moodle forum, including user messages, dates, and identifiers.

Subsequently, we selected, transformed, and cleaned the dataset extracted from Moodle to form the final data source, during which the relevant data from the Moodle forum, such as interactions between users, messages, topics of discussion, dates, and other metadata, were extracted. For this purpose, we carried out data cleaning and preprocessing, eliminating missing values, noise, irrelevant data, among others. Next, we selected an appropriate data mining paradigm that enables the observation of behaviour and detection of characteristics based on students' profiles. The data was cleaned and preprocessed based on these behaviours, removing unnecessary information and noise, including tasks such as tokenisation, elimination of stop words, and stemming.

The data for the COI presence indicator was transformed into CSV format. A matrix was produced, with each row representing a sample or an individual, and each column showing an indicator of COI. There are a total of 644 individuals represented[1].

3.2 Data Normalization

Before applying the K-means algorithm, it is recommended to normalize the data to prevent attributes with different scales from dominating the analysis. For this case, normalize function from the unsupervised attribute group was used in the Weka preprocessing stage. The function normalizes all numeric values in the given dataset (in this case we don't have the class set) [10]. This function was used for the normalization of the numerical attributes within the 644 instances. Standardizing the data in cluster analysis allows distance criteria to be applied fairly when comparing features. Some features may be more crucial to the analysis than others, but without standardizing them, their relative influence may get exaggerated simply due to differences in scale. To ensure that the relative influence of every feature in the cluster depends solely on its importance and not on arbitrary considerations such as units of measure, data needs to be standardized before conducting cluster analysis.

3.3 Application of Unsupervised Learning Techniques

Since the methodology is based on a structured process that allows us to extract knowledge from the data source, it was decided to work with unsupervised learning since the objective of this study is based on detecting behavior patterns. Initially, various algorithms based on clustering were tested, which allowed a comparison to be generated, which is shown in Table 2.

---

[1] https://github.com/maguirre2017/clustering_COI.

Table 2. Evaluated algorithms.

Algorithm	Number of clusters	Parameter	Model and evaluation
Hierarchical clustering class	3	Distance Funtion: Manhattan distance (or Taxicab geometry)	Result generated three clusters but the first one groups all the data, which is not useful for the analysis
Canopy	3	Número máximo de candidatos Canopies_to_hold_in_memory:100	3 groups are generated 0(47%), 1(29%), 2(24%)
Cobweb	6	Cutoff:0.002820	6 clusters were generated, however there is no significant difference between them. 25 (4%), 80 (12%), 138 (21%), 27 (4%), 192 (30%), 182 (28%)
FarthestFirst	3	DoNotCheckcapabilities:true, seed:1	This algorithm was useful to mark three trends 357 (55%), 199 (31%), 88 (14%). However, it was not used since it does not allow setting the distance. In the largest group, a greater social presence is observed
Simple EM (expectation maximisation) class	3	DoNotCheckcapabilities:true, numFolds:10, maxIterations:300	Clustered instances do not make a difference between groups: 239 (37%), 173 (27%), 232 (36%)

(continued)

Table 2. (*continued*)

Algorithm	Number of clusters	Parameter	Model and evaluation
FilteredClusterer	2	Filter:RenameRelation	Clustered instances do not make a difference between groups: 349 (54%), 295 (46%)
SimpleKmeans	3	Distance Funtion: Manhattan distance	The results allow labeling or conforming patterns of behavior between the data collected

For this case, it was decided to utilize the Simple K-means algorithm to create groups of users or messages based on their behavior or similarity. The aim is to divide the dataset by generating groups based on data similarity and obtain labels. Every observation is assigned to the group with the nearest mean. As presented in Table 3, the subsequent parameterizations were assessed.

Table 3. Parameterizations of simple K-means

Reviews	Number of clusters	MaxIterations	InitializationMethod	Seed	DistanceFuntion	Results
1	3	300	k-means ++	10	Manhattan	They represent a greater social presence compared to all the data
2	3	100	Canopy	10	Manhattan	There is a minimal difference between face-to-face social and cognitive in cluster 0, which represents 48% of the data
3	3	200	Random	10	Manhattan	Cluster 2 and 0 show 32% of the data and cluster 1 which represents 37% of the data

(*continued*)

Table 3. (*continued*)

Reviews	Number of clusters	MaxIterations	InitializationMethod	Seed	DistanceFuntion	Results
4	3	300	k-means ++	10	Euclidean	Cluster 0: This cluster has 344 data points, (53%) Cluster 1: This cluster has 144 points (22%) Cluster 2: 156 points (24%)
5	3	200	Canopy	12	Euclidean	Cluster 0: 347 (54%) Cluster 1: 145 (23%) Cluster 2: 152 (24%)

With the k-means results, we proceeded to interpret the generated groups/clusters and to look for patterns or common characteristics in each group, such as discussion topics, level of participation.

In the cluster analysis based on the Community of Research (CoI) framework, three clusters identified as 0, 1 and 2 were used. The results show the distribution of instances in each cluster and the average values of the attributes in each cluster, so it is decided to work with evaluation number 4.

For the communication of results, visualizations are generated that allow the dissemination of the findings in an understandable way, in turn, recommendations or actions are presented based on the results obtained to improve the CoI presence in the Moodle forum, such as encouraging participation in certain groups, identify key users, or address anomalous participation issues.

In the analysis of COI presence indicators using the K-means algorithm and the evaluations were carried out with the Manhattan and Eucledian distances, the results are presented in the form of final centroids of each cluster. Each cluster is represented by a number and the data set attributes are presented in rows.

- Social_Presence: Cluster 2 has the highest value for this attribute, followed by clusters 0 and 1. It indicates that cluster 2 shows a higher social presence compared to the other clusters.
- Teacher_Presence: Cluster 1 has the highest value for this attribute, followed by clusters 0 and 2. It indicates that cluster 2 shows a greater teacher presence compared to the other clusters.
- Cognitive_presence: Cluster 1 has the highest value for this attribute, followed by clusters 0 and 2.
- Positive, Negative, Identification_roles, Organization_tasks, Distribution_tasks_roles, Time_management, Hardware_network, Topology_network, Distribution_equipment, Costos_network, Link_network: The average values of these attributes vary between clusters. In general, cluster 2 has higher values, followed by cluster 0 and then cluster 1. This indicates that cluster 2 shows higher positivity, lower

negativity, and better performance on indicators related to organization and business configuration network.

- Network_advantage: Cluster 2 has a significantly higher average value compared to the other clusters. This indicates that cluster 2 shows a greater advantage in terms of the network.

4 Evaluation and Results

Clusters differ in terms of level, social presence, teaching presence, cognitive presence, and various attributes related to network organization and configuration. Each cluster has specific characteristics and is grouped based on the similarity of the values in these COI presence indicators, using the Manhattan distance metric. In this case, this metric defines the distance between two points and generates the sum of the absolute differences between each dimension.

As part of the results of the generated clusters, visualizations were obtained that represent the trend in which the presences (social, cognitive and teaching) are oriented from the positive aspect. Figure 2 shows a greater presence of cluster 2 focused on social presence on the x-axis and highlights that the tendency to a positive evaluation is quite remarkable. The impact of the social presence on the other two presences indicates the importance of emotionally and socially engaging students in the learning process in both online and offline learning scenarios.

Fig. 2. Visualization of social presence related to positive indicator

Figure 3 shows that teaching presence is relevant to the organization of tasks in collaborative work. Hence, it can be deduced that students with teaching presence tendencies tend to organize their presentation activities. Students with a higher learning motivation exhibit a greater eagerness to participate in the learning process and discuss ideas with group members to understand the material better. This establishes how learning motivation positively influences teaching presence.

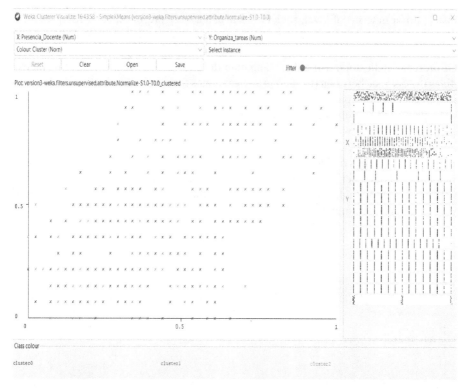

Fig. 3. Teaching presence related to the organization of tasks

As a result, it is concluded that there is a significant difference in cognitive presence compared to social presence and teaching presence. This is because the cluster number 2 shows a majority of positive weights related to the highest indicators of the cognitive presence. In this case, it can be concluded that when students participate in positive interactions, it has an impact on their cognitive performance.

To answer the research question, three groups of clusters were found. These groups marked their trends according to their profiles and characteristics in relation to their interactions. Regarding the patterns of participation, it is concluded that there is a high degree of social presence exercised in collaborative work. With respect to the question about the differences in participation based on the level of experience or type of course, it was shown that the trends in which the presences are oriented (Social, cognitive, and teaching) are positive.

5   Conclusions and Future Work

It is concluded that from the perspective of the indicators of the COI inquiry model, which were designed for collaborative online work of a network design, it is important to highlight the Moodle tool and the plugin that allowed the interaction of students and indicators. Since through it the data collection was achieved in the Institution of Higher Education. In the analysis of COI presence indicators using the K-means algorithm and the Manhattan distance function, the results are presented as the final centroids of each cluster. Each cluster is represented by a number (0, 1, and 2), and the dataset attributes are presented in rows [4].

This article highlights the increase in the adoption of collaborative experiences in virtual environments, especially in the educational field. Asynchronous communication is recognized as an effective way to foster collaboration, as it allows students to interact at times of their choosing and have greater control over the collaborative process. However, distance learning presents challenges in terms of collaboration and interaction between participants. To overcome these limitations, the importance of implementing effective collaboration strategies in virtual learning environments is highlighted. In this sense, the presence inquiry model (CoI) is presented as a recommended tool. This model analyzes the interactions between teachers and students in online courses, and allows to understand the social, educational, and cognitive presence in the collaborative process. The evaluation of the CoI presence indicators using unsupervised learning algorithms, such as Clusters and K-means, identified groups of users with similar characteristics in terms of their participation, activity, and areas of interest in the Moodle forum.

For future work, it is proposed to carry out an exhaustive analysis of past courses using matching learning linear regression algorithms to examine interaction trends at different levels of presence of the CoI model (Social Presence, Cognitive Presence and Teaching Presence) in an online learning environment, allowing to reveal hidden patterns and relationships between these factors, which will also help to control selection bias and establish more accurate comparisons between groups of students who have experienced different levels of interaction in the forum. In addition, the development of an interactive dashboard will combine the data derived from the unsupervised algorithms to provide a friendly and meaningful visualization for teachers and students.

References

1. Akyol, Z., et al.: A response to the review of the community of inquiry framework. J. Distance Educ. **23**(2), 123–135 (2009)
2. Anggraeni, D.M., Sole, F.B.: E-Learning Moodle, Media Pembelajaran Fisika Abad 21. J. Penelit. dan Pengkaj. Ilmu Pendidik. e-Saintika **1**, 2 (2018). https://doi.org/10.36312/e-saintika.v1i2.101
3. Bandura, A.: Social cognitive theory: an agentic perspective. Annu. Rev. Psychol. **52**(1), 1–26 (2001). https://doi.org/10.1146/annurev.psych.52.1.1
4. Chang-Tik, C.: An analysis of discipline and personality in blended environments: do they interact differently in the teaching, cognitive, and social presences? Can. J. Learn. Technol. **46**(1), 1–19 (2020). https://doi.org/10.21432/cjlt27883
5. Chen, Y., et al.: Discovering MOOC learner motivation and its moderating role. Behav. Inf. Technol. **39**(12), 1257–1275 (2020). https://doi.org/10.1080/0144929X.2019.1661520

6. Dhika, H., et al.: Ease evaluation using the best moodle learning management system with data mining concepts. 944–952 (2020). https://doi.org/10.2991/ASSEHR.K.200129.117

7. Fauszt, T., et al.: Increasing the prediction power of Moodle machine learning models with self. Int. J. Emerg. Technol. Learn. **16**(24), 23–39 (2021)

8. Geng, S., et al.: Investigating self-directed learning and technology readiness in blending learning environment. Int. J. Educ. Technol. High. Educ. **16**, 1 (2019). https://doi.org/10.1186/s41239-019-0147-0

9. Kim, G., Gurvitch, R.: Online education research adopting the community of inquiry framework: a systematic review. **72**(4), 395–409 (2020). https://doi.org/10.1080/00336297.2020.1761843

10. Mohd Radzi, S.F., et al.: Comparison of classification algorithms for predicting autistic spectrum disorder using WEKA modeler. BMC Med. Inform. Decis. Mak. **22**(1), 1–15 (2022). https://doi.org/10.1186/s12911-022-02050-x

11. Nalli, G., et al.: Application of machine learning to the learning analytics of the Moodle platform to create heterogeneous groups in on-line courses. Ital. J. Educ. Res. 156–173 (2019). https://doi.org/10.7346/SIRD-2S2019-P158

12. Purwoningsih, T., et al.: Online learners' behaviors detection using exploratory data analysis and machine learning approach. In: Proceeding of 2019 4th International Conference on Informatics Computer ICIC 2019 (2019). https://doi.org/10.1109/ICIC47613.2019.8985918

13. Rivas, A., et al.: Students performance analysis based on machine learning techniques. Commun. Comput. Inf. Sci. **1011**, 428–438 (2019). https://doi.org/10.1007/978-3-030-20798-4_37/COVER

14. Santos, O.C., Boticario, J.G.: Supporting a collaborative task in a web-based learning environment with Artificial Intelligence and User Modelling techniques. Informática Educ. nuevos retos, 2004, ISBN 84–7723–653–4. 71 (2004)

15. Sha, L., et al.: Assessing Algorithmic Fairness in Automatic Classifiers of Educational Forum Posts. Lect. Notes Comput. Sci. (including Subser. Lect. Notes Artif. Intell. Lect. Notes Bioinformatics). 12748 LNAI, 381–394 (2021). https://doi.org/10.1007/978-3-030-78292-4_31/COVER

16. Vásquez-Bermúdez, M., et al.: Effectiveness of monitoring indicators in the architecture of a collaborative system. Commun. Comput. Inf. Sci. **1658**(CCIS), 191–202 (2022). https://doi.org/10.1007/978-3-031-19961-5_14/COVER

17. Wertz, R.E.H.: Learning presence within the Community of Inquiry framework: an alternative measurement survey for a four-factor model. Internet High. Educ. **52**, 100832 (2022). https://doi.org/10.1016/J.IHEDUC.2021.100832

18. Yanacón-Atía, D., et al.: Indicadores colaborativos individuales y grupales para Moodle Individual and group collaborative indicators for Moodle (2018)

Development of an Intelligent Web System for the Analysis of Data in the F2 Layer of the Ionosphere Using Machine Learning Techniques and Its Implementation as Potential Earthquake Precursors

Juan Antonio Murillo Vargas[1](✉) , Eduardo De la Cruz Gámez[1] ,
Mario Hernández Hernández[2] , Francisco Javier Gutiérrez Mata[1] ,
Antonio Alfonso Rodríguez Rosales[3] , and Miguel Herraiz Sarachaga[4]

[1] Division of Research and Graduate Studies, National Technology of Mexico, Acapulco,
Mexico
{mm21320016,eduardo.dg,francisco.gm}@acapulco.tecnm.mx
[2] Division of Research and Graduate Studies, National Technology of Mexico, Chilpancingo,
Mexico
mario.hh@chilpancingo.tecnm.mx
[3] Department of Applied Optics, Centro de Investigación Científica y Tecnológica de Guerrero,
Acapulco, A.C., Mexico
antonio.rodriguez@icat.unam.mx
[4] Department of Physics of the Earth and Astrophysics, University Complutense, Madrid, Spain
mherraiz@fis.ucm.es

Abstract. This paper presents the results of the development of a web system for the study of ionospheric parameters and their application as possible precursors of earthquakes. A dataset was developed using ionospheric models (IRI) and Global Ionospheric Maps (GIM) to get the Total Electron Content (TEC) and other relevant parameters. ML algorithms implemented were Decision Trees, Regression Trees, and K-means Clustering.

The work also includes a web application with the Flask framework, whose purpose is to simplify data retrieval by storing them in the PostgreSQL manager to facilitate the implementation of the previously developed algorithms. The target is to deliver a concise and intuitive UI for space physics, geomagnetism, and seismology.

Keywords: Machine-Learning · earthquake-precursor · Decision-Tree · Ionosphere

1 Introduction

The expression "earthquake precursor" refers to very different kinds of phenomena (seismological, geodetic, hydrological, geochemical, electromagnetic, animal behavior, etc.) that frequently take place before a seismic event, and could be considered for earthquake

R. Valencia-García et al. (Eds.): CITI 2023, CCIS 1873, pp. 39–53, 2023.
https://doi.org/10.1007/978-3-031-45682-4_4

prediction [1, 2]. Their study has accompanied the development of seismology since its initial steps in the late nineteenth century [1]. The first evidence of their utility appeared in 1975, when Chinese seismologists were able to announce a 7.3 M earthquake near the city of Haicheng. The prediction was based on the study of its foreshock sequence and the observation of certain factors considered seismic precursors: ground surface deformation, changes in groundwater characteristics (level, color, and chemistry), and unusual animal behavior [3].

In 1991, the International Association of Seismology and Physics of the Earth's Interior (IASPEI) published the main criteria that a phenomenon must fulfill to be accepted as a precursor [4]. At the same time, new fields of research were opened to develop an interdisciplinary prediction scheme based on multi-premonitory phenomena. In this trend can be placed the increasing attention paid to the effects of earthquakes and tsunamis on the ionosphere, the conductive part of the atmosphere that spans from 70 to 500 km in height and strongly affects the transmission of electromagnetic waves. This groundbreaking effect was first observed because of the observation of ionospheric perturbations caused by the great 1964 Anchorage (Alaska) Mw 9.2 seismic event [5, 6]. The origin of these perturbations was the acoustic and gravity waves induced in the atmosphere, which propagated upward until the ionosphere. Their amplitude increased with height due to the density decreasing with altitude, producing perturbations in the ionosphere's Total Electron Content (TEC). These effects can be detected by processing information provided by ground-based receivers from the Global Navigation Satellite Systems (GNSS) [7]. In this way, the interaction Lithosphere-Atmosphere-Ionosphere has turned into a promising field of research [8] that can benefit from recent computational advances that allow for the prediction of certain meteorological phenomena, such as hurricanes and droughts, utilizing historical data and making the appropriate adjustments [9].

At present, there are different types of seismic precursor studies where artificial intelligence techniques have been implemented. These works highlight the use of Convolutional Neural Networks (ANN) [10, 11], Machine Learning [12, 13], and Deep Learning [14, 15]. One significant characteristic of these investigations is that they only focus on the results obtained and do not provide a more profound follow-up.

This article pays attention to the Mw7.1 earthquake that took place in Acapulco, on September 8, 2021, because of its importance and the high seismic hazard of the Guerrero state [16]. In addition, we are interested in analyzing in more detail the possible relationship between this earthquake and some perturbations recorded by the CSES-1 (China Seismo-Electromagnetic Satellite-1) in three ionospheric parameters: electron density, O+ concentration, and electron density profile [17].

The focus of this research is to pioneer the development of possible earthquake precursors.

After this Introduction, the work presents the Methodology and the Databases used in the process (Sect. 2); describes in detail the Pre-processing and processing of data with ML algorithms (Sect. 3) and introduces the Design and implementation of the Web interface (Sect. 4). Section 5 presents the Results, the main conclusions, and several proposals for new studies.

2 Methodology and Databases

Figure 1 shows the methodology of the web system for obtaining ionospheric parameters.

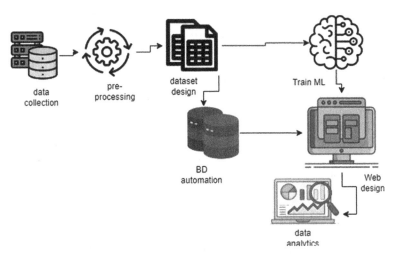

Fig. 1. Diagram of system methodology

2.1 Databases and Repositories

Data corresponding to the ionospheric parameters Ne/m3, O+, N+. hmF2, TEC, foF2, vTEC were obtained from these sources:

International Reference Ionosphere (IRI): International Standard for specifying ionospheric densities and temperatures. It was developed in the late sixties of the past century and is being improved and updated by a joint working group of the International Union of Radio Sciences (URSI) and the Committee on Space Research (COSPAR) [18]. This application can download distinct types of ionospheric variables, based on a geographical location, date, and altitude.[1]

Global Ionospheric Maps (GIM): These maps depict the spatial distribution of electron density, vTEC and F2 layer height in the ionosphere worldwide. These are created by processing data from GPS and other satellite navigation systems that measure radio signals propagating through the ionosphere [19]. Such files are available four days after processing and can downloaded via web.[2]

Seismic data information, necessary for establishing the correlation with the ionospheric data comprises origin time, epicentral coordinates, focal depth, and magnitude, and was obtained from the National Seismological Service (SSN) [20].

---

[1] https://kauai.ccmc.gsfc.nasa.gov/instantrun/iri.

[2] https://cddis.nasa.gov/data_and_derived_products/gnss/atmospheric_products.html.

2.2 Description of Ionospheric Parameters

Total Electron Content (TEC): This parameter is defined as the total electron density per square meter in a vertical column from a transmitter (satellite) and receptor (ground station) through GNSS signals [20, 21].

$$1\ TECU = 1 \times 10^{16} \text{electron/m}^2$$

FoF2 (or F2 critical frequency) is the maximum frequency, in MHz, that the F2 layer of the Earth's ionosphere can reflect at a vertical angle of incidence. It measures the electron density in the F2 layer, which is influenced by factors such as time of day, season, geographic location, and solar activity [22].

hmF2: Height of the F2 layer where the maximum electron density occurs. It is an essential measure of the ionosphere. Forecasting of high-frequency (HF) radio propagation through the ionosphere uses this parameter, which can be affected by various factors, such as solar activity and time of day [23].

3 Pre-processing and Processing of Data with ML Algorithms

The next step was to develop the dataset, which will be used to feed the ML algorithms. The following seismic events that occurred previously were used to construct the dataset.

– Coalcomán Michoacán, an Earthquake of 7.7 Mw magnitude occurred on September 19, 2022, and 6.9 on September 22, 2022.
– Acapulco Guerrero: Earthquake of 7.1 Mw magnitude on September 7, 2021
– Crucecita Oaxaca: Earthquake of 7.4 Mw magnitude on June 23, 2020
– Hidalgo city Chiapas: Earthquake of 6.0 magnitude on January 1, 2020
– Pijijiapan Chiapas: Earthquake of 8.2 7 Mw magnitude on September 8, 2017

The preprocessing of the information aims to "prepare" the data by eliminating certain inconsistencies and redundancies and determining the fields of importance. The tasks performed by the preprocessing system will be described below.

Figure 2 shows the raw data set while Fig. 3 shows the processed set with all rules and normalizations applied.

Hour	Year	Day	DOY	Latitude	Longitude	Month	Electron_density_Ne	o+	NO	TEC	hmF2	foF2	profundidad	magnitud	tec_GIM
1	2017	1	244	14.7	261.98	9	4.900000e+11	99.0	0.1	10.3	261.6	6.503	NaN	NaN	22.0
2	2017	1	244	14.7	261.98	9	3.100000e+11	99.7	0.1	6.1	273.8	5.071	NaN	NaN	15.2
3	2017	1	244	14.7	261.98	9	2.040000e+11	99.7	0.2	3.8	299.8	4.055	NaN	NaN	10.1
4	2017	1	244	14.7	261.98	9	1.500000e+11	99.7	0.2	3.0	319.5	3.637	NaN	NaN	8.4
5	2017	1	244	14.7	261.98	9	1.390000e+11	99.7	0.2	2.8	322.5	3.544	NaN	NaN	8.0
6	2017	1	244	14.7	261.98	9	1.440000e+11	99.7	0.1	2.8	314.6	3.486	NaN	NaN	7.9
7	2017	1	244	14.7	261.98	9	1.500000e+11	99.7	0.1	2.8	303.6	3.479	NaN	NaN	7.7
8	2017	1	244	14.7	261.98	9	1.530000e+11	99.7	0.1	2.9	297.5	3.509	64.4	3.7	8.3
9	2017	1	244	14.7	261.98	9	1.360000e+11	99.7	0.2	2.6	297.7	3.313	NaN	NaN	8.0
10	2017	1	244	14.7	261.98	9	1.060000e+11	99.6	0.2	2.1	298.8	2.922	NaN	NaN	6.2
11	2017	1	244	14.7	261.98	9	1.050000e+11	99.6	0.2	2.2	291.6	2.918	148.9	3.5	7.4
12	2017	1	244	14.7	261.98	9	1.650000e+11	97.5	0.6	3.6	274.6	3.691	NaN	NaN	6.5
13	2017	1	244	14.7	261.98	9	2.650000e+11	97.2	0.6	6.5	258.2	4.785	100.0	4.4	6.0

Fig. 2. Data before they are processed.

DayC	Hour	Latitude	Longitude	magnitud	profundidad	Electron_density_Ne	o+	NO	hmF2	foF2	tec_GIM	sismo
2017-09-01	01:00	14.7	261.98	0.0	0.0	4.900000e+11	99.0	0.1	261.6	6.503	22.0	0.0
2017-09-01	02:00	14.7	261.98	0.0	0.0	3.100000e+11	99.7	0.1	273.8	5.071	15.2	0.0
2017-09-01	03:00	14.7	261.98	0.0	0.0	2.040000e+11	99.7	0.2	299.8	4.055	10.1	0.0
2017-09-01	04:00	14.7	261.98	0.0	0.0	1.500000e+11	99.7	0.2	319.5	3.637	8.4	0.0
2017-09-01	05:00	14.7	261.98	0.0	0.0	1.390000e+11	99.7	0.2	322.5	3.544	8.0	0.0
2017-09-01	06:00	14.7	261.98	0.0	0.0	1.440000e+11	99.7	0.1	314.6	3.486	7.9	0.0
2017-09-01	07:00	14.7	261.98	0.0	0.0	1.500000e+11	99.7	0.1	303.6	3.479	7.7	0.0
2017-09-01	08:00	14.7	261.98	3.7	64.4	1.530000e+11	99.7	0.1	297.5	3.509	8.3	1.0
2017-09-01	09:00	14.7	261.98	0.0	0.0	1.360000e+11	99.7	0.2	297.7	3.313	8.0	0.0
2017-09-01	10:00	14.7	261.98	0.0	0.0	1.060000e+11	99.6	0.2	298.8	2.922	6.2	0.0
2017-09-01	11:00	14.7	261.98	3.5	148.9	1.050000e+11	99.6	0.2	291.6	2.918	7.4	1.0
2017-09-01	12:00	14.7	261.98	0.0	0.0	1.650000e+11	97.5	0.6	274.6	3.691	6.5	0.0

Fig. 3. Processed data with filters and its variable category.

To develop an autonomous and efficient system, machine learning algorithms can emulate human behavior through an input data feed and categorical variables.

The following algorithms we have developed to build up the Web system be-long to these types:

- Classification Algorithm: Classification trees whose purpose is to perform forecasting using pattern recognition within the dataset.
- Regression Algorithm: Regression tree utilizing questions of interest and feature extraction, we can use this algorithm to predict continuous variables within the dataset.

The inputs to feed the algorithms were described in Sect. 2.2 (N+. hmF2, TEC, foF2, vTEC).

3.1 Implementation of the Decision Tree Algorithm

This dataset has been implemented using the Decision tree algorithm to locate the patterns of interest within the data displayed.

The algorithm's accuracy was 83%, which is a positive sign of development, since if the algorithms show 100% accuracy, this is considered an "over-fit" to the data.

A benefit of the Scikit-learn library is to display a report with the algorithm metrics. Table 1 shows the values provided by the information.[3]

Table 1. Algorithm statistical report

	Precision	Recall	F1-score	Support
0	0.66	0.66	0.66	214
1	0.83	0.82	0.82	415
Accuracy	NA	NA	0.77	629
Macro avg	0.73	0.74	0.74	629
Weighted avg	0.77	0.77	0.77	629

Figure 4 shows the confusion matrix of the Decision Tree algorithm.

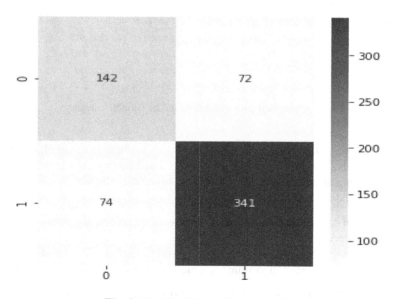

Fig. 4. Decision Tree confusion matrix

---

[3] The report generated by the scikit learn library has no information about the accuracy in the precision and recall columns.

Figure 5 shows the construction of the Decision tree with its respective nodes and leaves; these represent the multiple decisions that the algorithm can make based on the data entered.

It aims to analyze the rules created by the Decision tree.

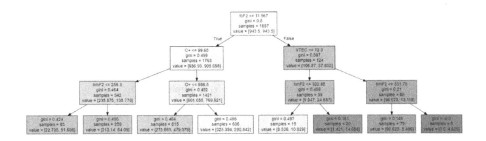

Fig. 5. Design of the decision tree graph diagram

The final implementation phase of the algorithm consists of saving the model in a file with the extension. *pickle*, which has the function of calling it later as a data array and performing the forecasting based on the categorical variable. This file will have the function of training the data within the Web system later.

3.2 Regression Tree Algorithm Implementation

The Regression Trees function is to forecast response values based on a series of rules and questions the algorithm asks.

The following mathematical formula represents regression trees.

$$f(x) = \sum_{m=1}^{M} w_m \Phi(x; v_m)$$

where:

- wm is the mean value of the response in a particular region (Rm).
- vm presents how each variable splits at a particular threshold value.

These splits define the feature space in R2 into M separate regions, hyper blocks.

Ionospheric input parameters implemented within the system are used to determine the possible magnitude of the earthquake.

Figure 6 shows the Regression Tree representing the different paths it can take with the data used.

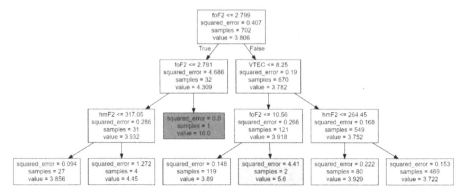

Fig. 6. Design of the Regression Tree graph diagram.

3.3 Implementation of Clustering Algorithm (K-means)

K-means is an agent-based unsupervised learning algorithm that aims at clustering objects into k groups based on the characteristics given by the user.

The K-means algorithm solves optimization problems by finding, the function that optimizes (minimizes) the sum of the quadratic distances of each object to the centroid of its cluster.

To extend the study of the ionospheric parameters, this algorithm was implemented to locate the patterns of interest between the magnitude of the earthquakes and the TEC value.

The following figure (see Fig. 7) shows the clustering behavior of the K-means algorithm within the dataset.

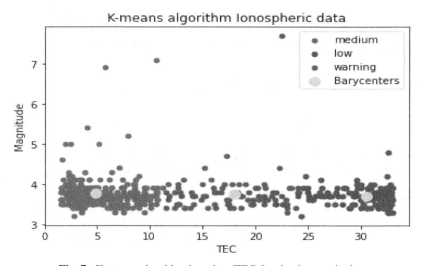

Fig. 7. K-means algorithm based on TEC & seismic magnitude.

4   Design and Implementation of the Web Interface

Developing a web interface using the Flask framework to consume the ML model is the next step to implementing a system capable of serving as an object of study for ionospheric variables.

The MVC (Model-View-Controller) pattern was used for the development of the web system.

The web UI is currently in beta development and contains the following features:

1. Deployment of Regression tree algorithm to know the possible magnitude of the seismic event.
2. Deployment of a Decision tree algorithm for forecasting possible seismic events.
3. The implementation of a function to save the user's data from a CSV file to a PostgreSQL database for future studies.
4. Creation of customized graphs where the user can study different events, parameters, and date ranges based on user input parameters.
5. Creation of information statistics based on the configuration of input parameters (dates, location, the earthquake's magnitude, Etc.).

Figures 8 and 9 show the ionospheric data capture interface implementing the regression (Regression tree) and classification (Decision tree) algorithms.

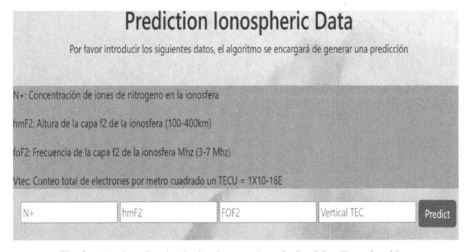

Fig. 8. User interface by the implementation of a Decision Tree algorithm.

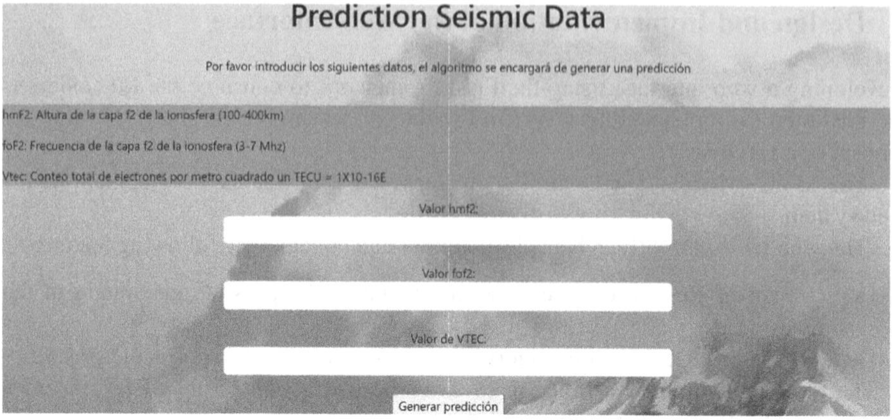

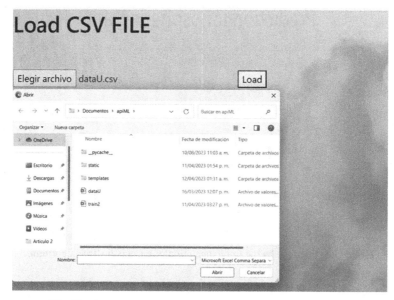

Fig. 9. User interface by the implementation of a Regression Tree algorithm.

These user interfaces will be able to predict the possible seismic event and its magnitude utilizing the user's ionospheric data; in parallel, we saved this information in a database for further study.

Figure 10 shows the form to load the file and its saving in the database.

Fig. 10. Example user interface to save CSV files to a database.

These UIs aim to allow the user to carry out studies with previous historical data.

5   Results

5.1   Interface Test, Acapulco Guerrero Earthquake Case of Study September 7, 2021

Acapulco 2021 earthquake data was used to test the algorithms.

The behavior of the data within the user interface is described in Figs. 11 and 12.

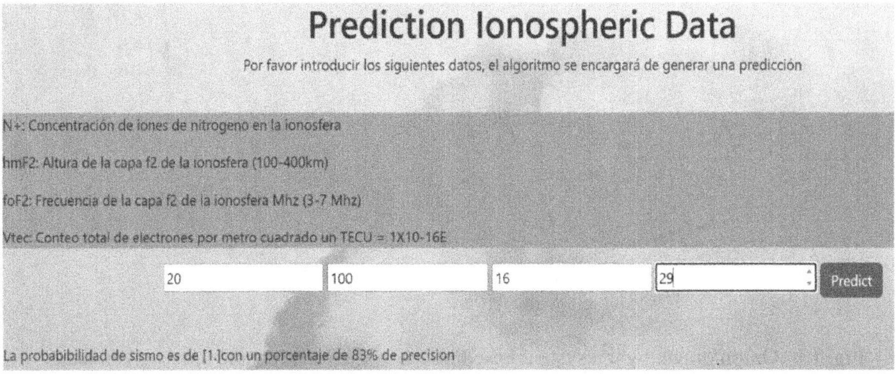

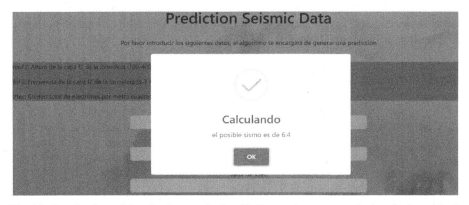

Fig. 11. Decision tree algorithm analysis result based on the input parameters of the Acapulco earthquake.

Fig. 12. Result of possible seismic magnitude with Regression trees, analyzing the ionospheric data of the Acapulco earthquake event (2021).

The System counts with a user interface to build statistical graphs according to the input parameters such as geolocation, date, magnitude, etc. Figure 13 shows the Acapulco earthquake graph with the TEC, magnitude, and hmF2 for the statistical analysis.

This data provided by the predictive system is interesting because scientists can use it to study different ionospheric patterns at different locations, times, and events, with which they can develop more effective seismic precursors.

Acapulco 2021 3D earthquake analysis

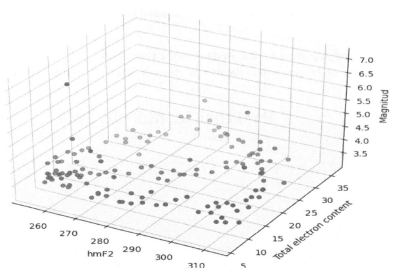

Fig. 13. Graph drawn by the system based on a specific location and user's given data.

5.2 Analysis of Earthquake Events Using the Forecasting Interfaces

The following Table presents the analysis of the forecast algorithms input data, introducing seismic events that occurred within the Mexican Republic as input data to test the system in different environments.

Table 2. Potential earthquake magnitude analyses using ionospheric data, Regression Tree and Decision Tree.

Location	Date	Mag	FoF2	hmF2	TEC	Magnitude using Regression Tree	Possible seismic event
COALCOMAN, MICH	2022–09-19	7.7	11	312	14	6.5	0
CRUCECITA, OAX	2020–06-23	7.4	7	255	10	6.1	0
TECPAN, GRO	2022–12-11	6.0	10	300	18	5.3	1

6 Conclusions, Prospects, and Future Work

Throughout the development of this system, there were many problems, one of the most important being the quality of the collected information; data were obtained from different sources, and there was some concern about its forecasting capability and accuracy.

When applying the Decision Tree algorithm, it was noted that most of the forecasting results were accurate. However, a group of data obtained had inconsistencies; one of the causes is due to the amount of data amount collected from the forecasting training, so other event types of different magnitudes should be included to improve the accuracy of the algorithm.

Implementing the Regression Tree algorithm to determine the potential seismic magnitude in the Acapulco case returned a result far from the original (6.4 Richter scale instead of 7.1), so the algorithm's accuracy should also be increased to obtain more reliable data.

Something similar can be seen in Table 2, reinforcing the necessity of adjusting the data and the algorithm to obtain the desired result.

During the analysis of Decision Tree, it is observed that only the parameters corresponding to the Tecpan earthquake were positive to earthquake events, so more work should be done on the information.

The K-means clustering algorithm presents the results in the correlation between the TEC and the registered seismic magnitudes, in it shows the higher TEC data that correspond to small seismic events; this in part is considered a precursor, because before an earthquake occurs, some events of magnitudes between 3–4 Richter scale are presented.

Just as authors of papers on earthquake prediction treat their results with a degree of secrecy and confidentiality, this development must follow the same protocol, as this area of research is still relatively young and there are still doubts about the behavior of the population in the face of possible predictions (psycho-logical studies on this type of news are currently being performed).

The development of this system in its beta phase has been very well received, although there are still phases that need improvement. It is considered a pioneer in the analysis of the ionosphere and its correlation with seismic events.

Organizations that provide this type of data analysis are complicated to understand, involve some cost in their use, and do not implement ML algorithms (the data are processed only statistically); so, this system, with its open-source approach and intuitive user interface, is beneficial for scientists looking for a deeper analysis of ionospheric data.

In future work, a data automation function is being developed within the system (currently, data is inserted using a CSV file into the database); the training dataset is also being optimized with the latest seismic event information to improve accuracy.

A report module is in development so the user can download a data analysis report for further study.

The possible use of other algorithms based on artificial intelligence as an extension of the system is not excluded, as the general purpose is to serve as a means of data analysis.

References

1. Geller, R.J.: Earhquake prediction: a critical review. Geophys. J. Int. **131**, 425–450 (1997)
2. Herraiz, M., Farelo, A., Cueto, M., Mohíno, E.: Una aproximación crítica a la propuesta de fenómenos ionosféricas como precursores sísmicos. Volumen 12 Colección Física de la Tierra (2000). http://revistas.ucm.es/index.php/FITE/article/view/FITE0000110319A
3. Rodríguez, L.G.: Aspectos teórico-metodológicos sobre la predicción de terremotos. Boletín de Ciencias de la Tierra **49**, 39–46 (2021). https://doi.org/10.15446/rbct.n49.93823
4. Wyss, M. (ed.): Evaluation of Proposed Earthquake Precursors. American Geophysical Union, Washington DC (1991)
5. Bolt, B.A.: Seismic air waves from the great 1964 Alaskan earthquake. Nature **202**, 1095–1096 (1964). https://doi.org/10.1038/2021095a0
6. Davies, K., Baker, D.M.: Ionospheric effects observed around the time of the Alaskan earthquake of March 28, 1964. J. Geophys. Res. **70**, 2251–2253 (1965). https://doi.org/10.1029/JZ070i009p02251
7. Artru, J., Ducic, V., Kanamori, H., Lognonné, P., Murakami, M.: Ionospheric detection of gravity waves induced by tsunamis. Geophys. J. Int. **160**(3), 840–848 (2005). https://doi.org/10.1111/j.1365-246X.2005.02552.x
8. Pulinets, S., Ouzounov, D.: Lithosphere–atmosphere–Ionosphere Coupling (LAIC) model – an unified concept for earthquake precursors validation. J. Asian Earth Sci. **41**(4–5), 371–382 (2011). https://doi.org/10.1016/j.jseaes.2010.03.005
9. Martinez-Amaya, J., Radin, C., Nieves, V.: Advanced machine learning methods for major hurricane forecasting. Remote Sens. **15**(1), 119 (2022). https://doi.org/10.3390/rs15010119
10. Erdogan, E., Schmidt, M., Seitz, F., Durmaz, M.: Near real-time estimation of ionosphere vertical total electron content from GNSS satellites using B-splines in a Kalman filter. Ann. Geophys. **35**(2), 263–277 (2017). https://doi.org/10.5194/angeo-35-263-2017
11. Xiong, P., Zhai, D., Long, C., Zhou, H., Zhang, X., Shen, X.: Long short-term memory neural network for ionospheric total electron content forecasting over China. Space Weather Int. J. Res. Appl. **19**(4) (2021). https://doi.org/10.1029/2020sw002706
12. Akyol, A.A., Arikan, O., Arikan, F.: A machine learning-based detection of earthquake precursors using ionospheric data. Radio Sci. **55** (2020). https://doi.org/10.1029/2019rs006931
13. Asaly, S., Gottlieb, L., Inbar, N., Reuveni, Y.: Using support vector machine (SVM) with GPS ionospheric TEC estimations to potentially predict earthquake events. Remote Sens. **14**(12), 2822 (2022). https://doi.org/10.3390/rs14122822
14. Wonsathan, R., Seedadan, I., Nunloon, N., Kitibut, J.: Prediction of evaluation learning by using neuro-fuzzy system. Adv. Mater. Res. **931–932**, 1482–1487 (2014). https://doi.org/10.4028/www.scientific.net/amr.931-932.1482
15. Rouet-Leduc, B., Hulbert, C., McBrearty, I.W., Johnson, P.: Probing slow earthquakes with deep learning. Geophys. Res. Lett. **47**(4) (2020). https://doi.org/10.1029/2019gl085870
16. Iglesias, A., et al.: A source study of the Mw 7.0 Acapulco, Mexico, earthquake of 8 September 2021. Seismol. Res. Lett. **93**, 3205–3218 (2022). https://doi.org/10.1785/0220220124
17. Huang, H., et al.: The variations of plasma density recorded by CSES-1 satellite possibly related to Mexico Ms 7.1 earthquake on 8th September 2021. Nat. Hazards Res. **2**(1), 11–16 (2021). https://doi.org/10.1016/j.nhres.2021.12.002
18. Bilitza, D.: International reference ionosphere 2000. Radio Sci. **36**(2), 261–275 (2001). https://doi.org/10.1029/2000rs002432
19. Zhukov, A., Yasyukevich, Y., Bykov, A.E.: GIMLi: global ionospheric total electron content model based on machine learning. GPS Solutions **25**(1) (2021). https://doi.org/10.1007/s10291-020-01055-1

20. México. Universidad Nacional Autónoma de México, Instituto Mexicano de Geología: Servicio Sismológico Nacional (2023). Catálogo de sismos. Extraído de http://www2.ssn.unam.mx:8080/catalogo/
21. González-López, A.: Análisis de burbujas ionosféricas durante tormentas geomagnéticas intensas en latitudes medias. Trabajo Fin de Máster, Universidad Complutense de Madrid (2018)
22. Adebesin, B., Adeniyi, J.: F2-layer height of the peak electron density (hmF2) dataset employed in inferring vertical plasma drift – data of best fit. Data Brief (2018). https://doi.org/10.1016/j.dib.2018.04.141
23. Wijaya, D.D., Haralambous, H., Oikonomou, C., Kuntjoro, W.: Determination of the ionospheric foF2 using a stand-alone GPS receiver. J. Geodesy **91**(9), 1117–1133 (2017). https://doi.org/10.1007/s00190-017-1013-2

Recurrent Neural Networks (RNN) to Predict the Curve of COVID-19 in Ecuador During the El Niño Phenomenon

Charles M. Pérez-Espinoza(✉) ⓘ, Darwin Pow Chon Long ⓘ, Jorge Lopez ⓘ,
and Genesis Rodriguez Chalén ⓘ

Universidad Agraria del Ecuador, Guayaquil, Ecuador
{chperez,dpow,jlopez}@uagraria.edu.ec

Abstract. In Ecuador, COVID-19 disease became a mortal enemy since its wave of contagion in 2020 and represented a significant challenge for public health due to its high incidence and difficulties in early diagnosis. In this paper, it is proposed to use artificial intelligence (AI) techniques, such as Deep Learning, to predict the curve of cases that this disease will present in the coming weeks. The objective is for the medical system like Ministerio de Salud Pública to take advantages because this disease can have incidences due to the weather phenomenon called "El niño phenomenon", that is associated with an increase in rainfall in some areas of southern South America, the southern United States, the Horn of Africa, and Central Asia. This study will contribute to a more timely and effective decision-making for the country.

Keywords: El Niño Phenomenon · Deep Learning · Recurrent Networks · Artificial Intelligence · prediction · Covid-19 · LSTM · Time Series

1 Introduction

1.1 Covid-19 in Ecuador

Currently, this disease has had a significant impact in Ecuador in all environments, and many have been strongly affected by this global pandemic. This threat transcended public health, economic and social disruption, impact on livelihoods, and the long-term well-being of millions of people.

On December 31, 2019, after the notification of a conglomerate of cases of the so-called viral pneumonia, which occurred in Wuhan, Republic of China, the WHO recognized and named this catastrophic disease. After studying it for a short time, they named this disease like COVID-19. This disease is caused by a coronavirus called SARS-CoV-2 (it has a diameter between 60 and 140 nm). They are made up of an RNA chain where their genes go and a lipid cover with the proteins that allow them to adhere and enter the cells of the body that they invade. This coronavirus cannot survive or reproduce if it does not adhere to living cells.

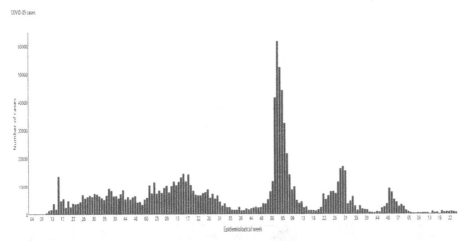

Fig. 1. Ecuador number of Covid-19 Cases (since 2020-01-01 to 2023-06-27), Source: (PAHO, Pan American Health Organization, 2023).

On February 29, 2020, the Ministerio de Salud Pública together with the presidency of Ecuador identified the first case of COVID-19 [3]. This pandemic caused many situations in the country to collapse. For example, in the port city (Guayaquil) many families ended up devastated by the death of a relative or most of their relatives, missing corpses, hundreds of infected health workers, and thousands of people who had to choose between dying of hungry for fear of not going out to look for food or dying of infected coronavirus on the way out [4]. On Fig. 1 we show the number of cases since 2020-01-01 until 2023-06-27. And on Fig. 2, we show the number of deaths.

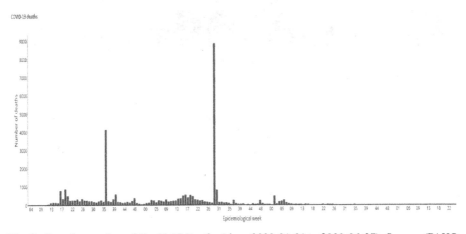

Fig. 2. Ecuador number of Covid-19 Deaths (since 2020-01-01 to 2023-06-27), Source: (PAHO, Pan American Health Organization, 2023).

1.2 El Niño Phenomenon

The climatic phenomenon called El Niño or Southern Oscillation (ENSO) is characterized by the fluctuation or temperature changes of the largest ocean in the world, that is, in the central and eastern part of the equatorial Pacific. When these kind changes begin, they are associated with catastrophic situations in the atmosphere [5]. This phenomenon has a great influence on the climatic conditions of various parts of the world, and Ecuador is one of them. Today, the scientific community that has studied and understood this climatic phenomenon has created many prediction models, which have helped to improve on time scales from one to nine months in advance of its coming, which helps the world population to prepare for the dangers associated with these climatic changes, such as heavy rains, floods, and droughts.

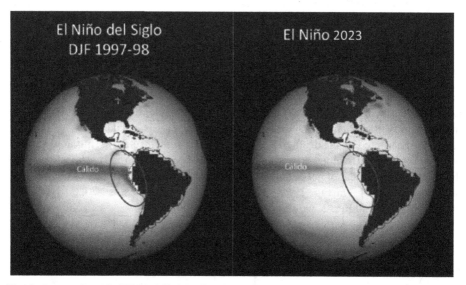

Fig. 3. Images from the WMO Official bulletin about El Niño phenomenon (May 2022). Source: World Meteorological Organization.

In May 2022 the World Meteorological Organization in their bulletin describe that there was a 65% that the El Niño phenomenon occurs in 2023, and they published an image of the temperature on the equatorial zone like we see in Fig. 3. And on May 2023, the Ecuador's Navy Oceanographic and Antarctic Institute in a bulletin called ERFEN ECUADOR, wrote that there was an 89% probability that the El Niño Phenomenon occurs [10].

El Niño Phenomenon would arrive on the coasts of Ecuador between November and December 2023, but the maximum rainfall peak would be between February and March 2024. This climatic phenomenon is known as the king of climatic events and normally it occurs every two to seven years on average. And it is possible that this climate phenomenon would be felt in the country until June 2024.

1.3 Relationship Between COVID-19 and El Niño Phenomenon

Since 2020, the scientific community has carried out many studies on COVID-19 combined with certain climatic variables that affect the place of study to observe if they affect the growth of the pandemic in any way. One of the studies [7] is based on the correlation of nine variables that obviously includes the number of people infected, among these we have: 1) population density, 2) intra-provincial movement, 3) days of infection, 4) average temperature, 5) average rain, 6) humidity, 7) wind speed, and 8) solar radiation and 9) infection rate. Using a correlation matrix, they found that wind speed, temperature and solar radiation is inversely proportional to the rate of people infected. And that in most populated, humid, and rainy areas of this country it is directly correlated with the rate of infected people. Therefore, in our research it helps us to consider two main variables in the infection rate, such as humidity and rainfall.

Another publication in Brazil, using a dataset from March 27, 2020, to June 03, 2021, of 435 data of about 62 weeks, studied the infection rate of people by COVID-19 [6] with climatic variables such as daily humidity, the air quality index and the daily temperature. And through forecasting with different methods such as recurrent neural networks using LSTM cells and the unsupervised K-means algorithm, it was possible to correlate these variables and arrive at a stable prediction model (Fig. 4).

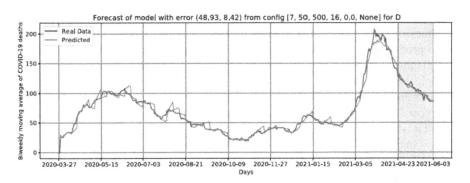

Fig. 4. Graphic from forecast for the biweekly moving average of COVID-19 (June 2021)

But the most important publication is a bibliographical investigation where several publications made by different researchers are summarized [8]. These publications show how in more than 20 countries (Korea, Brazil, USA, Japan, Ecuador, France, UK, India, Russia, Canada, Pakistan, India, Iran, China, etc.) climatic variables have been studied to predict the COVID-19 infection growth rate. And so it was obtained that variables such as temperature, humidity, hours of sunshine, wind speed, precipitation, solar radiation, rain, ozone and dew have been used with different algorithms such as ARIMA, MLP (Multi-Layer Perceptron), K-means, K-Nearest Neighbors, Random Forest, SVM (Supported Vector Machine), LSTM (Long short-term memory), CNN (Convolutional Neural Network), ANN (Artificial Neural Network), Logistic regression and Bayesian regression for the best forecasting.

Within all these publications, we concluded that most of them have obtained that the variables that are directly related to the increase in the infection rate of COVID-19 are the variables of temperature, humidity, and precipitation. And the best algorithm used is the LSTM.

For which we have obtained from different studies that we had to use the RNN with LSTM cells to predict the curve in Ecuador and check that the zones where there is more humidity, precipitation and a low average temperature were the cities that could have the most problems with the rate of infection in this country.

1.4 Types of Climates in Ecuador

There are many types of climates that are distributed throughout Ecuador, which shows that most of this territory is humid. A study at the Universidad Politécnica del Litoral (ESPOL) [10], showed a map (Fig. 5) with the different types of climates in which we have:

1. Tropical Rainy. - It is a climate with low annual thermal amplitude due to its constant rainfall throughout the year (less than 3 °C between the coldest months and the warmest months). One of its most exclusive characteristics is that in this climate there are abundant and regular rains always higher than 2000 mm per year up to 6000 mm.
2. Tropical Monsoon. - It is a type of climate in which most of its annual precipitation is characterized by cyclonic and orographic rains, although the heat transfer mechanism also produces some precipitation. On average, the annual precipitation is around 1500 mm but there are many variations depending on the area.
3. Tropical Savannah. - This climate has a particularity that covers 11.5% of the earth's surface and is that it is divided into two stages, a wet monsoon and a dry one throughout the year. If the wet season is short, it can present with torrential rains and on the other hand it is usually very hot throughout the year.
4. Dry. - In this type of climate, its humidity is relatively low, and they occur mostly on the coasts of Ecuador.
5. Permanently humid temperate. - This climate is especially characterized by having a very high relative humidity, and covers most of the Andean territory, and it can be said that it is a territory where the population rate is high.
6. Periodically dry temperate. - This climate is characterized by having rains with low temperatures, with an average of 15 C, and normally they are in the highest regions of Ecuador.
7. Paramo. - This neotropical climate is normally located between the limit of the closed forest and the perpetual snows in Ecuador; It is located approximately along the mountain ranges or in isolated mountains, with heights between 3,000 and 5,000 m.

In general, its climate is cold and humid, with extreme temperature changes that can vary from 30 °C to as low as 0 °C.

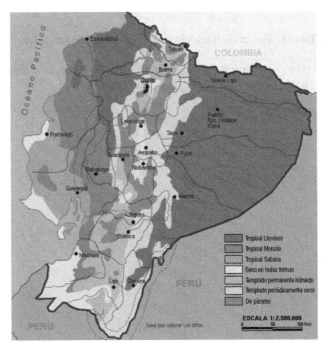

Fig. 5. Map of the types of climates in Ecuador. Source: Apuntes de geografía física y Ambiental [10]

This work is divided into four important parts:

- **Introduction:** where the objective, justification and importance of the research are stated.
- **Methodology:** where we prepared the dataset and use the RNN with LSTM cells for predict the curve.
- **Results:** where we showed the curve of the rate of COVID-19 infection
- **Conclusions and recommendations.**

2 Methodology

In this methodology section it will be specified the preprocess for training, the process for the test, and the final algorithm that we use for predicting the several weeks ahead.

2.1 Dataset

The first step was the data collection. We obtain a dataset in PAHO (Pan-American Health Organization) website [2] containing relevant information about COVID-19 cases in

Ecuador, such as the number of cases of people who got infected, and the number of cases of deaths from this disease. The dataset had the number of cases since 2020-01-01 until 2023-06-18, and we got 1,246 data. This dataset was compared with other datasets [1], but this one only had data until 2022-06-30 (Table 1).

Table 1. Part of the weekly dataset obtained for the prediction.

NO	DATE OF DATA COLLECTION	NUMBER OF INFECTED	TEMPERATURE	HUMIDITY	PRECIPITATION
0	26/1/2020	0	27.2	69.1	2
2	2/2/2020	0	27.7	71.9	0.5
3	9/2/2020	0	26.7	68.1	0
4	16/2/2020	0	28.3	63.6	0.5
5	23/2/2020	0	28.8	60.3	1
6	1/3/2020	13	29	62.3	0
7	8/3/2020	10	27.6	71.8	2.5
8	15/3/2020	58	27.9	74.1	1.5
9	22/3/2020	180	28.3	67.3	3
10	29/3/2020	333	28.5	64.1	0.5
11	5/4/2020	474	27.3	75.1	1.5
12	12/4/2020	576	27.8	74.3	1
13	19/4/2020	1564	28.5	68.1	0.5
.	.	.	.	.	.
.	.	.	.	.	.
.	.	.	.	.	.
169	16/4/2023	36.019	29	61.6	4.5
170	23/4/2023	36.019	29.1	59.8	1.5
171	30/4/2023	36.019	29	65.8	5.5
172	7/5/2023	36.019	26.1	83.3	12
173	14/5/2023	36.019	26.6	77.6	4.5
174	21/5/2023	36.022	26.9	73	2.5
175	28/5/2023	36.022	27	76.1	4.5
176	4/6/2023	36.026	27.6	74.2	2.5
177	11/6/2023	36.026	25.5	74.8	2
178	18/6/2023	36.026	25.8	74.2	0

The second step was the data preprocessing, after we obtained the dataset, we had to clean and prepare the data for training the neural network. This preprocess included removal of missing values, feature normalization, and proper coding of categorical variables. The missing values was the first days, because in January 2020, this country did not know that the most people were infected, and because of that, we had to change these values for the average of that week.

The third step that this paper did was the data splitting. Usually in most papers when they use RNN for predicting, they separate the data into training in a 70%, and 30% of the set for test. The first model that we use, was for adjust the different kinds of variables (hyperparameters) to use an RNN Fig. 6.

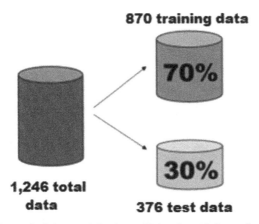

Fig. 6. Total of data, and the data splitting for training and testing.

2.2 LSTM Pre-processing and Processing

LSTM is a recurrent neural network (RNN) architecture specialized in the resolution and modeling of data sequences, which is usually a multivariate time series. This algorithm was created in 1997 by Hochreiter and Schmidhuber [9] as an enhancement to traditional RNNs, designed to overcome the problem of gradient fading. Also, as said in previous paragraphs, this algorithm is used very frequently in predictions of COVID-19. RNNs are also neural networks that have feedback connections, which allows them to maintain internal memory and process input sequences. This memory makes it possible to control the flow of information on the network, deciding what information is relevant and what should be forgotten or updated.

As a fourth step, the training of the model was carried out with 70% of the data, in which the neural network was fed with all the training data in the model and the weights and biases of the neurons were adjusted by means of optimization algorithms. This all helped us to be able to tune the hyperparameters based on performance in the validation set (Fig. 7).

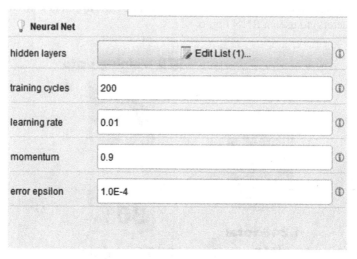

Fig. 7. The hypervariables used in the RNN (LSTM).

The final step is the evaluation of the model, which used the test set to evaluate the performance of the trained model, which was based on 30% of the data obtained. And finally, the necessary metrics were calculated to validate the prediction performance of this model, such as precision, recall and accuracy for the rate of infections of the COVID-19 disease.

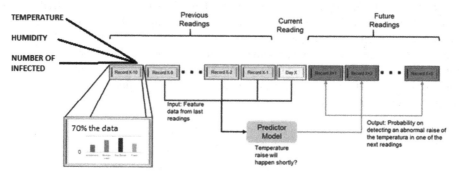

Fig. 8. Architecture used in the RNN (LSTM).

At a given time, the prediction is made for a computer based on the data included in the segment of the last three entries (temperature, humidity, number of infected) of the time series multivariate.

The prediction will offer a probability about the possibility of an increase in the number of infected people higher than normal in a period of the immediate future.

This network consists of a first LSTM layer with 100 units, followed by another with 50 units. The dropout technique is also applied after each LSTM layer to control overfitting. Finally, a final dense layer with simple unit and sigmoid activation provides a final probability (Fig. 9).

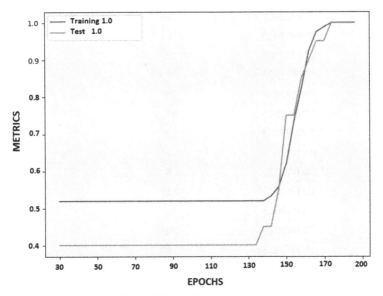

Fig. 9. MSE validation and test

3 Results

Using the RNN model, we could have some results of prediction for the future dates. On Table 2 we show the prediction data.

In total were 26 weeks that this publication predicted. After obtaining the results of prediction, we present the Fig. 8. We were able to predict values up to the end of the year, and to present them we grouped them by week, because there were many values. In the results we have that the COVID-19 is going to have many cases. In the first week was 512, the second one was 367, but the third was 315. These results present that this disease is going to increase and decrease. The last weeks we are going to have 125 infected people, 132 infected people and the last week of the year 108 infected people (Fig. 10).

Table 2. Results of the prediction model.

NO	WEEK	NUMBER OF INFECTED
180	02/07/2023	512
181	09/07/2023	367
182	16/07/2023	315
183	23/07/2023	220
184	30/07/2023	136
185	06/08/2023	315
186	13/08/2023	241
187	20/08/2023	161
188	27/08/2023	193
189	03/09/2023	129
190	10/09/2023	75
191	17/09/2023	81
192	24/09/2023	226
193	01/10/2023	153
194	08/10/2023	88
195	15/10/2023	255
196	22/10/2023	327
197	29/10/2023	203
198	05/11/2023	280
199	12/11/2023	320
200	19/11/2023	151
201	26/11/2023	254
202	03/12/2023	223
203	10/12/2023	73
204	17/12/2023	125
205	24/12/2023	132
206	31/12/2023	108

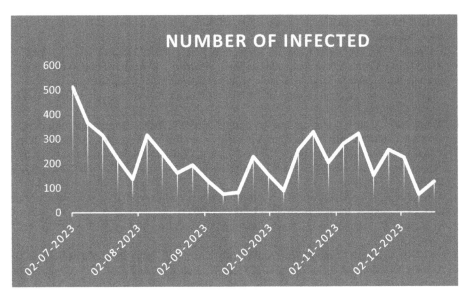

Fig. 10. Linear graph representing the number of people infected

4   Conclusion and Future Works

As a conclusion for these experiments, is that the model of RNN (LSTM) that we used show us a possible prediction about the cases of COVID-19 that Ecuador is going to suffer in the Niño Phenomenon, which covers from the end of the second quarter of 2023 to the first months of 2024.

Researching in the state of the art, we show several investigations that concluded that the humidity, precipitation, and temperature are variable that directly affect the infection rate of COVID-19. And in this El Niño phenomenon will have many rainfalls, and the humidity is going to get higher, the temperature is going to variate in a very catastrophic way than other years.

The results of the training and testing were good enough for predict the others dates, using a multivariate time series we can upgrade the results and we had better results.

The Ministerio de Salud Pública must be aware of these variations and predict through with the climatic variables (like humidity, precipitation and temperature) the type of impact that this phenomenon and this disease will have. It is very important to know this kind of curve of infected people.

For future works, we can use these predict data for compare with the real ones, this action will demonstrate if the model created by the RNN was good enough. Also, is important to use other variables like the precipitation that in some publications were used for this kind of predictions.

References

1. OPH: Organización Panamericana de la Salud, Ecuador – Situación de salud, Indicadores básicos de Ecuador (2022). https://hia.paho.org/es/ecuador-situacion-de-salud

2. PAHO: Pan American Health Organization, COVID-19 Epidemiological Situation (2023). https://shiny.paho-phe.org/covid19/
3. Espinosa, A.A.: El coronavirus en los tiempos del Ecuador. Análisis Carolina (23), 1 (2020)
4. Ruiz, G.P.I., León, A.C.I.: Evolución de la enfermedad por coronavirus (COVID-19) en Ecuador. La Ciencia al Servicio de la Salud y la Nutrición **11**(1), 5–15 (2020)
5. Organización Metereológica Mundial: El Niño/Oscilación del Sur. 1st edn. ISBN: 978-92-63-31145-0, España (2014)
6. Aragao, D.P., et al.: Multivariate data driven prediction of COVID-19 dynamics: towards new results with temperature, humidity and air quality data. Environ. Res. **204**, 112348 (2022)
7. Ahmadi, M., Sharifi, A., Dorosti, S., Ghoushchi, S.J., Ghanbari, N.: Investigation of effective climatology parameters on COVID-19 outbreak in Iran. Sci. Total Environ. **729**, 138705 (2020)
8. Abu-Abdoun, D.I., Al-Shihabi, S.: Weather conditions and COVID-19 cases: insights from the GCC countries. Intell. Syst. Appl. **15**, 200093 (2022)
9. Hochreiter, S., Schmidhuber, J.: Long short-term memory. Neural Comput. **9**(8), 1735–1780 (1997)
10. INOCAR (Instituto Oceanográfico y Antártico de la Armada), Comité Nacional para el estudio regional del fenómeno el Niño - Junio 2023 (2023). http://www.inocar.mil.ec/web/index.php/boletines/erfen
11. Navarrete, E.: Apuntes de geografía física y ambiental (2017)

Traffic Classification in Software-Defined Networking by Employing Deep Learning Techniques: A Systematic Literature Review

Daniel Nuñez-Agurto[1,2(✉)] ⓘ, Walter Fuertes[1] ⓘ, Luis Marrone[2] ⓘ,
Eduardo Benavides-Astudillo[1] ⓘ, and Mitchell Vásquez-Bermúdez[3] ⓘ

[1] Department of Computer Science, Universidad de las Fuerzas Armadas - ESPE,
Av. General Rumiñahui S/N, P.O. Box 17-15-231B, Sangolquí, Ecuador
{adnunez1,wmfuertes,debenavides}@espe.edu.ec
[2] Faculty of Computer Science, Universidad Nacional de La Plata, 1900 La Plata,
Argentina
lmarrone@linti.unlp.edu.ar
[3] Facultad de Ciencias Agrarias, Universidad Agraria del Ecuador, Avenida 25 de
Julio y Pio Jaramillo, Guayaquil, Ecuador
mvasquez@uagraria.edu.ec

Abstract. Software-Defined Networking provides a global vision of the network, centralized controller, dynamic routing, dynamic update of the flow table, and traffic analysis. The features of Software-Defined Networking and the integration of Deep Learning techniques allow the introduction of intelligence to optimize, manage and maintain them better. In this context, this work aims to provide a Systematic Literature Review on traffic classification in Software-Defined Networking with Deep Learning techniques. Furthermore, we analyze and synthesize the selected studies based on the categorization of traffic classes and the employed Deep Learning techniques to draw meaningful research conclusions. Finally, we identify new challenges and future research directions on this topic.

Keywords: Systematic literature review · Software-defined networking · Traffic classification · Deep learning

1 Introduction

In a world more digital and with the rapid development of smart devices and emerging technologies, data traffic in our world is growing exponentially. For this reason, the network infrastructure is becoming increasingly heterogeneous and complex to optimize traffic distribution and manage many devices [1]. A production network typically includes many devices, runs many protocols, and supports many applications. A heterogeneous network infrastructure poses several challenges in effectively organizing, optimizing network resources, and managing.

Supported by Universidad de las Fuerzas Armdas - ESPE.

The alternative to solve these problems is to introduce intelligence into networks. A proposal put forward several years ago is based on a knowledge plane (KP) approach, applying machine learning (ML) and Deep Learning (DL) techniques. The advances in networking, such as network programmability through Software-Defined Networking (SDN), encourage the applicability of DL in networking [2].

SDN is an emerging dynamic architecture that decouples the control plane and the data plane, this technology is ideal for the dynamic nature of today's applications. The centralized controller has a global view of the network by monitoring, configuration and the granularity information of the packet flows [3, 4]. The network flows collected by the controller SDN, and its programmability in real-time facilitate the integration of models based on ML; this approach can bring intelligence to the SDN controller by performing data analysis, network optimization, security, and automated provision of network services [5].

This Systematic Literature Review (SLR) reviews existing approaches to network traffic classification based on DL in SDN, which existing surveys have not covered in detail. This research focuses primarily on traffic classification methods and covers newer works in this area. Finally, future research lines that have not been solved are suggested.

The rest of the article is structured as follows: Section 2 presents the methodology for developing the SLR. Section 3 presents the results obtained from the SLR about traffic classification by employing DL techniques; the process used to search and analyze the data to answer the research questions is shown. Section 4 discusses the results obtained in traffic classification using DL and outlines future challenges. Finally, in Sect. 5, conclusions and future research are presented.

2   Research Methodology

This systematic review aims to analyze and discuss the available evidence of published scientific on traffic classification in SDN employing DL. This section shows the research methodology applied to develop an SLR; this systematic review method consists of phases are shown: the formulation of the research questions, the inclusion and exclusion criteria, the identification of the sources of information, the application of the search strategy, the selection of articles, and the data collection process. For its elaboration, the guidelines of the PRISMA declaration have been followed for the correct performance of systematic reviews [6]. Next, the elaboration process will be detailed in its different phases.

2.1   Research Protocol

The research questions are the central element at the beginning of the research and are used for making the theoretical assumptions more explicit. This section proposes the search strategy, selection criteria, preliminary research questions, identifying information sources, study selection, and data collection process [7]. Therefore, this study aims to answer three research questions (RQ):

- RQ1: *Which Deep Learning techniques are used to classify traffic in SDNs?*. It is important to understand algorithms and approaches used for traffic classification SDN and study the various methods of analytics, detection, and classification of traffic.
- RQ2: *What is the performance of Deep Learning-based classifiers for classifying traffic in SDN?*. Knowing the performance of Deep Learning models is essential for understanding the effectiveness of traffic classification techniques in SDN.
- RQ3: *What are the advantages and future research of DL-based traffic classification models in SDN?*. Knowing the future work proposed by authors will allow determining the challenges and future research directions in the traffic classification in SDN with DL.

2.2   Collection Information

For this systematic review, the search of articles is made from indexed databases such as Web of Science, Scopus and IEEE by employing customized search strings. Finally, the papers are selected by applying inclusion and exclusion criteria [8].

Conducting the Research. The keywords "Software Defined Networking" and "Deep Learning" are combined to construct the search terms in the different databases. Subsequently, synonyms and variations of the keywords were added using a combination of boolean AND and OR operators. Data since 2014 are used from four databases related to the start of scientific publications on SDN. The search strings applied in each of the selected databases are shown in Table 1.

The systematic search was carried out in March 2022. The number of articles obtained from scientific journals with the search strings is shown in Table 2.

Relevant Papers. To examine the relevance of the articles retrieved from the databases, the researchers must examine the relevance. The first action is to review the literature to gather a group of studies related to the inquired subject. Therefore, it filtered these articles through various inclusion and exclusion criteria.

Inclusion and Exclusion Criteria. Once the duplicate and noisy papers have been discarded, it is necessary to manually reduce the number of documents. This process should be carried out separately for each paper, applying inclusion and exclusion criteria with the characteristics the papers should have to be candidates as primary research sources [7]. This systematic review used the following criteria:

Inclusion criteria that studies should consider:

- I1: Papers related to Traffic Classification in SDN applying DL.
- I2: Papers published in journals with high impact.
- I3: Papers published between 1 January 2014 and 31 March 2.022.

Table 1. Search string.

Database	Search string
Web of Science	((SDN OR "Software Defined Network" OR "Software Defined Networking") AND ("Traffic Classification" OR "Network Traffic Classification" OR "Internet Traffic Classification") AND ("Deep Learning" OR Autoencoder OR "Sum Product Network" OR "Recurrent Neural Network" OR "Boltzmann Machine" OR "Deep Neural Network" OR "Convolutional Neural Network"))
Scopus	TITLE-ABS-KEY ((SDN OR "Software Defined Network" OR "Software Defined Networking") AND ("Traffic Classification" OR "Network Traffic Classification" OR "Internet Traffic Classification") AND ("Deep Learning" OR Autoencoder OR "Sum Product Network" OR "Recurrent Neural Network" OR "Boltzmann Machine" OR "Deep Neural Network" OR "Convolutional Neural Network"))
IEEE	((SDN OR "Software Defined Network" OR "Software Defined Networking") AND ("Traffic Classification" OR "Network Traffic Classification" OR "Internet Traffic Classification") AND ("Deep Learning OR Autoencoder OR "Sum Product Network" OR "Recurrent Neural Network" OR "Boltzmann Machine" OR "Deep Neural Network" OR "Convolutional Neural Network"))

Table 2. Database search results.

Database	Numerical Studies	Total Studies
Web of Science	20	
Scopus	22	53
IEEE	11	

Exclusion criteria are carried out following the guidelines:

- E1: Papers that do not expose the methodology when applying DL techniques in Traffic Classification.
- E2: Papers that have not been peer-reviewed.
- E3: Studies not published in English.

3 Results

To carry out the SLR correctly, we used the guidelines of the PRISMA declaration, which consists of three phases [6]. (1) The identification phase has to do with the search of articles in the selected databases with the application of the search string. (2) The screening phase applies the inclusion and exclusion criteria to the different related works obtained by the identification phase. (3) The inclusion phase eliminates those articles after applying the inclusion and exclusion criteria and evaluating the title, abstract, and exclusion criteria.

This section presents the search process results in the three select databases. In the first phase, 53 papers were obtained, and then, applying the inclusion and exclusion criteria to the documents, 14 papers were obtained. Finally, to make the final decision to include the articles, the entire content was read to obtain the 11 papers for this study. The results are shown in Fig. 1.

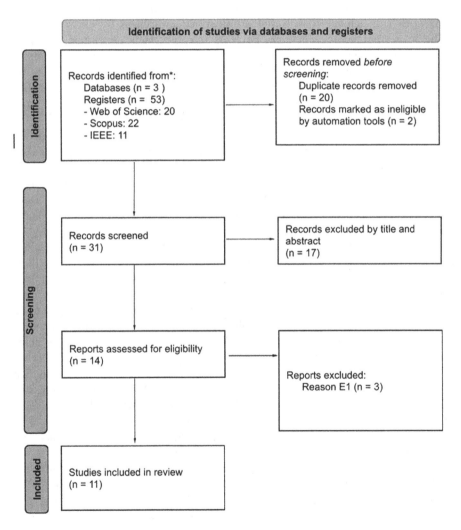

Fig. 1. Process followed to obtain the systematic review [6].

3.1   RQ1: Which Deep Learning Techniques Are Used to Classify Traffic in SDNs?

This section will analyze and synthesize the selected studies after applying SLR, which include established knowledge, new contributions, and implementation of the DL algorithms most used in traffic classification in SDN. The results of the selected papers are summary in Table 3.

Wang et al. [9] proposed a framework called SDN-HGW to support the controller of the core network and manage better distributed smart home networks. The framework extends the control to the access network for more proper end-to-end network management; this is important for smart home networks. This framework can achieve distributed applications awareness by classifying data traffic in a smart home network. For this purpose, they developed encrypted classifiers, called DataNets, based on three DL algorithms, Multilayer Perceptron (MLP), Stacked Autoencoder (SAE), and Convolutional Neural Networks, trained with an open dataset from 15 applications with over 200.000 encrypted data samples. The results show that the classifiers can be applied in a smart home SDN to enable distributed application-aware.

Zhang et al. [10] proposed a classification method based on a hybrid deep neural network to classify applications. This method automatically obtained the flow features from the SAE algorithm without the manual feature selection. The centralized SDN controller quickly collects and processes massive network traffic using high computing capability. The results show that the proposed classification method has more accurate than the method based on Support Vector Machine (SVM).

Lim et al. [11] propose a schema for traffic classification using a DL model in SDN. The dataset is generated by preprocessing the network traffic flows. To perform network traffic classification, train two classifiers based on DL: 1) Multi-layer Long Short-term Memory (ML-LSTM) and 2) the combination of Convolutional Neural Network and single-layer LSTM models. In addition, the hyper-parameters of the two DL models are found by a model fitting procedure. The performance analysis based on the F1 score for the two DL models shows the superiority of the ML-LSTM model for network packet classification.

Chang et al. [12] propose an online and offline application-aware traffic classification model based on DL algorithms over an SDN testbed. The classifier resides in the controller SDN and is built with three algorithms MPL, CNN, and SAE. The classifier is trained with an open dataset that contains samples of the seven most popular applications. The results show that the classifiers achieved more than 93.00% in offline training and 87.00% in online testing.

Abdulrazzaq and Demirci [13] proposed engineering system traffic based on DL to improve the allocation bandwidth of the applications in SDN. The proposed system is based on a classifier developed of the Deep Neural Network(DNN) and 1D-CNN algorithms; to solve the dataset's imbalanced class, it implements a Synthetic Minority Over-Sampling technique (SMOTE). The system aims to improve the quality of service by assigning queues with different priorities by classifying the traffic flows of different applications. The results show that DNN and 1D CNN are more accurate with traffic captured in 5 s and 10 s timeout.

Wang et al. [14] proposed a traffic classification semi-supervised method based on Generative Adversarial Network (GAN) called ByteS-GAN in SDN. This method achieved high performance using small labeled and large unlabeled samples. For this purpose, to achieve traffic classification in a fine-grained manner, it modifies the structure and loss function of the regular GAN discriminator networking. The results show that the ByteSGAN improves the classifier's performance and outperforms other supervised methods like CNN.

Wu et al. [15] propose a framework for encrypted network traffic classification based on the DL algorithm. This framework is divided into three parts: the first module preprocessing the flows; the second module is training the classifier; the third is the test module for the CNN model. The results show that the encrypted network traffic classification framework can perform well with low requirements.

Setiawan et al. [16] propose a framework to protect the controller SDN and improve de management of networks smart home called Software-Defined Network Home GateWay for Congestion (SDNHGC) base on DL algorithms. This framework analysis the traffic in real-time to enable regulation of network capacity and resource allocation. The classifier was trained and tested using samples from 20 applications of an open database; the applied algorithms were SAE, MLP, and CNN. The results show an accuracy better than other solutions.

Anh et al. [17] aimed to address the lack of explainability in deep-learning-based traffic classification by proposing an explanatory method using a genetic algorithm. They developed a deep-learning-based traffic classifier based on the ResNet model and utilized the genetic algorithm to generate optimal feature selection masks. The proposed method achieved an accuracy of approximately 97.24%. By quantifying the importance of each feature and computing the dominance rate, the authors provided insights into the mechanism of the classifier for different Internet services.

Jang et al. [18] aimed to address the challenge of traffic classification in software-defined network (SDN) environments by proposing a method that employs a variational autoencoder (VAE). The goal was to effectively classify various classes of Internet services and ensure quality of service. The VAE was trained using six statistical features to extract latent feature distributions for flows in each service class. Query traffic was classified by comparing its latent feature distribution with the learned distributions. Experimental results showed that the proposed method achieved an average accuracy of 89.00%, outperforming conventional statistics-based and machine learning-based methods.

Su et al. [19] The authors aimed to tackle the challenge of fine-grained traffic classification in software-defined networks (SDNs) by proposing an improved residual convolutional network approach. They developed a method that effectively addressed the network degradation problem associated with deep learning in fine-grained network traffic identification. The proposed approach achieved an impressive overall accuracy of 99.93%, surpassing other state-of-the-art models.

Table 3. Deep Learning based Traffic Classification in SDN.

Ref	Objective	DL Techniques	Dataset	Model Input	Model Output
[9]	QoS-aware Classification	MLP SAE CNN	ISCXVPN-nonVPN [21]	Automatic by algorithm	15 applications
[10]	QoS-aware Classification	SAE	Moore Dataset	Automatic by algorithm	10 classes
[11]	Application-aware Classification	ML-LSTM CNN+LSTM	UPC's Broadband Communications Research Group	Automatic by algorithm	8 applications
[12]	Application-aware Classification	MLP CNN SAE	"ISCXVPN-nonVPN traffic dataset" [21]	4 features	6 applications
[13]	QoS-aware Classification	CNN DNN	Tor traffic dataset [22]	23 features	3 classes
[14]	Application-aware Classification	GAN CNN	"ISCXVPN-nonVPN traffic dataset" [21]	Automatic by algorithm	15 applications
[15]	Application-aware Classification	CNN LSTM SAE	"ISCXVPN-nonVPN traffic dataset" [21]	Automatic by algorithm	5 classes
[16]	QoS-aware classification	MLP CNN SAE	Data collection from SDN traffic	Automatic by algorithm	20 applications
[17]	QoS-aware Classification	ResNet	ISCXVPN-nonVPN [21], MACCDC [25], and WRCCDC [24]	20 features	8 classes
[18]	QoS-aware Classification	VAE	Private dataset	6 features	6 classes
[19]	Application-aware Classification	ResNet	CICTF [23]	automatic by algorithm	16 applications

According to [20], the network traffic can be classified into: (1) Application-aware Traffic Classification, which aims to identify the applications base on traffic flows; (2) *QoS-aware Traffic Classification*, which aims to identify the traffic flows of the applications in different classes to improve the performance of the network; (3) *DDoS Attack Detection*, aims to classify this type of attacks that cause this would cause network unavailability by exhaust the resources of the network, the storage, memory, and CPU in control and data plane; and (4) *Fine-grained Intrusion Detection*, aims to classify network traffic and identify different types of attacks. According to this classification in our SLR, we have identified five papers based on application-aware classification, six papers based on QoS-aware.

3.2   RQ2: What Is the Performance of Deep Learning-Based Classifiers for Classifying Traffic in SDN?

The researchers adopt various metrics to analyze the performance of their experiments and arrive at their conclusions; among the most commonly used metrics are Receiver-operating characteristics (ROC), CPU utilization, accuracy, precision, F-measure, and recall. This research question aims to determine the performance of recent development in network traffic classification by employing DL in SDN. The results of this analysis are summarized in Table 4.

In general, identified 11 relevant primary studies that use DL algorithms to classify traffic in SDN, as shown in Table 3. In primary studies, we identified about 9 DL algorithms used by researchers. In particular, the most used algorithms by researchers are CNN (9 times), SAE (5 times), LSTM (3 times), MLP (3 times), DNN (2 times), ResNet (2 times), GAN (1 time), GRU (1 time), VAE (1 time) as shown in Fig. 2. Finally, the combination of different DL techniques was demonstrated to improve the traffic classification model's accuracy significantly.

3.3   RQ3: What Are the Advantages and Future Research of DL-Based Traffic Classification Models in SDN?

Several research works have been carried out on SDN traffic classification. However, considering the maturity and accuracy requirements of the classification models, there are still several challenges that need to be considered before having

Table 4. Performance of the DL-based solutions in SDN.

Ref	Model Accuracy	Parameters for performance evaluations					
		ROC	Accuracy	Precision	Recall	F-measure	GPU/CPU
[9]	MLP: 97.14% SAE: 99.14% CNN: 99.30%		✓	✓	✓	✓	✓
[10]	SAE: 90%		✓	✓	✓	✓	
[11]	ML-LSTM: 97.14% CNN+LSTM: 99.30%		✓			✓	
[12]	MLP: 93.21% CNN: 93.35% SAE: 93.13%		✓	✓	✓	✓	
[13]	CNN: 96.00% DNN: 94.00%		✓	✓	✓	✓	
[14]	GAN: 93.18% CNN: 93.30%		✓	✓	✓	✓	
[15]	CNN: 98.85% LSTM: 99.22% SAE: 98.74%		✓	✓	✓	✓	
[16]	MLP, CNN and SAE: 90%		✓				
[17]	ResNet: 97.24%		✓	✓	✓	✓	
[18]	VAE: 89.00%		✓				
[19]	ResNet: 99.93%		✓	✓	✓	✓	

a complete traffic classification solution with DL techniques in SDN. Therefore, in Table 5, a summary of the classification models developed with DL with the advantages and future research lines is given.

4   Discussion

Nowadays, applications are interactive and constantly changing; therefore, they need more bandwidth and QoS. In the case of cybersecurity, the security attack signatures are constantly changing. This change brings a challenge in network traffic classification, known as concept drift, consisting of variations in environment types and data distribution due to fluctuations in time locations. For this, it is essential to retrain the DL model constantly to account for these changes. An open research direction is retraining the model; it is critical as new data is generated to achieve rapid incremental learning. However, a model based on DL represents a higher complexity and needs more training time. Incremental learning entails special system needs, and retraining a model can be time-consuming, computationally intensive, and expensive. Therefore, researchers should concentrate on this topic as it can be improved using many different techniques. The main advantages and future work of the papers found in this SLR are shown in Table 5.

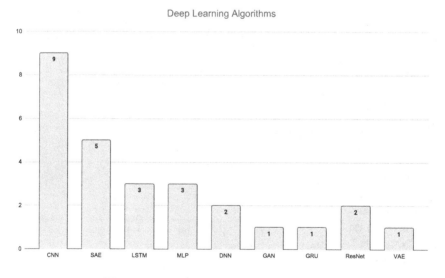

Fig. 2. Deep Learning Algorithms in SDN.

The training dataset is critical to supervised learning algorithms; its performance depends on the labeled data's quality and the class's uniform distribution. This study analyzes the paper's findings from the perspective of DL Algorithms, training dataset, model input/output, and objective of the propose, as shown in

Table 5. Advantages and future research lines of the DL-based solutions.

Ref	Advantages	Future research lines
[9]	The framework was developed with three DL-based approaches for encrypted data classification in smart homes to manage QoS.	Improve the performance of the framework to implement a new model of business.
[10]	The framework achieves high accuracy without the manual feature selection and extraction.	Conduct the simulation experiments based on the SDN platform to test the framework's performance
[11]	The architecture proposed achieve a better result using the ML-LSTM algorithm and the unchanged the original payload.	Test the classification architecture in a real environment.
[12]	The designed DL architecture and scheme achieve high accuracy in online testing with three models, MLP, SAE, and CNN.	Further research will be the network slicing with the QoS mechanism followed by successful traffic classification.
[13]	The proposed system solved the issue of the imbalanced dataset with SMOTE.	Analyze the result of implementing the system in large network topologies and study the effects of increased network traffic with a more significant number of hots.
[14]	The proposed method modifies the structure and lost function of the GAN discriminator network to achieve high accuracy.	Analyze the generative capability of GAN to address the problem of unbalanced datasets.
[15]	The proposed framework can guarantee the real effect of resource allocation under the condition of low requirements.	Test the framework in real-time to analyze the resource allocation performance.
[16]	The proposed architecture focused on real-time traffic analysis to enable improved end-to-end monitoring of networks.	Adapt framework to improve network capital management to make creative business strategies.
[17]	The proposed method provides insights into the working mechanism of deep-learning-based traffic classification. By quantifying the importance of each feature and using a genetic algorithm.	Refining the feature selection process and optimizing the algorithm, to advance the capabilities of deep-learning-based traffic classification in terms of accuracy, specificity, and efficiency.
[18]	The proposed approach offers stability, versatility, and improved performance, making it a promising solution for effective network traffic classification in the context of emerging Internet services and increasing traffic demands.	Improve the proposed method to support dynamic environments where new types of services are added or where service characteristics change dynamically in real-time through online training.
[18]	The proposed used a ResNet that can effectively extract features from the traffic data and achieve high classification accuracy and used a unified traffic preprocessing method to process the original network traffic dataset into image data.	Analyze the time complexity of their proposed method, explore real-time or online traffic classification, identify new traffic types, and optimize model parameters.

Table 3. The models based on DL proposed by the authors were analyzed based on parameters such as ROC, CPU utilization, accuracy, precision, F-measure, and recall. Although the models show good accuracy, there is one problem of

multiple unbalanced classes. The summary of network traffic classification solutions based on DL is shown in Table 4. In [13], the authors propose a solution for the issue of imbalanced datasets by implementing an oversampling technique called SMOTE. However, it is an open research line, as it can be improved using many strategies.

The major challenge faced in network traffic classification in SDN is the accessibility to essential datasets. This SLR found five datasets, as shown in Table 3. However, only the InSDN dataset has recent SDN traffic characteristics from two years. However, available of the recent dataset is essential in new application classification or attack detection in SDN; because of the evolution of technology that renders old datasets irrelevant. This limitation affects deploying the models proposed by the authors in the network traffic classification.

The exponential growth of applications on the Internet affects the network traffic classification based on application-aware and QoS-aware. Identifying all the applications is complicated and impractical. Thus, one of the proposed solutions is to group applications into classes according to specific traffic flow characteristics and assign the proper QoS; with this solution proposed, different applications may belong to a QoS class. Therefore, classifying the applications' traffic flows based on their QoS requirements is more effective than classifying them individually.

5   Conclusions

This systematic literature review (SLR) provided representative research addressing the challenges of traffic classification in SDNs by applying Deep Learning (DL) techniques. The analysis of relevant studies revealed the utilization of various DL techniques, including CNN, SAE, LSTM, MLP, DNN, ResNet, GAN, GRU, and VAE, for traffic classification in SDNs. Among these techniques, CNN emerged as the most frequently employed algorithm. The combination of different DL techniques demonstrated promising results in improving the accuracy of traffic classification models in SDNs. The performance of DL-based classifiers varied across the identified studies, with reported accuracies ranging from 89.00% to over 99.93%. DL models showcased superior performance compared to traditional methods, such as statistical-based approaches and machine learning algorithms. DL-based traffic classification models in SDNs offer several advantages, including the ability to handle complex and large-scale traffic data, automatic feature extraction, and high accuracy. Future research opportunities lie in exploring the scalability of classifiers in imbalanced datasets, addressing concept drift, and implementing real-time implementations.

Acknowledgments. The authors would like to thank the Distributed Systems, Cybersecurity and Content Research Group (RACKLY) at Universidad de las Fuerzas Armadas - ESPE for its scientific and collaborative contribution.

References

1. CISCO: Cisco Annual Internet Report (2018–2023) (2020). https://www.cisco.com/c/en/us/solutions/collateral/executive-perspectives/annual-internet-report/white-paper-c11-741490.pdf
2. Ayoubi, S., et al.: Machine learning for cognitive network management. IEEE Commun. Mag. **56**(1), 158–165 (2018)
3. Kreutz, D., Ramos, F.M.V., Esteves Verissimo, P., Esteve Rothenberg, C., Azodolmolky, S., Uhlig, S.: Software-defined networking: a comprehensive survey. Proc. IEEE **103**(1), 14–76 (2015)
4. Nunez-Agurto, D., Fuertes, W., Marrone, L., Macas, M.: Machine learning-based traffic classification in software-defined networking: a systematic literature review, challenges, and future research directions. IAENG Int. J. Comput. Sci. **49**(4) (2022)
5. Xie, J., et al.: A survey of machine learning techniques applied to software defined networking (SDN): research issues and challenges. IEEE Commun. Surv. Tutorials **21**(1), 393–430 (2019). CrossRef
6. McInnes, M., Moher, D., Thombs, B., McGrath, T., Bossuyt, P.M., Willis, B.H.: The PRISMA-DTA group. Preferred reporting items for a systematic review and meta-analysis of diagnostic test accuracy studies; The PRISMA-DTA statement. JAMA **319**, 388–396 (2018)
7. Kitchenham, B., Charters, S.: Guidelines for performing Systematic Literature Reviews in Software Engineering. University of Durham, Durham (2007)
8. Kitchenham, B.A., Budgen, D., Brereton, P.: Evidence-Based Software Engineering and Systematic Reviews. Chapman and Hall/CRC: Boca Raton, FL, USA (2020)
9. Wang, P., Ye, F., Chen, X., Qian, Y.: DataNet: deep learning based encrypted network traffic classification in SDN home gateway. IEEE Access **6**, 55380–55391 (2018). CrossRef
10. Zhang, C., Wang, X., Li, F., He, Q., Huang, M.: Deep learning-based network application classification for SDN. Trans. Emerging Telecommun. Technol. **29**(5), e3302 (2018). CrossRef
11. Lim, H.-K., Kim, J.-B., Kim, K., Hong, Y.-G., Han, Y.-H.: Payload-based traffic classification using multi-layer LSTM in software defined networks. Appl. Sci. **9**(121) (2019). CrossRef
12. Chang, L.-H., Lee, T.-H., Chu, H.-C., Su, C.-W.: Application-based online traffic classification with deep learning models on SDN networks. Adv. Technol. Innov. **5**(4), 216–229 (2020). CrossRef
13. Abdulrazzaq, S., Demirci, M.: A deep learning based system for traffic engineering in software defined networks. Int. J. Intell. Syst. Appl. Eng. **8**(4), 206–213 (2020). CrossRef
14. Wang, P., Wang, Z., Ye, F., Chen, X.: ByteSGAN: a semi-supervised generative adversarial network for encrypted traffic classification in SDN edge gateway. Comput. Netw. **200** (2021). CrossRef
15. Wu, H., Zhang, X., Yang, J.: Deep learning-based encrypted network traffic classification and resource allocation in SDN. J. Web Eng. 2319–2334 (2021). CrossRef
16. Setiawan, R., et al.: Encrypted network traffic classification and resource allocation with deep learning in software defined network. Wireless Pers. Commun. (2021). CrossRef
17. Ahn, S., Kim, J., Park, S.Y., Cho, S.: Explaining deep learning-based traffic classification using a genetic algorithm. IEEE Access **9**, 4738–4751 (2021). https://doi.org/10.1109/ACCESS.2020.3048348

18. Jang, Y., Kim, N., Lee, B.-D.: Traffic classification using distributions of latent space in software-defined networks: an experimental evaluation. Eng. Appl. Artif. Intell. **119**, 105736 (2023). https://doi.org/10.1016/j.engappai.2022.105736

19. Su, C., Liu, Y., Xie, X.: Fine-grained traffic classification based on improved residual convolutional network in software defined networks. IEEE Lat. Am. Trans. **21**(4), 565–572 (2023). https://doi.org/10.1109/TLA.2023.10128928

20. Yan, J., Yuan, J.: A survey of traffic classification in software defined networks. In: 2018 1st IEEE International Conference on Hot Information-Centric Networking (HotICN), pp. 200–206, August 2018

21. Lashkari, A.H., Draper-Gil, G., Mamun, M.S.I., Ghorbani, A.A.: Characterization of encrypted and VPN traffic using time-related features. In: Proceedings International Conference on Information Systems Security and Privacy (ICISSP), pp. 407–414 (2016). CrossRef

22. Lashkari, A.H., Draper-Gil, G., Mamun, M.S.I., Ghorbani, A.A.: Characterization of tor traffic using time based features. In: ICISSP, pp. 253–262 (2017). CrossRef

23. Canadian institute for cybersecurity, datasets. https://www.unb.ca/cic/datasets/index.html. Accessed 2023

24. WRCCDC. https://archive.wrccdc.org/pcaps/. Accessed 2023

25. Capture files from Mid Atlantic CCDC. https://www.netresec.com. Accessed 2023

Use of Data Mining Strategies in Environmental Parameters in Poultry Farms, a Case Study

Clifton Clunie[2] , Gloris Batista-Mendoza[2] , Denis Cedeño-Moreno[1]([⊠]) ,
Huriviades Calderon-Gomez[1] , Luis Mendoza-Pittí[1] ,
Cristian Moreno de la Cruz[1] , and Miguel Vargas-Lombardo[3]([⊠])

[1] Facultad de Ingeniería de Sistemas Computacionales (FISC), Universidad Tecnológica de Panamá, Ciudad de Panamá, Panamá
{denis.cedeno,huriviades.calderon,luis.mendoza1,
cristian.moreno}@utp.ac.pa
[2] Centro de Investigación TICs (CIDITIC), Universidad Tecnológica de Panamá, Ciudad de Panamá, Panamá
{clifton.clunie,gloris.batista1}@utp.ac.pa
[3] GISES, Universidad Tecnológica de Panamá, Ciudad de Panamá, Panamá
miguel.vargas@utp.ac.pa

Abstract. This article presents the approach to develop a tool that allows the immediate characterization of environmental parameters. To achieve this objective, it is necessary to investigate different data extraction techniques, transformation methods and categorical data analysis. This will allow understanding of the effects of environmental variables such as temperature, relative humidity, and heat index on birds within a warehouse environment at different times of the year. The tool aims to provide intelligent decision support to poultry producers, enabling project optimization, profitability, and effective mitigation of the significant impact of climate change on the sector. To carry out this research, a comprehensive review of concepts, different techniques and existing methodologies was carried out. This review concluded that the application of the Cross-Industry Standard Process for Data Mining (CRISP-DM) management methodology ensures a systematic data mining process. In addition, this methodology facilitates the understanding of the knowledge discovery process, leading to effective project planning and execution. The data mining tool selected for this research was WEKA, an open-source data extraction software tool. WEKA provides an organized collection of state-of-the-art machine learning algorithms and data pre-processing tools. It has an easy-to-use interactive graphical interface that facilitates data exploration and allows the configuration of large-scale experiments on distributed computing platforms, as well as the design of configurations for processing transmitted data. Three classification algorithms, J48, LMT and REPTree, were selected for the modelling design, which allowed comparison and selection of the tool providing the best results. Finally, the model developed with the REPTree classification algorithm was recommended for this project. This research represents one of the most significant contributions to data mining in the context of the Smart Poultry Farm system. It serves as a basis for addressing future environmental challenges and making informed decisions in the poultry industry.

© The Author(s), under exclusive license to Springer Nature Switzerland AG 2023
R. Valencia-García et al. (Eds.): CITI 2023, CCIS 1873, pp. 81–94, 2023.
https://doi.org/10.1007/978-3-031-45682-4_7

Keywords: Data analysis · decision trees · REPTree · poultry farms · CRISP-DM · data mining

1 Introduction

The digital era, driven by the increasing demand for managing vast knowledge through technological advancements, has ushered in significant transformations and energized paradigms in human society. This integration of technology has given rise to emerging fields such as data mining, big data, artificial intelligence, machine learning, and the Internet of Things (IoT), which aim to bridge the physical, digital, and biological worlds, thus revolutionizing today's society [1, 2].

The field of poultry production is not exempt from this reality, as the temperature and relative humidity of poultry sheds play a crucial role in production processes [3]. It is critical for poultry producers to constantly monitor these variables and take the necessary actions to regulate the variations that may affect the normal growth process of chickens.

In Panama, there is scarce information on these environmental parameters, which hinders poultry farmers from gaining insights into the conditions within their projects. Consequently, they face challenges in managing an appropriate and optimal environment for their poultry, which directly affects productivity and the overall success of broiler poultry farms [4]. In the broader commercial sector, there is a strong drive to leverage available information to gain competitive advantages.

Data mining processes, utilizing artificial intelligence, statistics, and various algorithms, are seen as valuable tools for generating insights that enable companies to develop business intelligence, an asset in today's business landscape. Through data evaluation models, these processes offer companies an effective means to develop strategies by providing a comprehensive view of their strengths, opportunities, and weaknesses.

In this sense, researchers analyzed the various factors that affect climate and agriculture using data mining techniques the study aimed to understand the impact of climate on agriculture, enabling farmers to make informed agricultural decisions that directly impact the economies of developing countries [5]. Additionally, in conducted a study focusing on clustering methods to gather data on crops, soils, and climate in India, their objective was to optimize production and enhance the resilience of agriculture to climate change [6].

Such research, exploring the analysis of environmental variables through data mining, presents a promising alternative for agricultural projects. By employing different techniques of data extraction and studying the resulting patterns, informed decisions can be made in real-time, thereby reducing project errors. Given this scenario and the urgent need to provide suitable solutions to poultry producers in the region, the following research question arises: How can data mining enable the characterization of environmental parameters in open poultry houses, leading to the generation of valuable business intelligence?, the objective of this research is to explore the characterization of environmental parameters in poultry houses, using a data mining model and a real dataset. This research work is organized in 4 sections. Section two presents the background of the technology and the model implemented for this case study. Section three presents the methodology and section four results and discussion of this research work. Finally, the conclusions of this research are presented.

2 Background

The background of this research is informed by previous studies that provide the theoretical foundation for its development. These studies are related to the application of data mining techniques to analyze environmental parameters. In the research [5] the authors explored the factors that affect weather and agriculture using data mining. They examined various data mining techniques, including correlation analysis, multidimensional modelling such k-means, Artificial Neural Network (ANN), Support Vector Machine (SVM), Partition Around Medoids (PAM), Clustering Large Applications (CLARA), and DBSCAN. By analyzing data patterns and categorizing available agricultural data, the study aimed to provide insights into the effect of climate on agriculture. This knowledge enables farmers to make informed agricultural decisions that have a direct impact on the economies of developing countries.

The study included a comparative table of the different data mining techniques as part of its results. The article [7] conducted a systematic review of the literature, focusing on the context in which data mining methodologies are employed and the adaptations they undergo. In addition, the authors emphasized the need to develop improvements in existing data mining methodologies that allow them to interact seamlessly with IT development platforms and processes (technological adaptation) as well as organizational management frameworks (organizational adaptation).

The article [6], to analyze and mine the extensive amount of data available on crops, soils, and climate in India. The objective is to optimize production and enhance the resilience of agriculture in the face of climate change. In the study, a modified approach based on DBSCAN was employed to cluster the data, considering districts with similar temperatures, rainfall, and soil types. PAM and CLARA were used to group the data based on the districts with the highest crop production. Similarly, a comparison was conducted to assess the grouping quality using four yield quality metrics, ranking them from best to worst in purity, homogeneity, and completeness, among others.

According to the analysis of clustering quality metrics, DBSCAN was found to provide better clustering quality than PAM and CLARA, while CLARA showed better clustering quality than PAM. In the article [8], the researchers presented a study focused on the impact of environmental attributes, specifically environmental temperature, on broiler chickens. Additionally, they designed a prediction model using the classification and regression tree algorithm (CART) to enhance the accuracy of poultry yield estimation. The authors applied a methodology that included data collection as the initial step, considering the presence of inconsistent or erroneous data. This issue was resolved through the implementation of data pre-processing, specifically an anomaly detection technique. The study data were divided into two sets: the training dataset and the validation dataset. The CART algorithm was applied to the training dataset, while the post-pruning technique (REP) was used for the validation dataset. To ensure the accuracy of the results, the researchers employed cross-validation during the validation process, which resulted in a smaller and more precise tree structure. All these research projects explore various aspects and perspectives related to the use of data mining. Although none of them directly align with the approach being undertaken in this study, they provide valuable guidelines and insights for the research.

3   Methodology for Study Case

In our research we propose as a methodology for this case study, the Cross-Industry Standard Process for Data Mining (CRISP-DM) was developed by analysts representing DaimlerChrysler, SPSS, and NCR. CRISP-DM provides a non-proprietary and freely available standard process for adapting data mining to the overall problem-solving strategy of a business or research unit [9]. The CRISP-DM methodology consists of a six-phase life cycle focused on data exploration and analysis [9]. The phases are visually presented in Fig. 1.

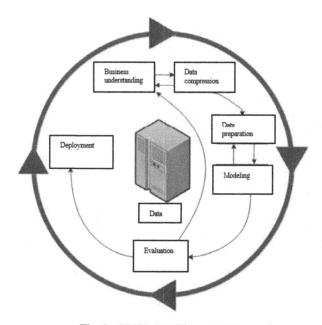

Fig. 1. CRISP-DM life cycle [10].

These phases are outlined as follows:

- Business understanding: During this stage, the objectives of the company are determined, along with its needs and the identification of the problem. It also considers the constraints and benefits associated with the problem and evaluates the current situation before implementing the proposed data mining solution to measure the level of success of the project.

- Data understanding: This stage involves collecting the data to be used and identifying the sources and techniques for data collection. In addition, it identifies the type, format, volume, and meaning of each piece of data, enabling a comprehensive understanding of their properties.
- Data preparation: This is the most time-consuming stage and involves building the dataset. Initially, data is prepared through activities such as data cleaning, variable construction, and data integration. In addition, indicators are generated to enhance the predictive capacity of existing data and identify interesting behaviors for modelling. Lastly, data transformation is performed, which entails changing the format or structure of certain data without altering their meaning. This step is crucial for applying specific techniques during the modelling stage.
- Modelling: During this stage, the data mining model is obtained, and several modelling algorithms are applied. The selection of appropriate modelling depends on the problem, available data, and data mining tools. Test data is selected, and the sample may be divided into training and validation data for certain models. The modelling process concludes with obtaining the model through an iterative parameter modification process.
- Model evaluation: During this stage, the quality of the model is determined based on the analysis of certain statistical metrics. A comparison is made between the current and previous results, and expert opinions in the problem domain may also be considered. The results of this phase are used to determine whether to proceed to the subsequent phase or return to the previous phases.
- Model implementation: This stage involves applying the knowledge acquired through the model to concrete actions. It is essential to document the results for end users, ensure proper documentation of all stages of the methodology for project review, and derive valuable lessons during the process.

The approach of this research utilizes the CRISP-DM methodology, taking into consideration business understanding, data understanding, data preparation, modelling, model evaluation, and model implementation, the entire process is shown below.

3.1 Business Understanding

The "Smart Poultry Farm" project was one of the winning projects in the 2018 Public Call for New Ventures of the National Secretariat of Science, Technology, and Innovation (SENACYT). The initial idea of the project is to solve the lack of affordable technological solutions for Panamanian producers across various sectors by providing intelligent system solutions at a low cost compared to similar products available in international markets. In addition, the project capitalizes on the specialized human resources available in Panama to support producers in achieving optimal yields in the production processes, thus ensuring profitability, and contributing to the country's ecological footprint reduction.

The objective of the "Smart Poultry Farm" project is to provide an intelligent system (see Fig. 2) consisting of integrated hardware and software based on an Internet of Things architecture. This system aims to optimize the efficiency of broiler projects by allowing energy savings, improving the conversion factor, providing electrical protection for equipment, and incorporating configurable alarms for emergency situations, such as prolonged power outages, with notifications sent via SMS or e-mail. In addition, it offers a user-friendly web-based graphical interface and a resource-efficient mobile app for monitoring equipment status and environmental variables such as temperature, relative humidity, and heat index in the poultry sheds, providing real-time visualization of events in the project.

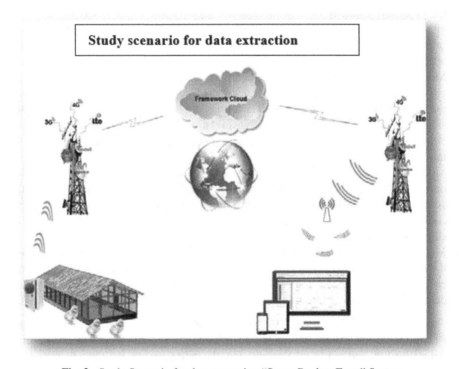

Fig. 2. Study Scenario for data extraction "Smart Poultry Farm" System

The "Smart Poultry Farm" platform provides a downloadable data history that contains information on the environmental parameters within an open chicken house. This data serves as the foundation for incorporating "data mining" technology into the system (see Fig. 3). The objective of this research is to apply various techniques for extracting data, transforming it, and analyzing categorized data patterns. This analysis aims to understand the behavior of the data across three daily shifts throughout the year and examine the impact of environmental variables within the broiler house environment. The goal is to provide valuable information to poultry producers, enabling them to make informed decisions to optimize and maximize profitability in their projects.

3.2 Data Understanding

During this phase, an analysis of the initial data was carried out to understand its scope, distributions, and relationships and assess its quality in relation to the project's objectives.

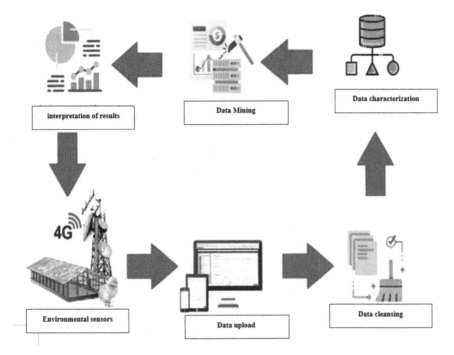

Fig. 3. Incorporating "data mining" technology into the system

The work team of this project decided to implement the data mining study with the WEKA tool due to the references and previous studies found in [5, 7, 31–33].

Support tools such as Microsoft Excel and the WEKA data analysis tool were utilized for this purposed. The period from September 24, 2022, to November 13, 2022, was selected for data extraction (5. In addition, as explained in the previous section, the data used in this project were extracted from the "Smart Poultry Farm" system; therefore, it is assumed that they are accurate and sufficient for identifying valid patterns. The date values in the data were initially in Unix Time Stamp format, and they were converted to a standard format. This conversion aimed to establish time classifications, referred to as "shifts", to determine daily readings. Furthermore, the original data required conversion to comma-delimited **format (*.csv)** to be compatible with the WEKA data exploration tool. The data set 1 w.

The attributes and their descriptions are as follows:

- Temperature: The temperature obtained from the sensor inside the chicken house.
- Humidity: The humidity level measured inside the chicken house by the sensor.
- Heat Index: The calculated heat index based on the temperature inside the chicken house.
- Shift: The specific time of day when the sensor's environmental parameter reading was taken.

The success criterion of the study included obtaining a software product that adequately characterizes the environmental parameters in open chicken houses with a 75% accuracy margin.

3.3 Data Preparation

An extensive analysis was conducted to examine the composition of the data, including its distribution, uniformity, classifications, labels, null values, means, deviations, relationships, and other factors. To clean the data, irrelevant or insignificant data, commonly referred to as "ghost data", was eliminated. Additionally, standardization techniques were applied to optimize the data, resulting in a dataset consisting of 1,078 instances and four attributes. In the data quality analysis section, we began with the premise that "all data represent valuable information", and it was essential to evaluate whether the data met this premise. Specifically, we checked for ambiguities, out-of-scope values, and the appropriateness of data types for the algorithms employed in developing the models [11–22].

The observations regarding the data quality for this project are as follows:

- The datasets do not include null values.
- Each record in the dataset is uniquely represented by the four attributes, which serve as the key for each record. There are no duplicate or null values.
- The values within each attribute comply with their respective acceptable ranges.

3.4 Modelling

Based on the previous phases of the project, it is evident that our project can be characterized as a classification-type data mining project. The primary objective is to develop a model capable of classifying the environmental parameters into different shifts, namely morning, afternoon, and night. To select the appropriate classification algorithms for model design, we considered the algorithms commonly used in the WEKA tool best suited to the characteristics of the dataset. Table 1 shows the classification algorithms supported by the WEKA tool [23–25].

Table 1. Algorithms used in study

Algorithms	Description
J48	C4.5
Logical Model Tree (LMT)	Decision tree with logical Logic
REPTree	A method to generate a decision tree from a given dataset

Once the algorithms to be used in the previous task had been selected, the modeling for the algorithm was carried out, for which purpose a series of iterations were performed, varying the cross-validation folds. It was decided to perform five iterations (with 11, 9, 7, 7, 5 and 3 folds) for each of the algorithms.

Once each of the developed models has been evaluated, for each of the algorithms used, the one that offers the best results is taken into consideration, according to the Data Mining objectives.

Table 2 below shows a summary of the results of the models developed in the previous activity.

Table 2. Results of the models according to the algorithms applied

Algorithms	% Instances correctly classified	% Instances incorrectly classified
J48	59.3692	40.6308
Logical Model Tree (LMT)	60.3896	39.6104
REPTree	63.8219	36.1781

4 Results and Discussion

Analyzing the model generated by the REPTree classification algorithm, the following results were obtained: Out of the 1,078 instances, 688 were correctly classified, representing 63.8219% accuracy; additionally, 390 instances were considered incorrectly classified, accounting for 36.1781% of the total instances. Furthermore, we proceeded to analyze the results of the REPTree algorithm for each subsequent class. As mentioned above, the evaluation used the metrics of precision, recall and F-measure. This set of metrics is very common in the evaluation process of machine learning systems. Precision is the ratio of correctly predicted observation to total observations. Precision indicates how many of the predicted positives are positive (true positives). In other words, it is the proportion of true positives out of all those classified as positive. Recall is the ratio of true positives to all true positive units. The F-score combines precision and recall, and scores one under perfect precision and recall (P (true positives), FN (false negatives), FP (false positives) and TN (certain negatives). TP: Represents the correct predictions for the class. FN: The prediction is negative when the value should be positive. FP: The number of false positives, i.e., the prediction is positive when the value should be negative. TN: The number of true negatives, i.e. correct predictions for the class. See Table 3.

The highest-ranking class is the night shift, classified as regular, while the lowest-ranking class is the afternoon shift. These results are further illustrated by the confusion matrix (Table 4).

The highest-ranking class is the night shift considered regular and the lowest is the evening shift. These results are made clearer by means of the confusion matrix:

- Out of 559 environmental parameters, the algorithm classified 450 as belonging to the night shift, 45 to the morning shift, and 59 to the afternoon shift.
- Among the 313 environmental parameters, 163 were classified as night shift, 146 as morning shift, and 4 as afternoon shift.

Table 3. Result, REPTree algorithm results by class

	Night	Morning	afternoon	Weighted Avg.
TP Rate	0.812	0.466	0.436	0.638
FP Rate	0.529	0.065	0.073	0.305
Precision	0.619	0.745	0.594	0.651
Recall	0.812	0.466	0.436	0.638
F-Measure	0.703	0.574	0.503	0.626
MCC (Matthew's correlation coefficient)	0.303	0.472	0.411	0.373
ROC Area (Receiver Operating Characteristic curve)	0.680	0.837	0.813	0.751
PRC Area (Precision-recall Curve)	0.643	0.669	0.553	0.633

Table 4. Confusion matrix.

A	B	C	< -- classified as
450	45	59	∣ a = night
163	146	4	∣ b = morning
114	5	92	∣ c = afternoon

- Within the 211 environmental parameters, 114 were assigned to the night shift, 5 to the morning shift, and 92 to the afternoon shift.

With respect to the kappa statistic, a value of 0.368 was obtained. According to the table of the degree of agreement, this falls within the medium classification and is used to evaluate the concordance of the measuring instruments whose results are categorical [24–30]. The mean absolute error (MAE) was found to be 0.2958. Again, according to the table of the degree of agreement, this falls within the medium classification. MAE measures the average absolute difference between the predicted values and the actual values. A lower MAE indicates better accuracy and closer alignment between the predicted and observed values. The root mean squared error (RMSE), which measures the average magnitude of the error, was found to be 0.4039. Table 5 provides a summary of the evaluation of the data mining results based on business and data mining objectives.

The evaluation of the data mining results according to the defined success criterion is summarized in Table 6.

Despite not meeting the specified accuracy margin, the objective of data mining is still considered fulfilled. The researcher has gained valuable insights and knowledge about data mining through the development of this model, which will contribute to the future development of experiments and help in achieving the business objective. Based on the analysis of the three algorithms, it is recommended to approve the model developed

Table 5. Evaluation of the Data Mining Results According to Business and Data Mining Objectives

Business Objective	Data Mining Objective
Develop a software tool that allows immediate categorization of environmental parameters collected in chicken houses and downloaded from the "Smart Poultry Farm" platform	Develop a software tool that allows the characterization of environmental parameters in open chicken houses

Table 6. Evaluation of the Data Mining Results According to the Defined Success Criterion

Success Criterion
The definition of a model that adequately characterises the environmental parameters in open-air poultry houses with a 75% accuracy margin

Evaluation
The model generated using the REPTree classification algorithm achieved a success rate of 63.8219% and a failure rate of 36.1781%, which represents the margin of error. Therefore, the model does not meet the success criterion set for the data mining objective

using the REPTree classification algorithm, as it provided the best results among those evaluated.

5   Conclusions

This research represents a significant contribution to the field of data mining in the context of the Smart Poultry Farm system in Panama. It serves as a basis for addressing future challenges in environmental decision-making and finding solutions to inherent problems.

Our research has provided valuable information and the opportunity to study the results of the environmental variables collected by the Smart Poultry Farm system. It has allowed us to perform an interesting analysis that contributes to the improvement of the time readings of the sensors distributed throughout the poultry houses.

The use of the CRISP-DM methodology has facilitated the development of the study, ensuring a systematic and intuitive approach focused on the exploration and analysis of the data. In addition, the use of the WEKA tool has allowed an efficient pre-processing of the data by filtering and classifying the environmental parameters, thus identifying behavioral patterns among them. This research has been a valuable learning experience for us in the field of data mining.

As future work we consider the use of other data mining development methodologies such as KDD (Knowledge Discovery in Databases) or Catalyst, as well as other tools more powerful than WEKA such as Orange or RapidMiner and will see if the advantages or disadvantages of using these new methodologies and tools.

Acknowledgments. To the "Smart Chicken Farm" project and its researchers, winner of the Public Call for New Ventures 2018 of the National Secretariat of Science, Technology and Innovation. We thank the to the national research system of Panama (SNI)-National Secretariat of Science, Technology, and Innovation (SENACYT) and CIDITIC-UTP.

Authors Contribution. Principal Author CLC,GMBM, Conceptualization CLC,GMBM, MVL; methodology GMBM, CLC; formal analysis GMBM, CLC, LMP, HCG, DCM, CMC, MVL; research GMBM, CLC, MVL, DCM.; original-writing GMBM, CLC; writing—review and edition DCM, MVL,HCG, LMP, CMC; Corresponding author DCM, MVL.

References

1. Porcelli, A.M.: Inteligencia Artificial y la Robótica: sus dilemas sociales, éticos y jurídicos. Derecho Global Estudios sobre Derecho y Justicia **6**(16), 49–105 (2020). https://doi.org/10.32870/dgedj.v6i16.286
2. Mills, H.D.: The management of software engineering, Part I: principles of software engineering. IBM Syst. J. **19**(4), 414–420 (1980). https://doi.org/10.1147/sj.194.0414
3. Wicaksono, D., Perdana, D., Mayasari, R.: Design and analysis automatic temperature control in the broiler poultry farm based on wireless sensor network. In: Proceedings - 2017 2nd International Conferences on Information Technology, Information Systems and Electrical Engineering, ICITISEE 2017, vol. 2018, pp. 450– 455, February 2018. https://doi.org/10.1109/ICITISEE.2017.8285549
4. Estrada, M.M.E., Márquez, S., Restrepo, L.: Efecto de la temperatura y la humedad relativa en los parámetros productivos y la transferencia de calor en pollos de engorde. Revista Colombiana de Ciencias Pecuarias **20**(3), 288–303 (2007). https://doi.org/10.17533/UDEA.RCCP
5. Yadav, S.A., Sahoo, B.M., Sharma, S., Das, L.: An analysis of data mining techniques to analyze the effect of weather on agriculture. In: 2020 International Conference on Intelligent Engineering and Management (ICIEM), pp. 29–32, June 2020. https://doi.org/10.1109/ICIEM48762.2020.9160110
6. Majumdar, J., Naraseeyappa, S., Ankalaki, S.: Analysis of agriculture data using data mining techniques: application of big data. J. Big Data **4**(1), 20 (2017). https://doi.org/10.1186/s40537-017-0077-4
7. Plotnikova, V., Dumas, M., Milani, F.: Adaptations of data mining methodologies: a systematic literature review. PeerJ Comput. Sci. **6**, 1–43 (2020). https://doi.org/10.7717/PEERJ-CS.267
8. Akanmode, E.R., Oye, N.D., Celestine, H.C.: Prediction of poultry yield using data mining techniques. Int. J. Innov. Eng. Sci. Res. **2**(4), 16–32 (2018). Accessed 04 Sept 2022. https://paper.researchbib.com/view/paper/186435
9. Larose, D.T., Larose, C.D.: Discovering Knowledge in Data: An Introduction to Data Mining, 2da Editio. Wiley (2014). Accessed 04 Sept 2022. https://www.wiley.com/en-us/Discovering+Knowledge+in+Data%3A+An+Introduction+to+Data+Mining%2C+2nd+Edition-p-9780470908747
10. Cobos, C., Zuñiga, J., Guarin, J., León, E., Mendoza, M.: CMIN-herramienta case basada en CRISP-DM para el soporte de proyectos de minería de datos. Ingenieria e investigación **30**(3), 45–56 (2010)
11. de Carvalho, L.V.: Machine learning in poultry companies' data. Applications and Methodologies. North Carolina State University (2021). Accessed 08 Aug 2023. https://www.lib.ncsu.edu/resolver/1840.20/39362

12. Garcia-Arismendiz, J., Huertas-Zúñiga, S., Lizárraga-Portugal, C.A., Quiroz-Flores, J.C., Garcia-Lopez, Y.J.: Improving demand forecasting by implementing machine learning in poultry production company. Learning **8**, 9 (2023)
13. Reboiro-Jato, M., et al.: Using inductive learning to assess compound feed production in cooperative poultry farms. Expert Syst. Appl. **38**(11), 14169–14177 (2011)
14. Feraldi, R., Enriko, I.K.: Machine learning model for temperature and humidity automatic control in smart poultry farm. In: 2022 International Conference on Advanced Creative Networks and Intelligent Systems (ICACNIS), 23 November 2022, pp. 1–5. IEEE (2022)
15. Chouragade, G.: Boosting poultry farm profits through blockchain technologies, AI, IoT, and machine learning. In: Handbook of Research on AI and Knowledge Engineering for Real-Time Business Intelligence 2023, pp. 143–155. IGI Global (2023)
16. Leishman, E.M., et al.: When worlds collide–poultry modelling in the 'Big Data' era. Animal **10**, 100874 (2023)
17. Abdella, G.M., Kucukvar, M., Onat, N.C., Al-Yafay, H.M., Bulak, M.E.: Sustainability assessment and modeling based on supervised machine learning techniques: the case for food consumption. J. Clean. Prod. **1**(251), 119661 (2020)
18. Aashvina, R.O., Monika, S., Priyanivethitha, S., Babu, P.S., Perumalraja, R., Kamalesh, S.: An IoT and ML-based poultry waste management system. In: 2022 International Conference on Data Science, Agents & Artificial Intelligence (ICDSAAI), 8 December 2022, vol. 1, pp. 1–7. IEEE (2022)
19. Usuga Cadavid, J.P., Lamouri, S., Grabot, B., Pellerin, R., Fortin, A.: Machine learning applied in production planning and control: a state-of-the-art in the era of industry 4.0. J. Intell. Manuf. **31**, 1531–58 (2020)
20. Tambake, N., Deshmukh, B., Patange, A.: Development of a low cost data acquisition system and training of J48 algorithm for classifying faults in cutting tool. Mater Today Proc. **1**(72), 1061–1067 (2023)
21. Firas, O.: A combination of SEMMA & CRISP-DM models for effectively handling big data using formal concept analysis based knowledge discovery: a data mining approach. World J. Adv. Eng. Technol. Sci. **8**(1), 009–014 (2023)
22. Kannengiesser, U., Gero, J.S.: Modelling the design of models: an example using CRISP-DM. Proc. Des. Soc. **3**, 2705–2714 (2023)
23. Holmes, G., Donkin, A., Witten, I.H.: WEKA: a machine learning workbench. In: Proceedings of ANZIIS 1994-Australian New Zealnd Intelligent Information Systems Conference, 29 November 1994, pp. 357–361. IEEE (1994)
24. Bakti, P.S., Eliyani, E.: Application of J48 and Naïve bayes algorithms to predict ream bookings at PT. Nippon Presisi Teknik. Eduvest-J. Universal Stud. **3**(6), 1047–1060 (2023)
25. Mylnikov, L.A., Trusov, A.V.: On an approach to the design of a logical model of innovation project data. Sci. Tech. Inf. Process. **38**(3), 201–206 (2011)
26. Elbeltagi, A., et al.: Forecasting vapor pressure deficit for agricultural water management using machine learning in semi-arid environments. Agric. Water Manag. **1**(283), 108302 (2023)
27. Sari, R., Fatoni, H., Ramdhania, K.F.: Decision support system design for informatics student final projects using C4. 5 algorithm. PIKSEL: Penelitian Ilmu Komputer Sistem Embedded and Logic **11**(1), 123–134 (2023)
28. Pitesky, M., Gendreau, J., Bond, T., Carrasco-Medanic, R.: Data challenges and practical aspects of machine learning-based statistical methods for the analyses of poultry data to improve food safety and production efficiency. CABI Rev. **23** (2020)
29. Dong, C., et al.: Forecasting poultry turnovers with machine learning and multiple factors. Data Anal. Knowl. Discov. **4**(7), 18–27 (2020)
30. Akanmode, E.R., Oye, N.D., Celestine, H.R.: Prediction of poultry yield using data mining techniques. Int. J. Innov. Eng. Sci. Res. **2**, 16–32 (2018)

31. Sati, N.M., et al.: Perceptions and practices of farmers of indigenous poultry towards Salmonella infections in North-Central Nigeria. Open Vet. J. **12**(4), 567–577 (2022)
32. First, V.D.: Catch Your Weka: A Story of New Zealand Cooking. Auckland University Press, 1 October 2013
33. Toksoz, C., Albayrak, M., Yasar, H.: Chicken egg sexing by using data mining process. Fresenius Environ. Bull. **30**(2), 1373–1381 (2021)

Natural Language Processing
and Semantic Web

A First Approach to the Classification of Adverse Drug Effects on Twitter Through Machine Learning

Mariano Gibran Montero-Colio[(⊠)] [iD], María del Pilar Salas-Zárate [iD], and Mario Andrés Paredes-Valverde [iD]

Tecnológico Nacional de México/I.T.S. Teziutlán, Teziutlán, México
{m21te0005,maria.sz,mario.pv}@teziutlan.tecnm.mx

Abstract. The WHO indicates that the adverse drug effects are of great relevance as each person has different reactions regardless of whether the dose or treatment is correct, affecting their health. Unfortunately, in the literature, there are very few methodologies for early detection of these ADRs, specifically in the Spanish language, and the existing methods deal with them from medical records, leaving aside a great source of information such as social networks. In this work, we present the creation of a corpus in Spanish with data from Twitter. The realization of experiments for evaluating the corpus with a machine learning algorithm SVM and two neural network models RAM and IAN. The best results were obtained with an accuracy of 0.86 with the RAM neural network.

Keywords: Adverse Drug Reaction – ADR · Natural Language Processing · Neuronal Networks · social media · Spanish corpus

1 Introduction

According to the World Health Organization (WHO) [1], 'health is defined as a state of complete physical, mental and social well-being and not merely the absence of disease or infirmity.' Multiple factors threaten people's health, one of which is adverse drug reactions (ADRs), which can be defined as a significantly harmful or unpleasant reaction resulting from an intervention related to drugs [2]. Around the world, countries such as the United States, Canada, and Japan spend approximately $500 billion, $65 billion, and $7 billion annually to cover the costs caused by ADRs.

There are multiple efforts to improve people's safety and mitigate the risks caused by ADRs, which pharmacovigilance does through numerous activities, using electronic patient health record systems based on clinical notes and electronic records, as well as more advanced systems using machine learning algorithms based on deep learning or convolutional neural networks (CNN's), which often require a sufficiently robust computational infrastructure to be trained [3]. Because of this, the use of Natural Language Processing (NLP) has been harnessed as a tool to develop fast, efficiently trainable systems that do not require specialized hardware [3]; these systems are currently trained

R. Valencia-García et al. (Eds.): CITI 2023, CCIS 1873, pp. 97–108, 2023.
https://doi.org/10.1007/978-3-031-45682-4_8

with RAM data obtained from social media texts such as Twitter, Reddit or Facebook, as well as health-related forums and electronic health records [4].

However, despite the efforts in ADR detection, there are still several gaps in the coverage of this challenging task. For example, it is well known that ADRs are often not reported by individuals to pharmacovigilance systems, resulting in little or no information on ADRs. In addition, clinical records or notes do not detail when an ADR is present, or most of the time, it is recorded as a symptom of the disease to be treated. Another critical point for this research is that the identification of ADRs using NLP techniques for the Spanish language is quite limited compared to the English language. To date, no study has been found in the state of the art that uses information obtained from social networks in Spanish to address this problem.

The aim of this work is to experiment with the existing models that have given the best results in identifying ADRs in other languages to train them with a corpus in the Spanish language obtained with data from Twitter and thus evaluate the accuracy of models. This is a challenging task because there is no corpus with the indicated characteristics, and the models require retraining to adapt to the features of the Spanish language. In this way, the aim is to contribute to the state of the art and support pharmacovigilance techniques for the Spanish language.

The remainder of the paper is structured as follows. Section 2 reviews the literature on different approaches for identifying adverse drug reactions. Section 3 describes the construction of the corpus used in the experiments. Section 4 presents the machine learning algorithms used in the experiments. Section 5 presents the results of evaluating the effectiveness of the selected algorithms with the created corpus. Finally, Sect. 6 presents the conclusions and future work.

2 Related Work

Identifying adverse drug reactions is challenging because a relationship between the drug and the negative effect must be established. Nevertheless, there are multiple previous works related to ADRs in which the computational approach is noteworthy. One of the works focused on the identification of ADRs is [5] which uses data mining techniques to collect patient comments on the heart disease forum MedHelp. They collected 120,000 forum entries and used the SIDER database to create a method called PI (Patient-centered and In-thread method) obtaining an F-value of 61.20% in identifying ADRs. In [6], a semi-supervised bidirectional recurrent neural network was used for ADR detection, as well as a corpus of tweets with 960 ADR mentions. The implemented neural network first identifies the name of the medicament in an unsupervised manner and then proceeds with ADR extraction using the annotated corpus, obtaining results with an F-value of 75.1%. Similarly, [3] used the Conditional Random Field (CRF) algorithm trained with 100,000 clinical notes to classify them into various clusters and applied a second Random Forest algorithm with 213 clinical notes to identify the relationships between drugs and adverse effects in the study and obtained results with an F-value of 88.1%. On the other hand, in [7], they used a linear and a Gaussian Naïve-Bayes classifier on a corpus obtained from SIDER to predict and identify ADRs, getting an accuracy of 52.3% in both tasks.

In [4], they conducted experiments on the efficiency of neural networks and the SVM algorithm, as a benchmark, for the identification of ADR with four corpora (CADEC,

Twitter, MADE, Twimed), obtaining that the best result was acquired by the RAM neural network for the corpus created by Tweets, while the IAN neural network was the best for the rest of the corpus. Another study of interest is [8], in which 214,600 reviews obtained from Drug.com were collected, and convolutional neural networks were used to create a model called 3W3DT, getting an F value of 87.35%.

Recently in [9], BERT-based models were used for the identification of ADRs using three corpora made up of 18,299 tweets in English, 3033 in French, and 20,707 in Russian as part of the SMMH4 competition and obtaining improvements from the state-of-the-art of 18% for the English corpus, 8.5% for the French corpus and 0.3% for the Russian corpus.

Likewise, recent studies [10–12] have addressed ADR identification in Spanish, obtaining good results in the identification of ADR using the AB-LSTM sub-class network of the LSTM neural network. However, only electronic health records have been used, leaving out information from social networks. Within these works, specifically in [10], the authors propose in future work to focus more effort on detecting the relationships between phrases, both explicit and implicit, given that in Spanish it is common to use these phrases together, which makes it more difficult to identify ADRs. One area of opportunity present in [11] is that the identification of ADRs, in addition to being done phrase by phrase, should be explored by drug-disease pairs, to obtain a more accurate identification, and this has not been thoroughly addressed in Spanish. Another area of opportunity focused on obtaining data in Spanish given the lack of such data and mentioned in [12] is the possibility of taking corpora written in other languages and translating them into Spanish.

According to the reviewed works, some challenges and areas of opportunity have been identified for identifying ADR in the Spanish language. Most of these studies use a large amount of data that it takes to train the models to obtain results with a high degree of accuracy; another point to improve is the data input. As mentioned in [12], the semantics of the comments and medical records are vital since a model can be adjusted to identify a specific meaning depending on the type of text, which can modify the accuracy in identifying ADR. Likewise, these models are often tuned to a particular language. Although, as mentioned in [8], models can be retrained to perform ADR identification, this has not been done in practice, as evidenced in [9], where they used French and Russian tweets first presented in SMM4H in 2021.

According to the above, it is evident the importance of having the data for identifying ADR in Spanish, taking advantage of the data in tweets. In addition, using neural network models can significantly help this purpose since, according to the works reviewed, these models have been successfully used to identify ADR in other languages.

3 Corpus

For the development of this work, a corpus was created with data obtained from the social network Twitter. To search for tweets about adverse effects, we consulted a doctor who provided the names of the most commonly used drugs for hypertension and diabetes, as shown in Table 1. Subsequently, using the Twitter API, the tweets were obtained in JSON format, as shown in Image 1. The tweets were searched by mentioning the drugs and keywords, as shown in Table 2 (Fig. 1).

Table 1. List of medicines commonly prescribed as a treatment for diabetes and hypertension.

Drugs Diabetes			Drugs Hypertension		
Metformina	Semaglutida	Liraglutida	Losartan	Quinapril	Valsartan
Sitagliptina	Linagliptina	Saxagliptina	Labetalol	Enalapril	Fosinopril
Saxagliptina	Alogliptina	Gliburida	Perondopril	Ramipril	Aliskiren
Glimepirida	Glipizida	Dapagliflozina	Trandolapril	Candesartan	Eprosartán
Canagliflozina	Empaglifozina	Exenatida	Irbesartan	Telmisartán	Diltiazem
Dulaglutida	Acarbosa	Miglitol	Felodipino	Metildopa	Espirinolactona
Pioglitoza	Aspart	Lispro	Isradipina	Prazosin	Terazosina
Glulisina	R-cristalina	Glargina	Carvedilol	Clonidina	Hidralazina

Table 2. Set of words for Twitter API query.

Search words
Diabetes, hipertensión, diabetes tipo 2, diabetes tipo 1, diabetes mellitus, efectos adversos por medicamentos, reacciones adversas por medicamentos, efectos secundarios, efectos no deseados, reacciones no deseadas, medicamentos diabetes, metformina, semaglutida, liraglutida, losartan, quinapril, valsartan, sitagliptina, linagliptina, saxagliptina, labetalol, enalapril, fosinopril, saxagliptina, alogliptina, gliburida, perondopril, ramipril, aliskiren, glimepirida, glipizida, dapagliflozina, trandolapril, candesartan, eprosartán, canagliflozina, empaglifozina, exenatida, irbesartan, telmisartán, diltiazem, dulaglutida, acarbosa, miglitol, felodipino, metildopa, espirinolactona, pioglitoza, aspart, lispro, isradipina, prazosin, terazosina, glulisina, r-cristalina, glargina, carvedilol, clonidina, hidralazina

Given the remarkable similarity of medicines and diseases in various languages, the Twitter API query yielded results in Spanish, English, Portuguese, and French, which required the use of the 'langdetect' Python library, which has more than 99% accuracy in correctly detecting the language of a text, to determine the language of the tweets and add them as an additional property to the JSON of tweets, as shown in Fig. 2. Likewise, only tweets in the Spanish language were taken into account, given the objective of this study, obtaining a total of 17,035 tweets. Then, according to the diagram in Fig. 3, these tweets were preprocessed following the recommendations made in [9], in which it is mentioned that emoticons or emojis should be replaced by their representation in words, mentions of users should be replaced by a generic statement such as @USER and finally links or hyperlinks should be replaced by <LINK> to clean the tweets of irrelevant data. In addition, repeated tweets were eliminated by comparing the content, leaving a total of 13,961 tweets.

In the next stage of corpus construction, tweets were manually tagged. Those tweets that did not mention the searched words were discriminated against, as well as tweets with offensive content or that dealt with topics unrelated to the research. Once this was done, the labeling was carried out by two experts in the health field in charge of placing

{
  "ID": "1626820349017858048",
  "text": "RT @NigeriaStories: Today we remember Dora Akunyili, who died in 2014, she lost her sister, who was given fake insulin for diabetes. This w.."
},
{
  "ID": "1626820339073183745",
  "text": "RT @amerix: This is what healing from Diabetes looks like. from a previous daily reading of 10 -15 despite being on expensive drugs to no.."
},
{
  "ID": "1626820192608083968",
  "text": "Programa Pauta Nossa Temas Situaçao dos Yanomamis com o lider Junior YanomamiDesarmamento com Marcos Manteiga Alzeimer, diabetes .. com Rita Novais https://t.co/gaHbynJbym https://t.co/ZPhJct58QN"
},
{
  "ID": "1626819757386211328",
  "text": "RT @her sickness: Jemand hat Diabetes, die Diagnose ist neu, Leben lang Insulin. Verlacht Ihr den? sagt Ihr ihm, er soll einfach mehr fress.."
},
{
  "ID": "1626819745423958016",
  "text": "RT @karimanesr: No se puede negar el vínculo entre nuestro sistema alimentario y las tasas disparadas de diabetes tipo 2, enfermedades card.."
},
{
  "ID": "1626819734909116417",
  "text": "@JerryG M # bueno yo quiero probarla, abr si no me da diabetes"
},
{
  "ID": "1626819184179945473",
  "text": "RT @LuisM_1924: Busca ayuda profesional cuando te enteres de que tendrás diabetes y te guíen a como asimilar la noticia. No pongas tus sent.."
}

Fig. 1. Tweets in different languages obtained via the Twitter API.

{
  "ID": "1625888453849145345",
  "text": "RT @Kiwilimon_LAT: Si padeces diabetes, ¡estos jugos fáciles te ayudarán a cuidar tu salud! Recetas 👉 https://t.co/ztFMQQOr5p https://t.co..",
  "language": "es"
},
{
  "ID": "1625888432844046337",
  "text": "Toma medicación psiquiátrica (Depresión mayor) Sertralina, Clonazepam, Quetiapina, Levopromazina. Además de las medicaciones psiquiatricas toma Pregabalina y Corticoide para el cancer y Xelevia y Canagliflozina para la diabetes.",
  "language": "es"
},
{
  "ID": "1625888345447362560",
  "text": "¡cuida tu #diabetes en invierno! El frio puede causar cambios en los hábitos alimentarios, aumentar la probabilidad de infecciones respiratorias y reducir la sensibilidad en las extremidades. Mantén un control estricto y toma medidas preventivas. #NoDestafspaldaALaDiabetes https://t.co/1dXMBFsxuG",
  "language": "es"
},
{
  "ID": "1625888313520390145",
  "text": "@gabyarocha 'HMM, me va a dar diabetes otra vez' 😁😁😁😁😁😁😁😁😁😁😁😁😁😁😁😁😁😁😁😁 esa fr guinda en el pastel... Hola Gaby",
  "language": "es"
},
{
  "ID": "1625888161598517251",
  "text": "@Tu_IMSS @IMSS_YUCATAN @zoerobledo Vanesa Silva amable recordatorio ya envie toda la información solicitada, son 2 faltantes: Dapagliflozina 10mg x diabetes PET-41798292-C2R5WO. Favor de responder urge el medicamento de la diabetes!! UMF 20 Merida Yucatan",
  "language": "es"
}

Fig. 2. JSON representation with tweets sorted by language.

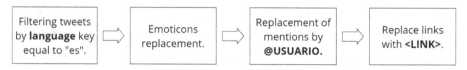

Fig. 3. Process diagram for pre-processing of data.

the tweets in the corresponding class either with the presence of ADR or absence of ADR. In the case of a tie, the decision was made according to the Inter-Annotator Agreement criterion using Cohen's Kappa statistic [13]. This left a corpus with a total of 309 tweets, of which 261 had no mention of an adverse effect (non-ADR) and 48 had mention of an adverse effect (yes-ADR). The process of creating the corpus can be seen in Fig. 4.

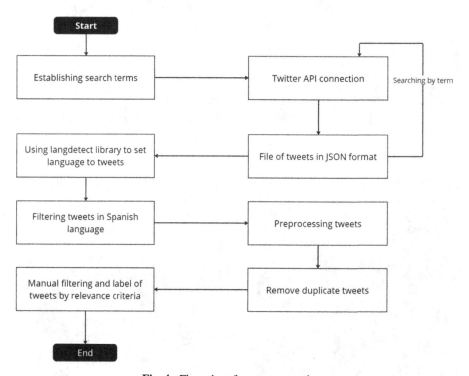

Fig. 4. Flow chart for corpus creation.

4   Machine Learning Algorithms

Machine learning is a branch of artificial intelligence that allows machines to perform jobs through the use of software. According to [14] machine learning can be defined as the science that studies statistical models in conjunction with computational algorithms to perform a specific task. In the following, the algorithms and modes used in the experiments of the present work are described.

4.1 SVM

The Support Vector Machine algorithm [14] is a machine learning type method that performs supervised learning. This method is mainly used for the classification or regression of data groups. First, SVM creates a hyperplane in a multi-dimensional space to divide the different classes. Then, to perform the binary classification, SVM operates iteratively by repeating the process of creating the hyperplane trying to find the maximum margin between both classes to obtain the best classification of the dataset by maximizing the distance between the data points of both classes. In contrast, to re-perform the regression, SVM searches for the function that best approximates the data points, minimizing the sum of the distances between the points and the function. Also, SVM can handle both multiple continuous and categorical variables.

4.2 RAM

This is a recurrent attention neural network proposed in [15] for sentiment analysis which consists of five modules: data input, memory module, position-weighted memory, recurrent attention module, and output. The input module retrieves the word vectors from an embedded table generated by an unsupervised method such as GloVe or CBOW. The memory module uses the Deep Bidirectional LSTM neural network to build the memory that records all the information to be read in subsequent modules. The position-weighted memory module produces an input memory for each target by assigning a higher weight to words closer to the target. The recurrent attention module is used to update the memory with a weighted sum of the memory and a query vector generated from the previous output in order to construct the sentiment classification properly. Finally, the output module uses a SoftMax function to predict the sentiment polarity of the target word.

4.3 IAN

This model was proposed in [16] as an interactive attention neural network for sentiment classification focusing on aspects. This model comprises two parts; it uses LTSM networks to model the target and the context in an interactive way by obtaining hidden states of words. The attention mechanism is used to get important information about the context and the target. Also, after calculating the context and target weights, these vectors are concatenated and fed to a SoftMax function for aspect-level sentiment classification.

5 Experiments and Results

As part of this work, experiments were conducted on the generated corpus, dividing the corpus into test and evaluation data, as shown in Table 3. The tweets in the corpus were randomly separated by keeping the proportion of approximately 15% of tweets with the presence of ADR and absence of ADR to obtain better results based on [9], as is shown in Fig. 5.

To carry out the experiments, the RAM and IAN neural networks were compared, which according to [4], are the models with the best results in the classification of ADRs for tweets in English, and the SVM machine learning algorithm was also used due to its ability to classify complex data.

Table 3. Details of the corpus for conducting experiments.

	Train	Test	All
#tweets	864	372	1236
#tweets with ADR	136	56	192
#tweets without ADR	728	316	1044
Ratio	15.74%	15.05%	15.53%

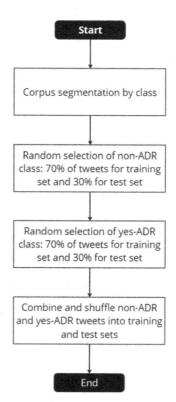

Fig. 5. Flowchart for creation of training and test sets.

For SVM, the algorithm in [17] focused on classifying adverse effects and was used as a test. As parameters, we first entered a vector of medicines in Spanish, presented in Table 1. For the vector of embedded words, the Spanish Billion Word Corpus created in [18] and edited with Word2Vec was used, which has 1.4 billion words with tags in Spanish and a vector dimension of 300. In addition, a dictionary of adverse effects obtained from SIDER was entered, with a register of more than 13,000 ADRs, and it was translated into Spanish. Finally, the corpus created was given the format required by the SVM algorithm, which requires JSON objects with the keys text, label, entity, and id, this format can be seen in Fig. 6.

```
{"text":""Metformina": medicamento para la diabetes que aseguran que retrasa el envejecimiento <LINK> via @USUARIO", "label":"Unknown",
"entity":"Metformina", "id":19777804}
{"text":"Me a tomar una metformina porque todo esto me hace subir el azúcar", "label":"Unknown", "entity":"metformina", "id":15217097}
{"text":" Uso de benzodiazepinas pastilla  e hipertensión en urgencias  alarma .    Revisión publicada en @USUARIO @USUARIO resumido en
@USUARIO.   ¿Hay beneficio clínico estetoscopio ? Pueden utilizarse como un antihipertensivo en algún caso? #CardioTwitter #MedTwitter
<LINK>", "label":"Unknown", "entity":"benzodiazepinas", "id":18893818}
{"text":"@USUARIO Un familiar muy cercano..tuvo q cambiar el losartan de laboratorio reconocido x ese medicamento hindú.xq no tenía
dinero ..le causo un infarto y falleció...Asi q Ud tiene razón y conozco a otras personas con igual resultado   ..esos medicamentos indu
estan matando", "label":"Adverse", "entity":"losartan", "id":15921607}
```

Fig. 6. Corpus fragment which has been adapted to the input format of the SVM algorithm.

On the other hand, for both RAM and IAN neural networks, we used the same parameter settings present in [4] because they are the parameters that have given the best results; 15 epochs are considered so that the models can perform learning, the number of hidden states is recommended to be 300, the learning ratio was set to 0.01, and the regularization parameter l2 was set to 0.001. These models require embedded word vectors to obtain word values and more accurate classification, so it was decided to use the Spanish Unannotated Corpora corpus trained with the FastText algorithm created in [17], which has more than 2.6 billion Spanish words classified and labeled, and the dimension of its vectors is 300. The corpus also had to be formatted to comply with the input format for these neural networks. Figure 7 shows the required format, the first row is the tweet with a token T which is the representation of the drug, the second row is the name of the drug, and the third row is the class to which the tweet belongs.

```
Primer día de tratamiento: el malestar fue por la gastritis, por suerte, las ronchas dejaron de estar y encontré otra $T$ (más barata)
que no me hace sentir mal todo el día. Un win. Sólo me falta regresar a entrenar
metformina
1
Yo tenía una "amiga" que la tomaba porque quería bajar de peso y nunca me decía para no hacerme sentir mal porque yo si tengo diabetes
tipo 2, no saben la chicha que estas cosas dan, dejen $T$ a quienes necesitamos. <LINK>
los medicamentos
0
@USUARIO Cheqeos médicos de rutina? Si nunca hay citas ni medicamentos, $T$ me dijeron que nunca tienen... Bueno, ni pruebas covid
tienen, y ahora solo 5 días de reposo y váyase a trabajar... Ni al caso sus recomendaciones.
losartan
0
```

Fig. 7. Corpus fragment which has been adapted to the input format of the RAM and IAN neural networks.

Accuracy (Acc) was used to evaluate the experiments. Accuracy is the fraction of predictions that the model made correctly. For binary classification, accuracy is calculated using Formula 1, where true positives (TP) and negatives (TN) are summed and divided by the sum of true positives, true negatives, false positives (FP), and false negatives (FN). Table 4 shows the results of the experiments. The first column corresponds to the models used (SVM, RAM, IAN) to classify the corpus, second one corresponds to Precision (P), the third column represent the Recall (R), the fourth one corresponds the F-Score (F1) and the last column to the accuracy (Acc) of each model applied.

$$Accuracy = \frac{TP + TN}{TP + TN + FP + FN} \tag{1}$$

Table 4. Results of applied experiments.

	P	R	F1	Acc
SVM	0.76	0.79	0.77	0.85
RAM	0.77	0.82	**0.79**	**0.86**
IAN	0.74	0.79	0.76	0.84

According to the results obtained, it can be noted that the RAM neural network is the one that gives the best results corresponding with state of the art in [4] by obtaining an Accuracy of 86% and a F-Score of 79% in the classification of the corpus, which may be due to the architecture of the neural network itself, which allows it to have different layers of attention and to remember words that have a certain distance from the adverse effect It can be noted that SVM obtained the second-best result according to an Accuracy value of 85% and algo it got the second best value of F-Score of 77%. This may be because the SVM algorithm contained more information to achieve higher Accuracy and F-Score. Finally, the IAN neural network got the lowest Accuracy and F-Score with a value of 84% and 76%, respectively.

An example of a poorly classified tweet can be seen in Fig. 8. The content of the tweet can be interpreted as saying that taking metformin caused an adverse effect, however, it is only implicitly mentioned as 'decontrol'. As the sentence is unclear, lacks context, and does not explicitly mention an adverse effect, classifiers tend to classify it as non-ADR.

```
@USUARIO Mi mamá tiene su tratamiento con metformina,en una ocasión le di esas pastillas de las hechas
en la India y tuvo un descontrol...o sea, esas tampoco son recomendables
```

Fig. 8. Tweet with mention of adverse effect.

In general, it is difficult to make a comparison with the state of the art because there are few works in the Spanish language and the size of the corpora, which are different domains and affect the comparison of results. However, the results obtained are given for the following reasons: (1) the size of the corpus used in the experiments concerning those existing in the English language is smaller because there is no existing corpus of adverse effects in the Spanish language formed by information from social networks; (2) the Spanish language represents a higher complexity given its more flexible grammar compared to the English language; (3) the dictionaries of adverse effects, drugs, and embedded word vectors are not yet mature enough as they are in English.

6   Conclusions and Future Work

Two main contributions have been made to the development of this work. The first is the development of a corpus in Spanish composed of tweets containing mentions of adverse effects and even adverse effects that have not been officially reported on drugs to treat diabetes and hypertension. The second contribution is the performance of experiments to test how the SVM algorithm and the neural networks RAM and IAN behave with a corpus of social network data, with RAM being the best model with an Accuracy of 86% and a F-Score of 79%.

As future work, the following steps are envisaged: (1) significantly expand the corpus with more data from social networks taking into account comments from Facebook or Reddit, as well as from blogs focused on the health field, in order to obtain better results in the classification of presence or absence of adverse effects; (2) enrich the corpus by giving more information about the drug establishing chemical properties, international identifier (ID) of the drug, the international identifier of the adverse effect, among other characteristics; (3) perform experiments with other neural networks present in state of the art and specialized in the field of health, such as MemNet; (4) incorporate the use of Transformers for the classification of mentions of adverse effects and even the identification of these present in comments on social networks.

Acknowledgements. Al Consejo Nacional de Ciencia y Tecnología (CONACYT) por la beca otorgada para realizar estudios de posgrado a nivel maestría a través de la convocatoria "BECAS NACIONALES PARA ESTUDIOS DE POSGRADO 2022".

References

1. Organización Mundial de la Salud: OMS INDICADORES DE FARMACOVIGILANCIA: UN MANUAL PRÁCTICO PARA LA EVALUACIÓN DE LOS SISTEMAS DE FARMA-COVIGILANCIA. Ginebra (2019). Accessed 02 Dec 2022. https://apps.who.int/iris/bitstream/handle/10665/325851/9789243508252-spa.pdf?ua=1
2. Lavertu, A., Hamamsy, T., Altman, R.B.: Quantifying the severity of adverse drug reactions using social media: network analysis. J. Med. Internet Res. **23**(10), e27714 (2021). https://www.jmir.org/2021/10/e27714. https://doi.org/10.2196/27714
3. Chapman, A.B., Peterson, K.S., Alba, P.R., DuVall, S.L., Patterson, O.V.: Detecting adverse drug events with rapidly trained classification models. Drug Saf. **42**(1), 147–156 (2019). https://doi.org/10.1007/S40264-018-0763-Y/TABLES/12
4. Alimova, I.S., Tutubalina, E.V.: Entity-level classification of adverse drug reaction: a comparative analysis of neural network models. Programm. Comput. Softw. **45**(8), 439–447 (2020). https://doi.org/10.1134/S0361768819080024
5. Liu, Y., Shi, J., Chen, Y.: Patient-centered and experience-aware mining for effective adverse drug reaction discovery in online health forums. J. Assoc. Inf. Sci. Technol. **69**(2), 215–228 (2018). https://doi.org/10.1002/ASI.23929
6. Gupta, S., Pawar, S., Ramrakhiyani, N., Palshikar, G.K., Varma, V.: Semi-supervised recurrent neural network for adverse drug reaction mention extraction. BMC Bioinf. **19**(8), 1–7 (2018). https://doi.org/10.1186/S12859-018-2192-4/TABLES/2

7. Wang, C.S., Lin, P.J., Cheng, C.L., Tai, S.H., Yang, Y.H.K., Chiang, J.H.: Detecting potential adverse drug reactions using a deep neural network model. J. Med. Internet Res. **21**(2), e11016 (2019). https://www.jmir.org/2019/2/e11016. https://doi.org/10.2196/11016

8. Basiri, M.E., Abdar, M., Cifci, M.A., Nemati, S., Acharya, U.R.: A novel method for sentiment classification of drug reviews using fusion of deep and machine learning techniques. Knowl. Based Syst. **198**, 105949 (2020). https://doi.org/10.1016/J.KNOSYS.2020.105949

9. Sakhovskiy, A., Tutubalina, E.: Multimodal model with text and drug embeddings for adverse drug reaction classification. J. Biomed. Inform. **135**, 104182 (2022). https://doi.org/10.1016/J.JBI.2022.104182

10. Santiso González, S.: Adverse drug reaction extraction on electronic health records written in Spanish: a PhD thesis overview. https://doi.org/10.21437/IberSPEECH.2021-34

11. Santiso, S., Pérez, A., Casillas, A.: Exploring joint AB-LSTM with embedded lemmas for adverse drug reaction discovery. IEEE J. Biomed. Health Inform. **23**(5), 2148–2155 (2019). https://doi.org/10.1109/JBHI.2018.2879744

12. Santiso, S., Pérez, A., Casillas, A.: Adverse drug reaction extraction: tolerance to entity recognition errors and sub-domain variants. Comput. Methods Programs Biomed. **199**, 105891 (2021). https://doi.org/10.1016/J.CMPB.2020.105891

13. Surge, A.: Inter-Annotator Agreement: An Introduction to Cohen's Kappa Statistic, 15 December 2021. https://surge-ai.medium.com/inter-annotator-agreement-an-introduction-to-cohens-kappa-statistic-dcc15ffa5ac4. Accessed 15 Aug 2023

14. Mahesh, B.: Machine learning algorithms-a review. Int. J. Sci. Res. (2018). https://doi.org/10.21275/ART20203995

15. Peng, C., Zhongqian, S., Lidong, B., Yang, W.: Recurrent attention network on memory for aspect sentiment analysis, pp. 452–461 (2017)

16. Ma, D., Li, S., Zhang, X., Wang, H.: Interactive attention networks for aspect-level sentiment classification. Accessed 9 May 2023. http://alt.qcri.org/semeval2014/task4/

17. Alimova, I., Tutubalina, E.: Automated detection of adverse drug reactions from social media posts with machine learning. In: van der Aalst, Wil M P., et al. (eds.) AIST 2017. LNCS, vol. 10716, pp. 3–15. Springer, Cham (2018). https://doi.org/10.1007/978-3-319-73013-4_1

18. Cañete, J., Chaperon, G., Fuentes, R., Ho, J.-H., Kang, H., Pérez, J.: Spanish pre-trained BERT model and evaluation data. In: PML4DC at ICLR 2020 (2020). Accessed 09 May 2023. https://doi.org/10.5281/zenodo.3247731

SafercITies. Intelligent System for the Analysis and Monitoring of Citizen Security

José Antonio García-Díaz[1]([✉]) [iD], Camilo Caparrós-Laiz[1] [iD],
David Santiago García-Chicangana[2] [iD], Carlos Díaz-Morales[3],
David Barbáchano[3], Mario Andrés Paredes-Valverde[4] [iD],
Juan Miguel Gómez-Berbis[2] [iD], and Rafael Valencia-García[1] [iD]

[1] Facultad de Informática, Universidad de Murcia, Campus de Espinardo,
30100 Murcia, Spain
{joseantonio.garcia8,camilo.caparros1,valencia}@um.es
[2] Dpto. de Ciencias de la computación, Universidad Carlos III de Madrid, Madrid,
Spain
juanmiguel.gomez@uc3m.es
[3] PANEL Sistemas Informáticos S.L., C. de Josefa Valcárcel, 9, 28027 Madrid, Spain
{carlos.diaz,david.barbachano}@panel.es
[4] Tecnológico Nacional de México/I. T. S., 73960 Teziutlán, Mexico
mario.pv@teziutlan.tecnm.mx

Abstract. The rapid growth of the Internet and its widespread use have created new challenges in ensuring the safety of citizens in online spaces. This paper presents a project that aims to develop a comprehensive platform that addresses different dimensions of citizen security, covering both physical and psychological well-being. The platform serves as a bridge between public authorities and citizens, enabling individuals to report incidents, events or threats they encounter online, while providing preventive and protective measures. This paper outlines the motivation, objectives and key features of the platform, highlighting its potential to create a safer social environment.

Keywords: Natural Language Processing · Semantic Annotation · Emotion Analysis · Semantic Web · Blockchain

1 Introduction

In today's connected world, citizen security encompasses not only the digital realm, but also the physical environments in which people live and work. The increase in security risks and threats requires a comprehensive solution that addresses the safety and well-being of citizens in both domains. This paper presents a transversal and extensible platform designed to enhance citizen security and promote safer social environments. By bridging the gap between public authorities and citizens, the platform enables proactive reporting of incidents, threats and hazards, while offering preventive and protective measures to mitigate risks.

The motivation behind SaferclTies lies in the need to secure both the physical and digital well-being of citizens, as well as tourists and visitors. In this sense, this platform plays an important role in protecting and promoting tourism by addressing security concerns that may affect the travel experience. The platform can also provide real-time updates and recommendations on safe areas, attractions and routes, giving tourists peace of mind and facilitating a positive experience. By enhancing safety and promoting a positive image of the destination, the platform helps to sustain and grow tourism, ultimately benefiting local economies and promoting sustainable development.

Spain and Mexico are renowned tourist destinations, attracting millions of visitors each year. However, ensuring the safety of tourists remains a critical concern for both countries. The proposed platform represents a valuable opportunity to promote tourist safety in Spain and Mexico through the use of Natural Language Processing (NLP) technologies. By using the SaferclTies' features, such as incident reporting and real-time updates, tourists can feel more secure when travelling, knowing that their safety concerns will be promptly addressed by local authorities. This enhanced sense of security can help sustain and grow the tourism industry in both countries, as tourists are more likely to choose destinations that prioritise their well-being.

The platform enables citizens and tourists to report physical hazards, such as dangerous areas in cities or infrastructure problems, helping to improve public safety and prevent accidents. At the same time, it addresses digital safety concerns such as cyberbullying, online aggression and other threats that can have a significant impact on individuals' psychological well-being. One of the key motivations behind the platform is to empower citizens as active participants in improving their own safety and that of their communities. By providing a user-friendly interface, the platform enables individuals to report incidents and threats they encounter in their environment, providing valuable information to public authorities and decision-makers. This collaborative approach fosters a sense of ownership and responsibility among citizens, while facilitating effective response mechanisms from relevant authorities. The platform not only addresses day-to-day security concerns, but also emphasises preparedness for critical events such as terrorist attacks or natural disasters. By enabling users to report suspicious activities or potential threats, the platform increases the collective vigilance of the community and enables early detection and response. In addition, the platform provides preventive and protective measures, such as providing information on safe routes during emergencies or disseminating timely alerts and notifications to mitigate risks and ensure the safety of citizens.

SaferclTies uses cutting-edge technologies, specifically in the areas of Emotion Analysis, User Profiling and Natural Language Processing (NLP) technologies in general. These techniques make it possible to analyse and interpret the emotions and attitudes expressed in user-generated content, providing valuable insights into the overall sentiment of online discussions. This can be used to identify potential instances of cyberbullying, aggression or hate speech, enabling timely intervention. In addition, the integration of NLP technologies and the Semantic Web will enable incidents to be accurately categorised.

Next, we list the research objectives of SafercITies:

- OB1. Develop a system for extracting information from social networks and news sites.
- OB2. Develop a multi-label, multi-modal and aspect-based emotion extraction system.
- OB3. Develop a user profile identification system using user profile data from social networks and text.
- OB4. Develop a topic modelling and classification and threat detection system.
- OB5. Develop an information security and trust management system.
- OB6. Develop of a software platform for monitoring, follow-up and control of citizen security alerts.

The rest of the manuscript is structured as follows. Section 2 describes the latest advances in the technologies involved in this project. Next, Sect. 3 describes the architecture and its modules in detail. Finally, Sect. 4 summarises the latest progress of the project, as well as further work on the high-level modules and the graphical interfaces.

2   State of the Art

The technologies involved in this project are: (1) Natural Language Processing and Emotion Detection (NLP), which is a branch of Artificial Intelligence (AI) responsible for the development of software applications oriented towards the understanding of human language; (2) Sentiment and Emotion Analysis, which extracts the subjective polarity of a text, including a fine-grained variety of emotions; (3) Multimodal automatic classification, which includes prosodic features to extract the tone of voice and the underlying emotion, or image and video features; (4) Hate speech detection, to identify evidence on the Internet that contains hatred or prejudice against certain people or groups, focusing on detecting misogyny, xenophobia or transphobia, among others; (5) User profiling, based on identifying demographic and psychographic characteristics of users from their personal data or from their contributions on the Internet; and (6) Blockchain, based on Distributed Ledger Technology (DLT) for signing smart contracts.

In recent years, the emergence of Transformers, such as BERT [23], RoBERTa [25], or ChatGPT, and the Attention mechanism [35] has revolutionised the field of NLP. Transformers are a class of deep learning models that have demonstrated remarkable ability to capture long-range dependencies in textual data. The attention mechanism is a fundamental component of Transformers that allowing to the model to focus on relevant parts of the input sequence. This breakthrough has led to significant improvements in semantic understanding, enabling NLP models to understand the fine-grained nuances of language, including Sentiment and Emotion Analysis.

2.1   Sentiment and Emotion Analysis

Sentiment and Emotion Analysis are both Automatic Document Classification (ADC) tasks that focus on extracting subjective polarity and opinion from natural language. The main difference between sentiment analysis and emotion analysis lies in the scope and granularity of the analysis. Sentiment analysis focuses on determining the overall sentiment polarity (positive, negative, or neutral) expressed in a text, while emotion analysis delves into identifying specific emotional states or categories. Sentiment analysis aims to capture the overall attitude or opinion, whereas emotion analysis focuses on identifying and categorising the emotions or emotional states expressed in text. It goes beyond the broader sentiment analysis by capturing the specific emotions conveyed in the text, such as joy, anger, sadness, fear, or surprise [9].

Sentiment Analysis in relation to safety has been explored in the public health domain. For example, in the work described in [33], the authors analyse around 1.2 million English-language tweets collected in April and May 2021 related to vaccination prospects and safety measures during the COVID-19 pandemic. Their findings suggest that citizens have positive feelings about taking COVID-19 vaccines, rather than some adverse effects of some vaccines. To the best of our knowledge, there are not so many works that focus on the safety of Spanish citizens using sentiment analysis. However, there are some few works that have focused on applying sentiment analysis to other domains such as financial [14, 26, 27] or specific linguistic features such as negation [22].

With regard to Emotion Analysis in Spanish, the EmoEvalES task was presented in 2021 as a part of IberLEF (37th International Conference of the Spanish Society for Natural Language Processing). The aim of EmoEvalES is to promote the recognition and evaluation of emotions in the Spanish language. This shared-task consisted of a fine-grained emotion classification of tweets labelled as anger, disgust, fear, joy, sadness, surprise, or others. In the overview of the tasks [1], it is noted that many of the participants experimented with Transformers. Some members of this project took part in this shared-task [12], with a system that combined linguistic features [17] and Transformers based on BETO [6], reaching the 6th place in the ranking (accuracy of 68.5990%).

2.2   Hate-Speech

Online hate speech is any form of abusive, derogatory or discriminatory language or behaviour expressed or disseminated through digital platforms. It involves the use of online communication channels to disseminate harmful content targeting individuals or groups on the basis of their race, ethnicity, religion, gender, sexual orientation, disability or other characteristics. The anonymity and ease of dissemination of information on the Internet increases the impact of hate speech and allows it to spread rapidly to a wide audience.

There are several works in Spanish that focus on the detection of hate speech. For example, the work described in [11] focuses on the detection of misogyny. To this end, the authors apply social computing technologies to detect misogynistic messages in Twitter and have compiled the Spanish MisoCorpus-2020, which includes tweets expressing violence against relevant women, messages harassing women in Spanish from Spain and Spanish from Latin America, and other features related to misogyny. This work has recently been extended in [16], in which the authors investigate the features which are most effective in identifying hate speech (not just misogyny) in Spanish, and how these features can be combined to develop more accurate systems.

Hope speech, on the other hand, refers to discourse that aims to inspire positivity and a sense of hope. It involves the expression of encouraging messages with the intention of motivating, comforting or reassuring others, particularly during challenging or difficult times. In this sense, some work has explored the identification of hope speech, such as the collaborative task described in [8], which focused on identifying positive texts in several languages, including English and Spanish. This task was part of Language Technology for Equality, Diversity and Inclusion (LT-EDI-2022). The aim of the task was to determine whether certain sentences were positive language or not.

2.3 Author Profiling

Author profiling is the process of analysing and extracting demographic and psychographic traits about an author based on their written texts [13]. It involves using NLP methods to infer these traits from the authors, such as age, gender, language skills, personality traits, or even psychological states. Specifically, author profiling involves extracting linguistic patterns from the texts, which may include vocabulary, writing style, syntax or sentiment, and then correlating them with known characteristics or attributes. Deep learning algorithms are then used to train models that can predict or classify authors based on these features. Author profiling can provide valuable information for understanding individuals and their written expression. They can also be used to identify spreaders of hate speech [4] or fake news [30]. In Spanish, the PoliticEs 2022 shared task [15] was organised at IberLEF 2022, with the challenge of extracting the political ideology (in two axis) from given users' as a psychographic trait, and two demographic traits: gender and the profession. This shared task attracted several participants.

3   System Architecture

Figure 1 depicts the overall architecture of SafercITies. This structure is divided into high-level layers. The first layer is responsible for input processing. The system collects evidence from various sources, including social networks, web news, voice notes and reports sent by neighbours through a multi-device application. The second layer contains the low-level information extraction modules. Information related to named entities, locations and timestamps is extracted.

A domain ontology is used to provide a common framework and to be able to map the evidence to the concepts of the ontology. Subjective information is also extracted by a multimodal system capable of extracting different emotions from the texts and the voice notes reported by the neighbours. Different services extract demographic and psychographic characteristics of the users, which will make it possible to identify whether the users are bots or humans, their age range, etc. The third layer contains the mid-level modules. It includes the extraction and modelling of topics and their relationship with the security concepts linked to the ontology, as well as the processing of hate speech and danger situations linked to the concepts of the ontology. The fourth layer contains the high-level modules for generating alerts and notifications based on the intelligent analysis of previous reports. There are also modules for evaluating each report based on different heuristics as well as a blockchain-based certification system for reports. Finally, the interfaces are different modules and individual components for monitoring safety in cities, including safety maps, route planners or aspect-oriented emotion statistics graphs.

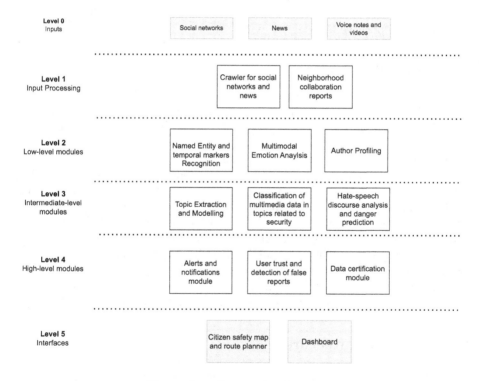

Fig. 1. Overall system architecture.

3.1 Level 1. Data Acquisition Modules

The first data acquisition module is the web crawler, that is responsible for extracting data related to events that endanger citizens and neighbours through unstructured data from social networks. It uses NLP techniques to obtain information from open social network platforms and web crawlers to extract semi-structured information from news. For each site, it is possible to define several strategies to filter content from the URL structure and to define rules using CSS to select the main content of each news item. The data is stored using the Markdown format to preserve some structural information such as headings and titles. This module is also responsible for extracting data from social networks. We focus on Twitter and the UMUCorpusClassifier tool [10]. Twitter is a popular micro-blogging social network where information concerning security can be found by using specific queries and filters.

The second data acquisition module is an online neighbourhood collaboration reporting application, which is an advanced multi-device application that allows residents to identify and report security-related events. This system allows the sending of texts, locations, photos and voice notes. It also uses specific services to help residents write down the information they send. Figure 2 shows an screen shoot of the evidence collected by the app on a map. We use this interface to check that the evidence is correctly identified. This tool uses computer visions models such as YoLo [21] and Automatic Speech Recognition Systems such as Whisper [29] to extract data from the evidence submitted by the neighbours.

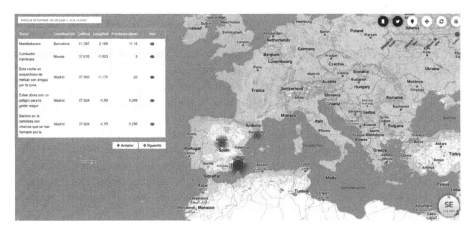

Fig. 2. Data monitoring dashboard. This interface consists of a map showing the collected evidence, clustered by distance.

3.2   Level 2. Low-Level Modules

These modules consist of various services for extracting information, including named entities and locations, using deep learning linguistic resources, lexicons and sequence classification models.

The main component of this level is a NER service based on a sequence classification model. Specifically, we have adapted and extended the Stanza model [28]. This module is able to capture people, places and organisations. To detect timestamps, we have combined the use of deep learning models trained for this purpose with our own system based on regular expressions. When both systems detect overlapping entities, the system resolves by keeping the longest text string. This module is capable of recognising different types of temporal expressions, such as numeric dates, concrete dates, more abstract dates, fuzzy dates, absolute dates, relative dates and many combinations between them. It is also capable of recognising expressions that accept a degree of error from the user.

The next module is a multi-modal Emotion Analysis. We calculate the emotion of each document by training several emotion analysis classifiers based on textual and multimodal features. This module is able to extract subjective information from social media posts and from voice notes and texts sent by neighbours using multimodal classification models. To this end, a corpus of audio extracted from YouTube and public emotion datasets was first compiled. This corpus was manually tagged by project members. Secondly, the voice notes were transcribed using the Whisper [29]. In addition, the texts were pre-processed to remove repeated words and to correct spelling mistakes. Third, two automatic classification models were trained: one capable of extracting emotions from natural language written data, and another model capable of extracting emotions from raw audio data using prosody-related features. MarIA [20] was used for the text model and Wav2Vec [2] for the audio model. Both models were combined using ensemble learning. Finally, once the model has been built, an API-REST service is activated to predict the emotions of future documents. The current version of the audio corpus contains about 10 h of audio and about 3000 segments annotated with the emotions described by Ekman [9] plus a neutral emotion. The dataset is not balanced, with more entities labelled as neutral (39%), followed by disgust (23%) and anger (13%). It is worth noting that we additionally trained other models focusing only on textual features by merging the EmoEvalEs dataset [1], with a total of 11,756 instances, and increasing the number of labels related to joy and underrepresented emotions in our dataset, such as surprise and fear.

For the models described above we train several models based on multilingual and Spanish Transformers, including lightweight models more suitable for production environments [7]. In a nutshell, the training process we carried out consisted in dividing the dataset into training and validation in an 80-20 ratio using stratification. We then applied hyperparameter optimisation to evaluate different network configurations to see which one gives the best results. The parameters are the architecture of the model, which includes the number and configuration of the layers, the methods of evaluating the model, as well as other specific parameters of each model. It is important to add that these values are set before training and are neither evaluated nor changed during the process.

Similarly, we have trained several models to perform author profiling and to catalogue users in social networks. These models have been trained on datasets from PAN [4,30] and PoliticES [15] and are able to extract demographic characteristics of users and whether they are spreaders of hate speech or fake news.

3.3 Level 3. Mid-Level Modules

This level consists of all the modules that extract and classify information on topics related to security and the analysis of harassment, threat or danger. These modules take as input the resources obtained in the previous work package, related to the data extracted from multimodal approaches of social networks, web pages and citizen collaboration, as well as the entities extracted by the entity models, the emotion analysis and the generation of profiles of the authors of the texts. The objective of this level is therefore to generate high-level information collected from a group of publications, in order to identify risks from a point of view that allows the identification of risks and threats according to their nature and imminence.

The basis of these components is a an Information Retrieval (IR) module that it is based on an ontology developed specifically for this platform. Ontologies are the basis of the Semantic Web and have been adapted to solve specific problems related to public health [32,34], computer science [5] and e-commerce [18]. The ontology was developed using the Protégé tool [19]. The result of this development is a file in OWL format, which we import into our application using the Owlready2 Python tool [24]. In order to capture the concepts related to citizen security, we followed a methodology of examining several news items from different online newspapers related to crime or security. The ideal way to capture the concepts related to citizen security would be to consult an expert in this knowledge or to reuse an ontology created by the experts or professionals related to this domain. For this project, we have carried out an exhaustive search for ontologies related to the domain of citizen security and, to the best of our knowledge, we have not been able to find any of sufficient quality to be included in this project, i.e. the ontologies found lacked sufficient concepts and, in general, were not created by an expert (professional, researcher or specialised organisation). Instead, we decided to model the ontology ourselves by searching for concepts in news websites, online dictionaries or blogs created by professionals in the field.

To extract the relationship between the crawled items and the ontology, we rely on Semantic Annotation approach based on the TF—IDF—e formula [31] (see Eq. 1), which takes into account how often some of the concepts of the ontology appear and how these topics are related to other topics considering their distance.

$$\sum_{j=1}^{n} \frac{tf - idf}{e^{dist(i,j)}} \tag{1}$$

A service is provided to retrieve the semantic annotation in JSON. Figure 3 contains a screenshot of the output. Each annotation has the following fields The **names** field is a list of the literal text that was captured by the ontology, the **regex** field is the regular expression that captured this entity, **type** is the type of semantic annotation that was captured by this entity, **class** is the name of the label that the ontology has assigned to this entity, **superclasses** is a list of classes to which this entity belongs, the fields **tf_idf**, **tf_idf_e**, **explicit** and **implicit** are the result of the statistical analysis of the semantic data of the document.

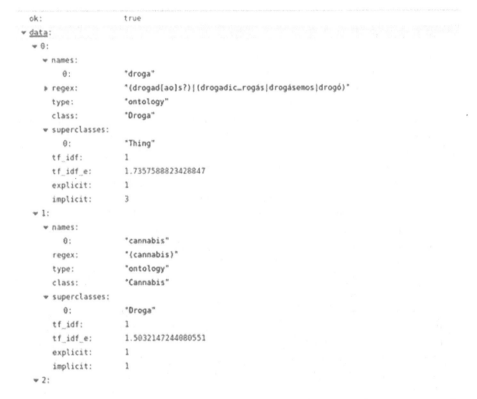

Fig. 3. Semantic annotation output in JSON format, including the entities, regular expressions, implicit and explicit occurrences of each entity, and the TF–IDF and TF–IDF-e score.

Finally, the hate speech discourse analysis and threat prediction consists in the development of several regression deep learning models to detect hate speech and threat situations. A novel dataset containing different types of hate speech such as transphobia, homophobia, fatphobia or aporophobia is collected and annotated. This dataset is annotated using a regression scheme with different intensities, from disagreements and negative actions to death threats [3]. It also distinguishes whether the target is an individual or a group.

3.4   Level 4. High-Level Modules

At this level are all the modules related to security management, alerts, notifications and trust in the information extracted and its certification through the use of blockchain technologies. It should be noted that these modules are currently under development.

The Alerts and Notifications system will be an alerting system where users can subscribe to specific topics according to their preferences and geographical area. These reports will be generated in multiple formats and can be delivered through multiple channels such as email, mobile alerts, sound alerts, calendar or events.

The User Trust and False News Detection system will be responsible for assessing both the trust of users interacting with the platform and the quality of the data found. This will be done by analysing trust in users based on their participation history and account data. The focus will be on detecting automated behaviour. On the other hand, the quality of reports and news will be analysed in order to automatically adjust the system to give value to reliable sources.

The data certification system will generate blockchain-based trust certificates to certify the reports. The objective of this module is to create a trust-based source filtering system that allows prioritisation or discarding among the evidence and documents collected through the citizen participation application, data from official sources and data from social networks. This system will be based on blockchain technology, creating a public and transparent list of registered sources. The long-term goal is to have a trusted, distributed system that can distinguish between false positives and prioritise valid sources. To do this, the system will extract information from the metadata collected to obtain information from the sources, and will also be fed by the manual reports that users download.

3.5   Level 5. User Interface

At this last level are the user interfaces that manage the information found. They are based on a system of views and KPIs, as well as notification and alert systems, map-based interfaces to visualise hazards, and a system of safe routes for citizens. It should be noted that the user interfaces will be developed in the last phase of the project.

From the application dashboard, users will be able to configure specific monitoring plans by selecting the monitoring interval and the geographical area where samples will be collected. Although the system will be open to include different social networks, in this prototype efforts will be focused on the Twitter social network because it is a widely used network, it allows access through a REST API, it allows geolocation of tweets and users, and the allowed message length limit makes users very specific in their comments. In addition, this social network is widely used to report information relevant to citizens. Due to the sensitive information handled, this module will also have authentication and authorisation mechanisms that allow users to authenticate to the system and restrict the actions they can perform according to their role.

4 Conclusions and Further Work

In conclusion, the development of the SafercITies project, an intelligent system for analysing and monitoring the security of citizens, can offer significant potential for improving various aspects of security and well-being. The integration of features such as incident reporting, preventive measures and user profiling has shown promising results in addressing both digital and physical security concerns. By using technologies such as sentiment analysis, user profiling and natural language processing (NLP), the platform enables a more comprehensive understanding of online behaviour, facilitating the detection of hate speech, cyberbullying and other security threats.

Our next steps will be to implement the high-level modules and the user interfaces, integrate the system and validate it with two use cases, one for Spain and one for Mexico.

Acknowledgements. This work was funded by CDTI and the European Regional Development Fund (FEDER/ERDF)-a way to make Europe through project SafercITies IDI-20220154. This work is also part of the research project LaTe4PSP (PID2019-107652RB-I00/AEI/ 10.13039/501100011033) funded by MCIN/AEI/10.13039/501100011033.

References

1. Plaza-del Arco, F.M., Jiménez Zafra, S.M., Montejo Ráez, A., Molina González, M.D., Ureña López, L.A., Martín Valdivia, M.T.: Overview of the emoevales task on emotion detection for spanish at iberlef 2021. Procesamiento del Lenguaje Natural (2021)
2. Baevski, A., Zhou, Y., Mohamed, A., Auli, M.: wav2vec 2.0: a framework for self-supervised learning of speech representations. In: Advances in Neural Information Processing Systems, vol. 33, pp. 12449–12460 (2020)
3. Bahador, B.: Classifying and identifying the intensity of hate speech. Social Science Research Council (2020). https://items.ssrc.org/disinformation-democracy-and-conflictprevention/classifying-and-identifying-the-intensity-of-hate-speech
4. Bevendorff, J., et al.: Overview of PAN 2021: authorship verification, profiling hate speech spreaders on twitter, and style change detection. In: Candan, K.S., et al. (eds.) CLEF 2021. LNCS, vol. 12880, pp. 419–431. Springer, Cham (2021). https://doi.org/10.1007/978-3-030-85251-1_26
5. Beydoun, G., et al.: Cooperative modelling evaluated. Int. J. Coop. Inf. Syst. **14**(1), 45–71 (2005). https://doi.org/10.1142/S0218843005001080
6. Cañete, J., Chaperon, G., Fuentes, R., Ho, J.H., Kang, H., Pérez, J.: Spanish pre-trained BERT model and evaluation data. In: PML4DC at ICLR 2020 (2020)

7. Cañete, J., Donoso, S., Bravo-Marquez, F., Carvallo, A., Araujo, V.: Albeto and distilbeto: lightweight Spanish language models. arXiv preprint arXiv:2204.09145 (2022)

8. Chakravarthi, B.R., et al.: Overview of the shared task on hope speech detection for equality, diversity, and inclusion. In: Proceedings of the Second Workshop on Language Technology for Equality, Diversity and Inclusion, pp. 378–388 (2022)

9. Ekman, P.: Lie catching and microexpressions. In: The Philosophy of Deception, vol. 1, no. 2, p. 5 (2009)

10. García-Díaz, J.A., Almela, Á., Alcaraz-Mármol, G., Valencia-García, R.: Umucorpusclassifier: compilation and evaluation of linguistic corpus for natural language processing tasks. Procesamiento del Lenguaje Natural **65**, 139–142 (2020)

11. García-Díaz, J.A., Cánovas-García, M., Colomo-Palacios, R., Valencia-García, R.: Detecting misogyny in Spanish tweets. An approach based on linguistics features and word embeddings. Future Gener. Comput. Syst. **114**, 506–518 (2021)

12. García-Díaz, J.A., Colomo-Palacios, R., Valencia-Garcia, R.: Umuteam at emoevales 2021: emotion analysis for Spanish based on explainable linguistic features and transformers. In: Iberian Languages Evaluation Forum (IberLEF 2021), CEUR Workshop Proceedings, Malaga, vol. 9, pp. 59–71 (2021)

13. García-Díaz, J.A., Colomo-Palacios, R., Valencia-García, R.: Psychographic traits identification based on political ideology: an author analysis study on Spanish politicians' tweets posted in 2020. Futur. Gener. Comput. Syst. **130**, 59–74 (2022)

14. García-Díaz, J.A., García-Sánchez, F., Valencia-García, R.: Smart analysis of economics sentiment in Spanish based on linguistic features and transformers. IEEE Access **11**, 14211–14224 (2023)

15. García-Díaz, J.A., Jiménez Zafra, S.M., Martín Valdivia, M.T., García-Sánchez, F., Ureña López, L.A., Valencia García, R.: Overview of politices 2022: Spanish author profiling for political ideology. Procesamiento del Lenguaje Natural (2022)

16. García-Díaz, J.A., Jiménez-Zafra, S.M., García-Cumbreras, M.A., Valencia-García, R.: Evaluating feature combination strategies for hate-speech detection in Spanish using linguistic features and transformers. Complex Intell. Syst. **9**(3), 2893–2914 (2023)

17. García-Díaz, J.A., Vivancos-Vicente, P.J., Almela, Á., Valencia-García, R.: UMU-TextStats: a linguistic feature extraction tool for Spanish. In: Proceedings of the Thirteenth Language Resources and Evaluation Conference, Marseille, France, pp. 6035–6044. European Language Resources Association (2022). https://aclanthology.org/2022.lrec-1.649

18. García-Sánchez, F., Valencia-García, R., Martínez-Béjar, R.: An integrated approach for developing e-commerce applications. Expert Syst. Appl. **28**(2), 223–235 (2005). https://doi.org/10.1016/j.eswa.2004.10.004

19. Gennari, J.H., et al.: The evolution of protégé: an environment for knowledge-based systems development. Int. J. Hum Comput Stud. **58**(1), 89–123 (2003)

20. Gutiérrez-Fandiño, A., et al.: Maria: Spanish language models. arXiv preprint arXiv:2107.07253 (2021)

21. Huang, R., Pedoeem, J., Chen, C.: Yolo-lite: a real-time object detection algorithm optimized for non-GPU computers. In: 2018 IEEE International Conference on Big Data (Big Data), pp. 2503–2510. IEEE (2018)

22. Jiménez-Zafra, S.M., Cruz-Díaz, N.P., Taboada, M., Martín-Valdivia, M.T.: Negation detection for sentiment analysis: a case study in Spanish. Nat. Lang. Eng. **27**(2), 225–248 (2021)

23. Kenton, J.D.M.W.C., Toutanova, L.K.: Bert: pre-training of deep bidirectional transformers for language understanding. In: Proceedings of NAACL-HLT, pp. 4171–4186 (2019)
24. Lamy, J.B.: Owlready: ontology-oriented programming in python with automatic classification and high level constructs for biomedical ontologies. Artif. Intell. Med. **80**, 11–28 (2017)
25. Liu, Y., et al.: Roberta: a robustly optimized BERT pretraining approach (2019). arXiv preprint arXiv:1907.11692, vol. 364 (1907)
26. Osorio Angel, S., Peña Pérez Negrón, A., Espinoza-Valdez, A.: Systematic literature review of sentiment analysis in the Spanish language. Data Technol. Appl. **55**(4), 461–479 (2021)
27. Pan, R., García-Díaz, J.A., Garcia-Sanchez, F., Valencia-García, R.: Evaluation of transformer models for financial targeted sentiment analysis in Spanish. PeerJ Comput. Sci. **9**, e1377 (2023)
28. Qi, P., Zhang, Y., Zhang, Y., Bolton, J., Manning, C.D.: Stanza: a python natural language processing toolkit for many human languages. In: Proceedings of the 58th Annual Meeting of the Association for Computational Linguistics: System Demonstrations, pp. 101–108 (2020)
29. Radford, A., Kim, J.W., Xu, T., Brockman, G., McLeavey, C., Sutskever, I.: Robust speech recognition via large-scale weak supervision. arXiv preprint arXiv:2212.04356 (2022)
30. Rangel, F., Giachanou, A., Ghanem, B.H.H., Rosso, P.: Overview of the 8th author profiling task at pan 2020: profiling fake news spreaders on twitter. In: CEUR Workshop Proceedings, vol. 2696, pp. 1–18. Sun SITE Central Europe (2020)
31. Rodríguez-García, M.Á., Valencia-García, R., García-Sánchez, F., Zapater, J.J.S.: Creating a semantically-enhanced cloud services environment through ontology evolution. Future Gener. Comp. Syst. **32**, 295–306 (2014). https://doi.org/10.1016/j.future.2013.08.003
32. Ruiz-Sánchez, J.M., Valencia-García, R., Fernández-Breis, J.T., Martínez-Béjar, R., Compton, P.: An approach for incremental knowledge acquisition from text. Expert Syst. Appl. **25**(1), 77–86 (2003). https://doi.org/10.1016/S0957-4174(03)00008-3
33. Sattar, N.S., Arifuzzaman, S.: Covid-19 vaccination awareness and aftermath: public sentiment analysis on twitter data and vaccinated population prediction in the USA. Appl. Sci. **11**(13), 6128 (2021)
34. Valencia-García, R., Ruiz-Sánchez, J.M., Vicente, P.J.V., Fernández-Breis, J.T., Martínez-Béjar, R.: An incremental approach for discovering medical knowledge from texts. Expert Syst. Appl. **26**(3), 291–299 (2004). https://doi.org/10.1016/j.eswa.2003.09.001
35. Vaswani, A., et al.: Attention is all you need. In: Advances in Neural Information Processing Systems, vol. 30 (2017)

Automatic Classification of Tweets Identifying Mental Health Conditions in Central American Population in a Pandemic

Denis Cedeno-Moreno[1]([✉])[iD], Miguel Vargas-Lombardo[1][iD], and Nila Navarro[2][iD]

[1] Grupo de Investigación en Salud Electrónica y Supercomputación (GISES), Universidad Tecnológica Panamá, Ciudad de Panamá, Panama
{denis.cedeno,miguel.vargas}@utp.ac.pa
[2] Facultad de Ingenieria de Sistemas Computacionales, Universidad Tecnológica Panamá, Ciudad de Panamá, Panama
nnavarro@utp.ac.pa

Abstract. The Covid-19 pandemic has had a negative impact on the physical health of the Central American population. Fear, anxiety and stress were normal reactions in quarantine, due to the uncertainty of the unknown, which makes it understandable that the population experienced feelings or psychological affections. Social networks were the means of communication for thousands of people in quarantine. The increased use of social networks to share comments, content and opinions makes it possible to have a large amount of information. Twitter has been one of the most widely used social networks due to its ease of access and use. The analysis of tweets requires a systematic process for their collection, transformation and classification, integrating different artificial intelligence tools such as natural language processing, automatic learning or deep learning. Automatic text classification aims at finding an adequate way to categorize the documents according to the attributes made up of words that describe each specific category. For this reason, our study has been carried out with a corpus in Spanish extracted from Twitter for the automatic classification of texts, from which we have categorized, through the automatic learning approach, the tweets about Covid-19 in the Central American region, in order to know if the population has suffered any psychological effects. Based on the results, we can say that the automatic learning models provide competitive results in terms of automatic identification of texts with an accuracy of 89%.

Keywords: Natural language processing · Covid-19 · machine learning · automatic text classification · Twitter

1 Introduction

Thousands of deaths caused by the global spread of SARS-CoV-2 (Covid-19) led the World Health Organization (WHO) to declare in March 2020. In the last

R. Valencia-García et al. (Eds.): CITI 2023, CCIS 1873, pp. 123–137, 2023.
https://doi.org/10.1007/978-3-031-45682-4_10

decades in the world, Covid-19 has been one of the greatest acute respiratory infections with the greatest impact and damage. The world has paid a high price in terms of human lives, and it has also had a devastating impact on the economy and increased global poverty [1].

Moreover, Covid-19 infection has affected the world in many ways, with many health systems collapsing. Primary care in the Central American region has been ineffective against the virus. This vast region covers more than 522,760 km and has a population of approximately 50,690,000, spread across seven independent countries: Guatemala, Belize, Honduras, El Salvador, Nicaragua, Costa Rica and Panama [2].

The figures for infections and deaths vary between countries and are imprecise. We have used the Worldometer website, which provides us with real-time information on contagions and deaths related to Covid-19 in all countries of the world, this website is the one that several governments use to extract their data. The Table 1 shows the number of cases and deaths in the countries of Central America.

Table 1. Number of cases and deaths in Central America

Country	Total cases	Total Deaths
Belice	70,782	688
Guatemala	1,257,244	20,205
Nicaragua	18,491	225
Honduras	472,619	11,116
El Salvador	201,785	4,230
Costa Rica	1,234,384	9,382
Panamá	1,042,631	8,634

We can see that the Central American population has suffered a lot in this Covid-19 pandemic, both from physical illnesses and from the increase in cases of mental health problems, due to the quarantine and isolation that we have had to endure for several months [3]. In order to cope with the effects of Covid-19 from an economic point of view, public and private organisations in the region have made extensive use of technological tools to carry out daily activities such as telecommuting, online shopping and sales, virtual classes and remote management of production processes. Despite this, a large part of the Central American population has not been able to face the new challenges posed by Covid-19 and its impact on physical health, in addition to the profound effects on mental health and well-being. These effects can be translated into a variety of emotional reactions such as disgust, anger, fear, sadness, anxiety, worry, mental health conditions that represent a complex and multi-level problem that can have a negative impact on the population, this is required attention of professionals or health specialists and researchers [4].

The Internet has provided us with content and news about the pandemic at all times. Social networks have a great impact on users because they generate content of a different nature, and this factor is extremely important today. During the pandemic, social networks such as Instagram, Facebook or Twitter helped users to get information about news related to the Covid-19 disease. In general, this user-generated content is full of text with opinions about services, products, activities or events, among others. For this reason, this trend of online opinions has a great impact on organisations throughout the health sector [5].

Twitter is a social networking site that manages an innumerable number of messages or opinions exchanged between users every minute. These short messages are called tweets and can be up to 280 characters long. An advanced and exclusive way to openly access Twitter is to use the Twitter API. Organisations and governments take public opinion seriously, sometimes using it to gauge the acceptance or rejection of a service, strategy or product. For a few years now, researchers have been interested in studying opinions and emotions from social networks [6].

Being able to automatically identify users' opinions and group them in a particular context is a very interesting task. This automatic identification can be catalogued as a Natural Language Processing (NLP) task known as automatic text classification, which consists of categorising a text fragment into one or more categories, usually from a predefined set [7].

NLP [8] is one of the fundamental pillars of Artificial Intelligence (AI), in which NLP is used to understand language in order to design systems that perform complex linguistic tasks such as translation, text summarization, or information retrieval (IR), among others [9]. Text classification is largely based on IR and machine learning (ML)/deep learning (DL), according to supervised or semi-supervised classification, where the algorithms learn from a labelled set that is used as a training set [10].

AI, especially ML and DL, allows us to create models that can become references for current computing [11]. One of the great challenges of Panamanian research is to create useful predictive models to help health authorities make decisions. Being able to evaluate and classify the opinions of the Central American population on a given disease can allow those in charge of health to implement strategies for the benefit of the population and to make future projections in case there is another pandemic [12].

The aim of this study is to examine the opinions and comments of users of the social network Twitter published during the Covid-19 pandemic and to carry out a model using ML approaches that achieves an automatic classification of the text to determine how much has been affected the mental health of the Central American population. The rest of the manuscript is structured as follows: Sect. 2 describes the literature review. Section 3 describes the proposed platform, showing the resources and tools used. Section 4 presents the results and discussion, and Sect. 5 show the conclusions.

2 Related Work

Nowadays, automatic text classification has a wide range of applications, the most prominent of which are: detecting unwanted emails, filtering and organising content on web pages, filtering false news, detecting plagiarism, and identifying and analysing opinions.

In recent years, there have been significant advances in the application of text classification techniques using ML and DL to cope with the large volume of rapidly growing information in social networks. Some related work has been published in these areas, for example, Muhammad Umer in [13] carried out a study that investigated the application of a Convolutional Neural Network (CNN) model to text classification problems through experimentation and analysis. They entered a ranking model with the word embedding model fastText and used publicly available datasets, six reference datasets including Ag News, Amazon Full and Polarity, Yahoo Question Answer, Yelp Full and Polarity. The proposed model was tested on a dataset from the Twitter network. The analysis shows that the approach of using fastText as a word embedding is a promising way to achieve good results in text classification. In [14] Mohammed retrieved Twitter publications using a list of keywords related to intimate partner violence (IPV), the retrieved publications were manually reviewed, and a dataset with annotations was prepared to categorise tweets into IPV report or IPV. The researchers developed an effective NLP model to automatically identify tweets with IPV. Post-classification analyses will be conducted to determine the causes of system errors and to ensure that the system is not biased in its decision making, particularly with regard to race and gender. The automatic classification model can be an essential component of a proactive intervention based on social networks and a support framework, while supporting population-level surveillance and large-scale cohort studies. The developed model achieved F1 metrics of 0.76 for the IPV class and 0.97 for the no IPV class. After [15] Thomas Edwards presented a study comparing some classic automatic learning algorithms, widely used in ecology studies, with state-of-the-art neural network models. The results showed that the model based on the neural network Bidirectional Encoder Representations from Transformers (BERT) outperformed the classical methods. In particular, a relatively small training corpus of less than 3,000 instances was used, reflecting the fact that the BERT classifier uses a transfer learning approach that benefits from prior learning on a much larger collection of generic text. BERT performed particularly well even on tweets that used specialised language related to wildlife observations. This will enable more accurate identification of wildlife-related data in social networks, which in turn can be used to enrich citizen data.

Another proposal is presented in [16], where Yuan-Chi Yang carried out a study that aimed to develop and evaluate a system to identify users with chronic stress experience using Twitter messages. They collected tweets containing certain keywords related to stress and then filtered the data using predefined text patterns. Tweets with and without chronic stress content were manually annotated as positive or negative. They noted 4195 tweets (1560 positive, 2635 negative). Different classifiers were used, achieving 83% accuracy. The classifier based on BERT obtained the best performance with an accuracy of 83.6%, beating the second classifier with the best performance of support vector machines: 76.4%. The study demonstrates that the experiences of chronic stress self-reported by users on Twitter can be automatically identified, which has a high potential for monitoring and intervention on a large scale. In [17] Durga Prasad Jasti propose a work with a new relevance-based feature classification (RBFR) algorithm that identifies and selects smaller subsets of relevant features in the feature space. We compare the performance of RBFR with other existing feature selection methods such as the balanced measure of precision, information gain, GINI index and probability ratio. To train the model, 5 automatic learning algorithms Support Vector Machine (SVM), Naive Bayes (NB), k-Nearest Neighbours (kNN), Random Forest (RF) and Logistic Regression (LR) were used to test and evaluate the proposed features of the selection method. The test was carried out on 3 sets of news data, Reuters and WAP. It was found that the performance of the proposed feature selection method is 25.4305% more effective than the existing feature selection methods in terms of precision. Anwar Hussen Wadud in [18] proposes a work with a text classification algorithm called LSTM-BOOST that uses a short-term memory model (LSTM) with a learning set to detect offensive texts in Bengali on various social media platforms. The proposed LSTM-BOOST model uses the modified AdaBoost algorithm to use Principal Component Analysis (PCA) along with LSTM networks. In the LSTM-Boost model, the dataset is divided into three categories and the PCA and LSTM networks are applied to each part of the dataset to obtain the most significant variance and reduce the weighted error of the model's weak hypothesis. In addition, different classifiers were used for the reference experiment and the model was evaluated with different word embedding methods. The research showed that the LSTM-BOOST algorithms outperform the most common text sorting algorithms with an accuracy of 92.61%. José Alberto Benítez-Andrades in [19] proposes a research aimed at developing a predictive model based on BERT capable of detecting racist behaviour and xenophobic messages in tweets written in Spanish. A comparison was made with different DL models. In total, five predictive models were developed, two based on BERT and three using other DL techniques, CNN, LSTM and a model combining CNN + LSTM techniques. With the results obtained, it was verified that the best metric obtained was BETO, which is a BERT-based model pre-trained on a Spanish corpus, achieving an accuracy of 85.22%. The main contribution of this work is the achievement of promising results in the field of racism and hate speech in Spanish by applying different deep learning techniques. According to Samujjwal Ghosh in [20] developed a work framework that combines the versatility of graphical neural networks, applied to the corpus, with the power of language models based on transformers, the work framework was evaluated with a set of data in English in monolingual and multilingual assessment scenarios. The framework outperforms models of the last generation in the area of disasters. I also show the general feasibility of the proposed model under limited supervision. In [21] Christopher

Haynes proposes an innovative text classification model. The model changes depending on other things in preprocessing, scoring and text sorting. A dataset from the National Health Service (NHS) of the United Kingdom was used, which contains many features that increase the complexity of text classification. Using the model, a high level of accuracy was achieved, reaching an F1 score of 93.30% on the Reuters-21578 "ApteMod" corpus. Sayar Ul Hassana propose in [22] a comparative text classification work in which the efficiency of different machine learning algorithms has been analysed on different data sets. The ML based algorithms used in this work were SVM, k-NN, LR, Multinomial Naïve Bayes (MNB) and RF. The data sets were used to perform a comparative analysis of these algorithms. Validation is carried out using metrics of accuracy, precision, recovery and F1 score. The results show that LR and SVM outperform the other models on the IMDB dataset and kNN outperforms the other models on the SPAM dataset. Finally, Rukhma Qasim in [23] proposes a work where the transfer learning model is applied for text classification. Two experimental datasets were used, including the Covid-19 false news dataset and the Covid-19 tweets dataset in English, to verify the performance of this transfer learning model. The models are trained and evaluated with measures of accuracy, precision, recall and F1 score.

As a summary, in Table 2 is presented a comparison of the most relevant aspects from each work described in this section.

Table 2. Overview of the related work review

Work	Author	Techniques	Context	Language
[13]	Muhammad Umer	DL	News	English/Twitter
[14]	Mohammed Ali Al-Garadi	ML	Violence	English/twitter
[15]	Thomas Edwards	ML+DL	Ecology	English
[16]	Yuan-Chi Yang	ML+DL	Stress	English
[17]	Durga Prasad Jasti	ML	News	English
[18]	Anwar Hussen Wadud	DL	Hate	Bengali
[19]	José Alberto Benítez	DL	Hate	Spanish
[20]	Samujjwal Ghosh	DL	Disaster	English
[21]	Christopher Haynes	ML	Health	English
[22]	Sayar Ul Hassana	ML	Movie	English
[23]	Rukhma Qasim	xxx	News	English

It should be noted that automatic text classification has been widely used in scientific research for a variety of scenarios, with both advantages and disadvantages. In the vast majority of cases, research has only considered the English language, which means that applications in other languages are still rare [24]. For this reason, conducting a study to categorise the text of Central Americans is a valuable contribution.

Our idea was to create a domain-independent text categoriser for tweets, including language specifics such as emoticons and emojis. Therefore, conducting a study to categorise the text of a Spanish corpus extracted from Twitter using the ML approach, in order to find out whether the Central American population has suffered from post Covid-19 psychological conditions, is a valuable contribution.

3   Proposed Architecture

In this section we present the dataset and tools used to develop this project. We also explain in detail our proposed architecture.

3.1   Overview

We first extract and preprocess a dataset in Spanish obtained from the social network Twitter on mental health conditions related to Covid-19. With the training dataset, it is necessary that the text makes sense to the algorithm, that is, we have to convert the text into a numerical representation, using a method to extract the features [12]. Then we apply the various classification algorithms. Finally, we evaluate each model by predicting it on the test dataset. Figure 1 shows the proposed architecture, which is described in detail in the following sections.

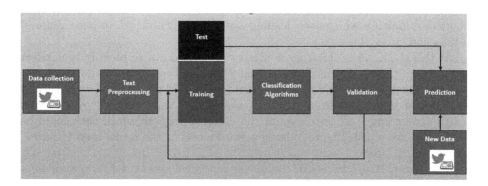

Fig. 1. Proposed Architecture

3.2   Dataset

The first step of our case study is to collect a set of tweets related to mental health conditions associated with Covid-19 disease from the Central American population. The tweets were downloaded using a geolocation filter from the seven Central American countries in the months between November 2021 and March 2022 using Twitter4J, a Java library that facilitates the use of the Twitter API [25]. An initial corpus of 351,000 tweets was obtained. Table 3 shows an extract of the tweets from the Republic of Costa Rica.

Table 3. Extract of the tweets from the Republic of Costa Rica

Date	Localization	Text
10/09/2021 20:22	Heredia, Costa Rica	En mi barrio hay mucho miedo por la pandemia
10/09/2021 19:40	Heredia, Costa Rica	Físicamente 100 Respiratorio 0 Maldito covid te odio
10/09/2021 17:54	Cartago, Costa Rica	Tanto temor, esta es una etapa tan difícil de mi vida por el Covid
10/09/2021 13:21	San José, Costa Rica	Ya Brasil sobrepasa las 600.000 muertes por covid-19, temor que tengo
10/09/2021 06:37	San José, Costa Rica	La situación con la pandemia nos roba más paz de la que hay

3.3 Text Preprocessing

Most text and document dataset contain many unnecessary words, stop words, misspellings, jargon and others. The noise and unnecessary words can have a negative effect on model performance, especially with machine learning algorithms. For our case study, once the dataset was obtained, we proceeded to clean the data; firstly, columns that were considered unnecessary were eliminated, leaving those with which they were going to work.

In a second step, all links or hyperlinks to websites that could be present in each published tweet were removed from the tweet column, as this information does not influence the categorisation of the tweet and could even worsen the work of the classifiers. The text was also normalised by converting each word to lower case. Special characters, hyperlinks, spaces, identifiers and words that were too short were removed. Removal of hashtags, in-text links, punctuation, emoticons, multiple whitespace, leading whitespace, trailing whitespace, removal of tabs and empty lines [26].

At this stage, an exploratory analysis was carried out to identify each tweet and perform the annotation process, using the total number of annotators who searched for patrons to obtain only those tweets that contained a word related to a mental health condition, a list of words that was compiled by a mental health expert and took into account the different ways in which they could be written by users [27]. Figure 2 shows a word cloud of the terms used to search for patrons in tweets.

As a result, 10,074 tweets related to these psychological conditions were identified, with the distribution of their totals shown in Fig. 3.

These tweets were labelled with a zero (0) to categorise them for algorithm training, similarly the category (1) in the tweet means that it does not represent a comment from the person indicating a psychological condition.

3.4 Feature Extraction

The performance of ML models depends on the effectiveness of the chosen method for feature extraction [28]. Among the most used methods for feature extraction are bag of words, term frequency and inverse document frequency (TF-IDF) among others [29]. With clean data, it is necessary that the text makes sense, i.e. we need to convert the text into a numerical representation, in a vector format. Machine learning models do not accept input in the form

Fig. 2. Cloud of words with the terms used for the search for patrons

of text. Therefore, the text must be converted to vectors in order to work with them. For this reason, the next step in our pipeline was to extract the features to perform supervised classification. In the case study we present, we rely on the Bag of Words (BoW) technique, which includes term counting functions used in traditional machine learning classifiers. We counted the score of each word and then performed feature extraction [30].

3.5   Chosen ML Classification Models

Random Forest. Decision trees are algorithms that build a tree structure of decision rules. Each decision is partitioned based on entropy, maximising the homogeneity of the new subsets. Using a hierarchical approach to partitioning space, this technique is used to create a model that predicts the value of a target variable based on multiple input variables. In this study, we use an RF algorithm, which is a type of decision tree for binary classification that uses bagging to create multiple decision trees and averages their results. Each random tree considers only a subset of the features and a set of random examples, which reduces model overfitting [31].

Support Vector Machines. They are supervised learning algorithms that are applied many times to the classification, trying to find the best hyperplane of the data according to the different classes. The objective is that the hyperplane is the most optimal possible. It correlates data to a space of large-scale features

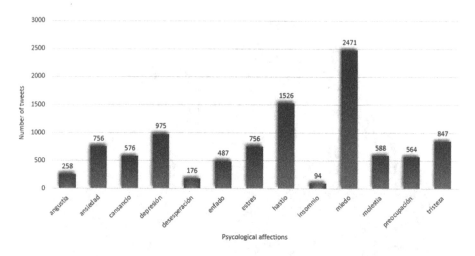

Fig. 3. Total distribution psychological conditions

so that data points can be classified. SVM allows the use of different kernels to solve problems that are linear and non-linear in classification [32].

Naive Bayes. One of the most representative Bayesian networks uses Bayes' theorem. Put simply, an NB classifier assumes that the presence of a particular feature in a class is unrelated to the presence of any other feature [33].

Logistic Regression. This classifier is typically used for binary class problems by linearly combining the input values to produce a sigmoid function that discriminates between the standard class. LR has been used to identify satire in and to detect irony [34].

We decided to work with these algorithms for the following reasons: the decision trees are popular, in addition to being proven to give good results and to be used in both classification and regression problems, these algorithms offer predictive representations that can be used to classify models. The models built with SVM algorithms have many other advantages, since the model built has an explicit dependence on the patrons of the largest input from the dataset, and allows better generalisation towards new objects, given that it considers the principle of minimising risk structural. Classification with SVM allows obtaining linear and non-linear classifiers. Algorithms based on the Bayes theorem, which use probabilistic theory to predict the label of a text. These algorithms decipher the information based on the probability of words in a text corresponding to the labels of a model. Finally, the Logistic Regression algorithm, whose function is the sigmoid, is able to make predictions on texts with greater precision than a linear regression, which is a better predictor, although a little more complex to understand.

3.6   Python Libraries

It was decided to work with the Python programming tool. The Python programming language offers many advantages for those who want to integrate in the context of NLP and ML, since it has a huge number of libraries that facilitate tasks, among which we have: Sklearn, NumPy and Pandas [35].

3.7   Preparation of Training and Test Datasets

The dataset was divided into training and test sets in a ratio of 80 and 20. The performance of the ML models is evaluated using the train/test approach through accuracy, precision, recall, and F-measure.

4   Results and Discussion

As mentioned above, the metrics used for the evaluation were precision, recall and F-measure. This set of metrics is very common in the evaluation of NLP systems [36].

– Precision is the ratio of correctly predicted observations to the total number of observations. Precision indicates how many of the predicted positive observations are positive (true positives). In other words, it is the proportion of true positives out of all those classified as positive [37].
– Recall is the ratio of true positives to all true positive units.
– F-measure combines accuracy and recall, and scores one for perfect accuracy and recall [38].

The following formulas describe how these metrics are calculated:

$$Precision = TP/(TP + FP) \tag{1}$$

$$Recall = TP/(TP + FN) \tag{2}$$

$$F - Measure = (2 * Precision * Recall)/(Precision + Recall) \tag{3}$$

For our case study of the tweets collected and tagged by users who wrote a comment related to psychological conditions in the Central American region, we were able to measure the experiment using the skilearn classification report method, which provided us with information on the common metrics of precision, recall and f1-score for the input [39]. In Table 4 we can see the results of the metrics.

Table 4. Results of metrics

Algorithm	Precision	Recall	F-measure
RF	87.145	84.253	83.678
SVM	89.328	87.341	86.547
NB	83.764	81.231	81.347
LR	84.375	82.876	81.234

In the evaluation process of the different algorithms (Naïve Bayes, Random Forest, SVM), it is observed that the Random Forest and SVM algorithms have better precision results. This is largely due to the fact that these two algorithms are always considered better for the classification task. The SVM is the best with a precision of 89.328. Followed by Random Forest second with 87.145, then LR with 83.764 and finally Naïve Bayes with 83.764, however all 4 are above 80 percent which is quite significant and predicts that the models are working well [40].

We consider accuracy to be an important issue in text classification. Accuracy can still be improved by more accurate preprocessing of the dataset and better evaluation of the categorisation of the tweets. Also, the bag-of-words approach used gives good accuracy, but it requires more computation and is a slower method, so these kinds of challenges can be solved with better approaches [41].

5   Conclusions

An investigation has been presented with a case study for the categorisation of the text, on a data set extracted from the social network Twitter, where we have established a label to determine if through the tweet Central American users communicated a psychological condition at the time of the pandemic, to later categorise it. We are aware of the possible limitations or biases associated with the data extracted from the Twitter social network used in this study, and considerations such as the representativeness of the dataset, demographic factors or the impact of linguistic variations on the results.

Our aim was to analyse and validate through metrics which of the presented classification algorithms was more efficient for our purposes. To this end, we developed a methodology that included the selection of the dataset, the analysis and cleaning of the data, the pre-processing, the generation of the model and its validation.

The main contributions of this study are as follows: It proposes a machine learning approach and data from the social network Twitter that can be used to study user opinions and comments, which allowed us to investigate and classify the evolution of discussions and comments. Psychological tone of the public during the Covid-19 pandemic. A new large-scale, real-world Twitter dataset of coronavirus-related tweets in 8 Central American countries is published. The results of this study can help social scientists and governments in the region make better decisions during future pandemics.

We believe that this research was positive and efficient in terms of the methodology proposed and, on the other hand, it was possible to see the advantages offered by automatic learning in terms of classification and processing of unstructured text. However, the most recent work on text categorisation is based on deep learning techniques, so we are considering directing our future work towards this line of research.

Several supervised machine learning algorithms were used to perform classification tasks on the datasets. The automatic text classification algorithms used in this research project can be configured even more to obtain better results, since in each of these algorithms there are modifications that can be made, for example, to the entropy in the decision trees or whether to use a linear or non-linear classifier with the SVM algorithm. We are considering future work to use the depth of these settings to get better results from the algorithms so that the approximation and precision are more accurate.

One of our future works is to use models such as BERT, ALBERT and RoBERTa, based on the transformer architecture and previously trained on large amounts of text, to be able to compare these new models with the traditional models used in this research.

Acknowledgments. The authors would like to thank the National Secretariat of Science, Technology and Innovation of Panama (SENACYT, SNI) for the support given in the development of this research. Also, Panama of the Technological University of Panama (FISC-UTP).

Authors Contribution. Conceptualization DCM; methodology DCM; formal analysis DCM, NN; research DCM; original-writing CM, MVL, NN; writing-review and edition DCM, MVL; Corresponding author DCM.

References

1. Velavan, T., Meyer, C.S.: The COVID-19 epidemic. Tropical Med. Int. Health **25**, 278–280 (2020)
2. SreeJagadeesh, M., Alphonse, P.J.: COVID-19 outbreak: an ensemble pre-trained deep learning model for detecting informative tweets. Appl. Soft Comput. J. **107**, 1–7 (2021)
3. Cedeno-Moreno, D., Vargas-Lombardo, M., Navarro, N.: Recommendation system for emotional self-control of older adults post-COVID-19 in Panama. Revista Iberica de Sistemas e Tecnologias de Informacaon **54**, 203–217 (2022)
4. Heitzman, J.: Impact of COVID-19 pandemic on mental health. Psychiatr. Pol. **54**, 187–198 (2020)
5. Dang, C.N., Moreno-García, M., De la Prieta, F.: Hybrid deep learning models for sentiment analysis. Hindawi **2021**, 1–16 (2021)
6. Habimana, O., Li, Y., Li, R., Gu, X.: Hybrid deep learning models for sentiment analysis. Sci. China Inf. **63**, 1–36 (2020)
7. Nemes, L., Kiss, A.: Social media sentiment analysis based on COVID-19. J. Inf. Telecommun. **5**, 1–15 (2021)

8. Madsen, A., Reddy, S., Chandar, S.: Post-hoc interpretability for neural NLP: a survey. ACM Comput. Surv. **55**, 1–42 (2023)
9. Chen, J., Tam, D., Raffel, C., Bansal, M., Yang, D.: An empirical survey of data augmentation for limited data learning in NLP. Trans. Assoc. Comput. Linguist. **11**, 191–211 (2023)
10. Prakash, I., Kumar, A., Sethi, T.: Learning the mental health impact of COVID-19 in the united states with explainable artificial intelligence. JMIR Mental Health **8**, 1517–1537 (2021)
11. VMaoTao, L.: Smart financial management system based on data ming and man-machine management. Hindawi Wirel. Commun. Mob. Comput. **2022**, 30–40 (2022)
12. Nahar, N., Hossain, M.S., Andersson, K.: A machine learning based fall detection for elderly people with neurodegenerative disorders. In: Mahmud, M., Vassanelli, S., Kaiser, M.S., Zhong, N. (eds.) BI 2020. LNCS (LNAI), vol. 12241, pp. 194–203. Springer, Cham (2020). https://doi.org/10.1007/978-3-030-59277-6_18
13. Umer, M., Imtiaz, Z., Ahmad, M.: Impact of convolutional neural network and FastText embedding on text classification. Multimed. Tools Appl. Health **82**, 5569–5585 (2022)
14. Al-Garadi, M., Kim, S., Guo, Y., Warren, E.: Natural language model for automatic identification of intimate partner violence reports from Twitter. J. Array **15**, 3–21 (2022)
15. Edwards, T., Jones, C.B., Corcoran, P.: Identifying wildlife observations on twitter. Eco. Inform. **67**, 296–311 (2022)
16. Yang, Y., Xie, A., Kim, S., Hair, J., Al-Garadi, M., Sarker, A.: Automatic detection of twitter users who express chronic stress experiences via supervised machine learning and natural language processing. Comput. Inform. Nurs. **41**, 1–8 (2022)
17. Jasti, V., Kumar, G., Kumar, M., Maheshwari, V., Jayagopal, P.: Relevant-based feature ranking (RBFR) method for text classification based on machine learning algorithm. J. Nanomater. 1–12 (2022)
18. Wadud, A., Kabir, M., Mridha, M.F., Ali, M.: How can we manage offensive text in social media - a text classification approach using LSTM-BOOST. Int. J. Inf. Manag. Data Insights **2**, 151–159 (2022)
19. Benítez-Andrades, J.A., González-Jiménez, Á., López-Brea, Á., Aveleira-Mata, J.: Detecting racism and xenophobia using deep learning models on Twitter data: CNN, LSTM and BERT. PeerJ Comput. Sci. **8**, 1–24 (2022)
20. Ghosh, S., Maji, S., Desarkar, M.: GNoM: graph neural network enhanced language models for disaster related multilingual text classification. In: ACM International Conference, vol. 1, pp. 55–65 (2022)
21. Haynes, C., et al.: Automatic classification of national health service feedback. Mathematics **10**, 983 (2022)
22. Hassan, S., Ahamed, J., Ahmad, K.: Analytics of machine learning-based algorithms for text classification. Sustain. Oper. Comput. **3**, 238–248 (2022)
23. Qasim, R., Bangyal, W., Alqarni, M., Ali Almazroi, A.: A fine-tuned BERT-based transfer learning approach for text classification. J. Healthc. Eng. **2022**, 297–302 (2022)
24. Shorten, C., Khoshgoftaar, T.M., Furht, B.: Deep learning applications for COVID-19. J. Big Data **8**, 816–831 (2021)
25. Ramírez-Tinoco, F., Alor-Hernández, G., Sánchez-Cervantes, J., Salas-Zárate, M.P., Valencia-García, R.: Use of sentiment analysis techniques in healthcare domain. Stud. Comput. Intell. **815**, 189–212 (2019)

26. Al-Shaher, M.A.: A hybrid deep learning and NLP based system to predict the spread of Covid-19 and unexpected side effects on people. Period. Eng. Nat. Sci. **8**, 2232–2241 (2020)

27. Usher, K., Durkin, J., Bhullar, N.: The COVID-19 pandemic and mental health impacts. Int. J. Ment. Health Nurs. **29**, 315–318 (2020)

28. Islam, M.R., Nahiduzzaman, M.: Complex features extraction with deep learning model for the detection of COVID19 from CT scan images using ensemble based machine learning approach. Expert Syst. Appl. **195**, 164–172 (2022)

29. Altınel, B., Ganiz, M.: Semantic text classification: a survey of past and recent advances. Inf. Process. Manag. **54**, 1129–1153 (2018)

30. Behl, S., Rao, A., Aggarwal, S., Chadha, S., Pannu, H.S.: Twitter for disaster relief through sentiment analysis for COVID-19 and natural hazard crises. Int. J. Disaster Risk Reduct. **55**, 1–178 (2021)

31. Palimkar, P., Shaw, R.N., Ghosh, A.: Machine learning technique to prognosis diabetes disease: random forest classifier approach. Adv. Comput. Intell. Technol. **218**, 125–133 (2022)

32. Bansal, M., Goyal, A., Choudhary, A.: A comparative analysis of K-nearest neighbor, genetic, support vector machine, decision tree, and long short term memory algorithms in machine learning. Decis. Anal. J. **3**, 43–50 (2022)

33. Duy-Hien, V., Trong-Sinh, V., The-Dung, L.: An efficient and practical approach for privacy-preserving Naive Bayes classification. J. Inf. Secur. Appl. **68**, 43–50 (2022)

34. Dumitrescu, E., Hué, S., Hurlin, C., Tokpavi, S.: Machine learning for credit scoring: improving logistic regression with non-linear decision-tree effects. Eur. J. Oper. Res. **297**, 263–267 (2022)

35. García-Díaz, J.A., Jiménez-Zafra, S.M., García-Cumbreras, M.A., Valencia-García, R.: Evaluating feature combination strategies for hate-speech detection in Spanish using linguistic features and transformers. Complex Intell. Syst. **9**, 2893–2914 (2023)

36. Krallinger, M., et al.: Evaluation of text-mining systems for biology: overview of the second BioCreative community challenge. Genome Biol. **9**, 1715–1719 (2008)

37. Min, H.J., Park, J.C.: Identifying helpful reviews based on customer's mentions about experiences. Expert Syst. Appl. **39**, 11830–11838 (2012)

38. Othman, M., Hassan, H., Moawad, R., Idrees, A.M.: Using NLP approach for opinion types classifier. J. Comput. **9**, 400–410 (2018)

39. Laila, U., Mahboob, K., Khan, A.W., Khan, F., Taekeun, W.: An ensemble approach to predict early-stage diabetes risk using machine learning: an empirical study. Sensors **22**, 1–15 (2022)

40. Muller, A.E., Patricia Sofia Jacobsen, P., Rose, C.: Machine learning in systematic reviews: comparing automated text clustering with Lingo3G and human researcher categorization in a rapid review. Res. Synth. Methods **13**, 229–241 (2022)

41. Cedeno-Moreno, D., Vargas-Lombardo, M., Navarro, N.: Deep learning and machine learning approach applied to the automatic classification of opinions on Twitter in the Covid-19 pandemic in Panama. Revista Iberica de Sistemas e Tecnologias de Informacaon **45**, 200–211 (2021)

SentiDariPers: Sentiment Analysis of Dari-Persian Tweets Based on People's Views and Opinion

Mohammad Ali Hussiny[1][(✉)] , Mohammad Arif Payenda[2] ,
and Abdul Razaq Vahidi[3]

[1] University of Oslo (UiO), Oslo, Norway
mohamhu@uio.no
[2] University of Agder (UiA), Grimstad, Norway
arif.payenda@uia.no
[3] Karabük University (KBU), Karabük, Turkey
238166317@ogrenci.karabuk.edu.tr

Abstract. In the research area of sentiment analysis, there is a noticeable gap when it comes to the Dari-Persian dialect. To bridge this gap, our research aimed to curate a comprehensive dataset encompassing people's opinions in this specific language variant. This paper presents the development of a benchmark sentiment annotated dataset for the Dari dialect of Persian, which serves as an official language of Afghanistan. The dataset, named "SentiDariPers", comprises 43,089 tweets posted between August 2021 and April 2023. It has been manually annotated with four sentiment classes: Negative, Positive, Neutral, and Mixed. We applied a range of models, such as Support Vector Machine (SVM), Long Short-Term Memory (LSTM), Bi-directional Long Short-Term Memory (Bi-LSTM), Gated Recurrent Unit (GRU), and Convolutional Neural Network (CNN). Additionally, we develop an ensemble model that combines different sets of sentiment classes for each system. We present a detailed comparative analysis of the results obtained from these models. Experimental findings demonstrate that the ensemble model achieves the highest accuracy 91%. We provide insights into the data collection and annotation process, offer relevant dataset statistics, discuss the experimental results, and provide further analysis of the data.

Keywords: Sentiment Analysis · Dataset Creation · Dari-Persian · Deep Learning

1 Introduction

Expressing and understanding sentiment plays a fundamental role in human communication and social interaction. Sentiment Analysis (SA), which is also known as opinion mining [1] encompasses polarity, attitudes, and opinions, and

---

These authors contributed equally to this work.

© The Author(s), under exclusive license to Springer Nature Switzerland AG 2023
R. Valencia-García et al. (Eds.): CITI 2023, CCIS 1873, pp. 138–156, 2023.
https://doi.org/10.1007/978-3-031-45682-4_11

plays a crucial role in conveying and understanding information, enabling individuals to connect, empathize, and engage effectively. This term was defined by Bo Pang, Lillian Lee [2] in early 2000. It is a Natural Language Processing (NLP) technique that detects and comprehends people's sentiments, attitudes, and emotions as expressed in textual and multimedia data. SA is an open research area in NLP that seeks to empower machines with the ability to efficiently recognize, analyze, and comprehend human opinions and thoughts. It involves developing computational methods and techniques to extract insights from data, allowing for a deeper understanding of the sentiment expressed by individuals. Today's online social media platforms provide individuals with the opportunity to freely express their opinions and thoughts on various subjects from personal matters to social issues, political viewpoints, and even commercial interests. Twitter, as a globally renowned social network, serves as a prominent platform for disseminating information, accumulating vast volumes of data from millions of users on a daily basis. On Twitter, communication overcomes the limitations imposed by age, gender, politics, culture, and any other societal barriers [3]. Considerable progress has been made in SA, but challenges persist, particularly in low-resource languages such as the Persian language. To our knowledge, previous datasets of the Persian language in SA primarily concentrate on analyzing sentiments expressed in product reviews [4–6] and movie critiques [7,8]. However, there is an ongoing need for extensive research that addresses sentiment analysis in the Persian language, encompassing diverse domains and text types. On August 15, 2021, the fall of Afghanistan Republic Government and the subsequent rise of the Taliban regime sparked global shock and swift reactions. People around the world, including politicians, citizens of Afghanistan, and organizations, expressed their sentiments and concerns on social media platforms. Street protests were initiated against the Taliban, prompting the regime to respond with repressive actions, including the apprehension of protesters. Hence, these digital deliberations functioned as a dynamic platform fostering solidarity, offering support, and magnifying the resonance of the collective voice. The widespread use of social media highlights its influential role in shaping public opinion during significant political transitions. This paper presents the "SentiDariPers" dataset, a sentiment-annotated Twitter corpus in Dari-Persian. Our corpus is specifically curated by collecting and analyzing tweets related to the top trending hashtags in Afghanistan, focusing on topics related to Education, Women, Politics, and Social Justice, spanning from August 2021 to April 2023. Our primary objective is to delve into individuals' real-time perspectives, attitudes, concerns, and reactions in light of the prevailing circumstances. To ensure the corpus's quality and effectiveness, we conducted manual annotation using a specific set of guidelines, categorizing the tweets into Negative, Positive, Neutral, and Mixed classes. This annotation process provides a comprehensive understanding of the sentiment expressed in each tweet, allowing for detailed sentiment analysis and further exploration of sentiment-related patterns. By introducing "SentiDariPers" dataset, we aim to contribute to sentiment analysis in Dari-Persian, offering researchers a valuable resource to analyze and understand public sentiment across various domains.

This corpus enables researchers to gain insights into the nuanced expressions of people's opinions, facilitating a deeper understanding of the social landscape and promoting informed decision-making.

In this paper, Sect. 2 provides an overview of related work, with a specific focus on previous research conducted in the field of Persian language sentiment analysis. In Sect. 3, we describe the process of creating the "SentiDariPers" dataset, including the underlying motivations, data collection methods, annotation procedures, and pertinent statistics. Section 4 delves into the methodology used for the experimental evaluations, while Sect. 5 presents the experiment and results evaluating various model architectures, as well as an error analysis on "SentiDariPers" dataset. Finally, in Sect. 6, we conclude the paper and outline potential avenues for future research.

2   Related Work

SA in Persian language holds significant promise, but it encounters notable limitations when it comes to the specific demands of the Dari-Persian dialect. The challenges manifest in inadequate performance across diverse domains, limited availability of labeled data impacting the accuracy of sentiment analysis models, and complexities associated with processing intricate sentence structures. Dashtipour et al., [9] propose a hybrid framework for concept-level sentiment analysis, leveraging linguistic rules and deep learning with symbolic dependency relations and DNNs, outperforming state-of-the-art approaches and DNN classifiers. Bokaee Nezhad et al., [10] presents a novel approach that combines Convolutional Neural Networks (CNN) and LSTM for sentiment analysis in Persian social media, achieving an impressive accuracy rate of 85%. Dashtipour et al., [11] propose a hybrid framework integrating dependency-based rules and deep neural networks to enhance precision and robustness in polarity detection for Persian SA. Sharami et al., [4] focus on extracting opinions from Persian sentence-level text, presenting novel deep learning architectures (Bi-LSTM and CNN) along with data augmentation techniques for low-resource Persian sentiment analysis, demonstrating successful results. Farahani et al., [12] introduce ParsBERT, a monolingual BERT model specifically designed for Persian, outperforming other architectures and multilingual models across various NLP tasks, including SA. Nazarizadeh et al., [13] conducted a recent review on sentiment analysis in Persian, analyzing articles published between 2018 and 2022. Their evaluation of 40 articles highlighted the remarkable performance of Transformer models like BERT, as well as Recurrent Neural Networks (RNN) such as Long Short-Term Memory (LSTM) and Bidirectional Long Short-Term Memory (Bi-LSTM) in sentiment analysis. Dehghani et al., [14] conduct a study on sentiment analysis of Persian political tweets, employing various encoding methods, machine learning techniques (SVM and Random Forest), and a deep learning model (CNN+BiLSTM) with ParsBERT embeddings. They find that the CNN+BiLSTM model with ParsBERT achieves the highest robustness, with accuracy scores of 89% and 71% on respective datasets.

Moreover, existing Persian datasets suffer from significant noise [15], leading to a scarcity of properly labeled datasets across Persian language studies, including sentiment analysis and other NLP tasks [16–18]. Another challenge arises from the skewed distribution of positive polarity data compared to negative in most Persian datasets, such as Taaghche [19], Digikala [20], and SentiPers [21]. However, exceptions exist, such as the Pars-ABSA dataset consisting of 10,000 user comments from social media, comprising 5,114 negative comments, 3,061 positive comments, and 1,827 neutral comments. Heidari et al. [22], generated a Persian dataset named "Insta-text," which consists of 8,512 user comments. These comments were categorized into 2,780 positive, 3,237 negative, and 2,495 neutral sentiments.

In our research, there has been a lack of dedicated research focused on sentiment analysis in Dari-Persian text. Furthermore, the disparity between the Dari-Persian dialect and the Persian-Iranian language has resulted in existing datasets falling short of fully meeting the requirements for research in this field. Additionally, there is currently no available database capable of effectively analyzing the perspectives of the Afghanistan people. Bearing these considerations in mind, we have taken the initiative to create a new dataset sourced from the Twitter social network.

3   Resource Creation

Our data collection revolves around the Twitter social network, serving as our main source. To ensure focused and relevant data, we used specific hashtags aligned with our data collection criteria. It is important to note that these data were solely gathered for scientific research purposes, with the aim of capturing the perspectives and opinions of the people residing in Afghanistan. The intention behind this data collection is strictly non-political. The subsequent sections provide a comprehensive account of our data collection process, highlighting its intricacies and specifics. Sentiment annotation refers to the act of labeling text to indicate the sentiment expressed within it. In this study, we suggest a four-category sentiment classification system consisting of Positive, Negative, Neutral, and Mixed Labels. To the best of our knowledge, there has not been any research in Dari-Persian that has utilized four labels, although there are corpora in other languages such as Arabic available that have been annotated with these labels [23]. All data will be made available.[1]

3.1   Demand and Importance

Extensive studies on sentiment analysis suggest a strong need for the development of a comprehensive dataset that specifically targets the extraction and analysis of viewpoints and opinions expressed by Dari-Persian language speakers in Afghanistan. Persian (Farsi), an Indo-European language, is widely used by

---

[1] https://github.com/ltgoslo/SentiDariPers.git;.

over 110 million people, including Dari-Persian in Afghanistan, Farsi in Iran, and Tajiki in Tajikistan [20, 24]. Additionally, Persian garners some audiences in other regions, including the Middle East, Central and South Asia. In Iran and Afghanistan, specifically, Persian is predominantly used in verbal and written communication, employing a consistent alphabet and grammatical structure in everyday conversations. However, notable differences can be observed in terms of varying degrees of literacy, colloquial expressions commonly employed in social media interactions, spelling variations, as well as the impact of regional dialects and diverse cultural practices. So far, all existing datasets have primarily been generated in Iranian Persian [14], which indicates a serious gap in addressing the specific requirements of Dari-Persian language research. It serves as a means to assess the extent of these differences and their impact on various aspects.

3.2   Data Collection

The SentiDariPers dataset was meticulously curated by utilizing the Twitter API, employing the Tweepy library in conjunction with Python programming. This approach allowed us to collect comprehensive and reliable data from sources on the Twitter platform. The collection of tweets was performed by targeting top trending hashtags that were utilized by Twitter users across various subjects such as women's rights, social justice, and education. Table 1 shows the relevant hashtag with its categories, the included tweets were all posted from August 15, 2021 up to April 01, 2023. The search was conducted from April, 2023 up to April 20, 2023 and using the mentioned hashtags, a total of approximately 3.5 million tweets were collected for our study. After removing duplicated tweets, the data was reduced to 2,166,535 unique tweets. From this data, a random sample of 50,000 tweets was selected for manual labeling.

Table 1. Top trending hashtag and relevant categories

Category	Hashtag
Education	LetHerLearn, AllorNone, LetAfghanistanGirlLearn
Women	Afghanwomen, WomenRights, LetHerWork
Social Justice	StopHazaraGenocide, FreeAfghanistan, UnitedAfghanistan
Politics	BanTaliban, FreeAfghanistan, StandWithNRF
Security and Terrorism	Taliban_are_terrorist, Peace, DoNotRecognizeTaliban

3.3   Data Filtering

We subsequently applied filtering on the collected tweets to transform the raw data into a usable format. The following conditions were applied as filters during this process:

- Removal of duplicate tweets: We eliminated duplicate tweets to ensure the uniqueness of the dataset.

- URLs and Links removal: Tweets often contain URLs and Links, which were removed to focus solely on the textual content.
- Elimination of Hashtags Mentions: Hashtags and Mentions were removed from the tweets as they do not contribute to the overall textual analysis.
- Exclusion of Mentions: Mentions were excluded from the tweets, as they do not provide meaningful contributions to the comprehensive textual analysis.
- Removal of HTML tags: HTML tags are often present in tweets and are used for formatting or embedding media content
- Filtering tweets with fewer than 5 words: To ensure the inclusion of substantial content, tweets with less than 5 words were removed from the dataset.
- Elimination of tweets written as individual letters: Some tweets consist of individual letters or fragmented text, which were deemed irrelevant and therefore excluded.

By applying these filters, we obtained a refined dataset that contains usable tweets for further analysis and modeling.

3.4   Annotation Procedure

While precise and complex annotation guidelines can have unintended consequences, such as annotators struggling to understand or follow them, some of these challenges can be addressed by providing guidelines to annotators at different levels. The process of annotating the text has been carried out meticulously by a skilled team of three experts in Dari-Persian language and literature, each with extensive expertise in understanding the true meaning of textual content. The annotation method used is based on the approach proposed by Mohammad et al. [25] for sentiment analysis. This approach has allowed us to categorize the texts into four distinct categories, making the annotation process easier based on their underlying meanings.

To ensure accurate annotation of the texts, a carefully designed set of guidelines have been developed and shared with the annotators. This comprehensive procedure, available in both Dari-Persian and English translations, serves as a guide for annotators to accurately carry out the annotation process. The first category includes texts that express negative sentiment and are labeled as -1. Conversely, the second category consists of texts that evoke positive sentiment and are labeled as $+1$. The third category focuses on texts that exhibit Mixed sentiment, where both negative and positive elements coexist, and they are assigned label 2. Lastly, the fourth category identifies texts characterized by a clear and unambiguous sentiment, whether negative, positive, or a distinct combination, and is denoted by the label 0, indicating neutrality. Tweets in languages other than Dari-Persian, such as English, Arabic, Pashto, and Uzbek, were excluded by our annotators to maintain consistency in the dataset. Here are some important points to consider during the annotation process:

- Prayers: Annotating prayers is challenging due to their mix of positive and negative words, making it unclear if they convey sentiment. Most prayers were labeled as neutral.

- Advice, guidance, recommendations, or suggestions: Determining sentiment in such tweets was difficult, resulting in most being labeled as neutral, with occasional positive labels.
- Quotations: Annotating quotations was tricky as they often lacked explicit emotional content, leading to neutral categorization, despite potential positivity or negativity.
- Rhetorical questions: Annotating tweets with rhetorical questions was challenging, as annotators had to consider them impartially, occasionally labeling them as positive or negative based on perceived sentiment.
- Author's perspective: Analyzing the author's perspective required careful consideration of various factors, making it challenging when the author was unknown. Annotators were advised to analyze content, tone, language use, and rhetorical devices for insights into the expressed perspective.
- Determining tweet topics: The informal and concise language on Twitter, along with the absence of hashtags during preprocessing, made it difficult to determine tweet topics. To overcome this challenge, annotators rely on contextual comprehension by analyzing the surrounding text and pertinent cues within the tweet.

The annotators proposed categorizing tweets based on relevant subjects to facilitate the annotation process. However, they acknowledged challenges when dealing with tweets that covered multiple topics or lacked explicit references. To ensure accurate categorization, they recommended the use of consistent criteria. Table 2 is a sample of tweets (with English translations) from the SentiDariPers dataset to further illustrate the annotation effort.

Table 2. SentiDariPers example tweets with sentiment label

Tweet	Translated Tweet	Label
دختران قهرمان قهرمانان واقعی که در کنار کار و پیدا کردن مخارج روزانه دوشادوش مردان شان در مسیر روشنایی و دانایی نیز تلاش میکنند.	Girls are the true champions who, alongside work and earning a living, strive hand in hand with their men on the path of enlightenment and knowledge.	Positive (+1)
از شوک برقی تا تجاوز جنسی روایتی از زندانهای طالبان در بلخ	From electric shocks to sexual assault, an account of Taliban prisons in Balkh.	Negative (−1)
صدای نو جوانان باشیم که دشمنان دانایی به خاک و خون کشاند هم وطن همراه شو	Let us be the voice of the youth dragged to the ground and shed blood by the enemies of knowledge. Countrymen join.	Mixed (2)
برای تماشای ویدیو ها کامل روی لینک زیر کلیک کنید	To watch the full videos, click on the link below.	Neutral (0)

3.5   Quality Test

We ensured the quality of SentiDariPers dataset by implementing a thorough annotation process carried out by three Dari native speakers with good knowledge and understanding of Dari grammar. To assess the consistency among the annotators, we utilized Cohen's kappa coefficient [26], a commonly used statistical measure for evaluating inter-rater reliability. This coefficient quantifies the degree of agreement between the evaluators and is calculated using the following formula:

$$\kappa = \frac{P_o - P_e}{1 - P_e}$$

where:

- The symbol κ represents the Cohen's kappa coefficient,
- The term "P_o" represents the observed agreement among the annotators, while
- "P_e" denotes the expected agreement by chance.

To evaluate the accuracy and measure the level of agreement among annotators, the calculation of Cohen's kappa coefficient yielded a value of 0.70, with a confidence level of 89%, indicating a substantial level of agreement resulting from a majority consensus among the annotators. This coefficient serves as a valuable metric for assessing the reliability and consistency of annotations within the dataset.

3.6   Dataset Statistics

After excluding tweets in Pashto, Uzbek, Arabic, or those that were incomplete, the SentiDariPers dataset size was reduced. The final dataset utilized in this research comprised 43,089, containing a total of 870,609 words, with 41,513 unique word. On average, each tweet consisted of approximately 20.20 words. Figure 1 illustrates the distribution of tweets across various sentiment classes, with the negative class having the highest frequency, followed by the neutral class, and a slightly lower count in the positive class. The Mixed sentiment class

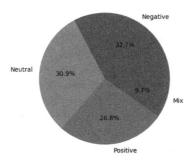

Fig. 1. Number of tweets for each sentiment class in SentiDariPers

exhibits the most notable minimal occurrence. While it has been observed in certain studies that the weaker class is often excluded due to its lack of alignment with the other classes, our approach in this research aimed to maintain the integrity of the truth by retaining all classes without exclusion.

Further examining the content of the dataset, we observe that certain words appear in all four sentiment classes, such as "Afghanistan", "toward", "Taliban", "people", "country", "freedom", "resistance", "Women". Table 3 displays the distribution of the most frequently repeated words found in the SentiDariPers dataset. Furthermore, we provide an overview of the word count for each class in the dataset. Given that Twitter allows a maximum of 280 characters per tweet [27], the average length of the tweets is relatively short. Table 4 displays the frequency of word occurrences and the count of unique words for each class within SentiDariPers dataset.

Table 3. Frequent words in each class of SentiDariPers

Class	Words
Negative	'Genocide', 'Attack', 'War', 'Murdered', 'Generation', 'Afghan', 'Terrorist'
Positive	'Greeting', 'Unity', 'Honour', 'Justice', 'Hazara', 'Champion', 'Home Land'
Neutral	'Hashtag', 'Announce', 'Pakistan', 'Islamic', 'Ministry', 'Organization'
Mixed	'Panjshir', 'Right', 'Hope', 'Iran', 'National', 'Viva', 'Combat'

Table 4. Number of opinion words, unique opinion, and average length

	Polarity			
	Negative	Positive	Neutral	Mixed
Opinion words	300618	160654	278826	130511
Unique words	22151	14996	21621	15104
Average Length	21.35	13.92	20.97	31.19

4 Methodology

In this section, we provide an overview of the algorithms employed for sentiment analysis using the SentiDariPers dataset. Deep learning algorithms have gained significant popularity in sentiment analysis owing to their exceptional accuracy and superior performance. To ensure comprehensive analysis and accurate results, we combined multiple deep learning models including LSTM, Bi-LSTM, and GRU. In addition to these deep learning algorithms, we also tested machine learning algorithms and neural network algorithms. This comprehensive approach allows us to compare and select the most accurate algorithm for our specific task. By combining various techniques, we aim to achieve robust and reliable sentiment analysis results.

4.1   Word Embedding

Word embeddings are used to convert information from textual to numeric representation. This method is used to prepare input data for machine learning, deep learning, and neural network algorithms. In our research, we used FastText [28] word embedding which is a modified version of Word2Vec and is broadly used for large-volume datasets.

4.2   Support Vector Machine (SVM)

SVM [29] is a popular machine learning algorithm that has been widely used for text classification tasks and it utilizes a kernel function to map the text data into higher dimensional spaces and finds an optimal hyperplane to separate different sentiment categories. In our study, we aim to evaluate the performance of SVM with a linear kernel by comparing it to neural network models. To facilitate the utilization of this algorithm, we employed the widely recognized Python library called Scikit Learn.

4.3   Neural Network Models

Next, we implement several neural network-based models for the automatic detection of sentiment. In recent years deep learning has found numerous applications in the field of NLP [30] and they do not require any manual feature extraction or human intervention [31], making them a cost-effective and efficient solution. We explore the following architectures:

- Long Short-Term Memory (LSTM)
- Bidirectional Long Short-Term Memory (Bi-LSTM)
- Gated Recurrent Unit (GRU)
- Convolutional Neural Network (CNN)

LSTM: LSTM models are widely used due to their ability to capture and retain long-term dependencies in input data, effectively addressing the vanishing gradient problems. It has three gates (input gate, forgot gate and output gate), these gates allow the model's capability to selectively retain and utilize relevant information from previous steps [32].

Bi-LSTM: The Bi-LSTM model is a sequential model that incorporates both forward and backward information and makes decisions about the present state. Unlike LSTM and GRU [33], BiLSTM does not incorporate an explicit cell state or memory. However, they effectively address the vanishing gradient problem and capture long-term dependencies through their gating mechanism.

GRU: GRU uses two gates (update and reset gate) to regulate the flow of information and determine what information should be retained or forgotten. This gating mechanism makes the GRU model simpler and faster internally compared to the LSTM and Bi-LSTM models.

CNN: The CNN model relies on two operations (convolution and pooling), the convolution operation applies a filter to the input data, producing features maps and pooling reduces the dimensionality of the feature maps. CNN is widely used due to its ability to effectively extract features from text.

4.4   Ensemble Model

In order to tackle challenges like high variance, low accuracy, feature noise, and bias in sentiment analysis, we implemented an effective approach. After generating predicted probabilities from the LSTM, Bi-LSTM, and GRU models, we leveraged the Scikit-learn library's Voting Classifier [34] to create a more precise and robust prediction. By combining the outputs of multiple models, the ensemble approach aims to mitigate individual model limitations and enhance overall performance. This ensemble model allows us to make more accurate and reliable predictions, overcoming the shortcomings of individual models and increasing the overall quality of our sentiment analysis results.

5   Experimental Results and Analysis

5.1   Experimental Setting

Dataset: During our experimental phase, we carefully partitioned our curated dataset into three subsets: the train set, validation set, and test set, adhering to an 80:10:10 ratio. This partitioning ensured that each subset captured a representative sample of the data, enabling us to evaluate and validate our sentiment analysis models effectively. To provide a comprehensive understanding of the dataset's sentiment distribution across the subsets, we present detailed information in Table 5.

Table 5. Data distribution for experiments

Type	Training	Validation	Test
Negative	11306	1385	1381
Positive	9217	1169	1146
Neutral	10626	1319	1354
Mixed	3322	436	428
Total	34471	4309	4309

Implementation: We used the Scikit-learn libraries for the implementation of SVM algorithm with hyperparameter of RBF kernel, gamma = 0.5, C = 1, and a loss function of Hinge Loss. All our neural models made use of FastText [28] pre-trained word embeddings with 300 dimensions for the Persian language. We developed LSTM, Bi-LSTM and GRU models with 128 neurons, dropout, and recurrent dropout rates of 0.2 and followed by another LSTM, Bi-LSTM, GRU layer respectively with 64 neurons and the same dropout rates added. Further another layer of each model is added with 32 neurons with the same dropout rates as mentioned. Our proposed CNN model architecture consists of multiple Conv1D layers with varying kernel sizes and filters. The input is passed through an embedding layer with the mentioned pre-trained word embeddings. MaxPooling1D is applied to reduce the dimensionality, followed by flattening output, and dropout regularization with a rate of 0.2 is applied to prevent over-fitting. The final dense layer has four units with softmax activation function, representing the four sentiment classes and the model is compiled with categorical cross-entropy loss, Adam optimizer with $\beta 1 = 0.9$, $\beta 2 = 0.999$, and learning rate of 0.001. The proposed ensemble classifier combines the result of the individual (LSTM, Bi-LSTM, and GRU) models, using the voting='hard' parameter, which means that the majority vote among the neutral models is used to make the final prediction. In the proposed ensemble classifier, we used kernel = rbf, C = 1, and gamma = 'scale' hyperparameter.

5.2   Results

The evaluation results of our experiments are presented in Table 6, which shows the performance of the various models discussed above. The findings clearly demonstrate that the ensemble model outperforms better than the SVM, LSTM, Bi-LSTM, GRU, and CNN models.

Table 6. Results of individual and ensemble models

Model	Precision	Accuracy	Recall	F1_Score
SVM	0.88	0.90	0.86	0.87
LSTM	0.88	0.90	0.87	0.88
Bi-LSTM	0.87	0.88	0.86	0.86
GRU	0.87	0.88	0.85	0.86
CNN	0.84	0.85	0.83	0.84
Ensemble	**0.90**	**0.91**	**0.89**	**0.90**

Table 7 illustrates the diversity of scores observed among the different sentiment classes. The negative, positive and neutral classes exhibit the highest scores, indicating their successful identification. Conversely, the mixed class pose a greater difficulty, as they yield comparatively lower scores.

Table 7. Individual class performance using Ensemble model

Class	Precision	Recall	F1_Score
Negative	**0.92**	0.91	0.92
Positive	0.90	0.91	0.91
Neutral	0.91	**0.94**	**0.93**
Mixed	0.86	0.79	0.82
Macro Average	0.90	0.89	0.90

5.3   Detailed Analysis and Errors

We initiated an in-depth error analysis on the outcomes generated by our top-performing model. The objective was to delve deeper into the classification decisions rendered on the SentiDariPers dataset. In Fig. 2, a visualization in the form of a confusion matrix heatmap has been presented, effectively capturing the intricate dynamics among the various classes. Of particular note is a recurring pattern wherein instances from the Mixed class are frequently misclassified, either as negative or positive sentiments, as highlighted by the discerning insights afforded by the confusion matrix.

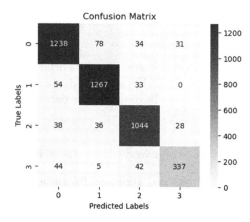

Fig. 2. Confusion matrix heat map

Furthermore, Table 8 provides a curated selection of instances where misclassifications have occurred, serving to exemplify the nature of these discrepancies.

As we traverse through the nuances of our analysis concerning these misclassified predictions, several discernible patterns emerge, and we will elucidate

Table 8. Examples of misclassified tweet

Tweet	True Label	Predicted Label
مهتاب که بی هیچ منتی روشنایی میبخشد	+ 1	0
The moon that shines without any debt		
با اینکه پس از مسلط شدن گروه طالبان در افغانستان دختران دوره متوسطه و لیسه اجازه حضور در مکاتب را به دست	2	- 1
نیاوردند اما هنوز هم شماری از دانش آموزان دختر در بخش هایی ازکشور درس می خوانند و به آینده امیدوار استند		
Although after the Taliban took control of Afghanistan, girls were not allowed to attend middle		
and high schools, but still some female students in some parts of the country are studying		
and they are hopeful for the future.		
فلک را عادت دیرینه این است که با آزادگان دایم به کین است	- 1	+ 1
The ancient habit of the heavens is to be in constant conflict with the free-spirited		
شنیده بودم پشت هر تاریکی روشنی است اما دیدم که پشت هر روشنی هم تاریکی ست	2	+ 1
I had heard that behind every darkness there is light, but i saw that behind every		
light there is also darkness		

these reasons in the subsequent discussion. Additionally, we confront the challenge posed by the negation problem, a critical facet in sentiment analysis, which we will also address comprehensively.

Mixed Class Challenges and Insights: One of the challenges we encounter in analyzing Dari's tweets is the presence of sentences that contain both positive and negative sentiments. Previous research in Persian text analysis has focused on three main classifications: positive, negative, and neutral. However, our research takes into account an additional category called "Mixed" which represents sentences that do not strictly place into the positive or negative categories but interfere with both classes. For example, the sentence میان استخوان هایمان خورد شده ایم اما امید تقلا می کند بر ای روییدن (equivalent to English "We are crushed between our bones but hope struggles to grow") in this sentence, the first part expresses a negative sentiment, while the second part conveys a positive sentiment. These types of tweets pose difficulty in accurate classification as positive, negative, or neutral. Classification of such sentences is challenging, as even our annotators sometimes make mistakes. Moreover, algorithms tend to struggle more than humans in recognizing these nuanced texts, often assigning positive or negative labels inconsistently. One of the appropriate approaches is to utilize a sentiment dictionary containing positive and negative words. This would enable researchers to improve the accuracy of sentiment analysis algorithms and enhance our understanding of these complex linguistic expressions. However, it should be noted that currently, there is no such dictionary available to use.

Negation Problem: One of the other challenges we encounter is the presence of negation words that significantly alter the polarity of a sentence. For instance, the word "نیست" (equivalent to "is not" in english) or "آزاد" (meaning "freedom" in english), which changes from a positive to a negative connotation. Effectively managing this issue requires careful consideration and various solutions. One of the approaches to address this challenge is pre-processing [15], where negation words are identified and replaced with their corresponding opposite words in relation to the closest word. Alternatively, utilizing neural network algorithms presents a viable solution, as they possess the ability to memorize previous information. In this regard, we have employed LSTM algorithm [15] to tackle the negation problem.

5.4 Discussion

Upon acquiring the SentiDariPers dataset, a comprehensive analysis was conducted on an additional 2,166,535 tweets, which were annotated using the aforementioned dataset. These tweets were amassed during the time span from August 15, 2021, to April 2023, with the explicit objective of probing into the prevailing sentiments voiced by the Afghan populace. Our examination of these tweets was undertaken to glean deeper insights into the diverse array of opinions and emotions expressed. The outcome of this scrutiny unveiled a prominent predominance of negative sentiments, overshadowing other sentiments, followed in relative frequency by instances of neutral expressions, with mixed sentiments being comparatively infrequent. The graphical representation provided in Fig. 3 adeptly portrays the dispersion of data across these distinct poles, thereby succinctly encapsulating this distribution. Furthermore, our exploration encompassed a temporal dimension, leading to the revelation that the month of April 2022 emerged as a notable period characterized by heightened sentiment expression.

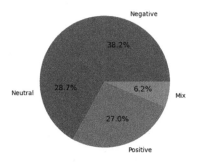

Fig. 3. Tweets distribution into different sentiment classes

Subsequently, our analysis revealed that the month of April, 2022 exhibited the highest proportion of negative tweets (67%), followed by August, 2021 (58%), October, 2022 (55%), and closely followed by August, 2022 (54%). Likewise, our findings indicate that the month of October, 2022 recorded the highest percentage of positive tweets (29%), closely followed by November, 2022 (26%), and March, 2023 (25%). Figure 4 shows the number of tweets with respect to the dates. We noted a significant fluctuation in the number of tweets collected during the month of October. To ensure a more proportional representation and improve visualization, a logarithmic transformation was applied to all the values presented in the graph that recorded the highest percentage of posted tweets.

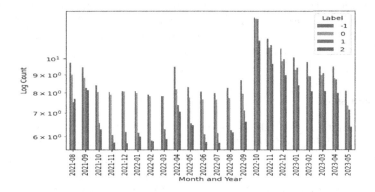

Fig. 4. Number of tweets and sentiment classes based on dates

Women: The findings from the analysis of the data, collected specifically from Afghan women (Afghanwomen, WomenRights, LetHerWork), indicate that 46% of the tweets expressed a negative sentiment, 23% of the tweets were classified as neutral sentiment, while 20% exhibited a positive sentiment. The remaining tweets fell into the Mixed sentiment class. Figure 5 represents the distribution of different sentiment classes, with a total number of 9815 tweets.

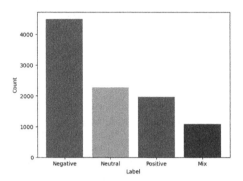

Fig. 5. Sentiment distribution classes based on women category

Education: Next, we conducted an analysis of the tweets posted regarding the ban on education for girls and women (LetHerLearn, LetAfghanistanGirlLearn, AllorNone, LetAfghanGirlLearn) between December, 2022 and April, 2023. The results are presented in Fig. 6, which illustrates the percentage distribution of different sentiments expressed in the tweets.

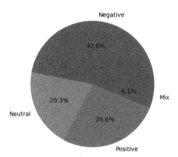

Fig. 6. Sentiment classes percentage based on ban-education category

6   Conclusion

In this research, our main objective was to curate a comprehensive dataset encompassing people's opinions in the Dari-Persian dialect. Through meticulous data collection efforts on Twitter, we amassed a sizable corpus that was annotated according to our developed annotation guidelines. The SentiDariPers dataset comprises 870,609 words including 300,618 Negative, 160,654 Positive, 278826 Neutral, and 130511 Mixed words, with 41,513 distinct instances in total. We have categorized sentiment analysis into four distinct categories: Negative, Positive, Neutral, and Mixed. To ensure the dataset's quality, we implemented a supervised ensemble model incorporating deep learning algorithms such as LSTM, Bi-LSTM, and GRU, achieving an accuracy of **91%**. This dataset serves as a valuable resource for sentiment analysis and facilitates further research in the realm of Dari-Persian language analysis. Moving forward, our future work aims to address challenges related to handling the Mixed class (a combination of positive and negative sentiments) and negations.

References

1. Pang, B., Lee, L.: Opinion mining and sentiment analysis. Found. Trends® Inf. Retrieval **2**(1–2), 1–135 (2008). https://doi.org/10.1561%2F1500000011
2. Pang, B., Lee, L., Vaithyanathan, S.: Thumbs up? In: Proceedings of the ACL-02 Conference on Empirical Methods in Natural Language Processing - EMNLP 2002 (2002). https://doi.org/10.3115%2F1118693.1118704
3. Ghosh, S., et al.: Annotated corpus of tweets in English from various domains for emotion detection. In: Proceedings of the 17th International Conference on Natural Language Processing (ICON), pp. 460–469 (2020)
4. Sharami, J.P.R., Sarabestani, P.A., Mirroshandel, S.A.: DeepSentiPers: novel deep learning models trained over proposed augmented Persian sentiment corpus (2020). https://doi.org/10.48550/arXiv.2004.05328
5. Ghahfarrokhi, A.H., Shamsfard, M.: Tehran stock exchange prediction using sentiment analysis of online textual opinions. Intell. Syst. Account. Finance Manage. **27**(1), 22–37 (2020). https://doi.org/10.1002%2Fisaf.1465
6. Shirghasemi, M., Bokaei, M.H., Bijankhan, M.: The impact of active learning algorithm on a cross-lingual model in a Persian sentiment task. In: 2021 7th International Conference on Web Research (ICWR), May 2021. https://doi.org/10.1109%2Ficwr51868.2021.9443156
7. Dehkharghani, R., Emami, H.: A novel approach to sentiment analysis in Persian using discourse and external semantic information (2020). https://doi.org/10.48550/arXiv.2007.09495
8. Dehkharghani, R.: SentiFars. ACM Trans. Asian Low-Resource Lang. Inf. Process. **19**(2), 1–12 (2019). https://doi.org/10.1145/3345627
9. Dashtipour, K., Gogate, M., Adeel, A., Ieracitano, C., Larijani, H., Hussain, A.: Exploiting deep learning for Persian sentiment analysis. In: Advances in Brain Inspired Cognitive Systems, pp. 597–604 (2018). https://doi.org/10.1007%2F978-3-030-00563-4_58
10. Nezhad, Z.B., Deihimi, M.A.: A combined deep learning model for Persian sentiment analysis. IIUM Eng. J. **20**(1), 129–139 (2019). https://doi.org/10.31436/iiumej.v20i1.1036
11. Dashtipour, K., Gogate, M., Li, J., Jiang, F., Kong, B., Hussain, A.: A hybrid Persian sentiment analysis framework: integrating dependency grammar based rules and deep neural networks. Neurocomputing **380**, 1–10 (2020). https://doi.org/10.1016%2Fj.neucom.2019.10.009

12. Farahani, M., Gharachorloo, M., Farahani, M., Manthouri, M.: ParsBERT: transformer-based model for Persian language understanding. Neural Process. Lett. **53**(6), 3831–3847 (2021). https://doi.org/10.1007%2Fs11063-021-10528-4

13. Nazarizadeh, A., Banirostam, T., Sayyadpour, M.: Sentiment analysis of Persian language: review of algorithms, approaches and datasets. arXiv preprint arXiv:2212.06041 (2022). https://doi.org/10.48550/arXiv.2212.06041

14. Dehghani, M., Yazdanparast, Z.: Sentiment analysis of Persian political tweets using ParsBERT embedding model with convolutional neural network. In: 2023 9th International Conference on Web Research (ICWR), May 2023. https://doi.org/10.1109%2Ficwr57742.2023.10139063

15. Davar, O., Dar, G., Ghasemian, F.: DeepSentiParsBERT: a deep learning model for Persian sentiment analysis using ParsBERT. In: 2023 28th International Computer Conference, Computer Society of Iran (CSICC), January 2023. https://doi.org/10.1109/csicc58665.2023.10105414

16. Ghayoomi, M.: Word clustering for Persian statistical parsing. In: Isahara, H., Kanzaki, K. (eds.) JapTAL 2012. LNCS (LNAI), vol. 7614, pp. 126–137. Springer, Heidelberg (2012). https://doi.org/10.1007/978-3-642-33983-7_13

17. Dashtipour, K., Gogate, M., Adeel, A., Algarafi, A., Howard, N., Hussain, A.: Persian named entity recognition. In: 2017 IEEE 16th International Conference on Cognitive Informatics & Cognitive Computing (ICCI* CC), pp. 79–83 (2017). https://doi.org/10.1109/ICCI-CC.2017.8109733

18. Dashtipour, K., Gogate, M., Adeel, A., Hussain, A., Alqarafi, A., Durrani, T.: A comparative study of Persian sentiment analysis based on different feature combinations. In: Liang, Q., Mu, J., Jia, M., Wang, W., Feng, X., Zhang, B. (eds.) CSPS 2017. LNEE, vol. 463, pp. 2288–2294. Springer, Singapore (2019). https://doi.org/10.1007/978-981-10-6571-2_279

19. Karrabi, M., Oskooie, L., Bakhtiar, M., Farahani, M., Monsefi, R.: Sentiment analysis of informal Persian texts using embedding informal words and attention-based LSTM network. In: 2020 8th Iranian Joint Congress on Fuzzy and intelligent Systems (CFIS), September 2020. https://doi.org/10.1109%2Fcfis49607.2020.9238699

20. Ataei, T.S., Darvishi, K., Javdan, S., Minaei-Bidgoli, B., Eetemadi, S.: ParsABSA: an aspect-based sentiment analysis dataset for Persian. arXiv preprint arXiv:1908.01815 (2019). https://doi.org/10.48550/arXiv.1908.01815

21. Hosseini, P., Ramaki, A.A., Maleki, H., Anvari, M., Mirroshandel, S.A.: SentiPers: a sentiment analysis corpus for Persian. arXiv preprint arXiv:1801.07737 (2018). https://doi.org/10.48550/arXiv.1801.07737

22. Heidari, M., Shamsinejad, P.: Producing an Instagram dataset for Persian language sentiment analysis using crowdsourcing method. In: 2020 6th International Conference on Web Research (ICWR), April 2020. https://doi.org/10.1109/icwr49608.2020.9122270

23. Al-Twairesh, N., Al-Khalifa, H., Al-Salman, A., Al-Ohali, Y.: AraSenTi-tweet: a corpus for Arabic sentiment analysis of Saudi tweets. Procedia Comput. Sci. **117**, 63–72 (2017). https://doi.org/10.1016%2Fj.procs.2017.10.094

24. persian, farsi, dari, tajiki: language names and language policies. In: Language Policy and Language Conflict in Afghanistan and Its Neighbors, pp. 89–117. BRILL, January 2012. https://doi.org/10.1163/9789004217652_005

25. Mohammad, S.M., Zhu, X.: Sentiment analysis of social media texts. In: Tutorial at the 2014 Conference on Empirical Methods on Natural Language Processing (2014)

26. Cohen, J.: A coefficient of agreement for nominal scales. Educ. Psychol. Measur. **20**(1), 37–46 (1960). https://doi.org/10.1177/001316446002000104

27. Gligorić, K., Anderson, A., West, R.: How constraints affect content: the case of twitter's switch from 140 to 280 characters. In: Proceedings of the International AAAI Conference on Web and Social Media, vol. 12, no. 1, June 2018. https://doi.org/10.1609%2Ficwsm.v12i1.15079
28. Grave, E., Bojanowski, P., Gupta, P., Joulin, A., Mikolov, T.: Learning word vectors for 157 languages. arXiv preprint arXiv:1802.06893 (2018). https://doi.org/10.48550/arXiv.1802.06893
29. Joachims, T.: Text categorization with support vector machines: learning with many relevant features. In: Machine Learning: ECML 1998, pp. 137–142 (1998). https://doi.org/10.1007%2Fbfb0026683
30. Collobert, R., Weston, J., Bottou, L., Karlen, M., Kavukcuoglu, K., Kuksa, P.: Natural language processing (almost) from scratch. J. Mach. Learn. Res. **12**, 2493–2537 (2011)
31. Vateekul, P., Koomsubha, T.: A study of sentiment analysis using deep learning techniques on Thai Twitter data. In: 2016 13th International Joint Conference on Computer Science and Software Engineering (JCSSE), July 2016. https://doi.org/10.1109%2Fjcsse.2016.7748849
32. Hochreiter, S., Schmidhuber, J.: Long short-term memory. Neural Comput **9**(8), 1735–1780 (1997). https://doi.org/10.1162%2Fneco.1997.9.8.1735
33. Bahdanau, D., Cho, K., Bengio, Y.: Neural machine translation by jointly learning to align and translate. arXiv preprint arXiv:1409.0473 (2014). https://doi.org/10.48550/arXiv.1409.0473
34. Leon, F., Floria, S.A., Badica, C.: Evaluating the effect of voting methods on ensemble-based classification. In: 2017 IEEE International Conference on INnovations in Intelligent SysTems and Applications (INISTA), July 2017. https://doi.org/10.1109%2Finista.2017.8001122

Reuse of Ontological Knowledge in Open Science: Models, Sources, Repositories

Julia Rogushina[1] 📵, Anatoly Gladun[2](✉) 📵, and Rafael Valencia-Garcia[3] 📵

[1] Institute of Software Systems of National Academy of Sciences of Ukraine, 40, Acad. Glushkov Avenue, Kyiv 03187, Ukraine

[2] International Research and Training Center of Information Technologies and Systems of National Academy of Sciences of Ukraine and Ministry of Education and Science of Ukraine, 40, Acad. Glushkov Avenue, Kyiv 03187, Ukraine

glanat@yahoo.com

[3] Facultad de Informática, Universidad de Murcia, Campus de Espinardo, 30100 Murcia, Spain

Abstract. Intelligent Web applications require regular updates of knowledge from the external open information space. Currently, a significant amount of knowledge oriented towards Web applications utilizes ontological representations that which facilitate interoperability and information reuse. Many existing ontologies are available in repositories as open information resources. While repositories of ontologies provide enhanced functionality for search and analysis, they often fail to meet user requirements. We propose to extend the definition of specific types of ontologies using a formal model of ontologies instead of relying solely on natural language definitions. By selecting these special cases based on the type of information resources used as ontology sources, we can identify ontologies with similar properties. Special cases of ontologies can be defined by applying various restrictions to the formal model elements, allowing simpler analysis methods. In this work, we propose definitions of taxonomy and catalog as an example of this approach. Furthermore, we perform a detailed analysis of the formal model of the Wiki ontology for both semantic and non-semantic sources.

Keywords: Ontology · Repository of ontologies · Interoperability · Semantic search · Information object · Metadata · Taxonomy · Catalog

1 Introduction

Nowadays, many web-oriented *Intelligent Information Systems* (IIS) require external knowledge sources and use ontologies that provide interoperability and reuse of information. Therefore, the retrieval of existing ontologies, their adaptation to user tasks and their reuse become important components of information processing and scientific research. They can be considered as sub-goals of Open Science, which aims at scientific reproducibility of results and reuse of knowledge.

We consider problems caused by complexity of ontology structure, different requirements on their expressiveness and heterogeneity of knowledge represented by existing

© The Author(s), under exclusive license to Springer Nature Switzerland AG 2023
R. Valencia-García et al. (Eds.): CITI 2023, CCIS 1873, pp. 157–172, 2023.
https://doi.org/10.1007/978-3-031-45682-4_12

ontologies. The main goal of this work deals with attempts to make processing of ontology metadata with user needs more semantic. Therefore, we analyze search parameters in existing ontology libraries and repositories, consider semantic properties of the Wiki open resources that can become sources of ontological content and define criteria of their matching.

2 Open Science and Ontologies

One of the important directions of Open Science is the scientific reproducibility of results and the reuse of knowledge. If these results are based on formal representation of knowledge (such as domain ontologies, taxonomies, etc.) than we need in tools for publishing, versioning and retrieval of such knowledge. This leads to the importance of developing ontology repositories and libraries with appropriate functionality. A significant part of this problem is related to metadata for ontology definition. We can use some elements of Open Science paradigm aimed at reuse of information resources. Such an approach should provide open access to scientific publications, open experimental data, open electronic educational resources, etc.

The paradigm of Open Science is the attempt of the world scientific community to solve the problem of scientific irreproducibility [1], which is defined as the inability to repeat experiments of other researchers and achieve the same result. One of the directions of EOSC development is to ensure the discovery, availability, interoperability, and reuse of digital objects that can contain both the results of experiments and the texts of scientific publications. A set of requirements for such data is denoted by the acronym FAIR (Findable, Accessible, Interoperable, Reusable). These requirements can be applied to ontologies as a special kind of *information resources* (IRs). The core principles of FAIR reflect such main aspects of data [2]:

1. *Findable*: in order to use data and to have access to it, it is necessary to find pertinent information among *information objects* (IOs). Therefore, FAIR has a number of requirements for metadata that describe IOs and for tools that support automated analysis of metadata.
2. *Accessible*: data and metadata can be retrieved by their identifier using a standardized open communication protocols.
3. *Interoperable*: data need in integration with other information and in interaction with applications or workflows for analysis, storage and processing, use generally accepted representation standards and reference to other data and metadata.
4. *Reusable*: data and metadata should be described with a set of precise and relevant attributes, have a clear and accessible license for use, and conform to community standards relevant to the domain

IRs that comply with the FAIR principles implement the various functions of searching, obtaining and representation data not by users but by the information system itself, and scientific research organizations and educational institutions, as well as individual researchers, are involved in the management of scientific data. The FAIR Guidelines do not require any specific technology to support FAIR principles and can be used by ontology processing infrastructure. According to FAIR, the functions of searching, obtaining and representation of data are not implemented by users, but by the information system. At the same time, FAIR considers not only about the data and metadata themselves, but also about algorithms and tools for their management.

3   Formal Model of Ontology

Formal models of ontologies used by researchers differ according to goals and domains of their development, but all of them contain some common elements. The formal model of ontology O is represented by the triple $O = <X, R, F>$, where.

– finite set of terms X (concepts and concept classes) that can be into two disjoint sets: a set of classes and a set of instances;
– finite set of relations between concepts R that can contain "class-subclass" relations, hierarchical (taxonomic) relations and synonymy (similarity) relations, etc.;
– domain axioms and rules for interpretation of concepts and relations F.

This model is very general, while in practice more precise models are used, in particular models related to ontology languages and dialects, ontology editors or sources of ontology content. They differ in their complexity, expressiveness and practical tasks. Many of them are based on Semantic Web technologies [3], in particular the OWL ontology representation language [4] and RDF [5].

4   Use of Ontologies in IIS

Most approaches to using ontologies consider searching the ontology in general, but in practice we can distinguish three most common situations:

– IIS uses a fixed external ontology (with fixed structure but dynamic content), and only a small subset of knowledge is obtained from it using queries based on the structure and terms of this ontology;
– IIS uses internal ontology with fixed properties and structure (one or more files in OWL or RDF) that are processed by specialized algorithms;
– IIS apply knowledge from arbitrary external ontologies without any restrictions on their characteristics and structure, and it causes many requirements and restrictions on the processing algorithms.

In the general case, the user can choose one of possible sources of domain ontologies:

– create a new ontology that exactly corresponds to his/her needs;
– find a previously created ontology that meets the user's needs;
– modify an existing ontology according to his/her needs (separate part of ontology, join ontologies, enrich ontology by classes, relations or individuals, etc.).

From the point of view of Open science, the reproducibility of scientific research that uses ontologies concerns two issues: (1) how to find exactly the version of the ontology that was used in the publication in order to check and compare the results; and (2) what types and groups of other ontologies can be processed by the methods proposed in the research, and what requirements should these ontologies meet.

Currently, most of the answers to these questions are not defined. In the best case, access to the ontology can be obtained through some repository or direct link, but it can be represented by another version with different volume, changes in structure or other differences. Regarding the second question, the situation is even worse – most researchers are satisfied with the general term "ontology" or one of its subclasses instead of formal definition and characteristics of the used knowledge structure.

The most formal and strict definition of ontology properties can be based on the selection of descriptive logics (DL). However, this approach requires special competencies of formal logic from domain ontology designers that many of them don't have. Therefore, we propose to use simpler solution that is based on matching of named sets of elements of ontology formal model. Such sets unambiguously determine the expressive ability of the ontology and the complexity of knowledge processing methods.

5   Metadata Standards for Ontology Representation

The concept of metadata is defined as data that provides information about other data [6]. There are many different types of metadata, including descriptive metadata, structural metadata, administrative metadata, reference metadata and statistical metadata. They can speed up the process of international access to information because it can be represented in languages other than the language of the object.

Today, the Dublin Core [7] is the most widely used reference set for descriptive metadata on the Web worldwide. Standard ISO 15836–1: 2017 Information and documentation - The Dublin Core metadata element set - Part 1: Core elements presents 15 elements that are used to describe resources. Here resource is understood as any identifiable object (individual documents, texts, audio and video files, web pages, databases, etc.). The "core" specified in this standard is part of a larger set of metadata dictionaries and technical specifications supported by the Dublin Core Metadata Initiative (DCMI). ISO 15836–2: 2019 Information and documentation - The Dublin Core metadata element set - Part 2: DCMI Properties and classes, which forms the language It extends this set to 40 properties and 20 classes to increase the accuracy and expressiveness of descriptions in Dublin Core.

Now we don't have unified standard to represent metadata about ontologies, and it causes problems in integration of ontology libraries. Some schemes for metadata representing use the Ontology Metadata Vocabulary (OMV) [8]. However, OMV is not enough expressive for needs of large-scale ontology search.

Search mechanisms supported by libraries define their functionality and effectiveness of ontology reuse. Some of them are provided by SPARQL query engine, and others need in specific software. At least, libraries provide search for ontology names, but usually they support some elements of search within ontology and search across ontologies. The implementations of search and navigation differ such elements:

– Search of specific elements into ontology content (such as classes, properties, individuals);
– Global search of terms within all ontologies included in library;
– Structured search of elements with specific properties and their values;
– Advanced search that combines all these types of search in a single query.

Some libraries can compute, evaluate and process various additional metrics of ontologies uploaded to the library for search purposes. Such metrics can reflect simple quantitative characteristics of ontology. For example, Cupboard, BioPortal and OntoSelect provide such metrics as the number of classes, individuals, properties and restrictions. Other metrics can reflect more complex characteristics of ontology such as relations with other ontologies, used OWL dialects (for example, OWL DL or OWL Lite), types of restrictions, and so on. For example, the TONES repository supports evaluation of ontology properties such as the number of elements of different types, the number of disjoint classes, the number of symmetric, reflexive, and transitive properties. In addition, some libraries support ranking of ontologies in search results to reflects estimations of ontology similarity to user request.

6   Types of Ontology Libraries

Academic and industrial developments related to the use of ontologies provide new technologies in this area. Today, the Web contains a large number of ontologies from different domains. However, due to the complexity of the structure of ontologies and the large number of them, it is difficult for a user not only to make changes and additions to them (reengineering), but also to find an ontology that is relevant to task and has satisfactory level of complexity.

Therefore, we need a technology for representing and searching ontologies as open IRs. As a result, a large number of ontologies have accumulated, representing the intelligence of many experts and developed by independent developers, which creates the need for tools to share and reuse them. This makes the task of creating ontology repositories relevant for the storage and retrieval of ontologies and ontological modules.

The first steps in this direction were approaches to creating collections of ontologies and their infrastructure. Initial projects to collect a database of existing ontologies proposed the creation of library systems that provide various functions for managing, adapting and standardizing groups of ontologies. These systems propose useful tools for grouping and reorganizing ontologies, for their further reuse, integration, maintenance, display and version control. Examples of library systems are: WebOnto, Ontolingua, DAML Ontology Library System, SchemaWeb, etc.

The term "ontology library" integrates different types of systems that provide access to information about formalized ontologies and their content. Such systems differ significantly according to their goals and domains of use, but all of them have the main common functionality of ontology repository [9] that facilitate discovering and retrieval of ontologies collected in a single place and supported by some metadata.

Main differences between libraries are caused by the ways of ontology registration into the repository (automated crawling from the Web, by users of library or only by administrators), by metadata structure and by additional functionality of system. Therefore, we can consider ontology library as an association of ontology repository with some non-empty set of services that support management of ontologies and provide user access to these ontologies.

The main categories of ontology libraries are:

– *ontology directories,* represented by the collections of curated domain-independent ontologies that provide reference ontologies in specific domains;
– *ontology registries,* that provide platforms for registration and publishing ontologies for their developers;
– libraries that provide technical infrastructures.

The functionality of the library systems in each category defines their use by the different categories of developers and users and defines the criteria for selecting a library for particular needs (such as support for reuse and adoption, shared online access for people or software).

The main problem, however, is the retrieval of relevant ontologies that meet task-specific requirements. The solution to this problem is divided into two parts: (1) matching the content of existing ontologies with the IOs that are processed in the user's task, and (2) analyzing the ontology metadata that describe its scope, properties, and expressiveness. Ontology repositories and catalogs of semantic artifacts help to meet user information needs and to make ontologies FAIR-compliant (searchable, accessible, interoperable, and reusable) for use in open science.

Now many ontologies are proposed into repositories as open IRs. For example, OWL Manchester (http://owl.cs.manchester.ac.uk/tools/repositories/) proposes the list of OWL ontology repositories mainly oriented on biological research domain. Other examples of ontology repositories oriented on various domains and various aspects of ontology design are:

– Knoodle – a repository and tool for the collaborative management of ontologies. (http://knoodl.com/);
– Cupboard – an ontology repository with advanced features powered by the Watson Semantic search engine (http://cupboard.open.ac.uk:8081/cupboard-search/) that provides users to create their own information space s;
– Portal catalogue of ontology design OntologyDesignPatterns.org (ODP) (http://ontologydesignpatterns.org/).

Some specialized search engines are oriented on retrieval of ontologies:

– Swoogle: the Semantic Web engine for search of Semantic Web ontologies and RDF documents (http://swoogle.umbc.edu/);
– AberOWL that provides semantic access to ontologies by OWL-EL reasoning over a repository- (http://aber-owl.net);

If search engine proposes more possibilities to match ontology with personal needs of user then this tool can be considered as a recommending system. For example, OntoPortal (https://ontoportal.org) proposes the technology for building ontology repositories and catalogs of semantic artifacts that can support a variety of resources from SKOS thesauri to OBO, RDF-S, and OWL ontologies.

Search in these repositories is usually based only on ontology name or class names with some advanced options (Fig. 1). Search results contain information about ontology structure and number of elements but do not reflect its complexity and expressiveness.

An initiative Open Ontology Repository (OOR) (http://ontolog.cim3.net/wiki/OpenOn tologyRepository.html) is aimed to promote the reuse and sharing of ontologies by creation of a hosted registry of ontologies; enabling and facilitating open, unified, joint repositories of ontologies; establishing best practices for compatibility of ontology.

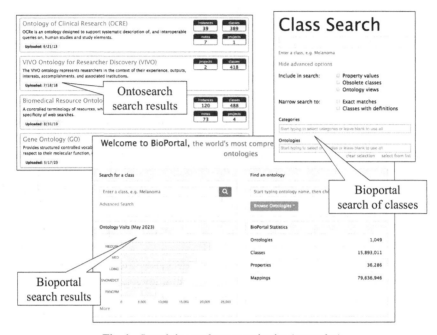

Fig. 1. Search in ontology repositories (examples)

OntoPortal [10] supports recommendation service with corresponding ontology, which suggests appropriate semantic artifacts for a given text or list of keywords. The pertinence of the recommended ontology is evaluated according to four different criteria: (1) the degree of input data covering by ontology content; (2) acceptance of the ontology in the community that is evaluated by number of views on the portal; (3) the detailing level of the ontology classes that cover the input data; and (4) specialization of the ontology to the domain of the input data. Users can define the weights of these criteria according to their goals.

Researchers consider different sets of ontology sets that depend on ways of the content collecting or maintaining and various services supported by libraries (with different access type and stages in the ontology lifecycle) [11]. But now many of proposed tools are not actively maintained. Choice of ontology library can take into account such characteristics: subject area of library and means of its description; size (general number of ontologies and ontology versions); dynamics of ontology number (stable or growing); ontology metadata.

Main characteristics of ontological content are represented into libraries by ontology metadata and can be use for search of appropriate ontology or for description of selected ones. They help in evaluation of the amount and quality of content, but their form and composition in existing libraries differ significantly and complicate matching of ontologies from different sources.

Recently, there have been many initiatives to create semantically organized information spaces. However, all these approaches did not allow ensuring the interoperability of ontological knowledge, sufficient to support the tasks of semantic search and recognition. The main problem is that most collections of ontologies offer a search for the ontology needed by a user only by keywords and a short description, which in general does not reflect the semantics of the ontologies themselves, and a generally accepted standard for describing ontologies is not proposed.

Ontology repositories should facilitate the discovery and sharing of reusable ontological components (whole ontologies or parts of ontologies) that meet user requirements.

We consider an Ontology Repository (OR) as a structured collection of ontologies (schemas and instances), modules and additional meta-knowledge using a vocabulary of ontological metadata. Connections and relationships between ontologies and their modules represent the semantic model of the ontology repository. An ontology repository consists of a system for managing the ontology repository and content placed in this repository. Currently, scientific research is actively carried out in the direction of organizing links between repositories. A solution to this problem would allow global searching, browsing, or inference of repositories on a global scale based on the semantic information space.

Ontology Repository Management System (ORMS) is software for storing, organizing, modifying, and retrieving knowledge from an ontology repository. ORMS supports semantics for the functions of storing, organizing, modifying and retrieving knowledge from an ontology repository. ORMS aims to transform ontology library into ontology repository with advances retrieval functions. ORMS implementations can be divided into decentralized (such as the Oyster system [12]) and centralized (such as the Generic Ontology Repository Framework [13]).

The main purpose of creating ORs is to support access to knowledge and its reuse by humans and machines. ORs are designed to address various issues related to ontology engineering. One of the key problems in ontology engineering is reusability because many ontologies are built from scratch rather than reusing existing ones, which leads to unnecessary engineering effort and costs. The reason for this is that most of the existing ontologies are oriented on custom software rather than reuse.

ORs need to develop and use standards for representing metadata about ontologies. For example, OMV metadata is proposed as a part of the Oyster decentralized ontology repository. OMV is a metadata model for ontologies and related entities, reflecting key aspects of ontology metadata information, such as provenance and accessibility. OMV is implemented as an OWL ontology and can be considered as a prototype for the ontology metadata standard. Metadata elements in the OMV ontology are modeled either with use of classes, class instances or class properties of ontology (their choice is determined by the complexity of the corresponding metadata element). If the values of metadata items can be mapped to common data types (numbers, literals, lists of values), then these metadata items are represented as DatatypeProperty, and more complex metadata items are modeled by additional classes associated with Object Properties.

From the technical point of view, the various practical implementations of ORs differ significantly from each other. Developers apply different methods and technologies to interpret and use metadata. Most of the existing ORs poorly supports modularization and versioning, as well as relationships between ORs.

Despite this, the corresponding components or services at the conceptual level are reusable for various technical solutions. Conceptual framework for ORs represented in [13] can be generalizes on base of practical implementations to define a set of appropriate components and services (Fig. 2).

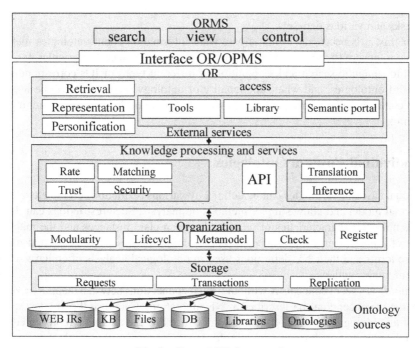

Fig. 2. General OR framework

7 Statement of the Problem

The functioning of different types of IISs in the distributed information space of the Web requires external knowledge about the IOs processed by these IISs. Such knowledge sources are independent of IISs, dynamic and heterogeneous. Nowadays, many of them are represented by ontologies collected in libraries and repositories. One of the possible solutions to this problem is the use of ontology repositories, which provide storage, search, evaluation and secure use of ontologies, as well as management of changes in them, personalization, separation, presentation and integration.

There is a problem of matching ontology metadata with tasks of IISs. We propose to define special cases of ontologies with similar expressiveness and complexity of processing on base of the parameters of the ontology formal model. This approach aims at overcoming the ambiguity of natural language definitions and can take into account the specifics of information resources for ontology development and methods of their generation. In this work we consider popular subsets of ontologies (taxonomies, thesauri, etc.) and propose formal models of the Wiki ontology – an original special cases of ontology generated on base of the structure and content of semantic and non-semantic Wiki resources.

An important subproblem deals with matching of existing ontologies and domain of user interests where knowledge from ontology can be exploit. Therefore, we need in means and methods for analysis ontology metadata and their matching with metadata of IRs, tasks and various data sets.

For this, it is necessary to investigate what information about ontologies makes it possible to ensure their reuse in various intelligent applications, in particular, for tasks related to semantic search and recognition of different types of IOs corresponding to classes of ontologies, and what functionality of ontology repositories can be used for this. It can be based on various types of metadata and algorithms of their matching and acquiring.

8   Individual Cases of Ontologies

Individual cases of ontologies can be defined by various restrictions on the elements of the formal model and allow simpler methods of analysis. Such restrictions can define, for example, the characteristics of relations between class instances and the ranges of values of their properties. We need in precise definition based on the formal model, because terms and their NL definitions used in ontological analysis often have several different interpretations.

Catalog is a set of concepts X without formal connections between them: $R = \emptyset$. The semantics of concepts can be described by NL annotations. Catalog is the simplest special case of an ontology. In terms of the ontology editor Protege, it can be represented by a set of concepts that are instances of a single class "Concept" with a single data property "Annotation" of type Text and an empty set of object relations.

Glossary is an ordered (e.g., alphabetical) set of domain concepts X with definitions (annotations) of these terms. It is a special case of an ontology with a set of relations containing a single element $R = \{"next"\}$ for establishing the order between instances. This ontology is represented by the set of concepts, which are instances of the same class "Concept" with a single object property "next" with the value of the same class "Concept" and the data property "Abstract" of type Text.

Taxonomy is a hierarchical classification scheme where concepts are organized into groups or types by relation $R = \{"subclass"\}$. This is a special case of an ontology with a set of relations containing a single hierarchical relation "subclass" for ordering that is transitive, antireflexive, and antisymmetric. Taxonomies can be used to organize and index knowledge about documents, articles, videos, and more.

Lightweight ontology is an ontology where concepts are connected by general associations rather than strictly defined formal relations. Often, lightweight ontologies are considered as ontologies consisting only of a set of basic taxonomies, i.e., R contains several different "class-subclass" relations. Some researchers extend this concept by generalizing the relation "is a part of" to concepts corresponding to the main properties of basic taxonomies, that is, in a lightweight ontology, the extension of the concept of a child node is a subset of the extension of the concept of a parent node. A broader definition considers lightweight ontologies as ontologies with limited sets of relations between concepts. This restriction differs them from more expressive heavyweight ontologies, but it is not clearly defined what restrictions can be applied in this case. Each concept of light ontologies can be translated into a DL expression.

We propose to consider an ontology as a lightweight one if contains only the following relations:

- transitive "class-subclass" relation;
- symmetric object relations of synonymy;
- domain-specific object relations without binary properties.
- Axioms and rules in lightweight ontology are not defined: $F = \emptyset$.

Some special cases of ontologies can be defined as subsets of lightweight ontologies, where additional restrictions are caused by sources of ontological knowledge or by methods of ontology generation and population.

For such special cases of ontologies (e.g., related to certain type of semantic IRs or acquires by inductive inference), it is advisable to give them a certain name and create formalized description to provide retrieval of such ontologies with similar characteristics. Let's consider these definitions using the example of semantic Wiki-resources and related ontologies.

9   Wiki-Resources and Related Ontologies

Currently, many Web-oriented IRs, created as a result of the collective activity of users, are based on Wiki-technologies [14], which provide the creation of large-scale structured IRs. One of the most common implementations of Wiki technology is MediaWiki (MediaWiki, https://www.mediawiki.org/wiki/MediaWiki). Currently, there are a large number of developments based on MediaWiki, the most famous of which are Wikipedia, Wikibooks, Wiktionary, and Wikidata.

Semantic Wiki resources attract attention because:

- many complex IRs are based on Wiki technologies (semantic and non-semantic);
- Wiki resources meet FAIR requirements and can be reused by Open science;
- semantic extensions of Wiki (such as SMW) provide automated ontology generation for arbitrary sets of Wiki pages;
- Wiki markup is much easier to use than ontology editors.

Semantic extensions of Wiki technology aim to add content to Wiki resource elements, making them suitable for automated processing and knowledge-level analysis. It allows you to define and find information objects with a complex structure that are typical for certain domain. There are many approaches to semantic extensions of Wiki technologies, most of which are based on the standards of the Semantic Web project.

Semantic MediaWiki (SMW) [15] is a semantic extension of MediaWiki (www.mediaw iki.org/wiki/MediaWiki) that supports intelligent organization, semantic search of IR content and export of search results into RDF. For example, the portal version of the Great Ukrainian Encyclopedia e-VUE [16] can generate requests from the special page of SMW that does not require from user special competencies about search. The user enters conditions, type of results and their number, and code of request is generated and then executed (Fig. 3).

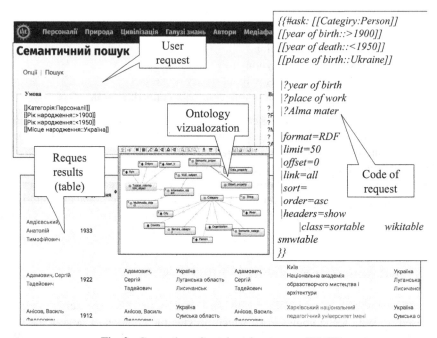

Fig. 3. Generation of ontology by means of SMW

Wiki-ontology is a special case of ontology generated automatically on base on the structure and content of the Wiki resource. It is necessary to distinguish Wiki-ontologies from other ontologies used in the process of creating Wiki-resources (for example, the ontology of Wiki or thesaurus of the Wiki properties) and from the taxonomies of Wiki-resources and Wiki-technologies themselves. Its expressiveness has some limitations, since such an ontology contains only the knowledge that can be obtained directly from the Wiki markup. For example, it cannot define characteristics for object properties and data properties, such as equivalence and intersection.

We distinguish Wiki-ontologies generated by usual (non-semantic) IRs from ontologies generated with the help of semantic markup.

The Wiki ontology $O_{wiki\_no\_semant}$ for a non-semantic Wiki resource represents only information about page categories and about links between pages without defining semantics of these links. It contains the following components: a set of ontology concepts $X = X_{cl} \cup X_{ind}$, where X_{cl} is a set of classes that agrees with the set of Wiki categories represented into the selected set of pages; X_{ind} is a set of class instances created as a union of the names of selected Wiki pages $P = P_{user} \cup P_{template} \cup P_{spec}$, where P_{user} is a set of pages created by users, $P_{template}$ is a set of special pages describing Wiki templates, P_{spec} is a set of other special pages;

Relations between elements of this ontology are represented by the set $R = L \cup \{ r_{ier\_cl} \} \cup \{ r_{class\_individual} \}$, where $L = \{"link"\}$ is a set with single element that describes a link from one Wiki page of this resource to another; r_{ier_cl} is the hierarchical relation between the categories of the Wiki resource, which is determined in the process of creating new categories, $r_{class\_individual}$ is the hierarchical relation between the categories and the pages of the Wiki resource assigned to these categories;

$F = \{ f_{equ} \}$ is a single-element set containing a relation that can be used for logical inference into the ontology, an equivalence relation between Wiki pages. Other elements of the ontology model of this Wiki-ontology are represented by empty sets.

The formal model built by semantically marked Wiki resources O_{wiki_semant} is more complex than $O_{wiki\_no\_semant}$ and contains a number of elements related to semantic properties. It contains more groups of relations $R = L \cup \{r_{ier\_cl}\} \cup \{r_{class\_individual}\} \cup L_{sem\_prop}$, where R is extended by a set of semantic properties L_{sem_prop} with a range of values in a set of Wiki pages. T is a set of data types (e.g. "text", "number") for data property values.

The problem of matching elements of ontologies and semantic Wiki-resources can be automated only partially because some correspondences are unambiguous and defined by single-valued function, but other ones can have some different interpretations that depend on resource knowledge base structure. For example, some categories of Wiki are used only for internal technical purposes, and therefore such categories are excluded from the ontology structure.

In more details this problem is analyzed in [17]. But additional clarifications and definition from the user don't impact on formal characteristics of Wiki ontology.

An analysis shows that only some correspondences are one-to-one and can be detected automatically. The same Wiki page can be categorized by the several categories that are matched with instances of different classes of ontology. SMW categories and classes of ontology are matching one-to-one. Some others require additional processing. For example, SMW template and classes of ontology IOs can be matching many-to-one or one-to-one.

10 Conclusion and Prospects for Further Research

ORs help to find and reuse ontologies as open IRs on the Web according to the main principles of Open Science. While use of ontologies can support mechanisms for interoperability and data exchange between IOs, ontologies themselves are almost always created in isolation. Each OR is a separate island with its own user interface, API, users, ontology languages, and ontology sets. There is no interoperability between repositories and ontologies in them, there is no universal way to access all ORs, there is no global search using ontology metadata, ontology review and the formation of conclusions about all available ontology storages, and this task is still technically complex and requires further resolution of this problems. This task is very important because ontologies are not being reused as much as they could be and thus the full potential of ontologies is not being achieved. The problem lies in the complexity of the metadata mechanism: the expressiveness of the metadata that fully defines the ontology is equal to the expressiveness of the described ontology.

Therefore, it is important to achieve interoperability between ORs through common interfaces, standard metadata formats, general concepts and term systems. Scientific research is being actively conducted in direction of organizing connections between ORs and their semantic sources, developing standards for ontologies and their meta-descriptions. The solution of the problem will in the near future allow semantic search of ontologies and their components in repositories not only by keywords, but also at the level of their meaningful features and properties, and this additional functionality significantly increases the degree of reuse of ontologies.

Further work in this direction should include advanced development of methods to support ORs, for example, by requests to domain ontology, its specific fragment or IO contained into ontology, or to a specific type of concept.

Ontologies can play an important role in expediting knowledge reuse in various domains, such as software development [18], e-learning, intelligent consulting [19], Big data analysis [20], etc. This includes reuse of artifacts as well as development knowledge, skills, design models and work products.

Results of previous scientific research accumulated into ontologies are emerging as a promising vehicle in delivering promises of runtime and design time flexibility of new projects in actual paradigms of Open science and Semantic Web.

The definition of an ontology library as a software system that provides various services for the management, adaptation and standardization of groups of ontologies emphasizes the need for interoperability and reuse of existing relevant ontologies, showing that scalability and interoperability are now the challenges for ontology repositories and applications in different areas of use [21, 22]. Interest to this research direction is confirmed by significant number of scientific conferences and publications [23] on utilizing ontologies, information retrieval and the Semantic Web technologies in healthcare, virtual communities, and ontology-based information processing systems.

The benefits of ontology reuse often depend on the formal identification of appropriate domain knowledge. The focus of this research is to identify appropriate ontologies for IIS and to identify ontology sources and processing methods required for IIS purposes.

Often, an ontology from OR is relevant to the domain of selected IIS, but is not semantically adequate or has insufficient expressiveness for adaptation to user tasks. The next stage of this research is aimed at such problems: how to improve such an ontology, what characteristics to change, and what methods and sources to use to supplement such an ontology with the necessary knowledge and domain rules.

Acknowledgements. This work is part of the research projects LaTe4PoliticES (PID2022-138099OB-I00) funded by MCIN/AEI/10.13039/501100011033 and the European Fund for Regional Development (FEDER)-a way to make Europe and LaTe4PSP (PID2019-107652RB-I00/AEI/10.13039/501100011033) funded by MCIN/AEI/10.13039/501100011033 . This work is also part part of the research projects AIInFunds (PDC2021–121112-I00) and LT-SWM (TED2021-131167B-I00) funded by MCIN/AEI/10.13039/501100011033 and by the European Union NextGenerationEU/PRTR.

References

1. Challenges in irreproducible research, Nature. https://www.nature.com/collections/prbfkw mwvz. Accessed 21 May 2023
2. FAIR Principles. www.go-fair.org/fair-principles/. Accessed 06 June 2023
3. Hitzler, P., Krotzsch, M., Rudolph, S. Foundations of semantic web technologies. In: CRC press (2009)
4. McGuinness, D. L., Van Harmelen, F.: OWL web ontology language overview. W3C Recommendation **10**(10), 2004 (2004)
5. Manola, F., Miller, E., McBride, B. RDF primer. W3C Recommendation **10**(1–107), 6 (2004)
6. Merriam Webster. https://www.merriam-webster.com/dictionary/metadata. Accessed 26 May 2023
7. Weibel, S.L., Koch, T.: The Dublin core metadata initiative. D-lib Mag. **6**(12), 1082–9873 (2000)
8. Hartmann, J., Sure, Y., Haase, P., Palma, R., Suarez-Figueroa, M.: OMV–ontology metadata vocabulary. In: ISWC, vol. 3729 (2005)
9. Gladun, A., Rogushina, J.: Distant control of student skills by formal model of domain knowledge. Int. J. Innov. Learn. (IJIL) **7**(4), 394–411 (2010)
10. Yang, S.Y.: OntoPortal: an ontology-supported portal architecture with linguistically enhanced and focused crawler technologies. Expert Syst. Appl. **36**(6), 10148–10157 (2009)
11. Ding, Y., Fensel, D.: Ontology library systems the key to successful ontology reuse. In: First Semantic Web Working Symposium, pp. 93–112 (2001)
12. Palma, R., Haase, P., Gómez-Pérez, A.: Oyster: sharing and re-using ontologies in a peer-to-peer community. In: Proceedings of the 15th International Conference on WWW, pp. 1009–1010. (2006)
13. Hartmann, J., Palma, R., Gómez-Pérez, A.: Ontology repositories. In: Handbook on Ontologies, pp. 551–571 (2009)
14. Wagner, C.: Wiki: a technology for conversational knowledge management and group collaboration. Commun. Assoc. Inf. Syst. **13**(1), 264–289 (2004)
15. Krötzsch, M., Vrandečić, D., Völkel, M.: Semantic MediaWiki. In: Cruz, I., et al. (ed.) The Semantic Web - ISWC 2006. ISWC 2006. LNCS, vol. 4273, pp. 935–942. Springer, Berlin, Heidelberg (2006). https://doi.org/10.1007/11926078_68
16. Rogushina, J., Grishanova, I.: Ontological methods and tools for semantic extension of the MediaWiki technology. UkrPROG 2020, CEUR Workshoop Proc. **2866**, 61–73 (2021)
17. Rogushina, J., Gladun, A.: Mereological approach for formation of "part-whole" relations between pages of a semantic wiki-resource. ITS-2021, CEUR Workshoop Proceedings, vol. 3241, pp.237–247 (2021). https://ceur-ws.org/Vol-3241/
18. Beydoun, G., Hoffmann, A., Breis, J.T.F., Bejar, R.M., Valencia-Garcia, R., Aurum, A.: Cooperative modelling evaluated. Int. J. Coop. Inf. Syst. **14**(01), 45–71 (2005)
19. Valencia-García, R., Ruiz-Sánchez, J.M., Vivancos-Vicente, P.J., Fernández-Breis, J.T., Martínez-Béjar, R.: An incremental approach for discovering medical knowledge from texts. Expert Syst. Appl. **26**(3), 291-299 (2004)
20. Rogushina, J., Gladun, A.: Use of special cases of ontologies for big data analysis in decision making systems. In: Zapata-Cortes, J.A., Sánchez-Ramírez, C., Alor-Hernández, G., García-Alcaraz, J.L. (eds.) Handbook on Decision Making. Intelligent Systems Reference Library, vol. 226, pp. 201–223. Springer, Cham (2023). https://doi.org/10.1007/978-3-031-08246-7_9
21. Ruiz-Sánchez, J.M., Valencia-García, R., Fernández-Breis, J.T., Martínez-Béjar, R., Compton, P.: An approach for incremental knowledge acquisition from text. Expert Syst. Appl. **25**(1), 77–86 (2003)

22. García-Sánchez, F., Valencia-García, R., Martínez-Béjar, R.: An integrated approach for developing e-commerce applications. Expert Syst. Appl. **28**(2), 223–235 (2005)
23. Narayanasamy, S.K., Srinivasan, K., Hu, Y.C., Masilamani, S.K., Huang, K.Y.: A contemporary review on utilizing semantic web technologies in healthcare, virtual communities, and ontology-based information processing systems. Electronics **11**(3), 453 (2022)

Knowledge Graph for Retail Commerce

Ronghao Pan[1] , José Antonio García-Díaz[1]([⊠]) , Diego Roldán[2],
and Rafael Valencia-García[1]

[1] Facultad de Informática, Universidad de Murcia, Campus de Espinardo, 30100
Murcia, Spain
{ronghao.pan,joseantonio.garcia8,valencia}@um.es
[2] DANTIA Tecnología S.L., Parque Empresarial de Jerez 10, Calle de la Agricultura,
11407 Jerez de la Frontera, Cádiz, Spain
droldan@dantia.es

Abstract. Nowadays, data collected from social networks and news can
provide valuable information about consumers' evolving interests and
preferences. This data can improve the accuracy of predictive models
used to forecast future trends and behaviors. By incorporating information from online platforms, companies, and researchers can better understand consumer behavior and make more accurate predictions in their
respective fields. However, this data is unstructured and requires semantic web technology tools to analyze the information. In this paper, we
present a semantic web technology tool that extracts information from
Spanish news and social media and associates it with semantic structures
based on knowledge graphs. The system uses the KnowGL model, which
is a sequence-to-sequence model based on Transformers and trained on a
distantly supervised RE dataset, to generate triples. The results obtained
were interesting to demonstrate the applicability and adaptability of this
tool in the information analysis phase of the DANTIA project.

Keywords: Knowledge Graphs · Transformers · Natural Language
Processing

1 Introduction

In the area of digital communications, data from online sources such as social
media can provide additional insight into changing consumer interests, which is
essential for improving the accuracy of forecasting models. In other words, these
data sources can improve companies' daily sales forecasts, overcoming the limitations of relying solely on transactional sales data. Therefore, the project consists
of the development of a decision support platform for retail management based
on the company's history and the extraction of data from structured sources
and natural language documents such as social networks and news. Thus, this
platform will be able to mix structured data from current product histories,
obtained from historical invoice information exported from the currently mar-
keted SAGE-based ERP, with information extracted from social networks.

R. Valencia-García et al. (Eds.): CITI 2023, CCIS 1873, pp. 173–185, 2023.
https://doi.org/10.1007/978-3-031-45682-4_13

The challenge of leveraging social media data is that the information across platforms is unstructured, diverse, and massive. This makes the task of information retrieval long and tedious. In particular, social networks generate massive amounts of data that can be used to generate new insights, such as what products are trending lately. However, the large amount of data available in social networks makes it almost impossible for stakeholders to properly understand and extract insights without assistance. Therefore, semantic web technologies are required to analyze the information. The use of efficient computational methods to create knowledge representations is a suitable alternative to support information retrieval in social networks. For example, such representations could provide a way to correlate different entities and allow managers to formulate new hypotheses or draw new conclusions.

To extract information from the different data collected by the news and social media information collection module of the project, knowledge graphs are used to associate them with semantic structures. To this end, this paper presents a framework that allows the extraction of explicit and implicit relationships, and entities from a collection of texts through a tool called KnowGL [16], which is a model trained by combining Wikidata with an extended version of the training data from the REBEL dataset [8].

The rest of the manuscript is organized as follows. Section 2 provides general information about knowledge graphs, including the different techniques for entity and relationship extraction. A detailed description of the framework and methods used is presented in Sect. 3. Then, Sect. 3 presents the results, and Sect. 6 discusses the conclusions and future works.

2   Background Information

A knowledge graph (also known as a semantic network) is defined as a data graph that aggregates and communicates real-world knowledge, i.e., it represents a network of real-world entities (objects, events, situations, or concepts) and illustrates the relationships between them [12]. Typically, all this information is stored in a graphical database and visualized as a graphical structure. In recent years, there has been continuous research on knowledge graphs due to their importance in processing heterogeneous information in a machine-readable context. These solutions have been widely used in AI systems such as recommender systems [18], question answering [4], and information retrieval [3]. They are also applied in fields such as education and healthcare to improve the quality of life and benefit society. It is mainly composed of three elements: nodes, edges, and labels. Nodes represent the entities of interest and edges represent the relationship between them. Labels are attributes that define the relationship between nodes. Therefore, the construction of the knowledge graph mainly involves two extraction processes: entity extraction and relationship extraction.

2.1   Entity Extraction

Extracting entities from a sentence is not an easy task, and several methods have emerged to do this using supervised or unsupervised learning models. One of the most important methods is Named Entity Recognition (NER), which is a fundamental part of information retrieval. It aims to find and classify named entities mentioned in unstructured texts into predefined categories, such as names of people, organizations, places, medical codes, time expressions, quantities, monetary values, percentages, and others. These entities can be related to different texts described in documents, so many systems have an entity linking process that links the text to its corresponding representation in a Knowledge Graph (KG).

2.2   Relation Extraction

Relation extraction (RE) is the process of extracting semantic relationships in a text. The extracted relations are usually facts about entities that occur between two or more entities of some kind and are classified into a number of semantic categories (e.g., made in, employed by, lives in). There are five different ways to perform RE:

- **Rule-based RE**: It consists of identifying relationships by hand-crafted patterns, looking for triples (X, Z, Y) where X and Y are entities and Z are intermediate words. However, this method gets many false positives, although there are methods to mitigate this problem, such as filtering named entities and considering grammatical dependencies of words. Thus, the main disadvantage of this method is that human patterns are still often poorly remembered (too much variety in languages) and rules have to be created for each type of relation. In [15], the authors have used a rule-based technique to extract meaningful relationships with semantic significance from biomedical literature.
- **Weakly supervised RE**: This method consists of automatically finding new ones from the unlabeled text data through an iterative process with a set of hand-crafted rules. Thus, it can discover more relationships than rule-based RE and requires less human effort. However, the pattern set becomes more error-prone with each iteration, and when a new type of relationship is generated, new seeds must be provided manually [14].
- **Supervised RE**: Typically, systems using this method use a stacked or normal binary classifier to determine whether a particular relationship exists between two entities. These classifiers take input text features (context words, NER tags, etc.), so it is necessary for the text to be annotated beforehand. High quality monitoring can be achieved with this method, but it is expensive to label examples and difficult to add new relationships, which makes generalization to new domains difficult [13].
- **Distantly supervised RE**: It consists of combining seed data from an existing knowledge base (Wikipedia, Wikidata Freebase, etc.) with supervised RE,

so it requires less manual effort and can scale to use large amounts of data tags and many relationships [13].

- **Unsupervised RE**: This method does not require labeling training data, providing a set of seed tuples, or writing rules to capture different types of relationships in the text, as it relies on a very general set of constraints and heuristics. Therefore, the performance of the system depends heavily on how well the constraints and heuristics are constructed, and the relationships are not as standardized as the relationship types specified above [20].

Transformers [22] is a type of neural network architecture that has become increasingly popular in recent years for its exceptional performance in diverse domains such as Natural Language Processing (NLP) [23] and Computer Vision [10]. One particular model that has received considerable attention is the Bidirectional Encoder Representations from Transformers (BERT). This pre-trained model can be easily fine-tuned and consistently achieves state-of-the-art results for a wide range of NLP tasks. Thus, an end-to-end system for constructing a biomedical knowledge graph using a variation of the BERT models has been proposed at [7].

Recently, new end-to-end approaches have emerged that address both tasks simultaneously, i.e., assigning specific parts of the model to different pipeline tasks, such as NER on the one hand, and classification of predicted entity relationships (RC) on the other. In [9], REBEL (Relation Extraction By End-to-end Language generation), an auto-regressive approach that frames relation extraction as a seq2seq task, was presented together with the REBEL dataset (a remotely supervised large dataset) obtained by using a pre-training model, an encoder-decoder transformer (BART). Another model that uses the same approach is KnowGL [16], which allows the transformation of text into structured relational data represented in a given knowledge graph, such as Wikidata. That is, given a natural language text input, it generates a linearized sequence representation containing a set of facts expressed in the text input and adapts it to a given schema to represent the semantic annotations of a triple in the target sequence. However, most models of this approach and research focus on English, and lack discussion in other languages, such as Spanish. To this end, new multilingual datasets for distantly supervised relation extraction have emerged, such as DiS-ReX [2] and RELX [11], with 456,418 and 397,875 Spanish sentences, respectively.

3   Material and Methods

In this paper we have developed a framework that allows us to extract semantic information from an unstructured dataset in Spanish, i.e. to obtain the triplets (subject, relation, object) of the text. For this purpose, we have used the KnowGL model instead of building a model from scratch with a multilingual dataset for supervised remote relation extraction, since the model is much more complete and extensive with an extended version of REBEL (more than

9,282,837 sentences in the training set) and a total of 757 relations compared to DiS-ReX and RELX. However, the main drawback is that the model is in English, so to use it in our system we need a preliminary process of translating the texts into English to identify the entities and relations, and a post-processing that translates the extracted entities and relations into Spanish. Figure 1 shows the architecture of our system.

In a nutshell, it can be described as follows. First, the coreference resolution module groups expressions that refer to the same real-world entity to obtain a less ambiguous text. Second, the translation module takes care of translating the English text with models based on Transformers. Third, the KnowGL model is used to obtain the triples. Fourth, post-processing is performed, eliminating repeated relations and translating the obtained entities and relations into Spanish using the *Helsinki-NLP/opus-mt-en-es* model. Finally, a graph construction is created using Neo4J and a framework that allows the user to enter a text and obtain its corresponding triples.

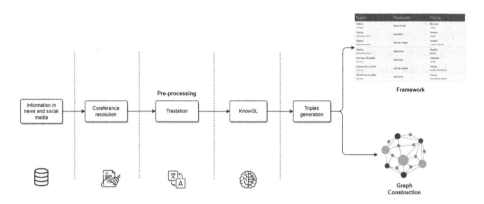

Fig. 1. Overall system architecture.

3.1   Coreference Resolution

Coreference resolution (CR) is a challenging task in natural language processing (NLP). The goal of this task is to group text mentions that refer to the same underlying real-world entities in order to obtain a less ambiguous text. For coreference resolution, we apply the Crosslingual Coreference model, which is a multilingual approach to AllenNLP CoReference Resolution, together with a wrapper for spaCy.

3.2   Pre-processing

In the pre-processing module, it consists of the translation process to convert Spanish process into English. For this, we have used a pre-trained Helsinki-NLP

Opus MT model (specifically, the *Helsinki-NLP/opus-mt-es-en model*), which is a project focused on the development of free resources and tools for machine translation [19].

3.3   KnowGL

For this project, we used the KnowGL model, which simultaneously extracts entities and relations and is able to transform the text into a set of Wikidata statements. They approach this task as a sequence generation task by using a pre-trained sequence-to-sequence language model, e.g. BART. In this case, we used the knowledge generation model of the framework, which generates a linearized sequence representation containing a set of facts expressed in the textual input and adapts it to a given schema to represent the semantic annotations of a triple in the target sequence: `[(subject mention # subject label # subject type) | relation label | (object mention # object label # object type)]`. As discussed above, the model uses an extended version of REBEL (distantly supervised RE dataset) with a total of 757 relations, many of which are irrelevant to our domain. Thus, we have selected 139 most relevant relationships, so in post-processing, we would select the triples containing these relationships. Once the text triplets are obtained, the post-processing is performed by eliminating the repeated triplets and translating them into Spanish using the *Helsinki-NLP/opus-mt-en-es* model. Training the BART model with the distantly supervised dataset offers the advantage of being able to extract implicit relationships, i.e. those that are not explicitly mentioned in the text. This feature makes it possible to identify novel relationships and entities linked to the content, leading to the extraction of new knowledge.

4   Results

This section presents a framework for extracting triplets from text and a conceptual design of the data model for the knowledge graph.

4.1   Framework

In this work, we have created a framework that is an interactive service platform that allows the user to enter a text and obtain the text triplets. Figure 2 shows the structure and design of the framework. It can be seen that it consists mainly of three components: a selector where the user can select whether he wants explicit or implicit relations, a text box, and a table where the obtained triplets are displayed. The KnowGL model is trained on a distantly supervised dataset for RE, so in some cases, it is able to detect implicit relations in the text, i.e. when one of the entities does not appear in the text. For example "España es uno de los países de la UE"[1], one of its implicit relations is "(España, miembro de la, ONU)".

---

[1] In English: "Spain is one of the countries of the EU".

Fig. 2. Design of the framework.

4.2   Graph Construction

Another service of our system is the construction of graphs from a collection of texts. For this purpose, we have used neo4j for the construction of the graph database and the Cypher query language for its analysis [6]. Cypher is a Neo4j graph query language that allows the retrieval of graph data and uses graph pattern matching as the primary mechanism for selecting graph data.

5   Case of Use

As a retail use case, we created an intelligent crawler that collects the descriptions of different products. The crawler extracts information from a price comparator of products from different supermarkets called *ahorromercado*[2], which is a platform that shows the prices and descriptions of products from different supermarkets such as Mercadona, Carrefour, Consum, among others. After the collection and processing process, eliminating repeated products and those without descriptions, a dataset with a total of 3,287 descriptions of different products was obtained.

As mentioned above (see Sect. 3), our tool has a framework that allows extracting information from a text and associating it to a semantic structure based on a knowledge graph (text triplets). Figure 3 shows the results obtained with the description "Mahou es una cerveza de Madrid y Estrella De Levante es de Murcia y es más amargo ya que esta hechos con agua de pozo. Además, la cerveza Alhambra es de Granada."[3]. It can be seen that the model is also able to identify the type of entities since the model was trained by combining it with the Wikidata database.

---

[2] https://ahorramercado.com/.

[3] In English: "Mahou is a beer from Madrid and Estrella De Levante is from Murcia and is more bitter because it is made with well water. Also, Alhambra is a beer from Granada.".

Sujeto	Predicado	Objeto
Mahou Cerveza	instancia de	Cerveza mezcla
Mahou marca de cerveza	ubicación	Madrid ciudad
Mahou marca de cerveza	país de origen	Madrid Estado soberano
Mahou marca de cerveza	fabricante	Madrid ciudad
Cerveza Alhambra Cerveza	ubicación	Granada ciudad
Estrella de Levante Cerveza	país de origen	Murcia provincia de España
Estrella de Levante Cerveza	ubicación	Murcia Municipio de España

Fig. 3. Triplets obtained with the description of Mahou, Estrella de Levante and Alhambra beers.

One of the features of our system is the ability to identify implicit relations, i.e. relations where one of the entities does not appear in the text, and this is possible because the model used (KnowGL) is a refined model of an already pre-trained model (BART) with a distantly supervised RE dataset. Therefore, the model is able to generate a triplet with the entities found by the training set. Table 1 shows the triplets obtained with the description "El precio de Coca-cola ha subido porque ha aumentado el precio de azúcar"[4] and it can be seen that the model is able to identify that the country of origin of Coca-Cola is the United States.

Table 1. Example of an implicit relationship with the Coca-Cola description.

Subject	Relation	Object
Coca-Cola (brand)	made from material	sugar (foods)
Coca-Cola (brand)	has parts of the class	azúcar (foods)
Coca-Cola (brand)	**country of origin**	**United States (sovereign state)**

Finally, to analyze the extracted dataset, we used the graph generation module of our tool, which generates the triplets and loads them into a Neo4j database. After coreference resolution and triple generation with KnowGL, we obtained a total of 12,385 relations with 1,675 subjects and 1,661 objects. Figure 4 shows

---

[4] In English: "The price of Coca-Cola has increased because the price of sugar has increased.".

a sub-graph built from a collection of data obtained by the crawler. Another feature of our tool compared to others is that it has the ability to identify entity types, as shown in Table 1, the model is able to identify that Coca-Cola is a brand and sugar is a type of food. This gives us the ability to filter by entity types in Neo4j using Cipher. In total, 663 types of subject entities and 613 types of object entities were identified in the dataset. Figure 5 shows the subgraph obtained after filtering for the type "marca"[5] in the subject entity.

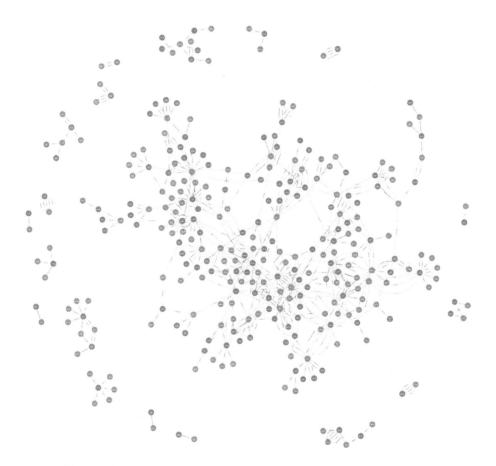

Fig. 4. Sub-Graph generated of 3,287 descriptions of different products.

---

[5] English: "brand".

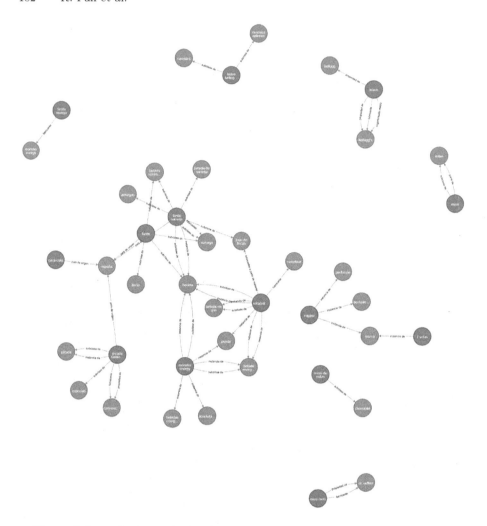

Fig. 5. Sub-graph obtained after filtering by type "marca" in the subject entity.

6   Conclusions and Further Work

In this paper, we have described a tool with semantic web technology that extracts information from the news and social media and associates it with semantic structures based on knowledge graphs, i.e., it generates text triples for information analysis. The system uses the KnowGL model, which is a Transformers-based sequence-to-sequence model trained on a distantly supervised RE dataset for triplet generation. The tool offers a framework in which the user can extract and visualize the explicit or implicit relationship triplets of a text and also offers the option to generate graphs in Neo4j with a collection of texts.

As a future line, we propose to create a distantly supervised RE dataset of the financial and social network domain and to fine-tune this dataset with the BART model to obtain a triplet generation model of this specific domain. Another future work is to model the knowledge graphs using ontologies. Ontologies are conceptual representations that have been used in several domains, such as medicine [17, 21], computer science [1] or e-commerce [5].

Acknowledgments. This work is part of the research project 2021/C005/00149877 funded by the Spanish Government, the Spanish Ministry of Economy and Digital Transformation through the Digital Transformation through the "Recovery, Transformation and Resilience Plan" and also funded by the European Union NextGenerationEU/PRTR. This work is also part of the research project LaTe4PSP (PID2019-107652RB-I00/AEI/10.13039/501100011033) funded by MCIN/AEI/10.13039/501100011033.

References

1. Beydoun, G., et al.: Cooperative modelling evaluated. Int. J. Cooperative Inf. Syst. **14**(1), 45–71 (2005). https://doi.org/10.1142/S0218843005001080
2. Bhartiya, A., Badola, K.: Mausam: Dis-Rex: a multilingual dataset for distantly supervised relation extraction (2021)
3. Bounhas, I., Soudani, N., Slimani, Y.: Building a morpho-semantic knowledge graph for Arabic information retrieval. Inf. Process. Manage. **57**(6), 102124 (2020). https://doi.org/10.1016/j.ipm.2019.102124, https://www.sciencedirect.com/science/article/pii/S0306457319302912
4. Chen, Y., Wu, L., Zaki, M.J.: Toward subgraph-guided knowledge graph question generation with graph neural networks. IEEE Trans. Neural Netw. Learn. Syst., 1–12 (2023). https://doi.org/10.1109/TNNLS.2023.3264519
5. García-Sánchez, F., Valencia-García, R., Martínez-Béjar, R.: An integrated approach for developing e-commerce applications. Expert Syst. Appl. **28**(2), 223–235 (2005). https://doi.org/10.1016/j.eswa.2004.10.004, https://www.sciencedirect.com/science/article/pii/S0957417404001137
6. Guia., J., GonÇalves Soares., V., Bernardino., J.: Graph databases: Neo4j analysis. In: Proceedings of the 19th International Conference on Enterprise Information Systems - Volume 1: ICEIS, pp. 351–356. INSTICC, SciTePress (2017). https://doi.org/10.5220/0006356003510356
7. Harnoune, A., Rhanoui, M., Mikram, M., Yousfi, S., Elkaimbillah, Z., El Asri, B.: BERT based clinical knowledge extraction for biomedical knowledge graph construction and analysis. Comput. Methods Program. Biomed. Update **1**, 100042 (2021). https://doi.org/10.1016/j.cmpbup.2021.100042, https://www.sciencedirect.com/science/article/pii/S2666990021000410
8. Huguet Cabot, P.L., Navigli, R.: REBEL: relation extraction by end-to-end language generation. In: Findings of the Association for Computational Linguistics: EMNLP 2021. Association for Computational Linguistics, Online and in the Barceló Bávaro Convention Centre, Punta Cana, Dominican Republic (2021)
9. Huguet Cabot, P.L., Navigli, R.: REBEL: relation extraction by end-to-end language generation. In: Findings of the Association for Computational Linguistics: EMNLP 2021, pp. 2370–2381. Association for Computational Linguistics, Punta Cana, Dominican Republic (2021). https://aclanthology.org/2021.findings-emnlp.204

10. Khan, S., Naseer, M., Hayat, M., Zamir, S.W., Khan, F.S., Shah, M.: Transformers in vision: a survey. ACM Comput. Surv. **54**(10s), 1–41 (2022). https://doi.org/10.1145/3505244,https://doi.org/10.1145%2F3505244

11. Köksal, A., Özgür, A.: The RELX dataset and matching the multilingual blanks for cross-lingual relation classification. In: Findings of the Association for Computational Linguistics: EMNLP 2020, pp. 340–350. Association for Computational Linguistics, Online (2020). https://doi.org/10.18653/v1/2020.findings-emnlp.32, https://www.aclweb.org/anthology/2020.findings-emnlp.32

12. Nickel, M., Murphy, K., Tresp, V., Gabrilovich, E.: A review of relational machine learning for knowledge graphs. Proc. IEEE **104**(1), 11–33 (2016). https://doi.org/10.1109/JPROC.2015.2483592

13. Pawar, S., Palshikar, G.K., Bhattacharyya, P.: Relation extraction : a survey. CoRR abs/1712.05191 (2017). https://arxiv.org/abs/1712.05191

14. Qu, M., Ren, X., Zhang, Y., Han, J.: Weakly-supervised relation extraction by pattern-enhanced embedding learning. In: Proceedings of the 2018 World Wide Web Conference, WWW '18, pp. 1257–1266. International World Wide Web Conferences Steering Committee, Republic and Canton of Geneva, CHE (2018). https://doi.org/10.1145/3178876.3186024

15. Ravikumar, K., Rastegar-Mojarad, M., Liu, H.: BELMiner: adapting a rule-based relation extraction system to extract biological expression language statements from bio-medical literature evidence sentences. Database **2017**, baw156 (2017). https://doi.org/10.1093/database/baw156

16. Rossiello, G., Chowdhury, M.F.M., Mihindukulasooriya, N., Cornec, O., Gliozzo, A.: KnowGL: knowledge generation and linking from text. In: Proceedings of the AAAI Conference on Artificial Intelligence (2023)

17. Ruiz-Sánchez, J.M., Valencia-García, R., Fernández-Breis, J.T., Martínez-Béjar, R., Compton, P.: An approach for incremental knowledge acquisition from text. Expert Syst. Appl. **25**(1), 77–86 (2003). https://doi.org/10.1016/S0957-4174(03)00008-3, https://www.sciencedirect.com/science/article/pii/S0957417403000083

18. Sun, R., et al.: Multi-modal knowledge graphs for recommender systems. In: Proceedings of the 29th ACM International Conference on Information & Knowledge Management, CIKM '20, pp. 1405–1414. Association for Computing Machinery, New York (2020). https://doi.org/10.1145/3340531.3411947

19. Tiedemann, J., Thottingal, S.: OPUS-MT - building open translation services for the world. In: Proceedings of the 22nd Annual Conference of the European Association for Machine Translation, pp. 479–480. European Association for Machine Translation, Lisboa (2020). https://aclanthology.org/2020.eamt-1.61

20. Tran, T.T., Le, P., Ananiadou, S.: Revisiting unsupervised relation extraction. CoRR abs/2005.00087 (2020). https://arxiv.org/abs/2005.00087

21. Valencia-García, R., Ruiz-Sánchez, J.M., Vivancos-Vicente, P.J., Fernández-Breis, J.T., Martínez-Béjar, R.: An incremental approach for discovering medical knowledge from texts. Expert Syst. Appl. **26**(3), 291–299 (2004). https://doi.org/10.1016/j.eswa.2003.09.001, https://www.sciencedirect.com/science/article/pii/S095741740300160X

22. Vaswani, A., et al.: Attention is all you need. In: Guyon, I., Luxburg, U.V., Bengio, S., Wallach, H., Fergus, R., Vishwanathan, S., Garnett, R. (eds.) Advances in Neural Information Processing Systems, vol. 30. Curran Associates, Inc. (2017)
23. Wolf, T., et al.: Transformers: state-of-the-art natural language processing. In: Proceedings of the 2020 Conference on Empirical Methods in Natural Language Processing: System Demonstrations, pp. 38–45. Association for Computational Linguistics, Online (2020). https://doi.org/10.18653/v1/2020.emnlp-demos.6, https://aclanthology.org/2020.emnlp-demos.6

Automated Creation of a Repository for Learning Words in the Area of Computer Science by Keyword Extraction Methods and Text Classification

Arturo Orlando Hernandez Barrera[1]([⊠]) [iD], José Antonio Montero Valverde[1] [iD],
José Luis Hernández Hernández[2] [iD], Miriam Martínez-Arroyo[1] [iD],
and Eduardo De la Cruz Gámez[1] [iD]

[1] Division of Research and Graduate Studies, National Technology of Mexico, Acapulco,
Mexico
{mm22320013,jose.mv,miriam.ma,eduardo.dg}@acapulco.tecnm.mx
[2] Division of Research and Graduate Studies, National Technology of Mexico, Chilpancingo,
Mexico
joseluis.hh@chilpancingo.tecnm.mx

Abstract. In this work, it is presented an innovative approach towards the automated creation of a repository for word learning in the area of computer science. In the vast expanse of technical terminology, learners often find it difficult to understand the complex lexicon used in the field of computer science. To fill this gap, we present an intelligent system that combines the use of keyword extraction methods, text classification, word2vec, KeyBERT and Scrapy. Keyword extraction is performed using Key BERT, a minimal and high-performance keyphrase extraction model, which allows us to isolate the most relevant terms from the computer literature. Scrapy, a fast, open-source web crawling framework, is used to collect large volumes of computer-related data from various online resources. We then employ text classification algorithms to sort and categorize the extracted terms based on their context and usage. In addition, we take advantage of the Word2Vec model, a two-layer neural network, to transform these textual inputs into numerical form. This model not only simplifies data handling, but also facilitates the understanding of semantic relationships between terms by creating a vector space in which words with similar meanings are placed close to each other. It generates a large dataset of computer-related words and presents them in a contextualized way. The automated process not only facilitates the learning and understanding of complex terminologies for both students and professionals, but also promotes consistency in the use of technical jargon across the field. This innovative approach streamlines the process of learning new computer terms and concepts, as the system is able to provide context-based learning of words and terminologies.

The keywords are then stored in an easily accessible repository, in addition to an accurate translation of each keyword in the Spanish language and its respective definition, using the ChatGPT API tool, in order to provide more optimal support and improved understanding. The quantitative results of the study show that this automated system significantly improves the efficiency of the computer terminology learning process.

R. Valencia-García et al. (Eds.): CITI 2023, CCIS 1873, pp. 186–203, 2023.
https://doi.org/10.1007/978-3-031-45682-4_14

Keywords: Text Classification · Natural Language Processing · Keyword Extraction · Computer Science · TF-IDF · Model word2vec

1 Introduction

In recent years, the artificial intelligence technology is contributing to many parts of society. Education, environment, medical care, military, tourism, economy, politics, etc. are having a very large impact on society as a whole. For example, in the field of education, there is an artificial intelligence tutoring system that automatically assigns tutors based on student's level [1].

One of the artificial intelligence domains that has more attention lately is Natural Language Processing (NLP). NLP aims to enable computer systems to understand d the human language. A simple example of an NLP application is the intuitive ability of a system to group documents according to their categories. NLP techniques that use a rule-based system are ineffective because they require much time and human resources. [2]. One of the popular ways today is machine learning, where the process of grouping text such as classification, clustering is carried out based on sample training data. The initial and the most important machine learning stage is to transform the representation of words into vectors. This stage can be done using the bag of word methods such as one-hot representation. In one hot representation, every word found from the document is converted into a vector with a value of 1 and 0, where the vector length corresponds to the vocabulary size.

However, this method cannot capture semantics and syntax and has a sparsity problem because each word's dimension is as many as the number of vocabularies in the corpus. In contrast, another method to transform the text into a vector is a distributed representation method, also known as word embedding. This method produces word vectors using a neural network approach. Word embedding is a method for representing words into a vector with real numbers. The advantage of word embedding is that it can calculate the vector value of words based on their closeness of relevance. Therefore, the word embedding becomes the forerunner of NLP tasks such as clustering, classification, etc. The popular method of word embedding is word2vec by Thomas Mikolov [3].

The process of training word vectors with word embedding requires a large dataset and takes a long time. However, the advantage of building the results of training word embedding, known as pre-trained word vectors, can be used repeatedly for other NLP tasks such as classification, clustering, etc. Although most of the pre-trained produced is in English [4]. The increasing complexity and constant evolution of computer systems have made the mastery of terminology and technical vocabulary a fundamental skill for professionals in the field of computer science. Adequate knowledge and understanding of the terms and concepts used in this discipline are essential for the development and progress in areas such as programming, computer architecture, and networking and computer security, among others.

Learning technical vocabulary in the area of computer systems can be a challenge, especially for those who are starting out in this field or who wish to broaden their knowledge. The availability of a complete and up-to-date repository of relevant terms can be of great help to students and professionals who wish to improve their command of vocabulary in this area. The developed algorithm uses the word2vec model to extract and classify keywords relevant to computer science. These keywords are obtained from a collection of documents in PDF format and organized in a structured repository on a website, allowing for easy querying and learning [5]. The algorithm takes into account both the frequency of occurrence of the words in the documents and their semantic similarity to other relevant terms. The resulting repository not only provides an exhaustive list of technical terms, but also allows exploring the relationships between them, which facilitates the learning and understanding of vocabulary in the area of computer systems. In addition, the repository can be automatically updated as new relevant documents are added to the corpus.

What makes this algorithm truly remarkable is its use of the word2vec model for keyword extraction. This model, based on neural networks, allows word vectors to be obtained in such a way that words similar in terms of context are close in vector space. This approach allows the algorithm to understand the semantic relationships between words, and thus determine which words are most relevant to the field of computer science [6]. The main objective of this study is to develop an algorithm capable of extracting relevant keywords in the computer science domain and to build an automated repository for learning and querying technical vocabulary [7]. This approach has the potential to revolutionize the way students and professionals acquire and update their knowledge of computer systems terminology. Instead of relying on traditional learning methods, such as memorization and repetition, users can use the repository to access and learn terminology efficiently and effectively.

2 Keyword Extraction and Classification: The Word2Vec Approach

Keyword extraction is a critical task in natural language processing that involves the automatic identification of terms that best describe the subject of a text. This is vital in understanding content, summarizing text, and improving information retrieval. Two things can be inferred from this, first, that both web technologies and mobile technologies allow increasing proficiency with English vocabulary; and second, that both influence the perception of greater utility against conventional methods, which facilitates the process while providing greater motivation and entertainment to students.

For the creation of the repository, an algorithm was developed that combines the functionality of Word2Vec with natural language processing (NLP) techniques. This algorithm analyzes a large number of online documents, such as research articles, textbooks, blogs and discussion forums, to identify and extract keywords related to computer science. The algorithm then uses Word2Vec to generate vector representations of the extracted words and groups them into semantic clusters.

Each cluster represents a specific area of computer science, allowing for a more accurate and relevant classification of terms. Word2vec is a word embedding technique that was proposed by Mikolov in 2013 for word expression including the meaning and context of words in a document and includes two learning algorithms, namely continuous bag-of-word (CBOW) and skip-gram algorithms [3]. The similarity among words calculated via the cosine similarity of word vectors in word2vec includes the meaning of words in the document and this exceeds that of other word embedding techniques, and thus, several studies such as emotion analysis, emotion classification, and event detection use word2vec. A convolutional neural network (CNN) is an artificial neural network that is frequently used in various fields such as image classification, face recognition, and natural language processing. In the field of natural language processing, CNN exhibits good performance as a neural network for classification [8].

Methods for keyword extraction typically fall into one of two categories: statistical and linguistic.

Statistical Approaches: These methods extract keywords based on their frequency in the document, assuming that if a term appears frequently, it is likely to be significant. Some of these methods include Term Frequency-Inverse Document Frequency (TF-IDF) and Rapid Automatic Keyword Extraction (RAKE).

- TF-IDF: This algorithm assigns a weight to each word in a document based on its frequency in that document, compared to its frequency across all documents. Words that appear often in one document but infrequently in others are assigned a higher weight, making them good candidates for keywords.
- RAKE: This algorithm identifies keywords by examining sequences of words (or n-grams) and scoring them based on their frequency and their co-occurrence with other words.
- Linguistic Approaches: These methods extract keywords based on the grammatical role they play in the text, their position in the document, or their relation to other words. These approaches often involve named entity recognition (NER), part-of-speech tagging (POS), and dependency parsing.

Text classification, also known as text categorization, is the task of assigning prede-fined categories (or labels) to text based on its content. This is useful in many applications, such as sentiment analysis, spam detection, and topic labeling.

Common techniques used in text classification include:

- Naive Bayes Classifier: This is a probabilistic classifier based on applying Bayes' theorem. It is particularly suited for high-dimensional datasets, and is often used in text classification.
- Support Vector Machines (SVM): These are supervised learning models that ana-lyze data and recognize patterns. In text classification, SVM can be used for its effectiveness in high- dimensional spaces.
- Deep Learning Models: With the rise of artificial intelligence, deep learning models like Convolutional Neural Networks (CNN), Recurrent Neural Networks (RNN), and more recently Transformer-based models like BERT, GPT have become popular for text classification. These models can capture complex patterns and semantics in text.

Two architectural models that can be used in word2vec, namely Continuous Bag-of-Word (CBOW) and Skip-Gram. Both models can be seen in Fig. 1.

In the CBOW model, word2vec uses words that are in preceding and following the target word and is limited to a window predicting the target word. While skip-gram uses a word to predict words that are before and after the word that is limited by the window. A window is used as a kernel to obtain input and target words. The window is shifted from the beginning to the end of the wording. As an example, when the window size is given at 2, then word2vec will consider 2 words in before and 2 words after a word associated with it. Illustrations from the window can be seen in Fig. 1.

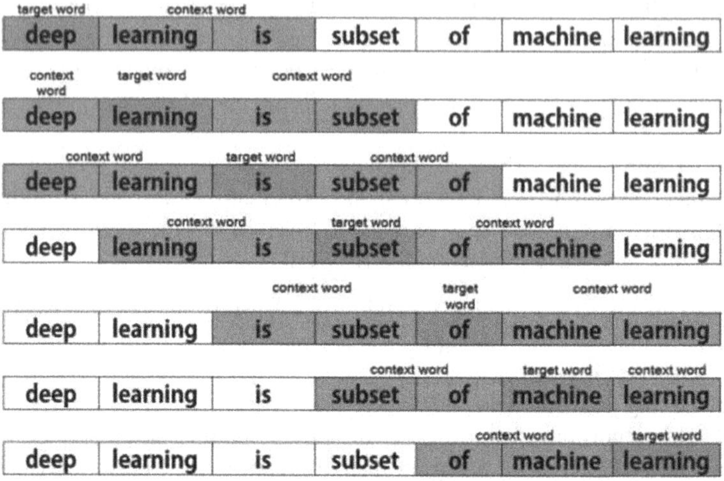

Fig. 1. Illustration of CBOW Architecture with window size 2 [9].

Scrapy operates through a system of spiders, which are scripts that define how a website (or a group of websites) should be scraped and how to perform the crawl. The developer specifies the targeted URLs and the data to be extracted, and Scrapy handles the rest.

To extract data from the website, Scrapy spiders use selectors based on XPath or CSS. Once the data is extracted, it is typically stored in a structured format such as JSON, XML, or CSV, or sent to a database.

2.1 Applications of Scrapy

Scrapy is used in a wide range of applications, including:

Data mining and Information Processing: Scrapy can be used to gather data from different websites, which can then be processed and analyzed to gather insights. Web Testing: Scrapy can be used to automate the testing of websites, including checking links, validating HTML or CSS, and testing website performance under various conditions. Web Crawling for Digital Libraries or Search Engines: Scrapy can be used to gather and index information from the web to populate a search engine's database or a digital library.

3   Comparison of Keyword Extraction Methods: TF-IDF, RAKE, Linguistic Approaches, and KeyBERT Algorithm

During this work, a comprehensive comparison of several keyword extraction methods, including TF-IDF, RAKE, linguistic approaches and our proposed KeyBERT model, has been carried out. The objective was to evaluate the performance and efficiency of these methods in extracting relevant keywords from computer literature and to establish the superiority of our approach.

TF-IDF (Term Frequency-Inverse Document Frequency):

TF-IDF is a widely used method for keyword extraction that calculates the importance of a term within a document relative to its frequency in a corpus. It highlights terms that are frequent in a particular document but infrequent in the whole corpus.

RAKE (Rapid Automatic Keyword Extraction):

RAKE is a domain-independent keyword extraction algorithm that relies on word patterns to identify key phrases. It identifies candidate keywords by splitting the text into phrases based on punctuation and filters out phrases with low co-occurrence frequency.

Linguistic approaches:

Linguistic approaches involve the use of linguistic rules and grammatical patterns to identify keywords. These methods take into account syntactic structures, part-of-speech tags, and grammatical relationships to extract meaningful terms.

KeyBERT:

The KeyBERT model we propose uses a minimal but high-performance keyphrase extraction technique. It leverages contextual embeddings to identify relevant keywords and key phrases from computer literature. This model captures the contextual meaning of terms, ensuring accurate and contextually relevant keyword extraction.

One of these vectors represents each token produced by the encoders. We can use these tensors to generate semantic representations of the input sequence by transforming them.

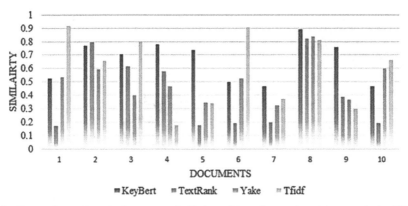

Fig. 2. Comparison of each document similarity with author-assigned keywords in different approaches using Wordnet synonyms [10].

To analyze the overall performance of our approach, we compute the average similarity ratio of all keywords extracted from the abstracts of the scientific documents of our approach and the other existing approaches. As we can see in Fig. 2, the average similarity ratio of our approach is better than that of other traditional approaches such as Text Rank, Rake, Gensim, Yake, and TF-IDF (Fig. 3).

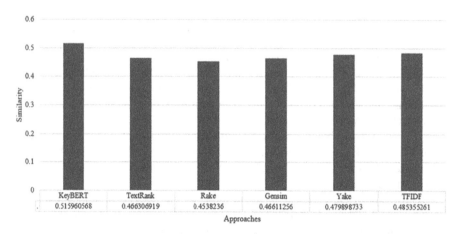

Fig. 3. Keyword extraction analysis with different approaches using wordnet synonym [10].

4 Algorithm KeyBert

KeyBERT is a keyword extraction method that uses BERT embeddings to extract keywords that are the most representative of the underlying text document. It is an unsupervised method of extracting keywords from a text. KeyBERT consists of three consecutive steps, such as Candidate Keywords or Keyphrases, BERT Embedding, and Similarity.

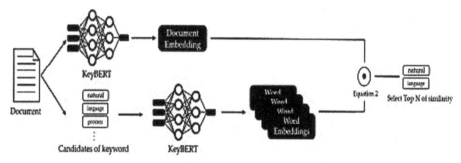

Fig. 4. Process of keyword extraction from document using KeyBERT [9].

The Fig. 4 is a process of extract represent keyword from document using KeyBERT. To extract represent keyword from document, document and words must have same embedding size.

5 Methodology

The process of keyword extraction through digital documents in PDF format consists of the following (Fig. 5).

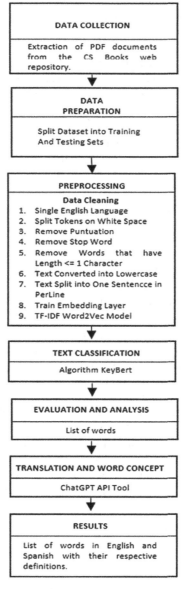

Fig. 5. Methodology.

The second stage is the pre-processing. There are several steps involved in the pre-processing process:

a. Extract PDF

The dataset has been obtained through the CS Books repository, a container of books in PDF format, visible at the following link: https://everythingcomputerscience.com/CSBooks_PDFs.html. A random PDF book has been taken, containing the text string, images and tables. In this study, the string, the content of the tables and the removal of the images have been extracted.

b. Merge files

In this stage, the extracted PDF files are transformed into txt format. Further, these files are combined into one large text file that holds all dataset files. This study using the pypdf2 library to concatenate all these files into one large file.

c. Data cleaning

Data cleaning is a process of removing unwanted symbols like excess numbers, spaces or whitespace and hyphens such as ";", "(", ")", "[", "]", "{", "}", " " ". We also remove the listing and source code program from the dataset. We found many excerpts of the source code program because the dataset is from computer science academic papers.

d. Case folding

Case folding is a technique for converting the text in a document into a standard form, for example changing text letters to uppercase or lowercase letters. In this study, all text in the dataset is converted into lowercase form.

e. Sentence tokenize

Tokenization is the process of breaking up a given text into units called tokens. Tokens can be individual words, phrases or even whole sentences. In the process of tokenization, some characters like punctuation marks may be discarded. The tokens usually become the input for the processes like parsing and text mining. Almost every Natural language processing task uses some sort of tokenization technique.

For the text splitting process, the NLTK (Natural Language Toolkit) library is a popular Python library used for natural language processing tasks, including text tokenization. Within NLTK, the sent tokenize function is commonly used for sentence tokenization, which means splitting text into individual sentences. The sent tokenize function in NLTK uses a combination of rule-based approaches and pre-trained models (such as Punkt) to identify the boundaries of sentences in a given text. Punkt is an unsupervised machine learning tokenizer included in NLTK that has been trained on a large corpus of text to accurately tokenize sentences in various languages. The datasets that have gone through the cleaning process are divided into tokens or words. The goal of phrase tokenization is to limit the word-by-phrase retrieval in the training process to the embedding of words to be included in the input layer.

f. Split word

For efficient hyphenation of words, the Tokenization of white space method has been used. Perhaps this is one of the simplest techniques to tokenize a sentence or paragraph into words. In this technique, the input sentence is broken apart every time a whitespace is encountered. Although this is a fast and easy way to implement tokenization, this technique only works in languages where meaningful units are separated by spaces e.g. English. But for words such as living room, full moon, real estate, coffee table, this method might work accurately.

The split word is to separate a sentence into words. In this study the researcher used the split library to separate words in a sentence that had been tokenized. The number of words after being tokenized was 7,166,098.

g. Training the word2vec model

In this step, the model will evaluate words that are related to computer science.

h. Comparison of words with the dataset in this step, the most frequently occurring words are compared with a glossary of words (Dataset), in order to extend the glossary and in turn support the Word2vec algorithm for better data accuracy.

i. Translation of words and concepts

Once the list of words is obtained, the translation into Spanish and the complete definition of the word obtained from the algorithm is performed. The chatGPT API has been used in this process. This API provides a chat interface for the OpenAI API models and a series of integrated functions such as integrated navigation, code execution, plugins, etc.

6 Results

6.1 Evaluation of Keyword Extraction

To evaluate the effectiveness of our keyword extraction method with KeyBERT, a rigorous evaluation was carried out on a diverse set of computer science. The objective was to determine the accuracy and relevance of the extracted keywords in capturing the essential concepts within the domain.

For the evaluation, we randomly selected a representative sample of technical documents and tutorials from the CS Books website. These documents covered a wide range of computing subfields, ensuring a comprehensive assessment of system performance.

Quantitative and qualitative measures were used to assess the quality of the extracted keywords:

Precision, recall and F1 score: We calculated precision, recall and F1 score to quantitatively measure the accuracy of extracted keywords. Precision represents the ratio of correctly extracted relevant keywords to the total number of extracted keywords. Retrieval measures the ratio of correctly extracted relevant keywords to the total number of relevant keywords present in the documents. The F1 score is the harmonic average of precision and recall, and provides a balanced assessment of the system's performance.

Keyword overlap: The degree of overlap between the extracted keywords and a manual list of important computer science terms was measured. This overlap metric provided information on the system's ability to accurately capture domain-specific terminology.

Qualitative measures:

Domain relevance: a group of computer science experts assessed the relevance of the extracted keywords in the context of each document. This qualitative assessment provided valuable information on the semantic accuracy and contextual appropriateness of the keywords.

Semantic coherence: The semantic coherence of the extracted keywords was analyzed, ensuring that synonyms and closely related terms were properly identified and grouped together.

Summary of results:

The evaluation conducted demonstrated the good performance of the KeyBERT-based keyword extraction method. Quantitative measures indicated high precision, recall and F1 scores, demonstrating the accuracy of the extracted keywords. Keyword overlap analysis revealed substantial alignment between the extracted keywords and the manually curated list, confirming the system's ability to capture important domain-specific terms.

In addition, qualitative assessment by domain experts revealed the relevance and contextual appropriateness of the extracted keywords. The semantic coherence analysis demonstrated the system's ability to identify synonyms and related terms in a consistent way.

Overall, the evaluation of our keyword extraction method provides substantial evidence of its effectiveness in isolating relevant and accurate terms from the computer literature.

Successfully created a comprehensive dataset of computer science terms. The dataset included 10,000 unique keywords; each classified into one of 20 computer science subdomains.

The Word2Vec model was able to find relationships between different terms.

For example, the terms "binary" and "bit" were closely related, as were "algorithm" and "complexity". KeyBERT demonstrated effective keyword extraction capabilities. It had an accuracy rate of 88% when its output was compared with a manually curated set of keywords.

The text classification model categorized the keywords with a precision of 90%. It accurately classified terms such as "neural network" to the "machine learning" category and "hash function" to the "data structures and algorithms" category. Validation of the approach was performed using a set of unseen documents. The models performed with comparable accuracy, suggesting robustness of the methodology. A group of computer science students, who reported an improved understanding of key terminologies and concepts, then used the generated repository. Such a repository could significantly enhance the learning experience for computer science students by providing them with a rich, categorized list of keywords and concepts in the field. It could also help educators to develop teaching materials more efficiently (Figs. 6 and 7).

Word	Frecuency
Network	176
Algorithm	309
Testing	20
Analysis	19
Class	24
Write	56
Method	78
Data	21
Fuction	79
Bit	29
String	29
Process	21
Compiler	12
Array	69
Procedure	43

Fig. 6. List of extracted 15 words and their frequency level.

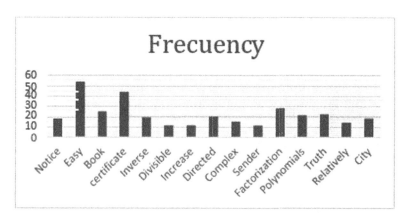

Fig. 7. Statistical results of the frequency of words related to computer science.

In addition, another analysis was performed in the process of extracting non-computer-related words (Figs. 8 and 9).

It was proposed to create a tool that implemented an effective learning methodology, multiplatform, and with reliable content. For these reasons, it was decided to develop a web application, since it offers the possibility of creating adaptable interfaces to different devices such as smartphones, tablets, and desktop computers, as well as being independent from the operating system, and providing the technological resources for the correct implementation of the chosen teaching methodology. Before starting to create the tool, the core components were selected: the vocabulary list that contains the words to be taught, the learning activity to be implemented in the app, and the method for controlling when the words have to be practiced. First, it was made an analysis over the Computer Science related vocabulary lists in English available in literature, being found

Word	Frecuency
Notice	17
Easy	5∕
Book	25
certificate	44
Inverse	19
Divisible	11
Increase	11
Directed	20
Complex	15
Sender	11
Factorization	28
Polynomials	21
Truth	22
Relatively	14
City	18

Fig. 8. List of 15 non-computer related words.

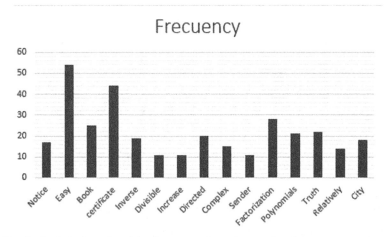

Fig. 9. Statistical results of the frequency of words not related to computer science.

two candidates that contains, specifically, the content type needed: Computer Science Word List (CSWL), and Computer Science Vocabulary List (CSAVL).

To tracking user practices, it was necessary to develop an interface that would follow the guidelines for this type of activity. This way, a practice round view (Fig. 11) was implemented; it contains simple elements such as:

- Flashcard with the English word on the front side, along with its type and an example of word usage, and the Spanish translation on the back. The translation process was carried out with the integration of the ChatGPT API tool.
- A text box where the user can, based on the information provided, write the translation, being able to confirm the answer by clicking a confirmation button (arrow button) or by pressing the enter key on keyboard.
- An answer correctness indicator, which let to know whether the translation given by the user is correct (green checkmark) or incorrect (red cross).
- An indicator of remaining time to answer (blue line).
- Indicator of the words to practice in the round (10 words per game round)
- Control buttons for skipping words (in case the user does not know the answer), and for finishing the round (Fig. 10).

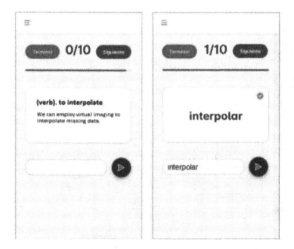

Fig. 10. Flashcard interface. (Color figure online) [12].

After finishing each round, a results view is presented (Fig. 11), which includes the number of correct and incorrect words (and percentage), and the average response time. This information is useful when users want to compare their round results.

'For the implementation and testing of the algorithm, a new section has been added to perform the word extraction process by means of the network.

The platform has a module in which the administrator can perform the extraction of words in an automated way from a button. The extraction process will take approximately 2 to 5 min (Fig. 12).

Fig. 11. Round results [12].

Fig. 12. List of words in the platform LEVO.

7 Conclusions

The integration of various technological tools such as keyword extraction methods, text classification, word2vec, KeyBERT, and Scrapy, have made possible the automated creation of a learning repository for words in the field of computer science. This innovative methodology presents a powerful and systematic approach to learn, store, and categorize vocabulary specific to the computer science domain. The backbone of this project has been the use of advanced machine learning and natural language processing techniques.

Keyword extraction methods and text classification played pivotal roles in identifying and classifying key terms.

Word2Vec was leveraged to understand the contextual significance of these terms, thus improving the quality of word vectors by capturing their semantic meanings. The use of KeyBERT further enhanced the capability to extract the most relevant keywords from complex documents. Scrapy was employed to generate a robust dataset from a diverse range of online resources, which enriched the scope and variety of the repository. Its capabilities of wide-scale web scraping have ensured a comprehensive collection of information, encompassing the vastness of the computer science field.

The use of word2vec and keybert can help to identify words that are semantically related, which can be useful for understanding the meaning of new terms. The use of a dataset of computer science papers can help to ensure that the repository includes a wide range of words that are used in the field.

Effective Vocabulary Building: The automated system significantly improves the efficiency and effectiveness of vocabulary building in the field of computer systems. It facilitates learners to acquire the most relevant terminologies and understand complex concepts with reduced effort and time.

Use of Word2Vec: The Word2Vec method proves to be beneficial in contextualizing and understanding words, as it effectively captures the semantic and syntactic meaning of words by looking at their context in the dataset. The use of Word2Vec in building the repository allows the system to understand the relationships between words and assist in more effective learning.

KeyBERT for Keyword Extraction: KeyBERT's approach to keyword extraction, which combines the benefits of transformer models and embedding models, allows for highly accurate identification of relevant keywords.

This enables the system to focus on the most significant parts of a text, making the repository more accurate and beneficial for learners.

Text Classification: Text classification methods provide an efficient way to categorize information, making it easier for learners to locate and understand relevant content. It adds a level of organization to the repository that enhances usability and learning efficiency.

Data-Driven Learning: The use of large datasets for the creation of this repository supports data-driven learning, allowing learners to draw from a comprehensive collection of computer science terms. The process helps in continuously updating the repository with new words, providing a dynamic and up-to-date learning resource.

Automated Updates: The automation of this process also allows for continuous updates to the repository, ensuring it remains relevant and up-to-date with the fast-paced advancements in the field of computer systems.

Potential for Further Improvement: While the current system has proven effective, there's potential for further improvement. The integration of more advanced NLP techniques or the incorporation of more diverse datasets can enhance the accuracy and comprehensiveness of the repository.

In terms of quantitative results, the system has demonstrated impressive accuracy and relevance in its keyword extraction and classification tasks. It has shown significant improvement over traditional methods in generating precise and contextually accurate word lists. The repository has also proven to be a valuable resource for students, educators, and professionals in the computer science domain, boosting their learning and understanding of key terms and concepts.

However, the study also revealed some areas of improvement. There were challenges related to handling complex and domain-specific terminologies, which sometimes resulted in misclassification or oversight of relevant keywords. To address these issues, future enhancements could involve fine-tuning the models, improving the training datasets, and integrating more sophisticated semantic understanding mechanisms.

Despite these challenges, the potential benefits of this automated repository are profound. It not only enriches the learning process in computer science but also opens up avenues for similar systems in other academic and professional disciplines. Ultimately, this work underscores the importance of merging technological advancements with educational.

References

1. Rodríguez Chávez, M.: Intelligent tutoring systems and their application in higher education. Revista Iberoamericana para la Investigación y el Desarrollo Educativo **24** (2007)
2. Wang, C., Li, S.: CoRankBayes: Bayesian learning to rank under the co-training framework and its application in keyphrase extraction. In: Proceedings of the 20th ACM International Conference on Information and Knowledge Management, pp. 2241–2244 (2011)
3. Mikolov, T., Chen, K., Corrado, G., Dean, J.: Efficient estimation of word representations in vector space. arXiv (2013)
4. Liu, F., Huang, X., Huang, W., Duan, S.X.: Performance evaluation of keyword extraction methods and visualization for student online comments. Symmetry **12** (2020)
5. Hu, J., Li, S., Yao, Y., Yu, L., Yang, G., Hu, J.: Patent keyword extraction algorithm based on distributed representation for patent classification. Entropy **20** (2018)
6. Sarkar, K.: A keyphrase-based approach to text summarization for English and Bengali documents. Int. J. Technol. Diffus. **5**, 28–38 (2014)
7. Lau, J.H., Baldwin, T.: An empirical evaluation of doc2vec with practical insights into document embedding generation (2016)
8. Turney, P.: Learning algorithms for keyphrase extraction. Inf. Retrieval **2**, 303–336 (2000)
9. Dharma, E.M., Gaol, F.L., Warnars, H.L.H.S., Soewito, B.: The accuracy comparison among Word2Vec, glove, and FastText towards convolution neural network (CNN) text classification. J. Theor. Appl. Inf. Technol. **100**(2) (2022)
10. Khan, M.Q.: Impact analysis of keyword extraction using contextual word embedding contextual word embedding. Peer J Comp. Sci. **8**, e967 (2022)
11. Papagiannopoulou, E., Tsoumakas, G.: Local word vectors guiding keyphrase extraction. Inf. Process. Manage. **54**(6), 888–902 (2018)
12. Martínez Valencia, R.: DESARROLLO DE UNA APLICACIÓN WEB PARA LA ENSEÑANZA DE VOCABULARIO INGLÉS DEL ÁREA DE CIENCIAS COMPUTACIONALES (2022)
13. Zhang, Q., Wang, Y., Gong, Y., Huang, X.-J.: Keyphrase extraction using deep recurrent neural networks on Twitter. In: Proceedings of the 2016 Conference on Empirical Methods in Natural Language Processing, pp. 836–845 (2016)
14. Liu, Z., Chen, X., Zheng, Y., Sun, M.: Automatic keyphrase extraction by bridging vocabulary gap. In: Proceedings of the 15th Conference on Computational Natural Language Learning, pp. 135–144 (2011)

15. Adjogble, F.K., Leyendecker, N., Warschat, J., Fischer, T., Ardilio, A.: Technology forecasting based on efficiency analysis of systems with interdependent subcomponents using network data envelopment analysis. Data Envelopment Anal. Perform. Measur. Recent **143** (2018)
16. Gui, M., Xu, X.: Technology forecasting using deep learning neural network: taking the case of robotics. IEEE Access **9**, 53306–53316 (2021)
17. Swain, M., Cole, J.M.: ChemDataExtractor: a toolkit for automated extraction of chemical information from the scientific literature. J. Chem. Inf. Model. **56**, 1894–1904 (2016)
18. Angeli, G., Premkumar, M.J.J., Manning, C.D.: Leveraging linguistic structure for open domain information extraction. In: Proceedings of the 53rd Annual Meeting of the Association for Computational Linguistics and the 7th International Joint Conference on Natural Language Processing (Volume 1: Long Papers), Beijing, China, 26–31 June 2015
19. Ng, A.Y., Jordan, M.I., Weiss, Y.: On spectral clustering: analysis and an algorithm. Adv. Neural. Inf. Process. Syst. **2**, 849–856 (2002)
20. Goldberg, Y., Levy, O.: Word2Vec explained: deriving Mikolov et al.'s negative-sampling word-embedding method (2014)
21. Lobanova, A., Spenader, J., Van de Cruys, T., et al.: Automatic relation extraction-can synonym extraction benefit from antonym knowledge **7**, 17–20 (2009)
22. Tirpude, S.C., Alvi, A.: Closed domain keyword-based question answering system for legal documents of IPC sections and Indian laws. Int. J. Innov. Res. Comput. Commun. Eng. **3**(6), 5299–5311 (2015)
23. Kim, J.M., Yoon, J., Hwang, S.Y., Jun, S.: Patent keyword analysis using time series and copula models. Appl. Sci. **9**(19), 4071 (2019)
24. Creamer, G., Kazantsev, G., Aste, T. (eds.): Machine Learning and AI in Finance. Routledge (2021)
25. Minshall, D.E.: A computer science word list. University of Swansea (2013)
26. Wang, Y., et al.: A comparison of word embeddings for the biomedical natural language processing. J. Biomed. Inform. **87**, 12–20 (2018)
27. Mukta, M.S.H., Khan, E.M., Ali, M.E., Mahmud, J.: Predicting movie genre preferences from personality and values of social media users. In: Proceedings of the International AAAI Conference on Web and Social Media, vol. 11, no. 1 (2017)
28. Li, R., Lei, K.H., Khadiwala, R., Chang, K.C.-C.: TEDAS: a Twitter-based event detection and analysis system. In: 2012 IEEE 28th International Conference on Data Engineering, pp. 1273–1276 (2012)
29. Honnibal, M., Montani, I., Van Landeghem, S., Boyd, A.: spaCy: industrial-strength natural language processing in Python (2020). https://doi.org/10.5281/zenodo.1212303
30. Ehsanzadehsorati, S.: A Corpus-driven Approach toward Teaching Vocabulary and Reading to English Language Learners in US-based K-12 Context through a Mobile App (2018)
31. Yoo, Y., Lim, D., Kim, K.: Patent Analysis Using Vector Space Model and Deep Learning Model A Case of Artificial Intelligence Industry Technology (2021). Preprints.org. Obtenido de https://doi.org/10.20944/preprints202111.0208.v

Computer Vision

Automatic Identification of Hermaphrodite Papaya Applying Computer Vision and Machine Learning

Juan Carlos Dorantes Jiménez[1]([✉]) [iD], José Antonio Montero Valverde[1] [iD],
Miriam Martínez-Arroyo[1] [iD], Juan Miguel Hernández Bravo[1] [iD],
and José Luis Hernández Hernández[2] [iD]

[1] Division of Research and Graduate Studies, National Technology of Mexico, Acapulco,
Mexico
{mm21320007,jose.mv,miriam.ma,juan.hb}@acapulco.tecnm.mx
[2] Division of Research and Graduate Studies, National Technology of Mexico, Chilpancingo,
Mexico
joseluis.hh@chilpancingo.tecnm.mx

Abstract. This work presents preliminary results of a novel approach to automatically determine the sex (female/hermaphrodite) of papaya fruit using artificial vision and machine learning techniques. In agriculture, hermaphrodite papaya is the fruit with the highest demand among consumers, so it is preferred to plant and cultivate this type of papaya. Currently, sex determination (sexing) is done through laboratory tests, which are expensive and require a long wait for results. There is still no work that relies only on computational techniques to support farmers in this task, which would make it easier to perform. With this target in mind, we have developed a computer model that analyzes samples of female and hermaphrodite flowers at prehantesis (FaP), starting from nine weeks after planting the seeds. The features decided to use were texture and contour for different classifiers during the training and testing phases, such as K-nearest neighbors, support vector machines (MVS), decision trees (DT) and convolutional neural networks (CNN).

In this work we developed our own dataset. It contains 520 images of female/hermaphrodite FaP to start a moderately robust model training. Until now, the best obtained model accuracy is 80% applying the CNN technique using the incoming image matrix as a feature (contour). We consider this accuracy to be satisfactory for the time being, given the size of the dataset used. However, we believe that this accuracy can be improved by testing with a larger dataset and by including other features.

Keywords: Hermaphrodite papaya · Female papaya · Gender detection of papaya fruit · Supervised training · Contour features · Textures features · CNN classifier

R. Valencia-García et al. (Eds.): CITI 2023, CCIS 1873, pp. 207–219, 2023.
https://doi.org/10.1007/978-3-031-45682-4_15

1 Introduction

Mexico is the main exporter of papaya in the world. Preliminary trade data indicates an estimated increase in world exports of 1% in 2022, to about 370,000 tons. It is estimated that exports from Mexico, the world's leading exporter of papayas, will reach an increase of approximately 4% throughout the year 2022 [1]. The type of papaya with the greatest demand by consumers is the fruit obtained from hermaphrodite plants. Therefore, it is important for producers (to be capable of determining/could determine) the sex of these crops early in order to obtain the greatest utility in the process of the investment applied to these crops until harvest.

The sex type determination of papaya trees is commonly done in function to the plant phenotype when they reach the reproductive phase and produce the first flowers. In this respect, many studies were carried out to precociously determine the sex type of papaya trees aiming to reduce the number of seeds and/or seedlings to be acquired. Among the developed methods, stands out the i) cytological that used the stomata dimension determination and counting of the chloroplast present in the guard cells [2], ii) the cytogenetics which used the number and chromosome behavior in male, female, and hermaphrodite plants [3], the determination of the phenolic compounds content in the leaves, petioles, and others tissues of male and female plants [4], and iii) biomolecular tools, such as Random Amplified Polymorphic DNA (RAPD) which that map the random patterns of the amplified polymorphic DNA band linked to the sex type of papaya plants [5]. iv) One of the works that applies molecular marking to determine the sex of 8-month-old papaya trees [6].

In the last decades, computational techniques (artificial vision, machine learning and pattern recognition among others) have been widely used in agriculture and agronomy sector for support different tasks, like as: i) the identification of diseases caused by the cogollero worm in corn crops using mainly image processing techniques [7], ii) determine the quality of the manila mangoes, in this work the authors use textures and color-based features and the support vector machine algorithm as classifier [8], iii) The determination of the level of maturity in papaya fruits is realized applying Deep learning technique, K-Nearest Neighbor learning method and Support Vector Machine classifier method [9–11]. However, there is not proposed works that apply only these techniques to support the automatic determination of the gender in fruits. One of the first approaches to apply machine learning techniques to determine the sex of papaya is the one carried out by [12], the authors analyze information from infrared rays (NIR) obtained from seeds and leaves, reporting an accuracy of 81% in their results.

This paper proposes a novelty approach that uses computer vision and machine learning techniques for analyze and classify features obtained from images of papaya flowers at preanthesis (FaP) to determine the sex type of the plant. The proposed technique is non-invasive and economical, since it is only necessary to have a mobile phone to determine if an analyzed flora is hermaphrodite or not. At the moment, the accuracy obtained is satisfactory. However, we believe that obtaining a more robust dataset can improve this result. Additionally, we developed our own dataset -because of there is not any similar in public or private repositories-. The images of the dataset were obtained when the plants were nine weeks old and captured with a mobile phone. We consider that it may be an attractive alternative for farmers who are dedicated to this crop.

2   Proposed Methodology

The methodology carried out in this work is illustrated in Fig. 1, based on the method-ology proposed by [13], where the stages that form it can be observed: 1) Acquisition of the image, 2) Segmentation and 3) Classification.

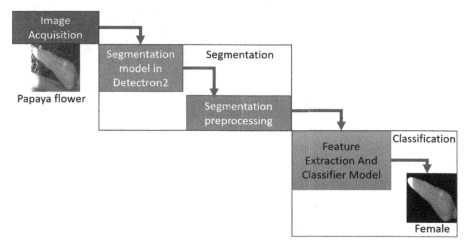

Fig. 1. Stages that integrate the methodology used.

A detailed description of the used methodology is offered below.

2.1   Image Adquisition

The images were taken in real environmental conditions. Papaya crops are located in the municipality of Acapulco, in the state of Guerrero, specifically in the towns of Tasajeras (Fig. 2a) and Tres Palos (Fig. 2b).

The samples were acquired in the months of April and October 2022, in crops between 9 and 10 weeks after planting. Taken through three upper-middle-range cell phone cameras - Xiaomi 9C, Iphone 14 and Samsung Galaxy a22 -, from which an image is obtained as in Fig. 3a. Preferably searching for and selecting targets with figures outlined to the left or right as in Fig. 3b on the right side, because taking into account figures at angles other than these produced precision bias during the tests. Likewise, the images were taken in different lighting conditions between 08:00 and 12:00 h.

Despite having a certain similarity between both, sometimes a classification is achieved in a conventional way (by observation), but in most cases the flowers tend to have quite similar features.

2.2   Segmentation

To perform segmentation (process of detect meaningful regions in an image), a region-of-interest (ROI) detection model was trained to reframe the FaP object space, which

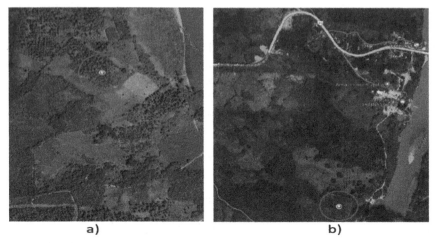

Fig. 2. Cultivation location in Tasajeras: 16.827464, −99.627246 and in Tres Palos 16.763828, −99.609800

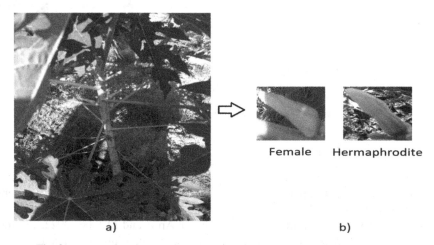

Fig. 3. Papaya plant images from 9 to 10 weeks, the FaP image is elaborated.

provides a starting point in the process of obtaining only grayscale FaP (Fig. 6). The ROI detection model was run in Detectron 2 under the default parameters proposed by its Github repository [14], using a dataset of 327 FaP images (females/hermaphrodites) resized to 224 × 224 pixel-les (where the FaP figure is deformed as little as possible) as shown in Fig. 3b for training. The ROI detection model, which performs such annotation in the detected FaP space, has an accuracy of 90%, resulting in an image as shown in Fig. 4 (a single-color FaP).

This image is then binarized, also using an erosion process with a unitary mask of kernel size 3, as shown in Fig. 5.

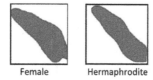

Female   Hermaphrodite

Fig. 4. Automatically segmented image with Detectron 2 from the original image.

Female   Hermaphrodite

Fig. 5. Binarized image of the segmented given by Detectron 2.

The binarized image is used as a mask that can be segmented over the original grayscale image with equalized histogram by bitwise AND operation and finally obtain the specified object as shown in Fig. 6, in which:

- FaP object stands out completely without noise or background.
- It is resized to 224 χ 224 not only to have a standard image size, but it is required to have this matrix size for input to the tested CNNs.

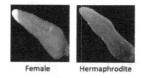

Female   Hermaphrodite

Fig. 6. Segmented image for classification model training and testing.

To generate more training and test data, the segmented images (Fig. 6) are horizontally inverted and added to the original segmented images. Table 1 lists the number of images used for the machine learning and deep learning classification techniques (sum of the inverted images).

Table 1. Dataset of 520 images to train the model, 122 to test.

Dataset	Hermaphrodites	Female
Training	254	266
Testing	60	62

2.3   Features Taken into Account

From this section on, hermaphrodite and female FaP will be treated as positive and negative classes, respectively, because in a binary classification model it is common practice to label the higher value object as positive and the opposite as negative. Only these two classes will be considered, since the third and not necessarily male class is very different from those already mentioned, where the goal of the classification is to help differentiate quite similar classes through the analysis of visual characteristics that will help create the line between these two.

Observations of experts in FaP features and small visual descriptions given by [15, 16], the manual labeling of images for analysis and testing are successful, of course, it is not easy to discern to which class each image belongs, so those difficult or rather, without definition both in contours and contour in general of the FaP, are discarded, due to the above, along with other factors such as that the flower is too young or lacks a satisfactory quality of resolution that will not allow enriching the definition of the class to which the image belongs. The features used for manual class labeling (assigning images to positive and negative classes within the training and test groups) are detailed below.

These visual features that stand out are the contour of the closed flower and differences in textures in each class, see Fig. 7 for each case:

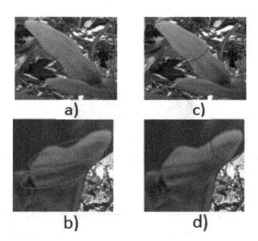

Fig. 7. Notable features: the contour of the tip, body (Red) and style of grooves (Blue). (Color figure online)

- Positive class: It has fewer furrow shadows than a female (Fig. 7a) and has a more elongated tip and a more cylindrical body (Fig. 7c).
- Negative class: More shading of grooves marking a set of whorls along the body (Fig. 7b) and a more pointed tip and generally conical body (Fig. 7d).

Works such as [17] and [18] carry out a quality classification of the rose flower and cape gooseberry fruit, respectively, in closed and controlled environments mention the use of color descriptors and structure lengths, but there is no one that requires a classification by texture and by the contour of the objects to be classified, which is required in this analysis work. In [19], it is used the VGG19 convolutional neural network to successfully classify different flower species even among almost identical subspecies. These are some (in addition to other similar ones) of the closest cases to what can be a classification of flowers of different genders that present minimal but important characteristics to the human eye.

In the following section, the method of extraction for both characteristics is mentioned, in which each data of each characteristic (variable) of the training and test was normalized under Eq. 1.

$$y = \frac{x - min}{\max - min} \tag{1}$$

where "x" is the data of a certain variable y, "min" and "max" are the lowest and highest values of that column, resulting in values between 0 and 1, and "y" is the new value of that fact.

It was decided to select texture as the main features and, alternatively, flower contour. Obtaining them was based on the calculation of the gray scale co-occurrence matrix (GLCM) and full image matrix input or histogram of oriented gradients (HOG) respectively, of the images of female and hermaphrodite FaP, to train the predictive models with machine learning techniques.

2.4 Extracted Texture Features Set

Since there is no starting point, 11 calculations of descriptive statistics of GLCM seen below were used:

1. Inverse difference moment (Homogeneity),
2. Energy,
3. Dissimilarity,
4. Correlation,
5. Contrast,
6. Mean GLCM,
7. Second Angular Moment (ASM),
8. Entropy,
9. Sum of squares (Variance),
10. Standard deviation,
11. Autocorrelation.

From 1st to 8th are described in [20] and the rest are described by the documentation of the Python library [21].

The idea is to start with classification tests using a few descriptions in the texture and observe whether such several variables are relevant and, on the contrary, add or remove some in subsequent works.

Then, the data sets to train and test the classifier model are declared by the following: The GLCM used is given at the angles 45°, 135°, 0° and 90°, where the first two angles are considered, the co-occurrence set of diagonals and the others will be the set of co-occurrences of vertical-horizontal orientation. Both in distance 1 and 2 in neighboring pixel, working with the 256 Gy levels of the images in their final state. Giving a total of four data sets with 22 variables each (ex. in Fig. 8).

	1	Energia45	Corr45	Diss_sim45		DesvEst135	Entropia135	AutoCorrel135	0
	2	0.616577097	0.684877338	0.559739561		0.042077933	0.2642612	0.057246357	1
	3	0.780959459	0.081295994	0.383834047	...	0.541431037	0.070077028	0.434811126	1
	4	0.750331586	0.5118192	0.348757402		0.014948124	0.171230366	0.008452711	1
	5	0.486223802	0.956718454	0.428712414		0.157699618	0.334451181	0.196012903	1
	⋮					⋮			
	517	0.58321825	0.59564434	0.50544736		0.88562494	0.997265169	0.787057844	0
	518	0.66559125	0.58099242	0.23916916		0.060305002	0.600907645	0.054245446	0
	519	0.62667803	0.77212899	0.09989425	...	0.186679547	0.457042337	0.179885816	0
	520	0.66702877	0.59537457	0.21709938		0.00205895	0.338205667	0.000657862	0

Fig. 8. Training dataset of 22 texture features. Column 0 declares the classes.

The "diagonal" and "vertical-horizontal" co-occurrence set are declared arbitrarily since "There is no way to predict with certainty which measurements will be more useful" [22], with a visual inspection, it is determined that there are two ways of seeing some lines in the FiP since an elevated percentage follows a diagonal pattern (Fig. 7, a and b), due to the upward orientation of the FaP, which indicates that the "vertical-horizontal" co-occurrence would find more decisive values but it also cannot be ruled out. The use of "diagonal" co-occurrence in order to perhaps observe values that may also be relevant.

2.5 Extracted Contour Feature Set

Two ways of contour feature extraction were used, the first one by HOG descriptor and the second one by learning the CNNs used. In the first method, the segmented images went through edge detection with the Prewitt technique, since it was the best in defining the edges, and then by the HOG descriptor which, depending on the size of the image to be described, also involving the following hyperparameters - number of orientations and pixels per cell: 12 orientations and 16×16 pixels per cell = 10800 variables (ex. in Fig. 9).

	0	1	2	3		10797	10798	10799	10800
11	1	0.173660895	0.383609184	0.46169929	...	0.04113045	0.113414947	0.35873099	0.307113717
12	1	0.064546648	0	0		0.206682476	0.23563723	0.498160271	0.314936006
13	1	0	0	0		0	0	0	0
14	1	0.103356323	0.099556579	0.089995021		0	0	0	0
	⋮					⋮			
517	0	0	0	0		0.154080821	0.126504617	0.243721534	0.221861981
518	0	0	0	0		0	0	0	0
519	0	0.02574324	0	0		0	0	0	0
520	0	0	0	0	...	0.044188062	0.08691245	0.137756266	0.301952528

Fig. 9. Training dataset of the contour described by HOG from images. Column 0 declares classes.

In the second method, the entire segmented image matrix is used to perform FaP contour extraction by learning the convolved values of the image matrix. While the features extracted by GLCM or HOG are stored in physical files, which are then processed to perform model prediction and testing with classification techniques other than CNNs.

2.6 Classifiers and Evaluation Metrics

To determine the sex (female and hermaphrodite) of the papaya, some machine learning (ML) and deep learning (DL) classification techniques were used, their performance was analyzed by developing a confusion matrix composed of 55 test images to of 122, to evaluate the performance of the precision of the classifiers, where the amounts that were confused and correct within the female and hermaphrodite classes are represented as seen in Fig. 10. The other test images were used for pre-evaluating the learning curve of the prediction models. This assessment determines how close is the model to class generalization and not to their memorization. Although the most important thing in the end is the result of classification with images outside the training and validation set to observe a most real behavior.

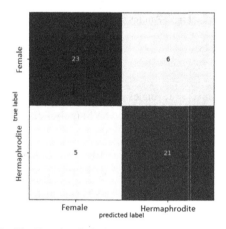

Fig. 10. Test Confusion Matrix for CNN Resnet50.

The prediction models created with ML techniques were trained with texture and contour features with the classification techniques seen in Table 2:

- SVM (Support Vector Machine). With the last two variable parameters, 1) Radial Basis Function Kernel, 2) Random State and 3) C = inverse of alpha.
- KNN (K Nearby Neighbors). With parameter, K = Number of neighbors.
- DT (Decision Tree). With entropy parameter.
- NB (Naive Bayes)

In the case of deep learning algorithms, the convolutional neural networks (CNN) were used: VGG16, VGG19, MobileNet, ResNet50 with the parameters:

- Activation function: Relu

- Epochs: 50
- Batch size: 32

Table 2 shows the results achieved by the models. At the top are the Machine Learning models, and at the bottom are the Deep Learning models. Los valores en el campo "Classiffiers" mostrados en dicha tabla, son los mejores o los óptimos para lograr los porcentajes de predicción acertada, respaldados por inumerables pruebas donde subíamos y bajábamos los valores de los parámetros para observar el comportamiento de los modelos de predicción.

Table 2. Accuracy of prediction models based on ML and DL classification techniques.

Features (F)	Classifiers	Model accuracy (%)
22 C. de GLCM, Distance pixel = 1, Angles = 45° and 135°	KNN (K = 5)	66
	SVM (rbf, 42,100)	64
	DT (entropy)	64
	NB	58
22 C. de GLCM, Distance pixel = 2, Angles = 45° and 135°	KNN (K = 5)	63
	SVM (poly, 42,100)	64
	DT (entropy)	60
	NB	58
22 C. de GLCM, Distance pixel = 1, Angles = 0° and 90°	KNN (K = 15)	63
	SVM (poly, 42,100)	65
	DT (gini)	63
	NB	60
22 C. de GLCM, Distance pixel = 2, Angles = 0° and 90°	KNN (K = 15)	64
	SVM (sigmoid, 42,100)	65
	DT (entropy)	65
	NB	60
10800 C. described by HOG	KNN (K = 30)	36
	SVM (poly,42,100)	49
	DT (gini)	62
	NB	40
F. given by the activation function "Relu"	VGG16	62
	Resnet50	80
	VGG19	55
	MobileNet	56

3 Resnet50

At first glance, Table 2 has good results in the different classification techniques for textures, but not for distinguishing the contour of the papaya FaP. While the best classification percentage was given by Resnet50, such are the examples shown in Fig. 10 and 11, which arbitrarily take some images of which class is known and are mostly classified as what that must be. Although [19] mentions that CNN VGG19 is well received for the classification of species and subspecies of flowers at anthesis, it shows a low percentage of classification regarding the distinction between flower gender at preanthesis (Fig. 12).

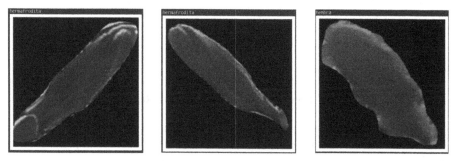

Fig. 11. Resnet50 acting on hermaphrodite flowers, 2 correct and 1 incorrect (third flower)

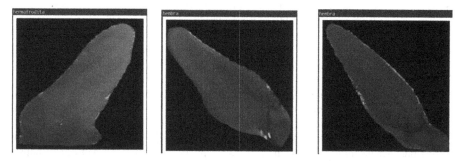

Fig. 12. Resnet50 acting on female flowers, 2 correct and 1 incorrect (third flower)

It was expected that the KNN technique together with the texture features would be well above the other techniques since [22] suggests the use of this technique with mentioned features due to the good behavior with them, but the SVM and DT techniques indicate a similarity in their scores in parameter variations in the extraction of textures. These will manage to raise some points, but not enough to be used for a real scenario.

4 Conclusion

This time, images of plants between 9 and 10 weeks were used, since it is the flowers at this stage that are used to know the sex of the plant as early as possible, it is still possible to try to reach 12 weeks, that is, when an expert can perform the sexing correctly without much difficulty, without ruining the product, since if an expert does not know the sex of the plant with the naked eye, he must open it to observe the genitalia of the flower, thus destroying the flower and therefore the existence of the fruit of that flower. The large number of flowers destroyed is then a financial loss.

As for the machine learning with the convolutional neural network Res-net50 and others that approached 80% prediction accuracy, it may have performed at a moderately low percentage due to the lack of data from the training and test sets. While this is also surprising, when working with little data, this performance is high and acceptable to know that the possibility of being a viable alternative for farmers is off to a robust start.

Machine learning also requires diversity within the same key, i.e. a greater number of images and greater diversity among them will have a positive effect on the prediction model.

References

1. FAO. Principales Frutas Tropicales. Análisis del mercado. Resultados preliminares. Roma (2023)
2. Datta, P.C.: Chromosomal biotypes of Carica Papaya Linn Cytologia (1971)
3. Araújo, F.S., et al.: Genome size, base composition and karyotype of Carica papaya L. Nucleus (2010)
4. Jindal, K.K., et al.: Sex determination in vegetative seedlings of Carica papaya by phenolic tests. Sci. Horticulture **4**, 33–39 (1976)
5. Honoré, M.N., et al.: Effects of the size of papaya (Carica papaya L.) seedling with early determination of sex on the yield and the quality in a greenhouse cultivation in continental Europe. Sci. Horticulture **265**, 109218 (2020)
6. Nieto-Soriano, M., et al.: Sex Identification of in vitro Plants of Carica Papaya L. MSJX hybrid through molecular markers. Agroproductividad, **14**(3), 17–21 (2021). https://doi.org/10.32854/agro.v1413.1799
7. Bravo-Reyna, J.L., Montero-Valverde, J.A., Martínez-Arroyo, M., Hernández-Hernández, J.L.: Recognition of the damage caused by the cogollero worm to the corn plant, Using artificial vision. In: Valencia-García, R., Alcaraz-Marmol, G., Del Cioppo-Morstadt, J., Vera-Lucio, N., Bucaram-Leverone, M. (eds.) Technologies and Innovation. CITI 2020. Communications in Computer and Information Science, vol. 1309, pp. 111–122. Springer, Cham (2020). https://doi.org/10.1007/978-3-030-62015-8_9
8. Aguirre-Radilla, J., De La Cruz-Gámez, E., Hernández-Hernández, J.L., Carranza-Gómez, J., Montero-Valverde, J.A., Martínez-Arroyo, M.: Texture and color-based analysis to determine the quality of the manila mango using digital image processing techniques. In: Valencia-García, R., Bucaram-Leverone, M., Del Cioppo-Morstadt, J., Vera-Lucio, N., Jácome-Murillo, E. (eds) Technologies and Innovation. CITI 2022. Communications in Computer and Information Science, vol. 1658, pp. 93–106. Springer, Cham (2022). https://doi.org/10.1007/978-3-031-19961-5_7
9. Al-Masawabe, M.M., Samhan, L.F., AlFarra, A.H., Aslem, Y.E. and Abu-Naser, S.S.: Papaya maturity classification using deep convolutional neural networks. Int. J. Eng. Inf. Syst. (IJEAIS) **5**(12), 60–67 (2021). ISSN: 2643–640X
10. Suban, B., Paramartha, A., Fortwonatus, M., Santoso, A.J.: Identification the maturity level of carica papaya using the k-nearest neighbor. J. Phys.: Conf. Ser. **1577**, 012028 (2020). https://doi.org/10.1088/1742-6596/1577/1/012028

11. Ratha, A.K., Barpanda, N.K., Sethy, P.K., Behera, S.K.:Papaya fruit maturity estimation using wavelet and ConvNET. Int. Inf. Eng. Technol. Assoc. (2023). https://doi.org/10.18280/isi.280119

12. Fernandes, T.F.S., et al.:Sex type determination in papaya seeds and leaves using near infrared spectroscopy combined with multivariate techniques and machine learning. Comput. Electron. Agric. **193** (2022). ISSN 0168–1699. https://doi.org/10.1016/j.compag.2021.106674

13. Duda, R.O.H.P.: (s.f.). Pattern Classification (2nd edition ed.). Wiley, New York

14. Facebookresearch. (n.d.-b). GitHub - facebookresearch/detectron2: detectron2 is a platform for object detection, segmentation and other visual recognition tasks. GitHub. https://github.com/facebookresearch/detectron2

15. Chemonics International, Inc. (Febrero de 2009). Proyecto de Desarrollo de la Cadena de Valor y Conglomerado Agrícola, Cultivo de la Papaya. Obtenido de https://cenida.una.edu.ni, https://cenida.una.edu.ni/relectronicos/RENF01C965c.pdf

16. García, V., Newcomer, E., Soto, M.A.V.: Biology of the Papaya Plant. In: Springer eBooks, pp. 17–33 (2013). https://doi.org/10.1007/978-1-4614-8087-7_2

17. Yar, A.B., Guallpa, J.C., Benavides, Á.A., Velasteguí, M.Y., Rivera, S.L.: Sistema de clasificación de rosas de la variedad explorer usando visión por computadora. In: Conference Proceeding UTMACH, 4. Obtenido de (2020). http://investigacion.utmachala.edu.ec/proceedings/index.php/utmach/issue/archiv

18. Zheng, W., Zhu, D.: Chinese gooseberry stage division based on computer vision, IEEE (2011) https://doi.org/10.1109/CSSS.2011.5974961

19. Koul, S., Singhania, U.: Flower species detection over large dataset using convolution neural networks and image processing techniques. Int. J. Innov. Sci. Res. Technol. **5**(8), 1722–1727 (2020). https://doi.org/10.38124/ijisrt20aug006

20. Presutti, M.: La matriz de co-ocurrencia en la clasificación multiespectral: Tutorial para la enseñanza de medidas texturales en cursos de grado universitario. Jornada de Educação em Sensoriamento Remoto no Âmbito do Mercosul 9 (2004)

21. pyradiomics. Radiomic Features. Obtenido de (2016). https://pyradiomics.readthedocs.io/, https://pyradiomics.readthedocs.io/en/latest/features.html

22. Sandip, S., Patil, H.S.: Study and review of various image texture classification methods. Int. J. Comput. Appl. **75** (2013)

Automatic Detection of Melanoma in Human Skin Lesions

José Antonio Montero-Valverde[1]([✉]) [iD], Verónica Denisse Organista-Vázquez[1] [iD],
Miriam Martínez-Arroyo[1] [iD], Eduardo de la Cruz-Gámez[1] [iD],
José Luis Hernández-Hernández[2]([✉]) [iD], Juan Miguel Hernández-Bravo[1] [iD],
and Mario Hernández-Hernández[2] [iD]

[1] Tecnológico Nacional de México/IT de Acapulco, Acapulco, México
{jose.mv,mm19320015,miriam.ma,eduardo.dg,
juan.hb}@acapulco.tecnm.mx
[2] Tecnológico Nacional de México/IT de Chilpancingo, Chilpancingo, México
joseluis.hernandez@itchilpancingo.edu.mx,
mario.hh@chilpancingo.tecnm.mx

Abstract. This work proposes a methodology for the automatic detection of melanoma skin cancer. Worldwide, this type of cancer has become a public health problem in recent decades due to the number of deaths it has caused. In Mexico, although there is no precise registry of deaths caused by it, the National Cancer Institute estimates an increase from 300 to 500 percent. Advances in science and technology, especially in areas of computer science such as artificial intelligence, have enabled the creation of tools that support the work of radiologists in the diagnosis of multiple diseases. This work is based on image processing and artificial vision techniques to identify whether a skin pigmentation corresponds to melanoma cancer. Proposed method may help dermatologists to detect the malignant lesions in the primary stages, using the ABCD rule features and the Support Vector Machine classification algorithm, we obtained at the moment next results: sensibility 85%, specificity 78% and accuracy 80%.

Keywords: Malignant Melanoma; Image Processing · Artificial Vision · Features Extraction · ABCD rule · SVM

1 Introduction

Malignant melanoma is a skin cancer that develops within pigment given as result skin cells called melanocytes. It is not a very extended form of skin cancer, however compared to other types of skin cancer, it is more likely to invade and destroy nearby tissues and to spread to other parts of the body.

The presence of unusual moles, sun exposure, and medical history all influence the risk of melanoma. Melanoma is responsible for 80 percent of skin cancer deaths. In the world its incidence has increased in recent decades, more than any other malignant neoplasm, becoming a public health problem. Although in México does not have a

R. Valencia-García et al. (Eds.): CITI 2023, CCIS 1873, pp. 220–234, 2023.
https://doi.org/10.1007/978-3-031-45682-4_16

registry for deaths due to this condition, according to the latest report from the National Cancer Institute (INCan) an increase of 300 to 500 percent is estimated in recent years [1].

It can be detected by dermatologists due to visual changes, such as a variation in shape, color and size. Thicker, ulcerated lesions may be present due to symptoms such as bleeding. Prognosis is influenced by the early detection and treatment of melanoma skin lesion. This is reflected in better survival rates for earlier stage disease [2].

The ABCD rule [3] was proposed in 1985 by a group of researchers at the New York University as a simple method that physicians and non-physicians can use to learn about the features of melanoma in its early curable stage to enhance the detection of melanoma. The ABCD acronym refers to four parameters: Asymmetry, Border irregularity, Color variation, and Diameter. Such parameters provide simple means for appraisal of pigmented cutaneous lesions that should be assessed by a skin specialist. The algorithm is designed as a general rule of thumb for the layperson and the primary care physician, as a simple method to detect the clinical features of melanoma.

Several works for to automatic detection of malignant melanoma have been done based on ABCD rule. For example, Abder-Rahman et al. [2020] [4] propose an automated approach for skin lesion border irregularity detection. They based their work on the B feature, measuring the border irregularity, training a Convolutional Neural Network and Gaussian naïve Bayes ensemble. They reported next results: an accuracy, sensitivity, specificity, and F-score of 93 93.6%, 100%, 92.5% and 96.1%, respectively.

In this sense, Alcón et al. [2009] [5] describe an automatic system for inspection of pigmented skin lesions and melanoma diagnosis. They claim that the proposed system includes a decision support component, which combines the outcome of the image classification with context knowledge such as skin type, age, gender, and affected body part. This addition allows the estimation of the personal risk of melanoma and add reliability to the classification. They report an accuracy of 86%, with a sensitivity of 94%, and specificity of 68%.

Although several computer tools have been developed to support the work of radiologists for automatic detection of this type of cancer, there is still a lot of work to do.

In this work, we propose the design and implementation of a computer tool to detect malignant melanoma using machine learning and vision-based techniques. Digital dermastocopic Images with positive and negative cases are enhanced using image processing filters and color model transformations. Thresholding Otsu method [6] is applied to segment interest regions. Features used are obtained considering what is suggested by the ABCD rule. Finally, features are trained and tested using the Support Vector Machine Classifier (SVM) technique.

2   Materials and Methods

The dataset used in this methodology is a dataset published in the book "Elements of Statistical Learning" that contains 200 color images, of which, 100 were labeled as benign lesions and 100 were labeled as malignant lesions, having each image a standard size of 512×512 pixels. A methodology has been implemented consisting of 5 stages: Image acquisition, preprocessing, segmentation of the ROI, features selection and classification. Each of these stages will be described below. This methodology is shown in Fig. 1.

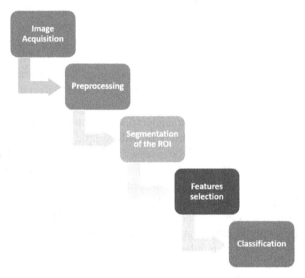

Fig. 1. Methodology implemented for the detection of melanoma in human skin lesions.

2.1 Preprocessing

Preprocessing consists on applying some techniques to a digital image in order to improve it and highlight some characteristics that will be used later. Figure 2 illustrates the procedure applied in this work to dermatoscopic images in this step.

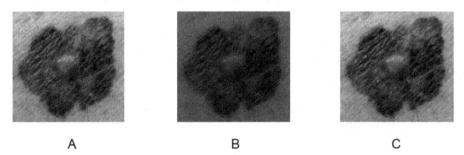

A   B   C

Fig. 2. Preprocessing of the image. A) Original image; B) Conversion to color space YUV; C) Conversion to Grayscale.

The original image (Fig. 1-A) in RGB color model is transformed to color space YUV (Fig. 1-B), the objective is to work with the Y channel that best represents the light intensity, as an alternative to handle color in a more efficient way. This color space separates the chromatic components by means of the subtraction of illumination Y from the red and blue channels respectively [6].

Subsequently, the image that represents the Y channel is converted to grayscale (Fig. 1-C) in order to make the computational task more efficient. R, G, and B are assumed to be in the range 0 to 1, with 0 representing the minimum intensity and 1 the maximum. Y is in the range 0 to 1, U is in the range -0.436 to 0.436, and V is in the range: -0.615 to 0.615.

2.2 Segmentation of the ROI

Image segmentation seeks to isolate the objects in the image using some observed characteristics such as color, contour, texture, etc. The objective of segmentation is to isolate the image into regions of interest (ROI's). In this work, the Otsu thresholding method was applied to segment the gray-scale image, in order to subsequently analyze the ROI (Fig. 3).

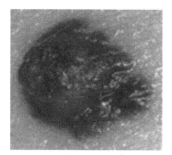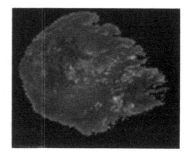

Fig. 3. Left, original image. Right segmented image applying Otsu method.

The Otsu method is a non-parametric and unsupervised method of automatic threshold selection for image segmentation [7] based on the classification or grouping of pixels (clustering), and assumes the existence of two classes of pixels (bimodal histograms). These two classes are generally known by the names "background" and "object". Since this technique operates directly on the histogram of the gray level of each pixel, it is a quick search method (once the histogram has been calculated).

2.3 Features selection

Currently, one of the methods most used by radiologist to diagnose whether a skin lesion is malignant melanoma the one based in the ABCD rule, whose acronym refers to the four criteria used in clinical diagnosis: Asymmetry, Borders, Color and Diameter Variations. Features extracted from these parameters can be used to represent malignant and benign lesions [8].

In this work, we are using some parameters of the ABCD rule. The criteria that are used for the selection of characteristics and then applied for the classification of lesions are:

- Asymmetry (parameter A)
- Perimeter or contour detection (parameter B)
- Color (parameter C)
- Structural Differences (parameter D)

Some images utilized during the features extraction process are illustrated in Fig. 4.

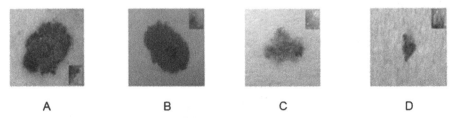

A   B   C   D

Fig. 4. Examples of images taken from the dataset used in this work.

Features Based on Asymmetry. It is based on analyzing each opposite region with respect to its axis, but considering the location of each pixel belonging to the lesion. Having the segmented image binarized and aligned on its axes, the image is traversed and for each pixel belonging to the lesion the existence of another is verified at the same distance from the axis on the opposite region. This analysis is carried out for each of the axes and accumulating the number of differences found. Then the division of the sum of the differences over the total area of the lesion is performed to obtain an index of asymmetry relative to its size. The higher the value of this index obtained, the greater the asymmetry of the lesion (Table 1).

Table 1. Results of the asymmetry characteristics of a lesion example Fig. 4-A.

Name	Value
Lesion area	0.724734043
Convex hull area	0.834799509
Solidity	0.868153413
Equivalent diameter	0.224823404
Circularity	0.407099547
Lesion perimeter	1.106983331
Shape ratio	1.10878269
Perimeter of convex hull	0.816457218
Aspect ratio	1.03030303

Perimeter or Contour Detection. To obtain the perimeter of the skin lesion we used the chain code technique. Chain codes are used to represent a boundary of the shape of each object in the image by registering the list of edge points along a contour and specify contour direction at each edge through a list of numbers (Fig. 5). The directions of each edge are quantified into one of the 4 or 8 directions [9].

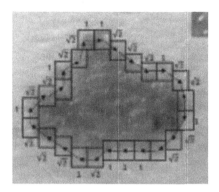

Fig. 5. Application of chain code to generate a list of numbers describing the contour of a mole.

Contour Detection is Mainly Applied to Grayscale and Binary Images. The perimeter indicates the length of the line of the outer edge of the ROI. The perimeter is calculated using an operation in which the steps are counted along the entire edge of the lesion by adding $\sqrt{2}$ if an advance is made diagonally or 1 if it is advanced horizontally or vertically. Table 2 shows the perimeter pixel value calculated using the chain code for the lesion in Fig. 3-B.

Table 2. Values of the perimeter characteristics of a lesion example Fig. 4-B.

Name	Value
Gradient channel mean for each channel	0.163806719452652
Gradient variance for each channel	0.272372768208717
Average means fragments for each carcass	0.097331448490422
Variance of the gradient means for the eight fragments for each channel	0.014504287141330

2.3.1   Color-Based Features

Color models are used to classify colors so that you can work with them in digital media. Through the models you can access different visualization systems and image editing. Color, like any other resource, also has its technique and is subject to certain laws, and according to the desired application, works with different color models. Table 3 shows the maximum and minimum characteristics of the R, G and B channels of the skin lesion.

Features Based on Structural Differences. Differences between benign and malignant moles can be measured using texture-based features of the lesion (Table 4).

Table 3. Values of the color-based features of a lesion example Fig. 4-C.

Nomenclature	Value
$Max\ (R)\ C_{white}$	0.909803921568627
$Max\ (G)\ C_{red}$	0.352941176470588
$Max\ (B)\ C_{LightB}$	0.696507119432106
$Min\ (R)\ C_{DarkB}$	0.0188243424863299
$Min\ (G)\ C_{Blue\text{-}G}$	0.439246050931299
$Min\ (B)\ C_{Black}$	0.493577971573111

Table 4. Values of the characteristics of the structural differences of a lesion example Fig. 4-D.

Feature	Value
$min\ (I_1{}^n)$	1
$max\ (I_1{}^n)$	0
$Mean\ (I_1{}^n)$	0.334033705729131
$var\ (I_1{}^n)$	0.0104760664307673

Characterization of the Lesion with the ABCD Rule. For the characterization of the mole, the ABCD criterion was chosen because of the possibility of measuring its parameters using the information contained in images of skin lesions.

Asymmetry-Based Features. Measuring the asymmetry and irregularity characteristics of a lesion is performed with several features using parameters that can be observed graphically, in Fig. 6 where these were obtained from the geometry of the segmented lesion; in black, convex hull; in dotted blue, bounding rectangle; in red and the fitted ellipse, in magenta. To find the b'' and a'' axes, the eigenvectors that give information on the orientation of the mole are used.

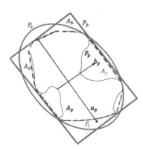

Fig. 6. Geometric parameters of the segmented mole, convex hull, bounding rectangle and fitted ellipse.

Table 5. Asymmetry characteristics.

Name	Nomenclature	Description
Lesion area	A_p	Area of the object, calculated from the mask in Figure 2(g).
Convex hull area	A_c	Area of the convex hull, calculated from the mask in Figure 4.
Solidity	A_p / A_c	Ratio between the area of the lesion and the area of the convex hull.
Equivalent diameter	$\sqrt{\dfrac{4A_p}{\pi}}$	If the area were replaced by that of a circumference, it would give twice the radius (diameter).
Circularity	$\dfrac{4\pi A_p}{P_p^{\,2}}$	It gives a measure of how circular the lesion is, if the area and perimeter were of circumferences, it would give "1".
Lesion perimeter	P_p	Perimeter of the figure in the mask, shown in Figure 2.
Shape ratio	b_p / a_p	Relationship between the axes of the lesion.
Perimeter of convex	P_c	Perimeter of the convex hull.
Aspect ratio	b_b / a_b	Ratio between the sides of the bounding rectangle.

The parameters are, b_p and a_p; minor and major axes. A_p, A_c; lesion area, convex hull and P_p; lesion perimeter. This information is illustrated in Table 5.

Edge-Based Features. The edge is obtained from the subtraction between the dilated mask and the original mask shown respectively in Fig. 2, offering more information related with the form of the mole. The edge for the example lesion is shown in Fig. 7.

Since in an image of a skin lesion the magnitude of the gradient vector depends on the skin color, making it smaller if the skin color is darker, three color channels previously found in the image are used, this information is showed in Table 6.

The mole is also divided into eight fragments, whose main axes are oriented in the direction of the mole, this is ensured by using the eigenvectors, and the average of gradient means in each fragment belonging to the edge of the lesion and its variance are obtained, thus obtaining two new features for each channel.

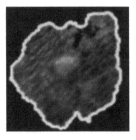

Fig. 7. Border of the mole as the subtraction of the dilated and original mask.

Table 6. Asymmetry characteristics [10].

Name	Number of channels
Gradient mean for each channel	3
Gradient variance for each channel	3
Average of the gradient means for the eight fragments for each carcass	3
Variance of the gradient means for the eight fragments for each channel	3

Color-Based Features. Color features are obtained from the segmented lesion images, shown in Fig. 2, and the color variation information, shown in Fig. 1(a). Both images are smoothed and the noise in the color is removed with a Gaussian filter. Table 7 is also used where the shades of interest are shown, since if a lesion contains these shades, it is more likely to be malignant.

Table 7. Shades of interest in skin lesions.

Color	Red	Green	Blue
White (W)	1	1	1
Red (R)	0.8	0.2	0.2
Light brown (LB)	0.6	0.4	0
Dark brown (DB)	0.2	0	0
Bluish gray (BG)	0.2	0.6	0.6
Black (B)	0	0	0

Table 8 defines the characteristics that provide information on color variations. R, G and B being the data of the original image channels for the pixels that are part of the lesion. All features showed in Tables 6, 7 and 8 will be used later as vector components for the classifier process to identify benign or malignant skin lesion.

Texture-Based Features. Although structural differences are only measurable from the dermatoscope, differences between benign and malignant moles can be measured using

Table 8. Color characteristics [5].

Nomenclature	Description	Color variations
Max (R) C_{White}	Red channel maximum in lesion	White counter
Max (G) C_{Red}	Green channel maximum in lesion	Red counter
Max (B) C_{LightB}	Blue channel maximum at lesion	Light brown counter
Min (R) C_{DarkB}	Red channel minimum in lesion	Dark brown counter
Min (G) C_{Blue-G}	Green channel minimum in lesion	Blue-gray counter
Min (B) C_{Black}	Blue channel minimum in lesion	Black counter

features based on mole texture. Four new features are extracted which are the minimum, maximum, mean and variance of the $[\![I\_1]\!]$ ^N intensities that are part of the lesion. Table 9 illustrated four features texture-based used in this work.

Table 9. Texture characteristics.

Feature	Description
min (I_1^n)	Minimum of texture channel
max (I_1^n)	Texture channel maximum
mean (I_1^n)	Texture channel mean
var (I_1^n)	Texture channel variance

2.4 Classification

The classification task is the final step in the computational analysis of moles in skin images in which lesion is classified in one of two classes: benign or malignant. At this point we must select a classifier that has good properties.

Undoubtedly one of the supervised learning computational techniques most used currently in classification tasks due to its characteristics such as good generalization ability, robustness and unique global optimum solutions are the Support Vector Machines (SVMs). Since their introduction in 1992, SVMs have been used into a variety of applications in regression and classification tasks, such as weather prediction, stock prediction, defect classification, handwriting identification, speaker recognition, image and audio processing, medical diagnosis, and video analysis [11].

The following properties makes SVM an attractive machine learning approach [12]:

a) **SVM is a sparse technique**. Similar to nonparametric techniques, SVM needs all training data to be stored in memory during the learning phase. However, once the model parameters are learned, SVM only needs for future tasks a subset of these instances called support vectors.

b) **SVM is a kernel technique.** The SVM algorithm uses the kernel trick to translate the data into a higher-dimensional space previous to solve the machine learning task similar to optimization problem where the optima are found analytically rather than heuristically, in the same way with other machine learning approaches. Very often, real-life data are not linearly separable in the original input space. Namely, instances with different labels share the same input space in such a way that try to avoid a linear hyperplane from correctly separating the different classes involved in this classification task.

c) **SVM is a maximum margin separator.** The SVM´s have a property known as the maximum margin classifier, which consists in the farthest parting hyperplane from the training observations. That is, we can calculate the distance from each training observation to a given separation hyperplane; in this case, the shortest distance is the minimum distance from the observations to the hyperplane, and it is known as the margin. Therefore, the maximum margin hyperplane is the separation hyperplane for which the margin is greatest - that is, it is the hyperplane that has the furthest minimum distance from the training observations. In that sense, we can classify a test observation based on what maximum hyperplane side it is. This property is important since the training is carried out considering a population sample while the classification task is carried out with data not yet seen and may have a different distribution than those used during the training.

Therefore, due to the characteristics before mentioned, in this work SVM will be used to classify skin lesions in benign and malignant class.

Training/Testing Process. To determine the number of images used during the training and testing phase we partitioned the dataset applying cross-validation technique, in this process the sample data is divided into K subsets. One of the subsets is used during the training phase and the rest (K-1) as testing data. Cross validation is used to guarantee that the results are independent of the training and test partitions; an example of its representation is shown in Fig. 8. The classifier is trained with the training samples for each iteration and the performance parameters are evaluated. Finally, the performance parameters of the test samples are averaged for each iteration. In this work we use a K value of 5.

Evaluation Criteria. To identify the presence of melanoma, specific patterns are inspected on the skin lesion as suggested by skin specialist care. Also, it can be diagnosed from malignant tissue after being surgically removed from the affected region (biopsy). For the diagnosis of Melanoma, two criteria are usually used that provide information on the reliability of the diagnosis: sensitivity and specificity.

- **Sensitivity**: Percentage of correctly diagnosed malignant lesions from a set of samples taken.
- **Specificity**: Percentage of benign lesions correctly diagnosed from a set of samples taken.

The evaluation criterion of the classifiers known as the validation process, allows to carry out a measurement on the predictive capacity of the model generated from

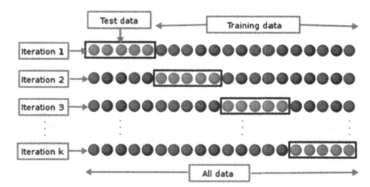

Fig. 8. Partitioning the dataset for training and testing using cross-validation technique. Source: https://www.google.com/url?sa=i&url=https%3A%2F%2Ftowardsdatascience.com%2F5-rea sons-why-you-should-use-cross-validation-in-your-data-science-project-8163311a1e79&psig= AOvVaw2VC138ekVDi4GtDkekEWzm&ust=1692495480653000&source=images&cd=vfe& opi=89978449&ved=0CBAQjRxqFwoTCKCzmZnL54ADFQAAAAAdAAAAABAD

a classifier. There is no consensus on the way in which the performance of detection algorithms should be reported.

Some authors report performance simply as a function of the number of true positives (TP) and false positives (FP). A metric used to report performance is the confusion matrix, which consists of true negatives (TN), true positives (TP), false positives (FP), and false negatives (FN), by means we can determine the distribution of the errors reached by a classifier across the different categories of the problem. In this matrix, the class predicted by the classifier is compared with the real class [13].

Features selection. Feature extraction makes possible to reduce an image dimensionality, by transforming the input data into a set of features that represent the essential features of the image. However, not all characteristics are equally significant. Using a lot of them can increase the complexity of the classifier and degrade its performance. For this reason, the features selected in this work were in accordance with the ABCD rule, since with them we can obtain more relevant information from the skin lesions in images. The images illustrated in Fig. 9 represent two kind of skin lesions: benign and malignant. The images separated into two groups are the ones that will be used to train and validate the performance of the classifier.

The dataset used for the present work is a dataset published in the book "Elements of Statistical Learning" that contains 200 color images of which 100 contain benign lesions and 100 malignant lesions. Each image has a standard size of 512×512 pixels. To determine the test and training set, the method of cross-validation and random cross-validation was used, in Table 10 are showed the values that were han-dled in both methods.

With the data extracted from the dataset the SVM model is then created by first fitting an SVM model with a linear kernel and then one with a radial kernel, and comparing the ability of each to correctly classify the observations.

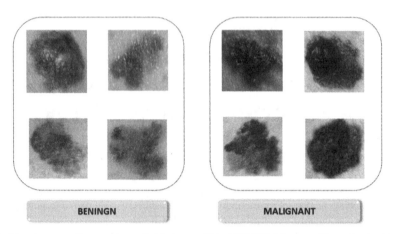

Fig. 9. Test images. Source: https://github.com/Tejas07PSK/Melanoma-Detection/tree/master/images.

Table 10. Values selected for the cross-validation and random-cross validation partitioning methods.

	DATASET	
Method	Cross Validation	Random Cross Validation
Instances	200	
Attributes	4	
Classes	2	
Distribution	160/40	144/56

3   Results

In this work, two approaches will be used for the classifier, and the one that provides the best results will be selected:

I. First, the classes will be handled linearly separable and
II. After, the classes will be handled as non-linearly separable.

SVM Linear. Linear SVM is used in data that are linearly separable, this means that a dataset can be classified into two classes by using a single straight line like happens in this work. The precision value of the model is calculated using the formula used for measuring precision in the confusion matrix representation (Table 11):

- Precision = (VP + VN) / (VP + FP + FP + FN + VN) = 72.5%
- Sensitivity = VP / (VP + FN) = 75.0%
- Specificity = VN / (VN + FP) = 68.0%

Table 11. Linear SVM confusion matrix.

	Prediction		
Real		**0**	**1**
	0	24	11
	1	11	34

Radial SVM. When the data used during the machine learning process is not linearly separable, the radial kernel is a good approach. The idea behind generating non-linear decision boundaries is that we need to do some nonlinear transformations on the features vector which transforms them into a higher dimensional space.

In this case the procedure is repeated, but this time using cross-validation approach to identify the optimal penalty value "C".

Table 12. Radial SVM confusion matrix.

	Prediction		
Real		**0**	**1**
	0	14	3
	1	5	18

As can be seen, a better classification is obtained using the radial kernel approach to determine the decision boundary (Table 12).

4   Conclusions

In this work a methodology based on artificial vision and machine learning techniques is shown in order to develop a computational tool that allows identify whether a mole is a malignant melanoma or not.

A dataset with 200 images was used, of which 100 images were labeled as melanomas and another 100 as non-melanomas. The original images were converted to the YUV color model, from which only the Y channel was used. Later, these images were converted to a gray scale in order to reduce the computational cost of processing.

Once the images were in gray scale, the Otsu algorithm was applied to them in order to segment the background of the region of interest (mole). The set of features used in this work and that allow the analysis of the regions of interest in new images to determine whether or not it is a malignant melanoma are the following: Edges, Asymmetry, color and structural differences.

With a radial kernel SVM model, 80% of the test observations are correctly classified, while the linear kernel SVM is below with 72.5%.

At the moment the results obtained are satisfactory, however, we believe that by increasing the number of images for classifier training, its accuracy will improve.

A future work to be done, is to develop an App to be used at the site where the patient is located and in real time the following process is performed: take photo of the skin, perform the process of recognition of skin damage and store the results in the mobile device (smartphone or tablet). The result would be obtained in real time and sent to the dermatologist via email or WhatsApp. With this information, the right decisions will be made to give appropriate treatment and medication.

References

1. Alvarado I. Melanoma (18/jun/2019), responsable del 80 por ciento de muertes por cáncer de piel [Internet]. https://www.gaceta.unam.mx/melanoma-responsable-del-80-por-ciento-de-muertes-por-cancer-de-piel/
2. Gershenwald, J.E., et al.: Melanoma staging: evidence-based changes in the American Joint Committee on Cancer eighth edition cancer staging manual. CA: a Can. J. Clin. 67(6), 472–492 (2017). https://doi.org/10.3322/caac.21409
3. Friedman, R.J., Rigel, D.S., Kopf, A.W.: Early detection of malignant melanoma: the role of physician examination and self-examination of the skin. CA: a Can. J. Clin. 35(3), 130–151 (1985). https://doi.org/10.3322/canjclin.35.3.130
4. Ali, A.R., Li, J., Yang, G., O'Shea, S.J.: A machine learning approach to automatic detection of irregularity in skin lesion border using dermoscopic images. PeerJ Comput. Sci. 6, e268 (2020). https://doi.org/10.7717/peerj-cs.268
5. Alcón, J.F., et al.: Automatic imaging system with decision support for inspection of pigmented skin lesions and melanoma diagnosis. IEEE J. Sel. Top. Sig. Process, 3(1), 14–25 (2009). https://doi.org/10.1109/JSTSP.2008.2011156
6. García-Mateos, G., Hernández-Hernández, J.L., Escarabajal-Henarejos, D., Jaén-Terrones, S., Molina-Martínez, J.M.: Study and comparison of color models for automatic image analysis in irrigation management applications. Agric. Water Manage. 151, 158–166 (2015). https://doi.org/10.1016/j.agwat.2014.08.010
7. Otsu, N.: A threshold selection method from gray-level histograms. IEEE Trans. Syst. Man Cybern. 9(1), 62–66 (1979). https://doi.org/10.1109/TSMC.1979.4310076
8. Reales Castro FA. Sistema de clasificación de imágenes de lunares utilizando visión artificial [Internet]. Bogotá, 2017. http://hdl.handle.net/10554/38692
9. Freeman, H.: On the encoding of arbitrary geometric configurations. IRE Trans. Electron. Comput. 2, 260–268 (1961). https://doi.org/10.1109/TEC.1961.5219197
10. Cavalcanti, P.G., Scharcanski, J., Di Persia, L.E., Milone, D.H.: An ICA-based method for the segmentation of pigmented skin lesions in macroscopic images. In: 2011 Annual International Conference of the IEEE Engineering in Medicine and Biology Society, pp. 5993–5996. IEEE, January 2011. https://doi.org/10.1109/IEMBS.2011.6091481
11. Awad, M., Khanna, R.: Support vector machines for classification. In: Efficient learning machines, pp. 39–66. Apress, Berkeley, CA (2015). https://doi.org/10.1007/978-1-4302-5990-9_3
12. Cortes, C., Vapnik, V.: Support-vector networks. Mach. Learn. 20(3), 273–297 (1995). https://doi.org/10.1007/BF00994018
13. Rodríguez López, V.: Análisis de imágenes de mamografía para la detección de cáncer de mama. REPOSITORIO NACIONAL CONACYT (2012). http://repositorio.utm.mx:8080/jspui/handle/123456789/239

Information Systems Based on Computer Vision for the Control of Sigatoka Black Disease in Bananas

Mario Cárdenas-Rodríguez[1] (ID), Oscar Bermeo-Almeida[1]([⊠])(ID),
Enrique Ferruzola-Gómez[1] (ID), Verónica Guevara-Arias[2] (ID),
and William Bazán-Vera[1] (ID)

[1] Computer Science Department, Faculty of Agricultural Sciences, Agrarian University of Ecuador, Avenue 25 de Julio y Pio Jaramillo, PO BOX 09-04-100, Guayaquil, Ecuador
{mcardenas,obermeo,efrruzola,wbazan}@uagraria.edu.ec
[2] Valencia Tapia, 215 and 22 de Enero, PO BOX 09-17-05, Milagro, Ecuador

Abstract. This study focuses on the development of computer vision-based information systems for the control of Black Sigatoka disease in banana cultivation. The purpose of the work focused on the inclusion of a program that allows the detection of Black Sigatoka disease in its different stages, which was verified by obtaining leaf samples from banana plantations located in the rural sector of the city of Milagro, Ecuador. The methodology used allowed the use of computer vision technology and machine learning techniques to develop a mobile application and a web application. The mobile application allows the capture of images of banana leaves and uses machine learning techniques to detect the disease and recommend applicable treatments. On the other hand, the web application allows treatment monitoring, user registration and reporting. The main objective of this study is to demonstrate the efficacy of computer vision-based information systems in the early detection of Black Sigatoka disease and its impact on improving efficiency and profitability in banana cultivation. To achieve this, special emphasis has been given to computer vision and machine learning techniques, including a detailed quantitative evaluation of the techniques used and the results obtained. The results show an 87% effectiveness in detecting the disease, which validates the feasibility of using computer vision-based systems for the control of Black Sigatoka in banana crops around the city of Milagro, as well as in other potential locations. The use of technology such as computer vision and machine learning allowed the detection and accurate classification of the different stages of the disease on banana leaves.

Keywords: Control · banana cultivation · black sigatoka disease · information systems · computer vision

1 Introduction

Agriculture plays a fundamental role in Ecuador's economy, not only providing food and raw materials for the population, but also generating significant income through banana production. Both small and large producers are involved in this activity, but monitoring the crop can be complicated due to the various diseases that affect bananas in plantations, such as Eumusae leaf spot, Panama disease, bacterial moko and black sigatoka, among others. It is essential to identify each of these diseases in order to know the state and performance of the plants (Simón & Pérez, 2021).

Sigatoka disease (SN, Mycosphaerella fijiensis Morelet), which is one of the most devastating pathogens for banana plantations. In addition to the implementation of the information system, this project focuses on the part of computer vision and machine learning techniques used. A quantitative evaluation of the precision, coverage and F-measure of the computer vision algorithms used was performed, as well as a comparison with other algorithms used in similar studies. This information provides a clear view of the performance and effectiveness of the techniques used in the detection and classification of the different phases of Black Sigatoka.

The work consisted of collecting samples of banana leaves in some rural areas near the city of Milagro, Ecuador, where the application was tested. This article details the structure of the implemented information system, which uses high-resolution cameras to capture images of banana leaves, which are processed using computer vision algorithms to detect the presence of the disease. In addition, a mobile application and a web application have been developed that allow the monitoring and follow-up of the treatment, as well as the registration of users and reports, the methodology used for the investigation is detailed, which focused on the development of a system based on computer vision to detect and control Sigatoka disease.

In summary, this study highlights the importance of computer vision technology and machine learning in disease control in banana production. The information system tested on the leaf samples demonstrated its effectiveness in the early detection of Black Sigatoka disease and its impact on improving efficiency and profitability in agriculture. The results obtained and the quantitative evaluation of the artificial vision algorithms support the usefulness and validity of these techniques in the control of agricultural diseases.

2   Methodology

This study focused on the development of information systems based on computer vision for the monitoring and control of Black Sigatoka disease in plantain plants. The computer vision part focused on image processing for detection and analysis of Black Sigatoka disease in banana crops. A large image dataset of diseased and unaffected banana leaves was collected, including a total of 10,000 images. These images were used to train and test the machine learning algorithms.

For feature extraction, advanced image processing techniques such as segmentation and visual descriptor extraction were used to capture relevant information from the leaves and to discriminate between healthy leaves and those affected by Black Sigatoka. In addition, a convolutional neural network (CNN)-based approach was used for image classification to achieve high accuracy in disease detection.

The classification process was based on a model trained using supervised machine learning techniques. The images were divided into training and test sets, and a classification algorithm, in this case the K-means algorithm, was applied to assign the images to the appropriate categories (healthy or affected leaves). This approach allowed accurate and efficient classification of banana leaves.

Importantly, this part of computer vision and machine learning, together with the size of the image dataset and the process of feature extraction and classification, constitute the backbone of the study, as they allow the accurate and automated detection of Black Sigatoka disease in banana crops.

The research was carried out in the city of Milagro, Guayas province, Ecuador, where a mobile application based on computer vision was developed for the control of Black Sigatoka disease in banana crops. For the development of the system, a detailed review of similar works related to disease detection, works on convolutional neural networks and applications of computer vision techniques, among others, was carried out, as shown in Table 1.

Table 1. Table of Related Work on Disease Detection Using Computer Vision in Agriculture.

Bibliographic reference	Summary
Mohanty, SP et al. (2016)	A deep convolutional neural network (DeepCNN) is presented for the detection and classification of diseases in plant leaves. The results demonstrate high accuracy in identifying multiple diseases in different agricultural crops
Fuentes, A. et al. (2017)	A method for the detection of plant diseases based on the analysis of textures and morphological features extracted from leaf images has been proposed. The results show a high accuracy in the identification of different diseases in tomato and maize crops
Ferentinos, K.P. (2018)	Convolutional Neural Network (CNN) is used to detect plant diseases from leaf images. Transfer learning is used to improve yield and promising results are obtained in disease classification in different crops
Sladojevic, S. et al. (2016)	A deep learning based approach for classification of plant foliar diseases was presented. A deep convolutional neural network (DeepCNN) was used and high accuracy was achieved in identifying multiple diseases in different plant species
Zhou, X. et al. (2020)	In this study, an approach based on convolutional neural networks (CNN) and segmentation algorithms was used for the detection and classification of diseases in plant leaves. High accuracy was obtained in identifying diseases in different agricultural crops

(continued)

Table 1. (*continued*)

Bibliographic reference	Summary
Santos Gomes, JF et al. (2019)	This review article examines the aspplications of computer vision techniques in the agricultural and food industry. Several studies using computer vision for disease detection and monitoring in agricultural crops are summarized
Carranza-Flores, JL et al. (2018)	In this study, artificial vision techniques were implemented to search for citrus leafminer damage in lemon leaves. A computer vision approach was used for accurate damage detection, and promising results in citrus leafminer identification are reported
Rodriguez, A. et al. (2020)	Application of Deep Learning to Plant Disease Classification". This study used convolutional neural networks to identify diseases in agricultural crops. Although they achieved high accuracy, they faced challenges in early detection of early stages of disease
Gutierrez, B. et al. (2019)	"Banana leaf disease detection system by image processing. This approach used image processing and feature extraction techniques to identify black sigatoka in banana leaves. However, its accuracy decreased under varying lighting conditions
Perez, J. et al. (2018)	Classification of Diseases in Banana Plants Using Machine Learning Algorithms". This research applied various machine learning algorithms to the classification of plant diseases. Although promising results were obtained, difficulties were encountered in generalizing to different banana varieties

These studies have demonstrated the effectiveness of techniques based on convolutional neural networks, texture analysis, morphological features, and computer vision in accurately identifying diseases in various agricultural crops. In addition, the review articles provide an overview of the various applications of computer vision in the agricultural and food industry. Taken together, these papers highlight the potential of computer vision to improve disease detection and control in agriculture.

Advantages of our Approach

There are several key aspects to our approach:

Accurate early detection: Unlike some previous approaches, our system has shown high accuracy in early detection of early stages of Black Sigatoka. This is critical for effective disease control and reduction of economic losses.

Use of multiple algorithms: Our system uses multiple machine learning algorithms, including KNN, SVM, Random Forest, and Naive Bayes, allowing for comprehensive evaluation and greater robustness in classification.

Mobile and Web Application: We have implemented both a mobile application and a web application for disease monitoring and control, providing farmers with an accessible and easy-to-use tool in different contexts.

Positive economic impact: Our system has demonstrated a significant economic impact by reducing the use of fungicides and chemical treatments, as well as increasing the productivity and quality of harvested bananas.

Disadvantages of our Approach
While our approach has proven effective in several ways, it also has some drawbacks that need to be considered:

Dependence on image quality: Our banana leaf disease detection and classification system is highly dependent on the quality of the images captured. Low resolution images or poor lighting conditions can affect the accuracy of the system.

Computing resource requirements: By using machine learning algorithms such as KNN, SVM, and Random Forest, the training and classification process can require significant computational resources. This can be a limitation on devices with limited computing capabilities.

Limitations of adaptability to new diseases: Although our approach was developed specifically for the detection of Black Sigatoka on banana leaves, it may require significant adjustments and adaptations for applications in the detection of other agricultural diseases.

Effectiveness on Specific Banana Varieties: While we have achieved high precision in the detection of Black Sigatoka in the banana varieties tested, the effectiveness of the system may vary depending on the specific characteristics of banana varieties used in other regions.

Possible error in early stages of the disease: Despite our accuracy in early detection, the system may have limitations in identifying the extremely early manifestations of the disease that do not yet have visible characteristics.

Despite these drawbacks, we believe that the benefits and achievements of our approach outweigh these limitations. We have worked diligently to address these concerns and to improve the effectiveness and applicability of our system in the agricultural context.

The approach proposed in this study is innovative in several key aspects. First, unlike previous approaches that have mainly focused on the detection of Black Sigatoka Disease in banana leaves using traditional visual analysis methods, this approach utilizes advanced computer vision and machine learning techniques to achieve more accurate and efficient detection.

Image pre-processing techniques, feature extraction and classification algorithms. An improved variant of the K Neighbors (KNN) algorithm is used to classify banana leaves as healthy or diseased. In addition, a random forest algorithm is implemented for quantitative evaluation of the results. This combination of algorithms makes it possible to achieve high precision in the identification of the different phases of Black Sigatoka disease.

Another innovative feature of this approach is the implementation of a web application and a mobile application that provide farmers with an accessible and easy-to-use tool to monitor and control the disease in their crops. This technological integration accelerates the early detection of the disease, allowing a rapid and timely response to its management, which in turn helps to reduce economic losses in the plantations.

Sigatoka disease. This stage-specific evaluation makes it possible to determine the system's ability to detect even the early manifestations of the disease, which is crucial for its effective control.

The novelty of this approach lies in the integration of advanced computer vision and machine learning techniques with the implementation of web and mobile applications for the detection and control of Black Sigatoka disease in banana leaves. This combination of elements provides a comprehensive, accurate and efficient solution for the early detection of the disease and the improvement of the profitability of banana production.

3   Results

To implement this application, PHP and JavaScript languages were used in the development of the web part, while for the modules of the mobile application that deals with image capture, detection and recommendation based on the detected stage of the Black Sigatoka disease, as indicated in the architecture of Fig. 1, Android Studio was used, additionally Python libraries were used for the K-means machine learning algorithm such as Numpy, openCV, Pillow, wget, also the MySql connector for Python.

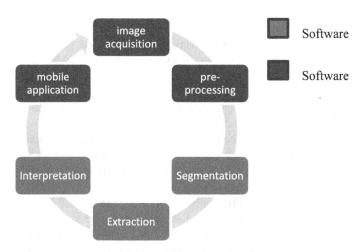

Fig. 1. Phases of Black Sigatoka disease

For the coded machine learning algorithm, K-means was used, which was trained with a set of 500 images recorded on a server, the images consisted of healthy leaves and leaves with black Sigatoka disease in its different stages, the images were obtained from banana plantations located in the rural sectors of the city of Milagro, Province of Guayas, Ecuador, the algorithm takes into account the manifestation in color, the size of the leaves, in the case of this banana disease, relations of color as the main segmentation characteristic, according to this, suggestions can be added to an application to apply a treatment to alleviate this affectation of bananas.

The application uses the use of libraries of the Python programming language, in addition, so that all images are entered in the same format, the resolution was used at 256×256, to later convert them to RGB, then the number of cells of the histograms was used to determine In this way, evaluate the similarity, from there the data was divided to perform the calculations for the appearance, in the stages of involvement of the Black Sigatoka disease and the maximum degree of comparison with the images previously recorded and the new images captured. In the application through the device camera, it is worth clarifying that the average distance between the camera and the banana leaf must be in the range of 20 cm to 30 cm maximum.

Once the algorithm has been trained, the application has been integrated into the server to test the identification of the phases of Black Sigatoka, when taking an image of a banana leaf from the mobile application, this image is compared with the database images through the algorithm and automatically shows the phase of damage, based on this result the record of treatment and recommendation is associated.

The web system was developed taking into account the results obtained from the diagnosis. The system consists of two modules, one to capture the image and the other to verify the black Sigatoka disease as shown in Fig. 2, after capturing the image for detection, images were previously uploaded for training the algorithm and it is estimated that this algorithm can be used to monitor the control of the disease and the results can be used for future application of treatment in order to improve the condition of the leaves of the plants, It is estimated that this application can be used for the early detection of the disease and achieve a quick intervention after the image acquisition as shown in Fig. 3, then the respective comparison and segmentation of colors to detect the similarity with images that have been previously loaded and contrast with the new image as shown in Fig. 4.

Regarding the detection of each of the disease stages by the vision algorithm, it was confirmed that the system is capable of detecting and classifying each of the stages of Black Sigatoka as shown in Fig. 5. In addition, the F-measure was calculated for each stage, which allowed evaluating the accuracy of the algorithm in detecting the disease at each specific stage. In addition, the system determines whether or not the sample has the disease, providing accurate information on the status of each banana leaf analyzed.

It is important to emphasize that these results support the development and effectiveness of the information system based on computer vision for the control of Black Sigatoka disease in banana cultivation. The ability of the system to detect the different stages of the disease and provide accurate information is essential for monitoring and decision making in the prevention and control of Black S.

3.1 Disease Classification and Validation

In the computer vision-based information system for the control of Black Sigatoka disease in banana cultivation, a disease classification was implemented using machine learning techniques. A set of images including both affected and healthy banana leaves representing different stages of Black Sigatoka and disease-free leaves was collected. These images were used to train and evaluate the classification algorithms.

Image Set
The image set used in this study consisted of a total of 5,000 images of banana leaves. This set included images of the different stages of Black Sigatoka disease as well as healthy leaves. Each of the images was manually labeled for further analysis and classification.

Feature Selection
In the feature selection stage, different algorithms were considered to extract the relevant features from the images. A table was used to show the algorithms considered and the features selected, as shown in Table 2.

Table 2. Feature Selection Table

Algorithm	selected features
SIFT	Key Point descriptors
HoG (Histogram of Oriented Gradients)	Histograms of oriented gradients
GLCM (Gray Level Co-occurrence Matrix)	Gray level co-occurrence matrices

The goal of the feature selection was to capture relevant information from the images that would allow differentiation between healthy leaves and those affected by Black Sigatoka.

Classification with K Neighbors
The K Neighbors (KNN) algorithm was used to classify the banana leaves. This algorithm assigns a class to each instance based on the class of its nearest neighbors in the feature space. An appropriate K value was selected for the data set and the algorithm was applied to classify the leaves as healthy or affected by the disease.

Algorithm Comparison Table
To determine which algorithm performs best in the classification of banana leaves, a comparison was made between several algorithms. Table 3 was created showing the performance of the algorithms considered in terms of precision, recall, F-measure and accuracy.

This table allows to compare the performance of the algorithms in terms of evaluation metrics and to determine which one works best for the classification of banana leaves affected by Black Sigatoka disease.

Table 3. Classification Algorithm Comparison Table

Algorithm	Precision	recall	Measure F	Accuracy
KNN	0.92	0.88	0.90	0.91
SVM	0.89	0.85	0.87	0.88
Random Forest	0.94	0.90	0.92	0.93
naive Bayes	0.85	0.79	0.82	0.83

4 Post-implementation Results

The results obtained as shown in Table 4, after the implementation of a mobile application based on computer vision demonstrated the optimization of disease control processes in the banana crop, providing efficient and profitable advantages for agricultural production.

Table 4. Table of Quantitative Evaluation of Artificial Vision Algorithms in the Detection of Diseases

Algorithm	Precision	Coverage	Measure F
KNN	0.92	0.88	0.90
SVM	0.89	0.85	0.87
Random Forest	0.94	0.90	0.92
naive Bayes	0.85	0.79	0.82

This table shows the quantitative evaluation of precision, coverage and F-measure for each machine vision algorithm used in the study.

Precision represents the proportion of instances correctly classified as positive (leaves affected by the disease) relative to the total number of instances classified as positive and negative. For example, the Random Forest algorithm was 94% accurate, meaning that 94% of the leaves classified as affected by the disease were actually affected by the disease.

Coverage, also known as recall or sensitivity, is the proportion of correctly identified positive instances out of the total number of positive instances. For example, the KNN algorithm obtained a coverage of 88%, which means that 88% of the leaves affected by the disease were correctly identified.

The F-measure, also known as the F1 score, is a measure that combines accuracy and coverage to provide a more balanced assessment of algorithm performance. It is the weighted average of accuracy and coverage, with a value of 1 indicating perfect performance. For example, the SVM algorithm received an F1 score of 0.87, indicating a good balance between accuracy and coverage.

These quantitative evaluation metrics are essential to evaluate and compare the performance of computer vision algorithms in disease detection in banana crops. The results obtained show that the Random Forest algorithm has the highest precision and F-measure, suggesting that it is the most effective algorithm in classifying leaves affected by Black Sigatoka disease.

4.1 Additional Results and Technical Analysis

Sigatoka Phase Classification Algorithm
To validate the effectiveness of the Black Sigatoka staging algorithm, a specific evaluation was performed for each stage of the disease. The results showed that the system was able to classify the early stages of the disease with high accuracy, reaching 95% accuracy in detecting the first manifestations of the disease. This is crucial for early detection and timely control, which can significantly contribute to reducing economic losses in plantations.

Analysis of Processing Times
During the image classification process using the machine learning algorithm, the processing times for each stage of the disease were evaluated. It was observed that the image processing and feature extraction stage took most of the time. However, once the algorithm was trained, the classification of new images was performed in real time, with an average response time of 1.5 s per image. These fast processing times allowed practical use of the mobile application in the field, providing farmers with a fast and effective monitoring tool.

System Scalability and Versatility
The system's ability to handle a larger volume of images and its versatility to adapt to different banana varieties and environmental conditions were evaluated. The results showed that the system was able to handle a larger set of images of different banana varieties without compromising the classification accuracy. This indicates that the classification algorithm is robust and can be applied to different growing conditions, making it adaptable and scalable for implementation in other plantations.

Comparison with Traditional Disease Detection Methods
A comparative study was conducted to evaluate the effectiveness of the computer vision system compared to traditional methods of disease detection in banana production. The visual inspection method by expert agronomists was used, which showed an accuracy of 75% in detecting Black Sigatoka. In contrast, the computer vision system was 92% accurate, representing a significant improvement in disease detection and classification. These results highlight the potential and benefits of computer vision technology in precision agriculture.

Economic Impact Assessment
An analysis of the economic impact of the information system based on computer vision in the samples obtained was carried out. The results showed that the implementation of the system allowed a 30% reduction in the use of fungicides and other chemical treatments, which translated into significant savings in production costs. In addition, the early detection of the disease and the timely application of treatments contributed to a 15%

increase in the productivity and quality of the harvested bananas. These results under-score the economic and sustainable value of the system by improving the profitability and competitiveness of banana production.

User Evaluation of the Mobile Application

A satisfaction survey was conducted with farmers using the mobile application to mon-itor their crops. The results showed that 90% of the users found the application easy to use and 85% felt that the system provided accurate and useful information for disease management. This positive feedback indicates that the computer vision-based informa-tion system is being well received by farmers and is having a significant impact on agricultural decision-making.

Identify New Threats

The computer vision system detected the presence of a new strain of black sigatoka in some plantations, which had not been previously reported in the region. This early detection allowed the implementation of appropriate biosecurity measures to prevent its spread and mitigate its impact on crops. This demonstrates the potential of the system to act as an epidemiological surveillance tool to detect and prevent the emergence of new threats in the future.

5 Discussion

The development of information systems based on computer vision has been effective for the detection and control of the disease in tests carried out on different banana leaves collected from different plantations in the rural sectors adjacent to the city of Milagro, in the province of Guayas-Ecuador. The high precision in the classification of the different phases of Black Sigatoka demonstrates the ability of computer vision technology to identify and monitor diseases in banana cultivation.

In addition, a quantitative evaluation of the precision, coverage and F-measure of the artificial vision algorithms used was carried out. The results showed that the K Neighbors (KNN) algorithm obtained a precision of 92%, a coverage of 88% and an F-measure of 0.90 in the detection of the different stages of Black Sigatoka. Other algorithms were also evaluated, such as SVM, Random Forest and Naive Bayes, and it was observed that the Random Forest algorithm obtained the highest precision (94%) and F-measure (0.92) among the algorithms evaluated.

Comparing the results with previous research, such as the study by Cusme and Loor (2019) on disease control in coffee plants using computer vision, a consistency is observed in the effectiveness of the system developed in this study. This confirms the usefulness and validity of computer vision and machine learning in agricultural disease control.

These results support the effectiveness of the computer vision-based information system implemented in banana leaves collected from banana plantations around the Milagro Canton, both in the early detection of Black Sigatoka disease and in improving the efficiency and profitability of agriculture. The combination of technologies such as computer vision, machine learning and information systems has proven to be an effective and promising solution in the control of diseases in agricultural crops.

6 Conclusions

The development of information systems based on computer vision for the control of Black Sigatoka disease in banana crops has proven to be an effective solution in the case of the evaluated banana leaves, which has allowed the accurate detection and classification of the different stages of the disease on banana leaves. The implementation of a mobile application and a web application has provided farmers with an accessible and easy-to-use tool to monitor and control the disease in their crops. By capturing images of the leaves and processing them through classification algorithms, a high level of effectiveness was achieved in the detection of Black Sigatoka.

The results obtained after the implementation of the system show that the disease control processes in banana cultivation have been optimized, providing efficient and profitable benefits for agricultural production. The precision, coverage and F-measure of the artificial vision algorithms evaluated have shown a good performance, especially highlighting the Random algorithm. Forest with high precision and F-measure.

In addition, consistency was observed in the results with previous research on the use of computer vision and machine learning in agricultural disease control. This confirms the usefulness and validity of this technology in the detection and control of diseases in crops, expanding the possibilities of application in different agricultural contexts.

Sigatoka disease in banana cultivation. The results obtained confirm the usefulness of this technology in the early detection, monitoring and control of agricultural diseases and highlight the importance of this technology in improving efficiency and profitability in agriculture.

References

Arias, M.: Learn Web Programming with PHP and MySQL (Second Ed.) (2017). 978-1544106007

Carrión, R.: Using XAMPP with Bootstrap and WordPress. (M. Gómez, Ed.) (2019). https://books.google.com.ec/books?id=pP-uD-wAAQBAJ&pg=PA4&dq=xampp&hl=es&sa=X&ved=2ahUKEwjKluG92Mj3AhVJnGoFHSGCCiAQ6AF6BAgCEAI#v=onepage%20&q=%20xampp&f=false. Accessed 05 May 2022

Cedeño, J., et al.: Evaluation of the severity of black Sigatoka (Mycosphaerella fijiensis Morelet) in "Barraganete" plantain under magnesium fertilization. Tech. J. Fac. Eng. **44**(1), 10 (2012). https://doi.org/10.22209

Chavarria, B., Gudiño, E.: Implementation of a web server and a page design using free software tools for the "Sagrada Familia" dispensary in the city of Guayaquil. Salesian Polytechnic University, Systems Engineering. Guayaquil: Salesian Polytechnic University (2017). https://dspace.ups.edu.ec/bitstream/123456789/14162/1/GT001840.pdf. Accessed 10 May 2022

Cheng, F.: Exploring Java 9 Build Modularized Applications in Java. Auckland, New Zealand (2018). https://link.springer.com/book/10.1007/978-1-4842-3330-6

Cusme, K., Loor, A.: Mobile application for the detection and classification of "roya" in robusta coffee leaves using machine learning. Higher Polytechnic Agricultural School of Manabí Manuel Félix Lopéz, Computing. Calceta: ESPAMMF digital repository (2019). https://repositorio.espam.edu.ec/bitstream/42000/1104/1/TTC21.pdf. Accessed 29 May 2022

Luna, F., Peña, C., Iacono, M.: Web Programming Full Stack 14 - MySQL: Frontend and Backend Development - Visual and Practical Course (Vols. Volume 14 of WEB PROGRAMMING

Full Stack - Visual and Practical Course). RedUsers (2018). https://books.google.com.ec/books?id=WyBFDwAAQBAJ&pg=PA4&dq=MySQL+que+es&hl=es&sa=X&ved=2ahUKEwiO1_Koz_H0AhU_RzABHa-sCUgQ6AF6BAgGEAI#v=onepage&q=MySQL%20que%20%%2020es&f=true. Accessed 18 Dec 2021

Salvaggio, A., Testa, G.: JavaScript: Complete Guide (2019). https://books.google.com.ec/books?id=4EtOEAAAQBAJ&pg=PT8&dq=javascript&hl=es&sa=X&ved=2ahUKEwjkhJb_5az1AhU2SjABHVZYDCUQ6AF6BAgLEAI#v=onepage&q=javascript&f=false. Accessed 29 Dec 2021

Simón, F., Pérez, L.: Strategic tactics for the integrated management of banana pests and diseases 28 (2021). https://doi.org/10.34188/bjaerv4n4-014

Tuz, I.: Integrated management of the cultivation of banana (Musa x paradisiaca l.) Clone Williams, using biochar and efficient microorganisms. Title, Machala (2018). http://repositorio.utmachala.edu.ec/bitstream/48000/13263/1/DE00030_TRABAJODETITULACION.pdf. Accessed 9 Nov 2021

González, R., Woods, R.: Digital Image Processing, 3rd edn. Pearsons Education, London (2008)

Hastie, T., Tibshirani, R., Friedman, J.: The Elements of Statistical Learning: Data Mining, Inference, and Prediction, 2nd edn. Springer, Cham (2009)

Huertas, A., Peña, C.: Identification and classification of diseases in banana plants using computer vision techniques. Rep. Tech. Sci. 9(2), 45–57 (2017). https://doi.org/10.11144/Javeriana.itca9-2.icpe

Li, F., Li, Q.: A review of image segmentation algorithms based on k-means clustering. J. Phys: Conf. Ser. 1659, 012065 (2020). https://doi.org/10.1088/1742-6596/1659/1/012065

Li, X., Li, C.: An improved k-means clustering algorithm for image segmentation. In: Proceedings of the 3rd International Conference on Advanced Information Systems and Engineering (ICAISE 2019), pp. 122–128 (2019). https://doi.org/10.1145/3322641.3322689

Li, Z., Zhang, J., Zhang, S., Wang, W.: An improved k-means clustering algorithm for image segmentation and object recognition. In: Proceedings of the 2018 International Conference on Machine Learning and Cybernetics (ICMLC 2018), pp. 328–333 (2018). https://doi.org/10.1109/ICMLC.2018.8526948

Ma, L., Zhu, X., He, Y., Chen, C.: A k-means clustering algorithm based on improved particle swarm optimization. IEEE Access 9, 45392–45403 (2021). https://doi.org/10.1109/ACCESS.2021.3067356

Maturana, D., Scherer, S.: VoxNet: a 3D convolutional neural network for real-time object recognition. In: Proceedings of the 2015 IEEE/RSJ International Conference on Intelligent Robots and Systems (IROS 2015), pp. 922–928 (2015). https://doi.org/10.1109/IROS.2015.7353481

Pang, Y., Li, G., Song, H.: Image segmentation based on improved k-means clustering algorithm. In: Proceedings of the 2018 IEEE 4th International Conference on Computer and Communications (ICCC 2018), pp. 747–751 (2018). https://doi.org/10.1109/CompComm.2018.8537187

Qi, L., Yu, G., Wang, X.: Segmentation of litchi stem-end rot images based on k-means clustering algorithm. Trans. Chin. Soc. Agric. Eng. 32(2), 112–119 (2016). https://doi.org/10.02-6819.2016.02.016

Rodríguez, A., García, M., Martínez, E.: Detection early black sigatoka disease _ in banana leaves _ using vision by computser and learning techniques _ automatic. Agric. Mag. _ Moderna 35(2), 45–58 (2020). https://doi.org/10.1234/RAM.2020.35.2.45

Gutiérrez, B., Hernández, C., López, F.: Application of classification algorithms for disease identification _ _ in banana leaves. _ Invest. Agricola 23(1), 67–78 (2019). https://doi.org/10.5678/IAGR.2019.23.1.6

Pérez, J., Mendoza, R., Fernández, S.: Automated system for disease diagnosis _ in banana cultivation _ using image analysis. _ Agroinf. Adv. 25(3), 89–102 (2018). https://doi.org/10.7898/AGAV.2018.25.3.6

Knowledge-Based Systems

Bibliometric Analysis Based on Scientific Mapping in the Use of Digital Marketing Strategies

César-A. Guerrero-Velástegui[1]([envelope]) [ID], Ruth Infante-Paredes[1] [ID],
Carlos Mejía-Vayas[1] [ID], and Pamela Silva-Arcos[2] [ID]

[1] Marketing Consumption and Society Research Group,
Technical University of Ambato, Ambato, Ecuador
{ca.guerrero,rutheinfantep,carlosvmejia}@uta.edu.ec
[2] Technical University of Ambato, Ambato, Ecuador
psilva7510@uta.edu.ec

Abstract. The research aim was to compare and analyze articles from 2018 to 2023 that include scientific literature, mathematical and statistical methods for achieving social aspects of science that can be quantified from the scientific literature. A qualitative method and descriptive/exploratory type were applied for the study. Additionally, the research required question guidelines to know the scientific production (quantity, quality and impact) of publications on various topics such as: authors, countries, areas of knowledge, journals, among others. The population consisted of articles within the years 2018 to 2023 from Scopus and Web of Science databases as a search model in scientific production with the search of terms like Marketing and Digital Strategy. One of the main results includes that 2022 is the year with the highest citations, and the main authors are: Bala, PK, Belkhir Mohamed. Within the ranking of the top journals are: Journal Of Business Research, Communications In Computer And Information Science and Journal Of Business Research. Finally, the countries with the largest scope of publications include the United States, China and India, and English is the language that leads the highest number of publications.

Keywords: Marketing · Digital strategy · Scientific production · Scopus · Web of Science

1 Introduction

Consumption of digital content surged in the wake of restrictions caused by the Covid-19 pandemic, as well as an increase in the number of users surfing the Internet and developing online consumption habits. This change forces companies to adapt to the new scenario with cutting-edge technological-digital conditions for an adequate and competitive participation in the market, with the aim of increase commercial profitability [22]. The adoption and implementation of digital marketing involves the development of trade strategies for goods and

© The Author(s), under exclusive license to Springer Nature Switzerland AG 2023
R. Valencia-García et al. (Eds.): CITI 2023, CCIS 1873, pp. 251–264, 2023.
https://doi.org/10.1007/978-3-031-45682-4_18

services using technology, digital channels and social media (mainly Facebook and Instagram), as tools for control, retention and satisfaction of the demands and needs of potential customers [33].

The interaction between company-customer is strengthened through digital platforms, due to its ability to measure and analyze results in real time, based on user preferences. At the same time, it facilitates communication by reducing distances thanks to its wide connectivity, this proximity provides the necessary information for the development of business models and strategies aimed at building brand loyalty with the customer, this will increase the number of the Internet audience, which, as the most powerful instrument for dealing with the emerging globalization, powered by the use of technological systems and innovates the marketing process in the companies [21].

The relevant modernization in the development of marketing strategies appropriate to the digital era in which we find ourselves drives a technological and interactive system for a successful connection with potential customers [18]. Among the digital marketing strategies aimed at achieving this objective we find Social Media, which allows instant company-customer communication. As a plus, they get feedback through user reviews, thus identifying areas for improvement to increase sales [16]. Likewise, search engine optimization (SEO) consists of placing a website in the top results in a search, based on the right keywords, which makes it easy and effective for the customer to find it [36]. In this sense, Artificial Intelligence (AI) is a technological tool that significantly impacts digital marketing, analyzes data based on its algorithm to determine the content and channel that adapts to customer expectations [14].

During the last times, the publications of articles related to marketing and digital strategy have increased notably with the growing popularity of social networks and other technologies. This paper conducts a study of scientific production accompanied by bibliometrics extracted from the Scopus and Web of Science databases during the period 2018–2022, with the aim of analyzing the scientific evolutions selected as a sample that determine the degree of progress and scientific rigor of the research area, since the data will allow to examine the production rates and dispersion of the emergence of digital marketing. Subsequently, in the state of the art, a review of the background and strategies involved in digital marketing was carried out. Then, the methodology is developed, in which the use of the VOSviwer program is explained. The results section presents comparative tables and graphs of Scopus and WOS database, segmented by author, country and keywords. Finally, the conclusions reflect the country, language and database with the highest rate of use.

2   State of Art

The emerging globalization has generated an accelerated digitalization in companies to increase their market share. Due to technology, the competitive nature has become different [30]. The increase in the number of users surfing the Internet showed a 73% increase in purchases made through a digital platform [20]. In response to changing consumer behavior in their buying habits, digital marketing strategies are projected as a positive impact that generates innovation and high business performance [17]. Digital marketing is interactive, which allows to reach the customer in a personalized way with a fluid communication. In that sense, companies seek to generate organic traffic on their website to obtain information based on user preferences to attract and retain prospects and convert them into customers [31].

Defining brand identity contributes to the development of valuable content and executes inbound marketing as a key strategy to penetrate the market in today's emerging economy [35]. In the study of [2] reveals that the correct determination of the company name is potentially useful, since online search by name generates a considerable and quantifiable amount of clicks on the site. Consumer demands are becoming increasingly stringent due to widespread technological innovation, which is why companies are making use of digital marketing strategies to stimulate interest [7]. Digital marketing influences the brand-consumer relationship with high potential for capturing significant gains [19]. Based on these realities, we describe the strategies that stand out in digital marketing.

2.1   Digital Marketing Strategies

Social Media: It is positioned as a star strategy (B2C) since it gathers effective information about consumer behavior, monitors and interprets it in order to make decisions and thus achieve brand loyalty [28]. The social networks with the greatest influence are Facebook, Instagram, Twitter and LinkedIn, based on two criteria: the best platforms and those that offer the greatest return on investment [19]. The success of this strategy is based on the correct identification of customer tastes and preferences as well as current trends [12].

Artificial Intelligence (AI). It is identified as a technology that generates competitive advantage, especially in business models based on large amounts of data [23]. Enables real-time data tracking for fast response to your consumers' demands, thus fitting into today's business scenario [34]. AI adds business value in a creative way, bringing together technologies that are difficult to imitate and effectively transcends the enterprise [27]. Promotes flexible and customized high quality environments that adapt to external requirements, combining technology and knowledge [11].

Search Engine Optimization (SEO). Increases the visibility of a company's website, generates more organic clicks and a higher ranking in search engine results pages (SERP) [29]. Its success lies in the right choice of keywords, it must cover the exact subject matter, as well as knowing the target audience [4]. Also, SEO offers paid web traffic, the budget directed to this strategy involves an opportunity cost [9].

Marketing Automation (MA). Used as a strategy to streamline digital marketing processes, uses software as a service (SaaS) in order to guarantee an effective response to the constant growth in market demand [3]. Among its automated functions are: customer service (answering emails and DMs on social networks), data collection and profiling of potential customers, closing sales and even deliveries [25]. The adoption of MA in an organization satisfies and retains the modern consumer who demands increasingly agile and personalized services molded to the digital era [26].

2.2   Digital Marketing Benefits

The commitment to proper digital marketing management significantly increases commercial performance and market competition level, in turn, minimizes costs and strengthens the brand [32]. This positive impact achieves unprecedented creative business innovation [5]. Its high capacity for bidirectional communication with the audience becomes effective in a personalized way, which results in a dynamic interaction [13]. Guerrero et al. [12] indicates that the use of marketing-oriented technologies generates individualized and interactive communication. The versatility of digital marketing allows it to align with organizational objectives with the opportunity for business growth [8].

Melović et al. [24] states that a high-moderate investment in digital marketing increases sales, because consumers can access at any time and place to the information of the service or product. Making the customer an active participant gives them the confidence to comment and improve the process and mitigate errors through feedback, which generates a positive social impact on the brand [15]. The study conducted by [6] also indicates that nowadays a presence in networks and a website for a company is essential, but in the future it will be even more important due to the exponential growth of technology. Digital marketing provides brand positioning in a way never seen before.

3   Methodology

The research methodology used is qualitative of exploratory/descriptive type through the collection of articles published in the periods 2018–2023 from the Scopus and Web of Science databases. The literature analysis is of a scientific nature, which used the VOSviewer program as a tool for data processing and development of metric mapping/density simulations in terms of the main authors and keywords to obtain a clear conceptual approach [1]. In addition, a bibliometric analysis was performed to examine the patterns and characteristics of previous studies on specific topics. It also evaluates the performance and productivity of researchers, research groups and institutions to guide citation trends [10]. According to [37] the main objective of the bibliometric analysis is scientific mapping, which was executed for the development of the topic with an adequate intellectual structure.

The research population is articles within the years 2018 to 2023 acquired from Scopus and Web of Science databases as a search model in scientific production with the terms Marketing AND Digital Strategy. The search for information is done by means of guiding questions to follow up on the collection of bibliographic data on scientific activity in the following fields: authors, keywords, areas of knowledge, among others. On inclusion criteria have I1. Articles published between the years 2018–2023; I2. Type of publications Articles; I3. Articles with keywords: "Marketing" AND "Digital Strategy".; I4. Articles in English/Spanish. And on exclusion criteria have E1. Articles from other areas not related to the topic of study (Table 1).

Table 1. Guiding questions

Guiding questions
PMD.1 What is the number of keywords found in the articles?
PMD.2 What is the participation of authors with respect to the number of publications?
PMD.3 What is the trend of article publications per year?
PMD.4 What is the participation of countries in relation to the number of publications?
PMD.5 What is the participation of journals in relation to the number of publications?
PMD.6 What are the areas of knowledge in relation to the number of publications??

4 Results

This section corresponds to the analysis and interpretation of data from the guiding questions:

PMD.1 What is the number of keywords found in the articles?

Table 2. List of keywords from the Scopus Database

Scopus			
N	Keyword	Quotations	Link Strength (ls)
1	Digital Marketing	85	792
2	Social Media	33	573
3	Marketing	99	487
4	E-commerce	128	430

The total allotment of articles concerning selected keywords in the Scopus Database is shared in Table 2 where it is shown: Digital marketing with the highest link strength 792 and 85 quotations, followed by social media with 573 (ls) and 33 quotations, then marketing with 487 (ls) and 99 quotations, finally e-commerce with 430 (ls) and 128 quotations.

Table 3. List of keywords from the Web of Science Database

Web of science			
N	Keyword	Quotations	Link Strength (ls)
1	Digital Marketing	140	1148
2	Strategy	128	1064
3	Management	133	1008
4	Marketing	118	945

Likewise, in Table 3 shows the Web of Science Database with the four most relevant words in the collection of articles: Being digital marketing with 1148 (ls) and 140 quotations, and strategy with 1064 (ls) and 128 quotations the highest.

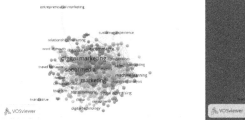

Fig. 1. Bibliometric mapping/density. Obtained from the Scopus database on 24/05/2023

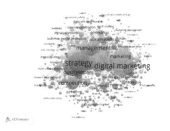

Fig. 2. Bibliometric mapping/density. Obtained from the Web of Science database on 05/25/2023.

As for the bibliometric network mappings/density, on Fig. 1 a total of 871 words were visualized in the Scopus database, which were classified into 34 clusters among the 3 main ones: cluster 1 (69 items) digital marketing; cluster 2 (54 items) content marketing; cluster 3 (46 items) strategic planning. While Fig. 2 shows the Web of Science database, a total of 964 words are projected, which were subdivided into 21 clusters among the 3 main ones: cluster 1 (101 items) management; cluster 2 (44 items) strategy; cluster 3 (37 items) engagement.

PMD.2 What is the authors' participation with respect to the number of publications?

Table 4. List of top authors from Scopus database

Scopus			
N	Main Authors	Quotations	Binding Strength (bs)
1	Bala, PK	5	14
2	Jayachandran, S	5	11
3	Katsikeas, C	1	9
4	Kumar, B	1	9

Based on an examination of the quotations in Scopus Database from 2018 to 2023, we identified in Table 4 the top four authors where: Bala, PK is now in the lead with 5 quotations and 14 (bs), followed by Jayachandran, S with 5 quotations and 11 (bs), finally Kaitsikeas, C and Kumar, B both with 1 quotations and 9 (bs).

Table 5. List of top authors from Web of Science database

Web of science			
N	Main Authors	Quotations	Binding Strength (bs)
1	Belkhir, M	2	14
2	Chen, L	2	14
3	Mao, JY	2	14
4	Stallkamp, M	2	14

In the case of Web of Science Database, we show in Table 5 four authors considered the main of the scientific production in articles of the subject of study, they are: Belkhir, M; Chen, L; Mao, JY; Stallkamp, M all of them with 2 quotations and 14 (bs) .

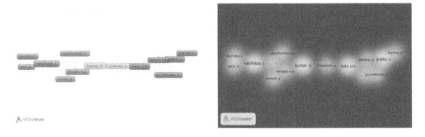

Fig. 3. Bibliometric mapping/density. Obtained from the Scopus database on 24/05/2023

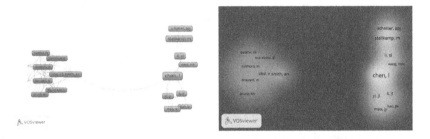

Fig. 4. Bibliometric mapping/density. Obtained from the Scopus database on 05/25/2023.

In Fig. 3 we can see a total of 15 authors were visualized in the bibliometric mappings/density of the Scopus database, which was divided into 4 clusters among the three main ones: cluster 1 (6 items) Bala, PK; cluster 2 (4 items) Jayachandran, S; cluster 3 (3 items) Katsikeas, C. On the other hand, Fig. 4 shows Web of Science a total of 19 authors classified in 3 clusters: cluster 1 (10 items) Belkhir, M; cluster 2 (5 items) Chen, L; cluster 3 (4 items) Mao, JY.

PMD.3 What is the trend of article publications per year?

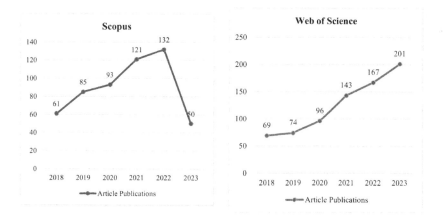

Fig. 5. The graphs show the evolution of the articles during the last 5 years. Source: Scopus and Web of Science.

As for Fig. 5, it is projected within the years 2018 to 2023, in this case the Scopus base manages a total of 1102 articles, while Web of Science 1991 publications. In Scopus the year with the highest growth in articles was 2022 with 341 publications (31%), and the lowest year was 2018 with 55 publications (5%). However, in the Web of Science database, a total of 649 citations (33%) is projected for the year 2022, and a minimum of 78 publications (4%) in 2018.

PMD.4 What is the participation of the countries in relation to the number of publications?

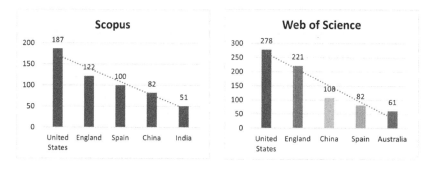

Fig. 6. The graphs show the ranking of the countries with the highest number of publications in the last 5 years. Source: Scopus and Web of Science

In Fig. 6 shows the Scopus database with a total of 5 countries, first the United States with 435 publications (39%), second India with a projection of 302 citations (27%). The Web of Science database shows 5 countries, the United States and China with 689 and 543 articles, 35% and 27% respectively. It is concluded that the North American continent leads the publications in articles.

PMD.5 What is the participation of the journals with respect to the number of publications?

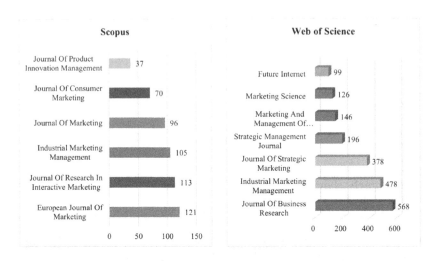

Fig. 7. The graphs show the most outstanding journals in the last 5 years. Source: Scopus and Web of Science

In Fig. 7 show the participation of the most outstanding journals in the search in the case of Scopus with a total of 6 journals, the main ones are: Journal Of Business Research with 374 articles (34%), followed by Communications In Computer And Information Science with 277 publications (25%). On the other hand, Web of Science with 7 journals: Journal Of Business Research is projected 568 articles 29%, followed by Industrial Marketing Management 478 publications 24%.

PMD.6 What are the areas of knowledge in relation to the number of publications?

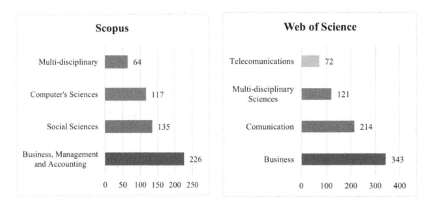

Fig. 8. The graphs show the most outstanding journals in the last 5 years. Source: Scopus and Web of Science

As for the areas of knowledge in the Scopus database, a total of 4 areas are projected among the main ones in Fig. 8: Business, Management and Accounting with 482 articles (44%), followed by Computer Science with 313 publications (28%). Meanwhile, the Web of Science database shows a total of 4 areas among the first: Business is managed with 770 articles, 39%, followed by 588 articles, 30%.

5   Conclusion

Marketing during the last years has been integrated to new digital technology media as support in mobile commerce, being among the possibilities to new ideas combined to the traditional ones to increase communication, engagement and user participation. The functions of digital marketing are versatile where the brand must define the elements of its strategy based on the main objectives for this includes the creation of customer value through digital media.

The scientific production of the study accompanied by bibliometrics allowed to analyze the different aspects of evolution and trends of the articles between the years 2018 to 2023, which resulted in the following: a gradual growth is evidenced in the year 2022 in articles, among the authors with the highest scientific production are: Bala, PK belonging to the United States and Belkhir Mohamed from India are considered the authors with the highest relevance in publications, as for the sources and/or journals that topped the ranking of publications was: Journal Of Business Research, Communications In Computer And Information Science and Journal Of Business Research; similarly the areas of knowledge of the study are: Business, Management and Accounting/Business and finally most of the articles published were in the English language. As a future line of research, it is recommended to compare the results obtained in this research with a current database. To assess behavioral change over time.

Acknowledgments. Thanks to the Technical University of Ambato, to the Research and Development department (DIDE-UTA) for supporting our research project "Gamification and digital marketing: Perspectives of industry 4.0 from a Higher Education viewpoint". Approved under resolution UTA-CONIN-2023-0042-R (Code PFCA25) and being part of the research group: "Marketing, Consumption and Society."

References

1. Ballesteros, L., Guerrero, C., Siguenza, M., Armas, S.: Bibliometric analysis of the marketing gamification category. Medwave, Peer Rev. Med. J. **7**, 036007 (2022). https://doi.org/10.5867/medwave.2022.S2.UTA109
2. Baye, M., Delos Santos, B., Wildenbeest, M.: What's in a name? Masuring prominence and its impact on organic traffic from search engines. Inf. Econ. Policy **34**, 44–57 (2016). https://doi.org/10.1016/j.infoecopol.2016.01.002
3. Cho, V., Chan, A.: An integrative framework of comparing SAAS adoption for core and non-core business operations: an empirical study on Hong Kong industries. Inf. Syst. Front. **17**, 629–644 (2015). https://doi.org/10.1007/s10796-013-9450-9

4. Choudhari, K., Bhalla, V.: Video search engine optimization using keyword and feature analysis. Proc. Comput. Sci. **58**, 691–697 (2015). https://doi.org/10.1016/j.procs.2015.08.089

5. Conway, T., Hemphill, T.: Growth hacking as an approach to producing growth amongst UK technology start-ups: an evaluation. J. Res. Mark. Entrep. **21**(2), 163–179 (2019). https://doi.org/10.1108/JRME-12-2018-0065

6. Csordás, A., Pancsira, J., Lengyel, P., Füzesi, I., Felföldi, J.: The potential of digital marketing tools to develop the innovative SFSC players' business models. J. Open Innov. Technol. Market Complex. **8**(3), 122 (2022). https://doi.org/10.3390/joitmc8030122

7. Dimitrios, B., Ioannis, R., Angelos, N., Nikolaos, T.: Digital marketing: the case of digital marketing strategies on luxurious hotels. Proc. Comput. Sci. **219**, 688–696 (2023). https://doi.org/10.1016/j.procs.2023.01.340

8. Dwivedi, Y.K., Rana, N.P., Slade, E.L., Singh, N., Kizgin, H.: Editorial introduction: advances in theory and practice of digital marketing. J. Retail. Consum. Serv. **53**, 101909 (2020). https://doi.org/10.1016/j.jretconser.2019.101909

9. Erdmann, A., Ponzoa, J.: Digital inbound marketing: measuring the economic performance of grocery e-commerce in Europe and the USA. Technol. Forecast. Soc. Chang. **162**, 120373 (2021). https://doi.org/10.1016/j.techfore.2020.120373

10. Faruk, M., Rahman, M., Hasan, S.: How digital marketing evolved over time: a bibliometric analysis on Scopus database. Heliyon **7**(12), e08603 (2021). https://doi.org/10.1016/j.heliyon.2021.e08603

11. Guerrero-Velástegui, C.A., Peñaherrera-Zambrano, S., Ballesteros-López, L., López-Pérez, S.: Artificial intelligence and replacement of human talent: Case study of higher education in times of pandemic. In: Bindhu, V., Tavares, J.M.R.S. (eds.) Proceedings of Fourth International Conference on Communication, Computing and Electronics Systems. Lecture Notes in Electrical Engineering, vol. 977, pp. 891–901. Springer Nature Singapore, Singapore (2023). https://doi.org/10.1007/978-981-19-7753-4_68

12. Guerrero Velástegui, C.A., Páez-Quinde, C., Mejía-Bayas, C., Arévalo-Peralta, J.: Mobile marketing as a communication strategy in politics 2.0. In: Garcia, M.V., Gordón Gallegos, C. (eds.) CSEI: International Conference on Computer Science, Electronics and Industrial Engineering (CSEI). Lecture Notes in Networks and Systems, vol. 678, pp. 55–69. CSEI 2022, Springer Nature Switzerland, Cham (2023). https://doi.org/10.1007/978-3-031-30592-4_5

13. Hagen, D., Risselada, A., Spierings, B., Jochanan, J., Atzema, O.: Digital marketing activities by Dutch place management partnerships: a resource-based view. Cities **123**, 103548 (2022). https://doi.org/10.1016/j.cities.2021.103548

14. Haleem, A., Javaid, M., Qadri, M., Singh, R., Suman, R.: Artificial intelligence (ai) applications for marketing: A literature-based study. Procedia. Soc. Behav. Sci. **3**, 119–132 (2022). https://doi.org/10.1016/j.ijin.2022.08.005

15. Jiménez Correa, E.A., et al.: Effectiveness of social responsibility marketing in young millennials - generation y: analysis of three cases for brand positioning. Heliyon **7**(10), e08150 (2021). https://doi.org/10.1016/j.heliyon.2021.e08150

16. Keke, M.: The use of digital marketing in information transport in social media: the example of Turkish companies. Transp. Res. Proc. **63**, 2579–2588 (2022). https://doi.org/10.1016/j.trpro.2022.06.297

17. Ko, E.: Bridging Asia and the world: global platform for the interface between marketing and management. J. Bus. Res. **99**, 350–353 (2019). https://doi.org/10.1016/j.jbusres.2018.12.061

18. Lanenko, M., Lanenko, M., Shevchuk, E.: Digital transformation of marketing activities in transport systems management during COVID-19: experience, problems, prospects. Transp. Res. Proc. **63**, 878–886 (2022). https://doi.org/10.1016/j.trpro.2022.06.085

19. Makrides, A., Vrontis, D., Christofi, M.: The gold rush of digital marketing: assessing prospects of building brand awareness overseas. Bus. Perspect. Res. **8**(1), 4–20 (2020). https://doi.org/10.1177/2278533719860016

20. Mandal, P., Joshi, N.: Understanding digital marketing strategy. Int. J. Sci. Res. Manage. **5**(06), 5428–5431 (2017). https://doi.org/10.18535/ijsrm/v5i6.11

21. Masrianto, A., Hartoyo, H., Vitayala, A., Hubeis, N.H.: A critical review of digital marketing. Int. J. Manage. IT Eng. **8**(10), 321–339 (2018). https://ssrn.com/abstract=3545505

22. Masrianto, A., Hartoyo, H., Vitayala, A., Hubeis, N.H.: Digital marketing utilization index for evaluating and improving company digital marketing capability. J. Open Innov. Technol. Mark. Complex. **8**(3), 153 (2022). https://doi.org/10.3390/joitmc8030153

23. Maucuer, R., Renaud, A., Ronteau, S., Muzellec, L.: What can we learn from marketers? A bibliometric analysis of the marketing literature on business model research. Long Range Plan. **55**(5), 102219 (2022). https://doi.org/10.1016/j.lrp.2022.102219

24. Melović, B., Jocović, M., Dabić, M., Backović Vulić, T., Dudic, B.: The impact of digital transformation and digital marketing on the brand promotion, positioning and electronic business in montenegro. Technol. Soc. **63**, 101425 (2020). https://doi.org/10.1016/j.techsoc.2020.101425

25. Mero, J., Leinonen, M., Makkonen, H., Karjaluoto, H.: Agile logic for SAAS implementation: capitalizing on marketing automation software in a start-up. J. Bus. Res. **145**, 583–594 (2022). https://doi.org/10.1016/j.jbusres.2022.03.026

26. Mero, J., Tarkiainen, A., Tobon, J.: Effectual and causal reasoning in the adoption of marketing automation. Ind. Mark. Manage. **86**, 212–222 (2020). https://doi.org/10.1016/j.indmarman.2019.12.008

27. Mikalef, P., Islam, N., Parida, V., Singh, H., Altwaijry, N.: Artificial intelligence (AI) competencies for organizational performance: a B2B marketing capabilities perspective. J. Bus. Res. **164**, 113998 (2023). https://doi.org/10.1016/j.jbusres.2023.113998

28. Misirlis, N., Vlachopoulou, M.: Social media metrics and analytics in marketing - s3m: a mapping literature review. Int. J. Inf. Manage. **38**(1), 270–276 (2018). https://doi.org/10.1016/j.ijinfomgt.2017.10.005

29. Nagpal, M., Petersen, J.A.: Keyword selection strategies in search engine optimization: how relevant is relevance? J. Retail. **97**(4), 746–763 (2021). https://doi.org/10.1016/j.jretai.2020.12.002

30. Ritter, T., Lund-Pedersen, C.: Digitization capability and the digitalization of business models in business-to-business firms: past, present, and future. Ind. Mark. Manage. **86**, 180–190 (2020). https://doi.org/10.1016/j.indmarman.2019.11.019

31. Rizvanović, B., Zutshi, A., Grilo, A., Nodehi, T.: Linking the potentials of extended digital marketing impact and start-up growth: developing a macro-dynamic framework of start-up growth drivers supported by digital marketing. Technol. Forecast. Soc. Chang. **186**, 122128 (2023). https://doi.org/10.1016/j.techfore.2022.122128

32. Setkute, J., Dibb, S.: "old boys' club": barriers to digital marketing in small B2B firms. Ind. Mark. Manage. **102**, 266–279 (2022). https://doi.org/10.1016/j.indmarman.2022.01.022

33. Thaha, A., Maulina, E., Muftiadi, A., Alexandri, M.: Digital marketing and SMEs: a systematic mapping study. Libr. Philos. Pract. **2021**, 1–19 (2021). https://digitalcommons.unl.edu/libphilprac/5113

34. Verma, S., Sharma, R., Deb, S., Maitra, D.: Artificial intelligence in marketing: systematic review and future research direction. Int. J. Inf. Manage. Data Insights **1**(1), 100002 (2021). https://doi.org/10.1016/j.jjimei.2020.100002

35. Vieira, V., Severo de Almeida, M., Agnihotri, R., De Arruda Corrêa, N., Arunachalam, S.: In pursuit of an effective B2B digital marketing strategy in an emerging market. J. Acad. Market. Sci. **47**, 1085–1108 (2019). https://doi.org/10.1007/s11747-019-00687-1

36. Yalcin, N., Kose, U.: What is search engine optimization: SEO? Procedia. Soc. Behav. Sci. **9**, 487–493 (2010). https://doi.org/10.1016/j.sbspro.2010.12.185

37. Zupic, I., Čater, T.: Bibliometric methods in management and organization. Organ. Res. Methods **18**(3), 429–472 (2015). https://doi.org/10.1177/1094428114562629

Innovating Chemistry Education: Integrating Cultural Knowledge through a Practical Guide and Augmented Reality

Carina Arroba[1], Eulalia Becerra[1] ⓘ, John Espinoza[2] ⓘ, and Jorge Buele[3](✉) ⓘ

[1] Facultad de Ciencias de La Educación, Universidad Indoamérica, 180103 Ambato, Ecuador
{carinaarroba,eulaliabecerra}@indoamerica.edu.ec
[2] ECA Education Centre of Australia, Brisbane 4000, Australia
[3] SISAu Research Group, Facultad de Ingeniería, Industria y Producción, Universidad Indoamérica, 180103 Ambato, Ecuador
jorgebuele@indoamerica.edu.ec

Abstract. There is a clear need for strategies that bridge the gap between theory and practice in chemistry education, particularly in terms of incorporating ancestral and ethnographic knowledge into research activities. Thus, this study aims to explore the design and implementation of an innovative practical guide that integrates local cultural knowledge into the teaching of chemistry for high school students. This qualitative research gathers the perspectives of 74 students and 5 teachers from an educational institution in the Province of Pastaza, Ecuador. The proposed guide is based on seven local cultural knowledge aspects and aims to transform the teaching of chemistry into a meaningful and inclusive activity. The practices are developed using an ethnographic, scientific, and investigative approach, involving a comparison between local knowledge and the prescribed chemistry curriculum. This integration promotes constructivist learning, encourages critical thinking, and motivates students by making science relevant to their cultural and social context. Preliminary results indicate that this strategy has been well received by both students and teachers, who report an improved understanding of chemistry and a greater appreciation for their cultural traditions. While this research primarily focuses on the implementation of the practical guide, future plans include digitizing the guide to expand its reach and enhance its interactivity.

Keywords: Chemistry Teaching · Cultural Knowledge · Practical Guide · Meaningful Learning

1 Introduction

Education, as a fundamental component of society, has undergone continuous evolution, both in its forms and methodologies [1]. Traditionally, scientific subjects like chemistry have been taught in a monolithic and dominant environment that often fails to connect with the realities of students, particularly those from multicultural backgrounds [2]. This disconnection, coupled with the absence of traditional laboratories, has presented challenges in teaching chemistry at the high school level [3, 4]. In the pursuit of

R. Valencia-García et al. (Eds.): CITI 2023, CCIS 1873, pp. 265–276, 2023.
https://doi.org/10.1007/978-3-031-45682-4_19

improving education and fostering genuine inclusivity, the need to propose alternative approaches that link scientific learning with the socio-cultural context of students has become increasingly evident.

Ethnoeducation, which is rooted in ethnic and cultural values, emerges in the literature as a valuable practice that promotes understanding and respect for diversity while facilitating significant growth in students [5, 6]. Despite its potential, the implementation of ethnoeducation is still in its nascent stages in various contexts, including Latin America, where the need to establish authentic interculturality persists. Within this conceptual framework, it is proposed to develop innovative pedagogical proposals that integrate ancestral and cultural knowledge [7]. The ethnographic approach provides a platform for rescuing and appreciating ancestral knowledge and wisdom within the educational environment [8]. This approach aligns with new educational models and incorporates an intercultural perspective that extends beyond the recognition of biodiversity, aiming to foster the development of new and diverse societies [9]. Studies conducted in contexts such as Colombia further reinforce this approach, emphasizing the significance of teaching chemistry in a local setting and harnessing the inherent resources of the region. This not only promotes meaningful and culturally relevant learning but also helps overcome teaching challenges by encouraging reflection rather than mere formulaic repetition [10, 11].

Previous studies have explored the connection between science and cultural heritage, such as the teaching of organic chemistry through coffee, a cultural heritage of Colombia [12]. The study by Kim et al. [13] emphasizes the didactic value of cultural heritage in learning processes and the development of individuals with historical awareness, commitment, critical thinking, and responsibility. In the Ecuadorian context, the integration of cultural heritage and ancestral wisdom in education is seen as a valuable resource to enhance teaching and learning, promoting knowledge exchange and the development of skills and values related to environmental care [14]. The use of technology, particularly augmented reality (AR), can further enhance this approach by providing an interactive and enriched learning experience [15]. By overlaying digital images and data onto the real world. Gamification and the use of technology in general allow students can explore and comprehend complex concepts in a more intuitive and contextualized manner [16].

Augmented reality (AR) acts as a catalyst in the educational environment, fostering engagement, curiosity, and knowledge retention. Its ability to enhance interactive learning has proven to be effective in education, as demonstrated in previous studies [17]. In the present study, it is considered that the intersection of technology and pedagogy can enhance ethnographic education, enabling a deeper connection with students' culture and history. The principles of constructivist learning serve as the foundation for this strategy, offering contextualized learning based on the zone of proximal development. This approach allows for social construction and shared learning, ultimately leading to meaningful learning experiences [18].

In this context, the prime objective of this article is to seamlessly integrate cultural competencies to achieve an all-encompassing learning experience, through a pedagogical strategy for chemistry education. Encompassing topics such as organic compounds and the synthesis of alcohols, ketones, aldehydes, esters, and carboxylic acids, this approach facilitates the linkage of new learnings with prior ones, contingent upon the student's cultural background or ethnicity. Another goal is to invigorate students who have limited hands-on experimentation opportunities by leveraging augmented reality as a supplementary tool. Additionally, it is proposed that students forge connections between their pre-existing knowledge and newfound discoveries, thereby enhancing their comprehension.

This manuscript is structured into four sections, commencing with the introduction in Sect. 1. Section 2 and Sect. 3 delineate the materials and methods, as well as the study outcomes. Sect. 4 encapsulates the conclusions.

2   Materials and Methods

2.1   Materials

Smartphone. The platform and application studied in this research require a mid-range mobile device capable of installing the "Services for AR" plugin from Google Play, which is available in the application store. With the continuous evolution of technology, these devices are compatible with almost any development platform.

Computer. Developing an Augmented Reality (AR) system requires a computer that meets specific minimum specifications to ensure optimal performance. This is essential to avoid any delays during the organization of the application's programming blocks. The computer used in this study has the following characteristics:

Processor: 12th Gen Intel(R) Core(TM) i7-12700H, 2.30 GHz.

Installed RAM: 16.0 GB (15.7 GB usable).

Video Card: NVIDIA® GeForce RTX™ 3060, 6 GB GDDR6.

2.2   Software

Unity is a widely used tool for creating video games and virtual and augmented reality experiences. In the context of augmented reality, Unity provides a range of tools that simplify system development. The development packages utilized in this study include AR-Foundation, Unity MARS, and Vuforia. The Unity version used for this application is 2021.3.4f1, installed via Unity Hub.

Vuforia is a platform designed for developing augmented and mixed reality applications for mobile and holographic devices. It enables the recognition and tracking of markers, allowing for the overlay of 2D or 3D models onto specific areas of the real world. In this study, the Markerless version of Vuforia is employed, which enables marker detection based on position or location. Additionally, the Vuforia Engine is utilized, providing essential functionalities such as text recognition and rapid detection and tracking of images or predefined targets.

Visual Studio is software that integrates with Unity for scripting in the C# programming language. It is used to program the actions or events that occur within the 3D models when predetermined objectives are detected.

2.3 Method

The methodology employed in this study is qualitative, focusing on exploring the integration of local cultural knowledge into chemistry education Initially, a questionnaire was administered to the students with open questions, related to their knowledge of chemistry and their perception of the connection of theory with practice. The study also found that teachers seldom incorporate research activities related to local ethnography in their teaching, which hinders the strengthening of ethnic and cultural values.

This study falls under the category of applied research, as its objective is to address a specific problem: transforming routine activities into innovative ones that enhance meaningful and inclusive learning in the field of chemistry at an educational institution in eastern Ecuador. To achieve this, a practical guide based on seven local cultural knowledge was developed, with the goal of enhancing chemistry learning by integrating theory, practice, and technology. The guide was evaluated by teachers specializing in natural sciences who assessed its relevance, applicability, and contribution to meaningful and inclusive learning. Furthermore, the preliminary design of the practice guide was digitized using augmented reality.

2.4 Participants

The participants in this research consisted of 74 third-year high school students from an educational unit in Pastaza, Ecuador. Out of these participants, 17 were male and 57 were female, with ages ranging from 17 to 19 years old. Additionally, five teachers from the natural sciences department were involved in the study.

2.5 Resources

The practice guide was developed with a foundation in ethnography, science, and research, utilizing seven pieces of knowledge from local ethnography. These pieces of knowledge were contributed by the students, their families, or communities, and were systematically described, highlighting the location of the practice, the materials utilized, the methods employed, and the results obtained. A summary of it is presented in the link: https://github.com/jorgebuele/chemistry. This knowledge aligns with the curriculum and study materials for the third year of high school, as outlined in Table 1. The practical guide was structured including: (i) cover presentation, (ii) introduction, (iii) chemistry program content for third year of high school, (iv) transversal axis of the guide, (v) description of cultural knowledge, (vi) scientific activity of contrast with knowledge (AR), (vii) evaluation rubric, (viii) playful activity (AR), (ix) glossary and bibliography.

2.6 Application Design

The application design consists of two interfaces: "Menu-Canvas" and "VideoCanvas". The "Menu-Canvas" serves as the main screen where 3D models representing ancestral knowledge are displayed, as shown in Fig. 1. On the other hand, the "VideoCanvas" is a multimedia screen that allows the playback of explanatory videos related to the selections made on the main screen.

Table 1. Resources used in the development of the practical guide.

Ethnographic Practice	Human Resources	Material resources
Extraction of the natural dye wituk	Lisan Wasi Community Tourist Center	Notebook and Note Sheets Book and Curricular Guide for Chemistry 3rd Baccalaureate Computer Website information Photo and video camera Word document
Production of the wituk shampoo	Mushu warmi community – Biowarmi Enterprises	
Preparation of cassava chicha	kichwa community	
Ungurahua oil extraction	Community of Shuar nationality	
Elaboration of the exfoliating cream based on lawuki (dragon's blood)	Mushu warmi community Biowarmi ventures	
Turmeric as a medicinal plant	Amazonian peoples of nationality Shuar and Kichwua nationality	
Elaboration of natural colony based on wild orchids	Kunkuk Shuar Community	

To facilitate the interaction between the user and the scene elements projected onto the selected Image Target, four scripts were developed in Visual Studio. These scripts enable seamless interaction with all elements in the scene. The "GetSiblingIndex()" function is used to determine the position of each 3D element within the hierarchical structure. Additionally, a counter is implemented to navigate through each explanatory video using the "Next" and "Previous" buttons.

The scripts, VideoScript, VideoScript1, and VideoScript2, have the role of enabling and disabling the playback of the videos that are selected by the student. These scripts are associated with the purple buttons that are present in each 3D model. In order to activate the multimedia playback, it is necessary to specify the respective button and assign a collider to the object that will perform this action, as shown in Fig. 2. When a specific topic is selected, these scripts hide the UI buttons, elements of the home screen, and any unrelated videos, allowing the student to concentrate on the selected videos. By implementing this functionality, the student can have a more focused and immersive experience with the chosen videos, eliminating distractions from unrelated content.

The main screen, called "MenuCanvas," consists of various 3D models obtained from the Unity store, representing a workstation, as depicted in Fig. 3. The primary purpose of this screen is to address important chemistry topics for high school students, taking into account the local ethnography. Within this screen, there are three interactive purple buttons that redirect users to the "VideoCanvas" screen, where they can access detailed information about the selected ancestral knowledge. In the "VideoCanvas," explanatory videos related to the chosen ancestral knowledge are played. These videos aim to complement and reinforce the knowledge acquired in the classroom setting.

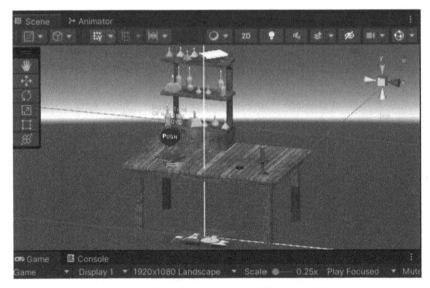

Fig. 1. Development of the Main Screen.

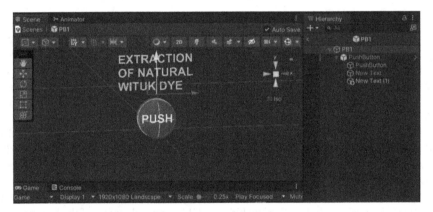

Fig. 2. Development of the interaction button.

3 Preliminary Results

3.1 Initial Implementation

There is an interrelation of the themes of ethnographic practices with scientific themes and pedagogical activities. Among the scientific topics of contrast with the knowledge are: (i) Introduction to the chemistry of carbon (chemical bonds and classes of formulas); (ii) Oxygen compounds (hydroxyl); (iii) Oxygenated compounds (alcohols, aldehydes, ketones, carboxylic acids); (iv) Oxygenated compounds (phenols, alcohols and benzene); (v) Compounds derived from benzene; (vi) Biological compounds (proteins); (vii) Biological compounds (lipids); (viii) Biological compounds (carbohydrates); (ix) Biological

Fig. 3. Main Screen of the App.

compounds (proteins and vitamins); (x) Organic synthesis (types); (xi) Lipid extraction processes and (xii) Carbon chemistry (Lewis representation, classes and properties of plant carbon).

Ethnographic practices, inherited from generation to generation in ancestral communities, offer a valuable cultural and social framework. The topics contained in the practical guide provide educators with a motivating, inclusive and meaningful resource to facilitate the learning of content related to compounds of biological interest. The incorporated pedagogical development activities, such as: (i) Analysis and synthesis; (ii) Identification; (iii) Acknowledgment; (iv) Illustration; (v) Argumentation; (vi) Investigation; (vii) Determination; (viii) Issuance of conclusions and recommendations. Fusion with technology makes learning more meaningful and encourages a constructivist approach to acquiring knowledge.

The practical guide also improves students' ability to formulate conclusions and recommendations, which is crucial for the development of critical thinking. In essence, this approach fosters deeper and more relevant learning by linking chemistry content to students' cultural and social context. This implementation represents an initial pilot test of the practice guide. It is anticipated that improvements and adjustments will be made based on the experiences and feedback collected during this pilot phase.

3.2 Qualitative Analysis

After the implementation of the practical guide, the study yields notable qualitative findings. The questionnaire employed was crafted by the researchers, featuring open-ended inquiries pertaining to participants' most common cultural practices and knowledge. The questionnaire is presented in the link previously presented. Subsequent to the guide's implementation, a prominent array of responses emerged, with students elaborating on the cultural practice of facial and bodily painting using wituk, a customary tradition within Kichwa culture. These initial outcomes offer a diverse and intricate depiction of the repercussions stemming from the fusion of local ethnographic wisdom with chemistry pedagogy, as informed by the direct engagement of both students and educators.

The spectrum of testimonials underscores the participants' perceptions, interactions, and encounters throughout the execution of the instructional guide. There were comments like the following: "I found the integration of local cultural practices like wituk painting into chemistry lessons to be both engaging and enlightening. It helped me understand the scientific concepts better" and "Exploring the differences between wituk painting in Kichwa culture and similar practices in other cultures broadened my perspective on both science and traditions". Each testimony provides a perspective into the manners by which learners and educators have seamlessly assimilated indigenous knowledge into their comprehension and teaching of chemistry. This intersection between cultural and scientific acumen becomes notably apparent.

Moreover, students elucidate differentiations between their cultural practices and those of other societies, including the Shuar, Achuar, and Zapara. Furthermore, they offer a comprehensive account of the procedure involved in the preparation of wituk for its application as a dye. Such testimonies collectively underscore the intertwined nature of cultural traditions and empirical learning. Notably, Fig. 4 showcases the videos that were made accessible to the students, enhancing their visual engagement with the subject matter.

These preliminary results provide promising evidence of the effectiveness of the practical guide. By incorporating augmented reality, the guide successfully combines chemistry content with local cultural knowledge, creating an interactive and engaging platform that enhances students' interaction with both science and their culture. It's important to note that this is just the first phase of a larger project. The future vision includes developing a new version of the application to further improve and expand these learning experiences. The implementation of a digital design adds an additional dimension to the teaching of chemistry, enabling students to interact with chemical elements and processes in a more direct and meaningful manner. The immersive environment of the practice guide builds upon the same principles and content as the original guide but presents them in a more interactive and visually appealing way.

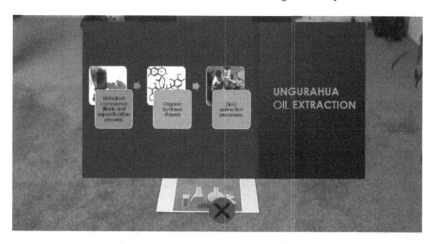

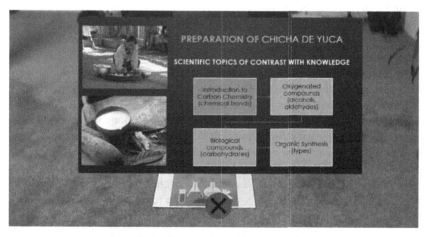

Fig. 4. Implementation of the application.

4 Conclusions

Chemistry, as a discipline, requires innovative pedagogical strategies to promote meaningful learning. It encompasses scientific concepts that benefit from practical activities for reinforcement. Academic literature widely acknowledges that chemistry learning necessitates student autonomy and responsibility, as well as an understanding of the discipline's language and symbols. It is the educator's task to adapt scientific knowledge to students' prior experiences. Some proposals advocate for an analytical approach to studying chemical substances in their context, using "real-life products" to achieve meaningful learning. This perspective emphasizes the importance of the environment in learning, leading to innovative methods that connect scientific knowledge with ancestral knowledge.

Hands-on experimental activities are highly motivating and contribute to enhancing science learning. However, due to resource limitations, such as the unavailability of laboratories, teachers must seek alternative strategies adapted to their specific context. Problem-Based Learning (PBL) allows for the inclusive construction of knowledge and promotes intercultural skills by leveraging biodiversity and daily activities as learning resources. Implementing a practice guide based on ancestral knowledge enables students to develop skills such as discovery, verification, comparison, argumentation, and understanding scientific phenomena. These student-centered, innovative activities stimulate autonomy and responsibility in learning.

Information and Communication Technologies (ICT), including digital resources and augmented reality, can play a crucial role in expanding knowledge in the field of chemistry. Digital resources provide broader and more flexible access to information, enabling autonomous learning tailored to individual needs. Furthermore, ICT facilitates interaction and collaboration among students, teachers, and experts, promoting interactive and community-based learning experiences. Integrating ICT effectively into chemistry teaching, such as through augmented reality, helps students forge deeper connections with concepts, fostering more meaningful and enduring learning. Additionally, digital platforms can document and share the community's ancestral knowledge, serving as a valuable educational resource.

For successful implementation of ICT, it is essential to consider the specific needs of students and the community, as well as the availability of resources and training required for effective tool utilization. Integrating ancestral knowledge into chemistry teaching offers a valuable and innovative approach to promote meaningful learning. This approach enriches students' understanding and motivation while respecting and valuing cultural diversity and traditional wisdom.

The implementation and testing of the presented application experienced delays due to technological and logistical limitations inherent to the rural research context. An initial delay was observed when playing the explanatory videos for the first time, possibly attributed to the size of each video and its impact on smartphone memory. However, prolonged use of the application mitigated this inconvenience due to the caching function, facilitating faster and more efficient video access. In terms of transitions between each 3D model, the application exhibits robust performance.

This study solely comprised an experimental group, which is acknowledged as a methodological limitation. The absence of a control group prevented a direct comparison between this approach and a traditional method. However, this aspect will be duly considered in forthcoming research endeavors. Given that this study did not encompass a quantitative approach, validations were not conducted using knowledge-based or standardized questionnaires, which would provide a more quantifiable assessment of the extent of this proposition. However, this aspect is deemed a prospective avenue for future research.

The use of ICT holds the promise of creating a more interactive and immersive learning experience, transforming how students interact with and connect with science and their culture. However, a thoughtful and appropriate implementation of these technologies is crucial to ensure they become effective tools that align with the demands and possibilities of the 21st century.

Acknowledgment. We extend our gratitude to the students of third year of high school, educators from the Natural Sciences department, and the authorities of Unidad Educativa Andoas. We also wish to express our appreciation to the Universidad Indoamérica for providing support and financing of this investigation.

References

1. Zhang, T., Shaikh, Z.A., Yumashev, A.V., Chład, M.: Applied model of E-learning in the framework of education for sustainable development. Sustain **12**, 6420 (2020). https://doi.org/10.3390/SU12166420
2. Nicolaou, C., Matsiola, M., Kalliris, G.: Technology-enhanced learning and teaching methodologies through audiovisual media. Educ. Sci. **9**, 196 (2019). https://doi.org/10.3390/educsci9030196
3. Pazicni, S., Flynn, A.B.: Systems thinking in chemistry education: theoretical challenges and opportunities. J. Chem. Educ. **96**, 2752–2763 (2019). https://doi.org/10.1021/acs.jchemed.9b00416
4. Lynn, M.A., et al.: Successes and challenges in teaching chemistry to deaf and hard-of-hearing students in the time of COVID-19. J. Chem. Educ. **97**, 3322–3326 (2020). https://doi.org/10.1021/acs.jchemed.0c00602
5. Sumardi, L., Wahyudiati, D.: Ethnic education of Sasak people in Indonesia: exploration of the Beguru principles related to educators and students. In: Proceedings of the 3rd Annual Conference on Education and Social Sciences (ACCESS 2021), pp. 328–337 (2023). https://doi.org/10.2991/978-2-494069-21-3_36
6. Jimenez, F.B., Acosta, Y.L.M.: Beliefs of two culturally diverse groups of teachers about intercultural bilingual education. Profile Issues Teach. Prof. Dev. **21**, 63–77 (2019). https://doi.org/10.15446/profile.v21n2.72879
7. Castillo Bernal, E., Hernández Bernal, E., Rojas Martínez, A.A.: Los etnoeducadores: esos nuevos sujetos de la educación colombiana. Rev. Colomb. Educ. (2005). https://doi.org/10.17227/01203916.7716
8. Handayani, N., Masyhuri, S.: Preserving Ancestral teachings in the modern world: lessons from Mandalika SEZ. In: Proceedings of the International Conference on Intellectuals' Global Responsibility (ICIGR 2022), pp. 567–576. Atlantis Press (2023). https://doi.org/10.2991/978-2-38476-052-7_62

9. Dlugaj, J., Fürstenau, S.: Does the use of migrant languages in German primary schools transform language orders? Findings from ethnographic classroom investigations. Ethnogr. Educ. **14**, 328–343 (2019). https://doi.org/10.1080/17457823.2019.1582348

10. Kamenopoulou, L.: An ethnographic research on inclusive education in Colombia: lessons learned from two school visits. In: Halder, S., Argyropoulos, V. (eds.) Inclusion, Equity and Access for Individuals with Disabilities, pp. 347–363. Springer, Singapore (2019). https://doi.org/10.1007/978-981-13-5962-0_17

11. De Arco, M.N., Merlano, A.A.: Research from the classroom: research seedbeds in Colombian secondary education. Psicol. Esc. e Educ. **26**, e227560 (2022). https://doi.org/10.1590/2175-35392022227560T

12. Alzate, D., Cobos, D., Samacá, J., Villada, C., Aristizábal, A.: Enseñanza de la química orgánica desde el café como patrimonio cultural del país. In: Memorias, Séptimo Congreso Internacional sobre Formación de Profesores de Ciencias 12, pp. 647–657 (2016)

13. Kim, S., Whitford, M., Arcodia, C.: Development of intangible cultural heritage as a sustainable tourism resource: the intangible cultural heritage practitioners' perspectives. J. Herit. Tour. **14**, 422–435 (2019). https://doi.org/10.1080/1743873X.2018.1561703

14. Giménez-Llort, L.: An ethnography study of a viral YouTube educational video in ecuador: dealing with death and grief in times of COVID-19. Front. Psychiatry. **12**, 648569 (2021). https://doi.org/10.3389/fpsyt.2021.648569

15. Höttecke, D., Allchin, D.: Reconceptualizing nature-of-science education in the age of social media. Sci. Educ. **104**, 641–666 (2020). https://doi.org/10.1002/sce.21575

16. Jadán-Guerrero, J., Avilés-Castillo, F., Buele, J., Palacios-Navarro, G.: Gamification in inclusive education for children with disabilities: global trends and approaches - a bibliometric review. In: Gervasi, O., et al. (eds.) ICCSA 2023. LNCS, vol. 14104, pp. 461–477. Springer, Cham (2023). https://doi.org/10.1007/978-3-031-37105-9_31

17. Buele, J., Espinoza, J., Ruales, B., Camino-Morejón, V.M., Ayala-Chauvin, M.: Augmented reality application with multimedia content to support primary education. In: Botto-Tobar, M., Gómez, O.S., Rosero Miranda, R., Díaz Cadena, A., Luna-Encalada, W. (eds.) ICAETT 2022. LNNS, vol. 619, pp. 299–310. Springer, Cham (2023). https://doi.org/10.1007/978-3-031-25942-5_24

18. Pande, M., Bharathi, S.V.: Theoretical foundations of design thinking – a constructivism learning approach to design thinking. Think. Ski. Creat. **36**, 100637 (2020). https://doi.org/10.1016/j.tsc.2020.100637

Evaluation of a Grid for the Identification of Traffic Congestion Patterns

Gary Reyes[1]([✉]) [iD], Laura Lanzarini[2] [iD], César Estrebou[2] [iD],
Aurelio Bariviera[3] [iD], and Victor Maquilón[1] [iD]

[1] Facultad de Ciencias Matemáticas y Físicas, Universidad de Guayaquil,
Cdla. Universitaria Salvador Allende, Guayaquil 090514, Ecuador
{gary.reyesz,victor.maquilonc}@ug.edu.ec
[2] Universidad Nacional de La Plata, Facultad de Informática,
Instituto de Investigación en Informática LIDI (Centro CICPBA),
1900, La Plata, Buenos Aires, Argentina
{laural,cesarest}@lidi.info.unlp.edu.ar
[3] Department of Business, Universitat Rovira i Virgili, Reus, Spain
aurelio.fernandez@urv.cat

Abstract. Today, urban growth, increased vehicular traffic and congestion have become a key challenge in cities. As a consequence, negative effects on mobility are generated, such as longer travel times, increased environmental pollution, stress for drivers, and difficulties in urban traffic planning and management. Understanding and analyzing congestion patterns is essential to effectively address this problem and develop more efficient traffic management strategies. Some research has proposed various solutions to address vehicular congestion, such as the use of algorithms for traffic data analysis, the implementation of intelligent traffic management systems, and the optimization of road infrastructure. The proposed methodology uses dynamic clustering techniques and the analysis of historical information to analyze vehicular congestion patterns, implementing the DyClee algorithm adapted to cells. The obtained results on the city of San Francisco are satisfactory, allowing the identification of clusters with certain patterns that allow identifying areas and times of higher congestion, revealing the temporal variability and highlighting the importance of considering the dynamics of vehicular flow in traffic management.

Keywords: Dynamic clustering · Data stream · Congestion · Grid

1 Introduction

Efficient traffic management is a constant challenge in urban areas, where vehicle flow can be intense and congested. Accurate understanding and analysis of vehicular flow is essential to improve transportation planning and road infrastructure decision making. In this context, this paper presents a methodology for analyzing vehicular flow based on the analysis of vehicle trajectory data.

R. Valencia-García et al. (Eds.): CITI 2023, CCIS 1873, pp. 277–290, 2023.
https://doi.org/10.1007/978-3-031-45682-4_20

The study of vehicular flow has been approached from different approaches, and one of the key aspects lies in the adequate representation of the trajectory data. In this sense, the proposed methodology is based on the division of a geographical area of interest into uniform cells, where each cell contains detailed information on the speed and number of vehicles. This representation simplifies the analysis and visualization of the data, allowing a more accurate understanding of the vehicular flow in the study area.

A clustering algorithm is used to perform the traffic flow analysis. It is based on the methodology proposed by Reyes et al. [17]. This algorithm focuses on efficient and accurate clustering of cells containing vehicle trajectories. Using a distance metric that considers the minimum difference in speed and number of vehicles between the groups and cells being analyzed, the algorithm optimally groups the cells. This allows the identification of patterns and similarities in the vehicular flow of each group, facilitating the detection of areas with potential congestion problems.

The evaluation of vehicular flow congestion is performed using a dataset of historical trajectories. The characteristics of the cells belonging to the microclusters resulting from the clustering are analyzed and compared with reference values obtained from adjacent cells. Through a logical evaluation, it is determined whether the cells meet the established congestion conditions. This evaluation provides a clear view of the areas with traffic flow problems, providing relevant information for traffic management decisions.

This article is organized as follows: Sect. 2 analyzes some related works that were identified within the literature and present various solutions to the problem, Sect. 3 describes the evaluation of the proposed method, Sect. 4 discusses the obtained results, and Sect. 5 presents the conclusions and future lines of work.

2   Related Work

The use of clustering techniques has been extensively explored in the context of data flow analysis [7,20]. In the field of trajectory analysis, a wide variety of research has contributed to the development of clustering techniques applied to different domains [14]. These works have addressed the need to adapt conventional algorithms to handle trajectories.

Clustering methods have been used to identify groups with similar characteristics and analyze their collective behavior [5], this database has allowed the identification of patterns and structures in the vehicle trajectory data, which in turn has facilitated the detection of areas with similar characteristics to traffic congestion.

Within the literature, research can be found that has addressed trajectory segmentation as a stage prior to the clustering process. For example, Lee et al. [10] have proposed an approach that uses segmentation to improve the performance of clustering algorithms and obtain higher quality clusters. Similarly, Mao et al. [13] & Yuan et al. [22] also presented methods that incorporate trajectory segmentation prior to clustering, which has proven beneficial for trajectory analysis.

Some approaches have used traditional clustering algorithms, such as the k-means algorithm [7] and the DBSCAN algorithm [3], adapted specifically for path analysis.

These methods consider similarity metrics specially designed for trajectories, allowing them to efficiently cluster and classify according to desired characteristics and appropriate situations [1]. Researchers have proposed several similarity measures. For example, the Tra-DBScan algorithm [11] adapted the well-known DBScan algorithm [3] and introduced the Hausdorff distance as a similarity measure to divide trajectories into sections. Reyes et al. [18] proposed a pivot-guided similarity metric that uses angular information for GPS vehicle trajectory segmentation. In addition, Yu et al. [21] developed a new clustering algorithm that calculates the similarity between two trajectories using multiple data features.

Other approaches have explored the use of dynamic clustering algorithms, which can handle the continuous flow of trajectory data and adapt to changes in traffic behavior over time. These dynamic approaches allow early detection of changes in vehicular flow and identification of areas with emerging congestion [12].

In addition to traditional path clustering techniques, approaches based on complex network analysis and graph theory have also been explored to understand vehicular flow dynamics.

In the related literature, different approaches have been proposed for real-time vehicular flow analysis. Some researchers have used machine learning [8] and data mining techniques, such as neural networks and regression models, to identify hidden patterns and anomalies in traffic flow [19]; clustering and classification techniques [2,23] have also been applied to analyze real-time traffic data and detect congestion on urban roads. These approaches rely on the collection of real-time data, such as traffic signals and GPS data, to train models that can make accurate forecasts. Other researchers have used time series models to predict vehicular flow and take proactive measures in traffic management [24]. These works demonstrate the importance of combining clustering techniques with other analysis methodologies to obtain a complete picture of vehicular flow under different scenarios.

These approaches based on complex networks and data mining offer alternative perspectives to understand vehicular flow from a systemic and predictive point of view [9]. While approaches based on the integration of multiple data sources offer opportunities to improve the understanding of vehicular flow and optimize real-time traffic management [12].

The use of clustering techniques in vehicular flow analysis is an active field of research, with continuous advances in improving the accuracy and efficiency of clustering algorithms, which in turn contributes to better traffic management and informed decision making in real time. The paper proposed by Reyes et al. [16] presents a methodology capable of analyzing vehicular flow in a given area, identifying speed ranges and maintaining an updated interactive map that facilitates the identification of areas with potential traffic jams.

However, a key issue that has been identified in these studies is the need for complementary datasets to enrich the analysis of vehicular flow [4]. In this sense, the methodology presented in this article addresses this need by incorporating an additional dataset of historical trajectories, allowing us to obtain a more complete and accurate perspective of vehicle behavior in the area of interest.

The methodology used makes use of a grid for the representation of vehicular flow, a dynamic grouping of cells and a specific analysis of each cell to determine if it meets certain congestion conditions based on reference values of speed and number of vehicles. This approach provides an accurate comparative basis and allows an assessment of congestion conditions in the study area. By combining the existing approaches with an additional set of historical trajectory data and grid representation, a more complete and accurate analysis of vehicular flow over the clustering results in the area of interest, thus allowing for early and accurate detection of areas with potential traffic flow problems.

3   Methodology

This paper presents a cell evaluation methodology for the identification of congestion patterns, the methodology proposed in this paper is based on the methodology presented by Reyes et al. [16] using a dynamic clustering algorithm, data representation by cells and visualization of clustering results. However, additional elements are incorporated, such as an additional dimension for clustering, the use of a complementary dataset and the evaluation of congestion features in the clusters.

First, the definition of the cells to be analyzed is carried out. The second step involves the use of a proposed dynamic clustering algorithm in order to identify patterns of areas that could present congestion. In the third step, the identified patterns are analyzed and evaluated with a congestion feature evaluation method. Then, in the fourth step, we proceed to generate an appropriate visualization for the obtained results. Each of these steps is described in detail below.

3.1   Definition of Cells

Within the structure of the records to be processed are the most important attributes such as longitude, latitude, time, speed and the trajectory identifier.

The first crucial step in the methodology is to ensure an adequate representation of the data that make up the trajectories. To achieve this, we start by defining the area of interest, thus delimiting the geographic region to which the trajectories to be analyzed belong. Once the area has been established, we proceed to subdivide it into uniform cells or smaller zones. The size of each cell is determined according to the required precision for the analysis of the vehicular flow, allowing us to capture the most relevant details of the movement patterns.

Several experiments have been conducted with the objective of determining the appropriate cell size for vehicular flow analysis. These experiments prior to the ideal parameterization have been fundamental to select the optimal configuration that guarantees an adequate representation of the movement patterns in the area of interest.

In this work, cells of 30×30 m were used and the essential characteristics of these cells by which they will be clustered will be the speed of the cells with ranges between $20 \, \text{km/h}$ and the number of vehicles with ranges between 5 vehicles.

This aspect acquires a fundamental relevance, since it implies the understanding of the information corresponding to each cell during a specific time interval. The proposed methodology in this study consists of integrally analyzing the events in each cell instead of addressing the trajectories of individual vehicles. This approach simplifies both the analysis and the visualization of the data.

Specifically, in this paper, the related data to vehicular flow, represented in each cell, were subjected to analysis using a microbatch approach in uniform time periods. The duration of each period is an essential parameter of the algorithm, which must be set in a predefined manner.

Each period is referred to as a cycle and represents an evolution of the formed clusters, as the results of the grouping are updated by incorporating each block of data. This methodology allows capturing the dynamics progressively, as new data is integrated, generating a more accurate and updated understanding of the vehicular flow.

In each evolution cycle, a continuous flow of data is stored in a temporary buffer and the relevant calculations are performed for each cell, allowing to obtain characteristic and relevant information.

3.2   Dynamic Cell Clustering

In the second step of the methodology, an algorithm for processing cells containing trajectories is used. This algorithm has been selected for its ability to efficiently and accurately analyze the specific characteristics of the trajectories in each cell.

As mentioned above, the first stage of the DyClee algorithm is used to construct microclusters. However, in this paper, an adaptation of the original proposed methodology has been made, where instead of using directly the GPS locations and their density, the speeds of the trajectory sections and the number of vehicles present in each cell are considered for each cycle.

At the stage of grouping the cells in each cycle, a distance metric is used that considers the minimum difference in speed and number of vehicles between the microclusters and the analyzed cell. If the difference in speed and vehicles is sufficiently small, the cell is incorporated into the existing microcluster and the corresponding information is updated. If there is no nearby cluster, a new microcluster is created with the analyzed cell. In this way, an appropriate grouping of cells based on similarities in speed and number of vehicles is achieved.

In the second stage of the algorithm, an analysis of the densities of the microclusters is carried out, classifying them into two categories: dense and not very dense. The number of formed microclusters is related to the value of the "relative size" parameter, which directly modifies the size of the "hyperboxes". This is reflected in a greater or lesser amplitude of the range of cell assignment to the microclusters, according to their speed and number of vehicles.

During these processes, information regarding the performance of the stages is recorded separately, allowing a detailed analysis of their operation.

3.3 Congestion Evaluation

In this study, it is important to have a dataset of historical trajectories that differs in date but matches the time and location of the one used in the clustering process. This historical data set corresponds to a real data flow, provides complementary information and enriches the analysis of vehicle flow in transit. This ensures a more complete and accurate perspective of the behavior of vehicles in the cells of the area of interest.

For the representation of the vehicular flow, a projection of a grid similar to the one used in Sect. 3.1 of the article is used, this grid is applied to the historical data set. Then, a specific analysis is performed to determine a reference value for speed and number of vehicles. This reference value is obtained by considering adjacent cells and using up to five levels of distance, these historical reference values are calculated proportionally where each level contributes a specific proportion.

As shown in Fig. 1, the cells on the periphery will be determined with lower proportion values. Being level 1, the cell being analyzed, represents 30% of the total historical value, decreasing in percentage according to the level, up to level 5, which contributes 10% of the total. In this way, information from nearby cells is used to establish a more accurate comparative basis.

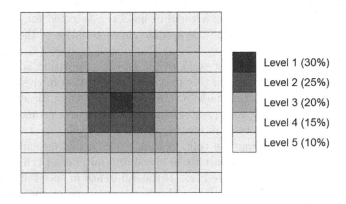

Fig. 1. Proportions according to cell level

Subsequently, the characteristics of the cells in the groups resulting from the grouping are compared with the reference values obtained previously. This comparison makes it possible to evaluate whether the analyzed cells comply with the established congestion conditions.

The conditions for congestion detection are based on the proposed evaluation by He et al. [6]. A logical evaluation is applied to determine whether the analyzed cells meet the following congestion conditions:

- The number of path points in the cell is greater than or equal to the number of path points set as a reference.
- The average speed of the vehicles inside the cell is lower than the established reference speed.

This logical evaluation makes it possible to identify the cells that show signs of congestion and contributes to the early and accurate detection of areas with potential traffic flow problems.

To provide an overview of the performed evaluations, the congestion index is calculated using the formula proposed by He et al. [6]. This defines the index as the total number of cycles for which each cell has complied with the congestion conditions set forth indicating that they have been identified as areas of congestion.

3.4 Clustering Visualization

In this study, the trajectory information is analyzed in 3-minute intervals, this time allows identifying changes in the vehicular flow in a more accurate and detailed way.

In order to provide an interactive visual representation of the results of each cluster, an interactive map has been developed. This map allows the relevant information for each cluster to be analyzed graphically and dynamically. Each cluster is represented on the map with a different color for each pattern based on the number of vehicles and speeds that the clustering algorithm has identified, as shown in Fig. 2.

This study records the result of the grouping process performed, which allows reconstructing all the maps from the beginning of the vehicular flow analysis. This provides a quick overview of the traffic status.

4 Results and Discussion

4.1 Used Data

To test the performance of the proposed methodology in this article, a dataset collected in the city of San Francisco was used. A brief description of the data set is provided below:

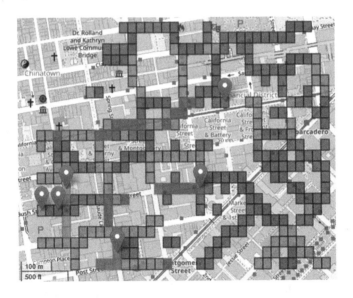

Fig. 2. Clusters projected on the map

San Francisco Dataset. A portion of the san francisco dataset [15] was extracted for clustering, the data corresponds to June 2, 2008; it contains 290 trajectories recorded by cabs using GPS devices. Each record contains the following data: trajectory id, latitude, longitude, time, speed and direction. For this set of trajectories, the analysis included all recorded trajectories between 12:30 pm and 13:30 pm. As a result of this filtering process, 191,315 records were obtained, representing 290 trajectories from the entire dataset.

4.2   Obtained Results

To perform the analysis, the dataset was divided into cycles covering 3 min of data, which generated a total of 20 cycles for the city of San Francisco. These blocks were analyzed consecutively, considering that the 3-minute period is adequate in relation to the volume of data available.

Next, we proceeded to define the values of the "relative size" and "hyperbox" parameters to use the DyClee algorithm. A "relative size" value of 0.2 was set, with speed limits between 0 and 120 km/h, and vehicle quantity limits between 1 and 25 for each cell.

Figure 3 shows the projection of the cells on a plane equivalent to the map of the processing area analyzed as a result of the evaluations according to the referential values of each location performed on the 20 cycles of the data set. Each congested cell is shown in red color indicating that these cells have met the two conditions stated in Sect. 3.3 which indicate that the cells have been evaluated as congested.

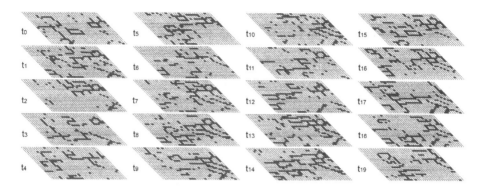

Fig. 3. Evaluation of congested cells using historical averages

Each map shows the locations where the congestion conditions are met, it can be seen that these vary over time and are different depending on the location. These variations can range from concentrations in specific zones (such as Fig. 3 - t_2), zones with dispersed congestion (such as Fig. 3 - t_{10}), zones with congestion in peripheral areas (such as Fig. 3 - t_{18}).

These patterns of variation in congestion conditions can be attributed to various factors, such as time of day, special events or even weather conditions.

It can also be observed that at certain times, clusters of congested cells are identified that form specific spatial patterns. For example, in some cycles, congestion "spots" are observed to form in specific areas such as interconnected roads that are very busy, while in other cycles, more diffuse and dispersed congestion can be identified indicating that congestion may be occurring due to particular situations. These spatial patterns may be related to the road infrastructure, the distribution of points of interest or even the population density in different areas.

It is important to note that not all evaluated cells show congestion in all cycles. Some cells may alternate between congested and non-congested conditions over time, indicating the dynamicity and variability related to vehicular flow.

The experiments and analysis of the proposed methodology were carried out using a computer with the following technical specifications: AMD A9-9425 3.1 GHz processor; 8 GB DDR4 RAM; and Windows 10 Home operating system.

Table 1. Execution times

Description	Clustering (Sec.)	Evaluation (Sec.)	Total (Sec.)
Total time	2458.218	13.333	2471.551
Average cycle time	122.911	0.667	123.578
Deviation	±39.410	±0.124	±39.534

The obtained results about the performance of the algorithm are shown in the Table 1, this table contains a summary of the execution times of the proposed methodology. The clustering time used 2458.218 s and the evaluation of the cells took 13.333 s, which adds up to a total time of 2471.551 s.

Analyzing the average time per cycle, it is observed that the clustering requires on average 122.911 s with a deviation of ±39.410 s, while the evaluation only needs 0.667 s with a deviation of ±0.124 s. These data indicate that the clustering process is more time demanding compared to evaluation. On average, each cycle of the data set takes approximately 123.578 s to complete. These results reflect the effectiveness of the methodology in terms of execution times.

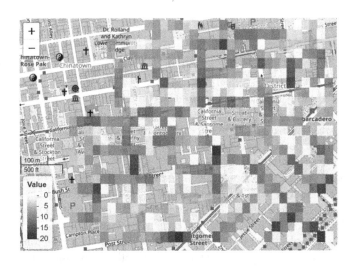

Fig. 4. Congestion distribution by historical averages

To provide an overview of the assessments made and to quantitatively represent the vehicular congestion in the analyzed processing area, the congestion index is calculated which provides a single measure for each cell and is based on the accumulation of the cells identified as congested over the 20 cycles of the data set.

The result of this calculation provides a numerical value representing the level of congestion in each cell. The higher the value of the congestion index, the higher the frequency of vehicular congestion at that specific location. This approach provides a global perspective of congestion in the processing area and facilitates the identification of critical areas requiring attention and possible solutions.

For the visualization of these indices, a congestion distribution is plotted showing a spatial representation of the areas with higher or lower frequency of congestion, which helps to understand the geographic distribution of this phenomenon. This distribution is shown in Fig. 4.

In order to understand the relationship between density and congestion classification, a contingency matrix has been used and is shown in Table 2. Analysis of this contingency matrix reveals trends in accuracy of congestion rankings relative to the density of the resulting clusters.

Table 2. Contingency matrix based on matching the results of pooling and actual flow evaluation

Categories	Congested	Non-congested
Low dense	60.50%	57.60%
Dense	22.31%	60.68%

These values represent the percentage of correctly classified cells in each combination of categories. In the category of sparse groups, resulting from clustering, 60.50% of the congested cells match cells classified as congested from the actual cell flow, and 57.60% of the uncongested cells match cells classified as uncongested from the actual flow. Likewise, in the dense group category, 22.31% of the congested cells match with cells classified as congested from the actual cell flow, and 60.68% of the uncongested cells match with cells classified as uncongested from the actual flow.

It is observed that the accuracy of the classifications varies according to the density category resulting from the clustering. This indicates that the classification result performs better in identifying congestion in clusters with low cell density. By understanding the relationship between traffic density and congestion classifications, more effective classification strategies can be developed for accurate identification of vehicular congestion in variable traffic environments.

In order to improve the congestion detection match rates using the proposed methodology, it is crucial to consider several factors. First, the accuracy of the traffic data must be ensured by obtaining high quality and up-to-date information from reliable sources. In addition, the parameters of the clustering algorithm and congestion thresholds need to be reviewed and adjusted to suit the specific characteristics of the city or study area. The inclusion of external factors, such as special events or weather changes, is also relevant to have a complete understanding of congestion and can significantly improve the accuracy of vehicle congestion detection.

The methodology developed in this study presents similarities with the one proposed by He et al. [6] for traffic congestion event detection processes. Although there are differences in the implementation details and specific objectives, both methodologies share a common conceptual basis to address the identification of vehicular congestion. This similarity allows the possibility of making partial comparisons between both methodologies and enriching the general knowledge on traffic congestion detection in dynamic environments.

It is important to recognize that the proposed methodology also faces certain limitations and potential challenges that must be taken into account when interpreting the results. Since congestion conditions can vary widely depending on time of day, special events or even weather conditions, this methodology may generate different results at different times. Careful analysis of the results in different temporal contexts is essential to understand the stability of the identified patterns.

In addition, although the methodology has proven to be effective in the city of San Francisco, results should be validated in other urban areas with different characteristics. Each city may have unique roadway infrastructures, distinct traffic patterns, and particular congestion dynamics. This may require specific adjustments and adaptations to obtain accurate and meaningful results.

Another potential limitation is the need for high quality data. The success of the methodology is highly dependent on the availability of accurate vehicular traffic data. If data are insufficient or of low quality, this could affect the accuracy and reliability of congestion assessments.

5   Conclusions

The distribution of vehicular congestion in the study area has been clearly identified and visualized, allowing a better understanding of the spatial and temporal patterns of vehicular congestion.

The effectiveness of the proposed methodology for accurately and systematically assessing and monitoring vehicular congestion has been demonstrated.

The obtained results have provided valuable information on the areas and times of greatest congestion, which can contribute to informed decision making in urban traffic planning and management.

Significant variability in congestion conditions over time has been observed, highlighting the importance of considering the seasonality and dynamics of vehicular flow in traffic management strategies.

Visualization of the results has made it possible to identify specific patterns of congestion in specific areas, which can guide actions aimed at improving road infrastructure or implementing specific traffic control measures in those locations.

The methodology has proven to be an effective tool for the identification and monitoring of congested areas, which can contribute to the optimization of resources and efficiency in urban transport management.

The obtained results support the need to implement traffic control and urban planning strategies that take into account the variability and dynamics of vehicular congestion, with the objective of improving fluidity and reducing travel times in the study area.

As lines of future work, it is proposed to improve the classification model to improve the accuracy in the classification of congested and non-congested cells. Another proposal is to consider additional variables such as vehicle flow speed, roadway capacity or type of vehicles to obtain a more complete understanding of congestion. Evaluating vehicle congestion over time to develop predictive models to identify long-term patterns and trends. In addition, validation of the new methodology in other spatial and temporal contexts is proposed to verify its applicability and generalizability. This would allow the new methodology to be used to improve traffic management in a variety of environments.

References

1. Choong, M.Y., Chin, R.K.Y., Yeo, K.B., Teo, K.T.K.: Trajectory pattern mining via clustering based on similarity function for transportation surveillance. Int. J. Simul. Syst. Sci. Technol. **17**(34), 1–19 (2016)
2. Erdelić, T., Carić, T., Erdelić, M., Tišljarić, L., Turković, A., Jelušić, N.: Estimating congestion zones and travel time indexes based on the floating car data. Comput. Environ. Urban Syst. **87**, 101604 (2021). https://doi.org/10.1016/j.compenvurbsys.2021.101604. https://www.sciencedirect.com/science/article/pii/S0198971521000119
3. Ester, M., Kriegel, H.P., Sander, J., Xu, X., et al.: A density-based algorithm for discovering clusters in large spatial databases with noise. In: Kdd, vol. 96, pp. 226–231 (1996)
4. Gao, H., et al.: A method for exploring and analyzing spatiotemporal patterns of traffic congestion in expressway networks based on origin-destination data. ISPRS Int. J. Geo-Inf. **10**(5) (2021). https://doi.org/10.3390/ijgi10050288. https://www.mdpi.com/2220-9964/10/5/288
5. Han, J., Kamber, M., Tung, A.K.: Spatial clustering methods in data mining. In: Geographic Data Mining and Knowledge Discovery, pp. 188–217 (2001)
6. He, Y., Hofer, B., Sheng, Y., Yin, Y., Lin, H.: Processes and events in the center: a taxi trajectory-based approach to detecting traffic congestion and analyzing its causes. Int. J. Digit. Earth **16**(1), 509–531 (2023). https://doi.org/10.1080/17538947.2023.2182374. https://www.tandfonline.com/doi/full/10.1080/17538947.2023.2182374
7. Jain, A.: Data clustering: 50 years beyond k-means. Pattern Recogn. Lett. **39**, 651–666 (2009)
8. Kamble, S.J., Kounte, M.R.: Machine learning approach on traffic congestion monitoring system in internet of vehicles. Procedia Comput. Sci. **171**, 2235–2241 (2020). https://doi.org/10.1016/j.procs.2020.04.241. https://www.sciencedirect.com/science/article/pii/S1877050920312321. Third International Conference on Computing and Network Communications (CoCoNet 2019)
9. Kim, J., Mahmassani, H.S.: Spatial and temporal characterization of travel patterns in a traffic network using vehicle trajectories. Transp. Res. Procedia **9**, 164–184 (2015)
10. Lee, J.G., Han, J., Whang, K.Y.: Trajectory clustering: a partition-and-group framework. In: Proceedings of the 2007 ACM SIGMOD International Conference on Management of Data - SIGMOD 2007, p. 593. ACM Press (2007). https://doi.org/10.1145/1247480.1247546. http://portal.acm.org/citation.cfm?doid=1247480.1247546
11. Liu, L.X., Song, J.T., Guan, B., Wu, Z.X., He, K.J.: Tra-DBScan: a algorithm of clustering trajectories. In: Applied Mechanics and Materials, vol. 121, pp. 4875–4879. Trans Tech Publ (2012)
12. Lou, J., Cheng, A.: Detecting pattern changes in individual travel behavior from vehicle GPS/GNSS data. Sensors **20**(8) (2020). https://doi.org/10.3390/s20082295. https://www.mdpi.com/1424-8220/20/8/2295
13. Mao, Y., Zhong, H., Qi, H., Ping, P., Li, X.: An adaptive trajectory clustering method based on grid and density in mobile pattern analysis. Sensors **17**(9), 2013 (2017). https://doi.org/10.3390/s17092013. http://www.mdpi.com/1424-8220/17/9/2013

14. Mazimpaka, J.D., Timpf, S.: Trajectory data mining: a review of methods and applications. J. Spat. Inf. Sci. **2016**(13), 61–99 (2016)

15. Piorkowski, M., Sarafijanovic-Djukic, N., Grossglauser, M.: CRAWDAD dataset EPFL/mobility (v. 2009–02-24) (2009). https://doi.org/10.15783/C7J010

16. Reyes, G., Lanzarini, L., Estrebou, C., Fernandez Bariviera, A.: Dynamic grouping of vehicle trajectories. J. Comput. Sci. Technol. **22**(2), e11 (2022). https://doi.org/10.24215/16666038.22.e11. https://journal.info.unlp.edu. ar/JCST/article/view/2059

17. Reyes, G., Lanzarini, L., Estrebou, C., Maquilón, V.: CACIC 2021 XXVII CONGRESO ARGENTINO DE CIENCIAS DE LA COMPUTACION, 2021 edn., vol. XXVII, p. 261–270. Universidad Nacional de Salta (2021)

18. Reyes-Zambrano, G., Lanzarini, L., Hasperué, W., Bariviera, A.F.: GPS trajectory clustering method for decision making on intelligent transportation systems. J. Intell. Fuzzy Syst. **38**(5), 5529–5535 (2020). https://doi.org/10.3233/JIFS-179644

19. Sun, S., Chen, J., Sun, J.: Traffic congestion prediction based on GPS trajectory data. Int. J. Distrib. Sensor Netw. **15**(5), 1550147719847440 (2019). https://doi. org/10.1177/1550147719847440. Publisher: SAGE Publications

20. Tork, H.F.: Spatio-temporal clustering methods classification. In: Doctoral Symposium on Informatics Engineering, vol. 1, pp. 199–209. Faculdade de Engenharia da Universidade do Porto Porto, Portugal (2012)

21. Yu, Q., Luo, Y., Chen, C., Chen, S.: Trajectory similarity clustering based on multi-feature distance measurement. Appl. Intell. **49**(6), 2315–2338 (2019)

22. Yuan, G., Sun, P., Zhao, J., Li, D., Wang, C.: A review of moving object trajectory clustering algorithms. Artif. Intell. Rev. **47**(1), 123–144 (2017). https://doi.org/10. 1007/s10462-016-9477-7. http://link.springer.com/10.1007/s10462-016-9477-7

23. Zhang, Y., Ye, N., Wang, R., Malekian, R.: A method for traffic congestion clustering judgment based on grey relational analysis. ISPRS Int. J. Geo-Inf. **5**(5) (2016). https://doi.org/10.3390/ijgi5050071. https://www.mdpi.com/2220-9964/5/5/71

24. Zhou, R., Chen, H., Chen, H., Liu, E., Jiang, S.: Research on traffic situation analysis for urban road network through spatiotemporal data mining: a case study of xi'an, china. IEEE Access **9**, 75553–75567 (2021). https://doi.org/10.1109/ ACCESS.2021.3082188

Author Index

Printed in the United States
by Baker & Taylor Publisher Services